The Holy See and Hitler's Germany

Also by Gerhard Besier

Das Europa der Diktaturen. Eine neue Geschichte als 20. Jahrhunderts

Der SED-Staat und die Kirche, Vols 1–3

Die Kirchen und das Dritte Reich: Vol. 3

Religion, State and Society in the Transformations of the Twentieth Century

The Holy See and Hitler's Germany

Gerhard Besier with the collaboration of Francesca Piombo

Translated by W. R. Ward

First published as *Der Heilige Stuhl und Hitler-Deutschland*
© 2004 by Deutsche Verlags-Anstalt GmbH, München.
This edition published 2007 by
PALGRAVE MACMILLAN
Houndmills, Basingstoke, Hampshire RG21 6XS and
175 Fifth Avenue, New York, N.Y. 10010
Companies and representatives throughout the world

PALGRAVE MACMILLAN is the global academic imprint of the Palgrave
Macmillan division of St. Martin's Press, LLC and of Palgrave Macmillan Ltd.
Macmillan® is a registered trademark in the United States, United Kingdom
and other countries. Palgrave is a registered trademark in the European
Union and other countries.

ISBN-13: 978–1–4039–8831–7 hardback
ISBN-10: 1–4039–8831–5 hardback

This book is printed on paper suitable for recycling and made from fully
managed and sustained forest sources. Logging, pulping and manufacturing
processes are expected to conform to the environmental regulations of the
country of origin.

A catalogue record for this book is available from the British Library.

Library of Congress Cataloging-in-Publication Data
Besier, Gerhard.
    [Heilige Stuhl und Hitler-Deutschland. English]
    The Holy See and Hitler's Germany / Gerhard Besier and Francesca Piombo ;
    translation by W.R. Ward.
        p. cm.
    Includes bibliographical references (p.) and index.
    ISBN-10: 1–4039–8831–5 (cloth)
    ISBN-13: 978–1–4039–8831–7 (cloth)
    1. Catholic Church—Foreign relations—Germany. 2. Germany—Foreign
    relations—Catholic Church. 3. National socialism and religion. 4. Catholic
    Church—Foreign relations—Europe. 5. Europe—Foreign relations—Catholic
    Church. 6. Fascism and the Catholic Church. 7. Pius XII, Pope, 1876–1958.
    I. Title.
    BX1536.B4713 2007
    327.456′3404309043—dc22   2007060009

10   9   8   7   6   5   4   3   2   1
16 15 14 13 12 11 10 09 08 07

Printed and bound in Great Britain by
Antony Rowe Ltd, Chippenham and Eastbourne

Contents

Preface

Since Rolf Hochhuth's drama *The Representative* (1963)[1] reproaches against the Pacelli-Pope Pius XII have crackled continuously: he failed solemnly and publicly to protest against the persecution and murder of European Jewry, and was 'silent' in the face of this and other crimes of National Socialism and Fascism. His judgement had been clouded both by anti-semitism[2] and by the one-sided anti-Bolshevism[3] of the Roman Catholic Church – attitudes which he himself shared. The real roots of this cynical behaviour lay in the doctrine and tradition of Christianity itself: in numerous passages of the Bible and two thousand years of old imperial striving for domination over the thoughts and feelings of mankind.[4] This history of the establishment of Christianity has left behind a broad trail of blood, and is the basis of the intolerance of Western culture.[5] Meanwhile this dominant negative historical picture, represented mostly by Anglo-Americans and disseminated by influential presses, has until recently been too much for the defences mounted by the Roman Catholic Church.[6]

The critics of Hochhuth, however, often overlook the fact that the then-unknown 32-year-old author in 1963–64 was exposed to the most violent criticism and massive professional injury, because he had ventured to overthrow a largely positive image of Pius XII hitherto held to be valid. Hannah Arendt who received a copy of the play in the autumn of 1963 from the Heidelberg philosopher, Karl Jaspers, broke a personal rule of life in order to help the young poet: she gave a television interview.

Jaspers later drew a connection between the Hochhuth case and the Arendt case – the resentment at her unemotional, sober and ironic account of the Eichmann trial in Jerusalem. Jaspers wrote:

> The persecution directed against you is dreadful [...] a frightful symptom of our situation, the situation of the Western world and of our role in it. Whoever speaks the truth is ostracized, unless no one listens to him. I am firmly convinced that this campaign to destroy your reputation will not succeed. [...] Hochhuth's *The Representative* has caused a great stir here. [...] Two days ago I took part, with him

and six other people [...], in a radio discussion [...] Much hate on the Catholic side [...] I was delighted to see this thirty-year-old German, self-taught [...] passionately engaged with the question of the murder of the Jews. In detailed knowledge he was so far superior to the Catholic professor [Rudolf Morsey][7] that he silenced him with facts and questions. [...] You are both living now behind a façade that you show the world. I am with you in my heart.[8]

Hannah Arendt's contribution was to get rid of misunderstandings and to highlight the real problem. On 25 February 1964, she published an article in the *New York Herald Tribune* saying among other things:

If we judge the Pope simply as a temporal head of state, he behaves no differently from most if not all of his peers under such circumstances. For the church as one institution among others is inclined to make an arrangement with every regime stressing its readiness to respect the property and privileges of the church [...] and understandably this has become almost a principle of faith of Catholic political philosophy [...] But the minuscule temporal power of the Papacy is connected with the 'spiritual sovereignty of the Holy See', which is another matter, and represents in the world an extraordinarily great, if also imponderable, spiritual authority.[9]

With his note – 'Church and Pope are for us human institutions. They have behaved no better and no worse than all other political authorities'[10] – Karl Jaspers touches the real neuralgic point. For unlike him, the tenor of Hochhuth's piece – one may say in agreement with faithful Catholics – implies a quite different expectation, namely, that the representative of God on earth, the head of the universal Roman Catholic Church, is to be assessed by standards other than those held by the world.

In any case a short period of peace had scarcely begun when a new wave of literature hostile to Pacelli caused fresh excitement and ran up against the beatification proceedings which had been running for more than seven years. These presupposed a holy life. Scholars reportedly argued that important information on Vatican diplomacy between 1933 and 1945 could be derived from the archives of the Papal State. Meanwhile the Vatican was the only European state to deny the world's interested historians free use of the archive up to February 2003, and persisted in a restrictive period of 80 years. Not even the historical commission set up in October 1999 jointly by the Vatican Commission for religious relations with Judaism and by the International Jewish Committee for Inter-faith Contacts received unhindered access to important Vatican documents for the period after 1922. As a result the commission of six Jewish and Catholic historians provisionally ended their work in July 2001.[11]

Since mid-February 2003 the following resources of the Vatican Secret Archive have become accessible: Archivio della Nunziatura Apostolica in Monaco [Munich] (di Baviera) – from 1922 to May 1934, Archivio della Nunziatura Apostolica in Berlino – to December 1929, Affari Ecclesiastici Straordinari, Baviera – from 1922 to the end of 1939.

These were followed in June 2002 by the opening of the Cardinal Faulhaber Archive in the Archepiscopal Archive of Munich and Freising. This enabled some gaps in the ecclesiastical historiography of the Nazi period to be filled.

The archive of the German National Church Santa Maria Dell'Anima, which includes among other things the papers of its rector, Alois Hudal, who played an important role in the periods under consideration, is, by contrast, not freely accessible. The Vatican preferred to appoint a commission to sift and evaluate the material first.[12]

Knowledge of the period after 1939 is limited to the 11-volume edition of documents (1965–81) and the narrative based on them in 1997 by Pierre Blet SJ[13] and will only be extended by more far-reaching archival studies. But the archives for the period of Pius XII (1939–58) are substantially closed. Sources and monographs so far published of course rule out the allegation that Pacelli was 'Hitler's Pope'. Pacelli's conduct in the mid-1930s precisely supports the view that he, the highest Vatican diplomat, could reach an understanding in the interests of his church and its faithful with Léon Blum's Popular Front government in Paris, equally with the American President Roosevelt, or with the European dictators, Mussolini, Franco and Hitler. The object of his policy was to strengthen or to widen the opportunities to develop Catholic life in the countries concerned. Partly against the wish of the respective episcopates in the individual national states, the Cardinal Secretary of State had to be prepared to deal with almost every political tendency. At all events these are aspects of a comprehensive estimate of Pacelli and his work.

The memoirs of Harold Tittmann Jr, Myron C. Taylor's assistant, which recently appeared, redress the balance further in favour of Pius XII, for they restore to their context many quotations which had been torn from it, and give a brilliant testimony to Pacelli who saved many lives.[14] These and other publications[15] seem to herald a new phase of research into this period. This is less a question of anything spectacular than of an honest historiographical attempt to understand the role of Pacelli and that of the Roman Catholic Church in the age of the dictatorships. 'My own sense is', wrote Joseph Bottum in an essay on *The End of the Pius Wars*, 'that the anti-Pius books are coming to an end'.[16]

The present book concentrates on the period between 1917 and 1939, and especially on those years on which new documents are to hand. It is of course a disadvantage that only the documents on the diplomatic business between the German nunciatures and the Vatican were opened, while the correspondence with the other European nunciatures remains closed. But since the diplomacy of the Holy See was conceived on a European scale, further material will have to be assembled on the other European states. This is particularly important for those countries which, as aristocratic Catholic states, laid claim to an especial ideological closeness to the Vatican, such as the fascist Italy of Mussolini.

The new documents offer no real 'sensations', but include some surprises. The new material succeeds in closing gaps in the research and helps to complete our knowledge of the 1920s and 1930s. The picture of the Vatican, the thought and dealings of its actors, gains in profile and hence in clarity. This is particularly true of Pope Pius XI, Pacelli and Cesare Orsenigo, the successor to Pacelli in the office of the Berlin imperial nuncio. In tracing the processes of decision the Vatican's veil of secrecy is demythologized.

Our best thanks are due to the archivists (of both sexes) who met us with constant kindness, and sometimes also generously let us work beyond the normal opening hours. We are particularly grateful to Fr Sergio Pagano, the Director of the Vatican Secret Archive, who facilitated our access to the Pacelli documents, and to Dr Peter Pfister, the director of the Archepiscopal Archive of Munich and Freising, who in personally difficult circumstances opened the Cardinal Faulhaber Archive to us.

We have to thank our colleagues at the Hannah-Arendt-Institut for manifold assistance. Hannelore Georgi and Katarzyna Stokłosa for the translations from the Russian and Polish, Hans Jörg Schmidt and Petra Tallafuss for going back to the German archives, for further translations, checking the notes and the index. Kai Krause has tirelessly struggled with books from the Dresden libraries, prepared numerous copies and, together with our librarian, Claudia Kegel, has looked after the inter-library loans. Stefanie Friedrich helped proofreading, and

Daniela Heitzmann provided the Index of Names. To Uwe Backes we owe references to important sources and literature; and to him and finally to Gerhard Lindemann we owe the revision of the MS and valuable suggestions. Thanks are due to Ulrich Volz of the Deutsche Verlags-Anstalt for careful sub-editing of the manuscript, and to W. Reginald Ward for his excellent translation. Last but not least, our thanks go to Michael Strang of Palgrave Macmillan publishers, and to our excellent reader, Peter Andrews.

Dresden, April 2007.   Gerhard Besier and Francesca Piombo

1
The German and European Policy of the Vatican 1904–20

1.1 Eugenio Pacelli: State–Church lawyer, diplomat and specialist in canon law

Almost uniquely as a leading priest, the Roman Eugenio Pacelli bore the impress of the Vatican and its history. The sphere of the boy Pacelli, who was born in 1876, was unequivocally determined and defined by his grandfather, father and brother, who served the Church-State in manifold ways as lawyers and officials.[1] The downfall of the Papal States in 1871, the taking of Rome by the troops of Garibaldi, the foundation of the state of Italy in 1870, and the theological measures taken within the Church by the Papacy to compensate for loss of diplomatic power, were in the background of hearsay or personal experience of one who grew up in a three-generation family of grandees.

All his life Pacelli was connected with Santa Maria in Vallicella, the church of his childhood, where he had assisted at Mass as a server. His parents sent him to the Ennio-Quirino-Visconti Lycée which offered a classical education, but was well known for its anti-curial, Italian nationalist attitude.[2] Yet the *laïque* spirit could have little purchase upon a boy with deep religious roots. Firmly resolved to become a priest, he took up theological study at the Papal Gregorian University, which he completed in 1899. On 2 April of the same year, on Easter Sunday, he was ordained priest; the following day he celebrated his first Mass. Cardinals and bishops took part in both events, which underlined again the close contacts of his family with the Holy See. The young, intellectually gifted priest was not attracted to parish service; he went back to the university, and in 1901 concluded his studies with a doctorate in law, civil and canon.

On the recommendation of Cardinal Vincenzo Vannutelli, the former papal ambassador at the court of the Tsar, and a friend of the Pacelli family, Eugenio began his professional career as a member of the Congregation of Extraordinary Church Affairs. Its influential Secretary was the titular Archbishop and internationally renowned church lawyer and canonist, Pietro Gasparri.[3] He had served from 1880 to 1897 as professor at the Institut Catholique in Paris and then as papal delegate in Peru, Bolivia and Ecuador.[4] The Congregation which was founded in 1814 reported to the Cardinal Secretary of State, dealing with questions of diocesan boundaries, nomination of bishops and similar objects. Regulations of this kind were of great significance when the Holy See was negotiating with national states and concluding bilateral treaties. Thus at just 24 years of age, Pacelli was in a crucial area of Vatican foreign policy. Already in 1903 he was nominated a staff member (Ital. *Minutante*) in the papal Department of Secretary of State, and made an adviser in the Vatican Foreign Ministry; in this way he began a career as an official in the papal Curia. Through this official work he acquired a basic insight into curial administration and papal diplomacy.

If the papal Foreign Office obtained an enduring significance from the formation of new national states, this was even more true of its Secretary. For Gasparri, the great hope of the 'progressive' cardinals,[5] did more than exercise the functions of an important office. He was also secretary of the 16-strong commission of cardinals called by Pope Pius X in 1904 to compile a new code of canon law, the Codex Juris Canonici (CIC). From the beginning he associated his colleague Pacelli in this business,[6] and took the 26-year old with him as he himself rose, continually backing him (Pacelli). On account of his work in connection with the CIC – he was credited with being the creator of the church legal code finally promulgated in 1917 and operative till 1983[7] – Gasparri was made a Cardinal in 1907, and in 1914 under Benedict XV[8] rose to be Cardinal Secretary of State. Pacelli was also at hand in 1906 when his mentor Gasparri drafted the White Book against the French law of 1905 separating Church and State;[9] in the wake of all this the Vatican unilaterally revoked the Concordat of 1801. This religious and political development in what had been 'Catholic France', a guardian of the Holy See, was bound to have a traumatic effect upon the papal diplomats. An abiding outcome of the French Revolution at the end of the eighteenth century was a division of the people into Catholics and laicists. Already in 1880 the French government had cancelled the legal validity of the 'church' Sunday as a regular holiday, and in 1906 replaced it by a secular rest day. From 1900 it took concrete measures to force the wealthy and powerful Catholic orders out of the educational system, and deprive them of the possibility of supporting anti-government activities. To this end Parliament passed a law in 1901 making the existence of religious orders dependent on legal permission. After France had finally broken off diplomatic connections with the Holy See, it was bound to seem that, from the political angle, the country was lost to the Curia.

Already in 1904 Pacelli had undertaken a private journey to France. Whether this was connected with the decision in Paris on domestic policy is uncertain. Despite the shock, Pacelli remained the complete diplomat, pursuing with pragmatism and perseverance the interests of the Holy See in regard to France.[10] For still nothing was lost.[11]

In fact there was a ferment in France at the turn of the century. The dominant climate of *Kulturkampf* favoured Charles Maurras and the reactionary *Action Française* – a movement rooted in the Dreyfus Affair, and aiming at a patriotic, anti-democratic, anti-revolutionary, monarchical and religious France.[12] It also combated the beginnings of Christian democracy, which it could assess only as an offspring of the Revolution. In the Vatican *Action Française* was taken very seriously. Maurras cultivated good relations with the upper clergy. Pius X made no secret of his sympathy for the movement. But Maurras had also attracted powerful criticism in Rome with his radical views; his enemies had several of his writings placed on the Index of forbidden books. Up to the breach of the Vatican with *Action Française* in the mid-1920s their relationship oscillated in a peculiar way.[13]

On 20 July 1903 Leo XIII died. In connexion with the papal election another Catholic great power, namely, Austria-Hungary, sought to block the candidature of Cardinal Secretary of State Mariano Rampolla by using its veto – the so-called Right of Exclusion – and opposed the candidature in the conclave.[14]

From a political point of view, the Dual Monarchy was rightly defending itself against a candidate who as the Vatican 'Foreign Minister' had wanted to prevent the Triple Alliance with Germany and Italy;[15] the alliance did not seem to him conducive to a solution of the unsettled 'Roman Question'.

With the veto the Dual Monarchy exercised no decisive influence on the election, but damaged its own case, for the affair leaked out. Even in liberal circles critical of the Church, the intervention was badly received. The Austrian Foreign Minister, Count Gołuchowski, was commissioned to attempt an appeasement. His claim that the Right of Exclusion was only a statement of wishes and a warning without obligatory force, was rejected in the *Osservatore Romano*.[16] Austria had asserted a 'traditional right', but one which had become an anachronism in the modern period.

The Vatican gazette here took up a line of argument which the young Pacelli, whose standing had risen in the Congregation for Extraordinary Church Affairs, had worked out in a study of the theme on Gasparri's instructions. In it Pacelli pointed to the late origin of the Right of Exclusion in the seventeenth century, to its establishment as a rule since the election of Innocent XII in 1691, and above all to the fact that secular states continued to make unceremonious use of the Right of Exclusion while at the same time insisting on the separation of Church and State; this separation ought to be based on liberty for both sides.

The cardinals of the Congregation for Extraordinary Church Affairs consequently agreed to the abolition of the right of veto. The explanations which Gołuchowski had made shortly before, not only suggested abolition but also offered it. This was felt the more strongly as the Church now, after the loss of its former territories, no longer regarded itself as a temporal, but only as a spiritual, authority. Hence the intervention of temporal states in the conclave concerned areas of spiritual jurisdiction, a thing no longer acceptable. Cardinal Secretary of State Raffael Merry del Val proposed to issue a second Constitution to regulate the other papal constitutions for the conclave. Hence in 1904 two constitutions were issued – on 20 January the *Commissum nobis* which condemned the right of veto, and on the 25 January the *Vacante sede apostolica* which did away with all but two (*Commissum nobis* and *Praedecessores nostri*) of the earlier Constitutions of the conclave.[17]

Pacelli was thus commissioned at the end of 1904 to acquaint the nuncios with the new constitution. They were instructed in no case to inform their respective governments about the content of the constitution – since it was a question of an internal matter affecting the conclave – but only to produce the text if they were later asked for it.[18] Only later did Pacelli, now Pope himself, succeed in completely forbidding the interference of other states in the proceedings of papal elections.

Under Pius X who followed Leo XIII on 4 August 1903, the Curia discontinued its demand for the restoration of the pre-1870 frontiers and fought instead for diplomatic recognition of the Church as an independent free entity on the juristic level.[19] The abolition of the right of veto in papal elections claimed by temporal Catholic rulers through which the Church asserted its independence of the Catholic great powers, Austria-Hungary, France and Spain, followed logically from this policy.

Pacelli rapidly advanced his career under Pius X. In October 1903, aged 27, he became on the proposal of Pietro Gasparri a colleague in the Congregation for Extraordinary Church Affairs, which as an independent authority led by a secretary, was directly subject to the Cardinal Secretary of State, and had the functions of a foreign ministry. In 1908 this congregation was incorporated in the Secretariat of State as its first division. In 1904 Pacelli rose to be house-prelate of the congregation, in 1911 he became Under-Secretary, and finally in 1914 Secretary. Pacelli was reckoned a reliable and capable representative of the policy of Pius X, and this certainly contributed to his rapid rise.[20]

In each of these offices he succeeded the ultra-conservative Monsignor Umberto Benigni. Unlike his predecessor, he put the weight not on anti-modernist and theological matters, but on the law of Church and State. Although he was doubtless an adherent of Pius X's integralist line, in this phase of his life he consistently kept out of current theological and political questions. This abstinence paid handsomely at the change in pontificate in 1914, for he was able under the new Pope Benedict XV and his Cardinal Secretary of State, Gasparri, to hasten further up his career ladder. In the first decade and a half after the turn of the century, integralism, the ecclesiastical counter-model to reform Catholicism and modernism, reached its peak. In this it became 'a sort of religious totalitarianism',[21] aiming to subject every area of faith, culture and politics to the direct authority of the Church. With the express approval of Pius X, Benigni constructed an 'espionage network over the whole of Europe',[22] the *Sodalitium Pianum*, an organization described by critics as a system 'of perfect espionage and defamation'. In this way 'covert' modernists in the Church were to be tracked down and got out of their appointments. Among those who were denounced was Angelo Giuseppe Roncalli, the future Pope John XXIII.

When the conclave met in the first weeks of the war to elect a new Pope, Cardinal Giacomo della Chiesa, the Archbishop of Bologna, was backed by the cardinals who advocated a rapid end to the modernist struggles. And in fact (and also on account of the war) after Benedict XV's accession the modernist witch-hunts faded into the background; in 1921 the Pope abolished the *Sodalitium Pianum* altogether. Of course there is no suppressing the facts that 'integralism' and 'fundamentalism' survived throughout as powerful currents in the Church, especially in high clerical circles.

After his nomination to be Secretary to the Congregation for Extraordinary Church Affairs in 1914, Pacelli was entrusted with the concordat negotiations with the kingdom of Serbia.[23] These he pursued in the name of the Cardinal Secretary of State, Raffael Merry del Val, but in fact largely independently.

The negotiations with Serbia had begun after the conclusion of a concordat with Montenegro (1886), the independence of which had been agreed in 1878 at the Congress of Berlin.[24] These first diplomatic contacts, however, had run into the sand, and were only resumed after the Balkan wars of 1912 and 1913.[25] Austria-Hungary seemed no longer to be in a position to represent the interests of the Catholic minority in the areas conquered by the Serbs. Hence the desire to protect the Catholics living there by a concordat. Belgrade had no basic objections to the Catholic faith; but locally Catholics were discriminated against because they were suspected of having political connections to Austria-Hungary. From this time on the Balkan state tolerated no intervention on the side of their Habsburg rivals. Thus the Serbian side was open to a concordat in the belief that this would impose limits to the influence of Vienna on its internal affairs.

Contact began via the nuncios of the two countries and through diplomatic channels. The Vienna nuncio, Raffaele Scapinelli di Leguigno, advocated a concordat, arguing that it would augment the influence of the Catholic Church upon Orthodox territory, even if it reduced the influence of the Danube monarchy in the region; but in the first instance Rome decided against it, in the belief that the negotiations would bring no immediate advantage to the Serbian side. But Austria-Hungary, the reliable Catholic protecting power would, it was feared, be weakened by such a step.

Yet – possibly because Vienna altered its attitude – there was support for a concordat, if the negotiations were conducted in complete understanding with the Dual Monarchy. At the beginning of 1914 the Holy See took the first official steps.[26]

The background was that the Curia had long ceased to pursue concordat negotiations. Pacelli therefore produced guidelines for a 'perfect and complete concordat' based on the Codex Juris Canonici, which was then in progress.[27] In these he embodied the following principles: free exercise of worship for the diaspora Catholics, freedom of the local church to keep contact with the Papal Curia, free admittance of religious orders, legal security of church and clerical property, state stipends for clergy and teachers of religion, and regulation of clergy training in Serbia. In the negotiations with the Serbian government, Pacelli completed this catalogue with the right to conversion and the maintenance of Austrian rights of patronage over the Catholic Church in Serbia. By permission of Cardinal Merry del Val, Eugenio Pacelli conducted the negotiations with the ambassadors from Belgrade. Vienna insisted on the maintenance of her traditional rights, such as the prayer for the Emperor during the Mass; Rome was ready to back the 'just' demands of the monarchy, but not to relax its own grip on the reins. Serbia, however, would not hear of any preservation of privileges of protectorate, and threatened to break off negotiations. At a meeting on 7 June 1914, the Cardinals decided to continue negotiations, and drop the Austrian claim to patronage rights. They were seeking to protect the Albanian Catholic minority in Serbia, and gave this higher priority.[28]

On 24 June 1914, in the presence of the negotiator Pacelli, Cardinal Merry del Val and the Serbian minister, Milenko R. Vesnitch, signed the concordat.[29] As a consequence a church province of Serbia was created, the limits of which corresponded to those of the kingdom of Serbia, and which guaranteed to those of the Roman Catholic confession free and public exercise of their faith. Candidates for bishops' sees must first be nominated to the Serbian government and take an oath of loyalty before their accession to office.

Circumstances altered dramatically four days later when Franz Ferdinand, the heir to the Austrian throne, was murdered in Sarajevo. It was Merry del Val who recommended Vienna not to recognize the concordat which had just been signed; ratification took another year – and then required pressure from Great Britain.

1.2 Pacelli becomes Apostolic Nuncio in Munich (1917) and represents the Pope's peace initiative

In autumn 1914 Gasparri was nominated Cardinal Secretary of State. He was to hold this office not only under Benedict XV but also under his successor Pius XI. From the beginning the new pope and his Cardinal Secretary of State were concerned to bring about an end to the war. Already five days after his election, on 8 September 1914, Benedict XV sent an appeal to all Catholic Christians world-wide.[30] In his accession encyclical of 1 November 1914 he besought the warring powers again to put a stop to the shedding of blood.[31] In the following year he formulated in the Secret Consistory a series of principles which should lead to a 'just and enduring peace'. Preeminent among these was the constructive compromise by which 'all parties should reduce or surrender the war aims already announced or the advantages they have previously hoped for'. Yet in the church parades there was no mention at all of the urgent words of the Catholic Supreme Head; and in the newspapers they received little or no notice.[32] In this appeal and proposals the Papacy viewed itself entirely as an unerring, impartial, moral great power. It is today uncontested that Benedict XV stuck strictly to the principle of impartiality, avoided all attempts to drive him into a corner – even by those of parties in the Vatican – and concentrated upon ending the war, working for the relief of misery and destitution; but each of the alliances reproached him in turn with supporting the other side. The French Prime Minister, Georges Clemenceau, abused him as 'le pape boche' – the German Pope – and in the German Supreme Command Erich Ludendorff spoke derisively of 'the French Pope'.[33] This was exactly the impression which Benedict XV continually wished to avoid; in the meantime he, for example, did not support a peace appeal of any side which contained no concrete proposals for the settlement of the conflict.[34] Above all under pressure from France, which since the breach of 1905 had maintained no diplomatic representation at the Holy See, Great Britain[35] and the Netherlands which had not up to 1914 maintained diplomatic relations with the Holy See now established them. Although Italy's entry into the war on the side of the Entente Powers caused many cardinals and bishops to back off towards the Western powers, the Pope and Gasparri practised a strict neutrality towards all sides.

For the Holy See conditions in Italy now took an extremely difficult turn. Pope Benedict XV complained to a Swiss prelate: 'Four-fifths of the clergy [in Italy] are anti-war and anti-government. Every sermon would be [...] under police surveillance; if a priest were to venture to offer up a prayer for peace or interpret the war as a judgment of God, he would be fetched down from the pulpit, locked up and made a subject of proceedings'.[36]

The entry of Italy into the war proved extremely inconvenient to the Vatican – not least because it was a considerable hindrance to papal diplomacy.[37] The ambassadors accredited to the Holy See by those states which found themselves at war with Italy had to leave Rome in May 1915 after the Italian declaration of war on the Central Powers.[38] They went off to Switzerland which thus became an important nerve centre of Vatican foreign policy. The diplomatic representatives of the Central Powers now settled in Lugano: the envoy of Prussia, Otto von Mühlberg, the envoy of Bavaria, Otto Ritter zu Groenesteyn, and the ambassador of Austria-Hungary, Prince Johann von Schönburg-Hartenstein. Only after the defeat of the peace initiative of the German Chancellor Theobald von Bethmann-Hollweg and that of the American President Thomas Woodrow Wilson – at the end of 1916 and the beginning of 1917 – did a new situation arise as a consequence of the US entry into the war on 3 February 1917. This intervention followed shortly upon the diplomatic failure and was immediately caused by it. The USA had been the last neutral great power which might have acted as a peace broker; she had now joined one of the warring sides. There now remained only the Holy See. Benedict XV and Gasparri wished to introduce their new peace mediation through the European nunciatures. Of all things, however, the Munich nunciature had, since the recall of Andreas Frühwirth,[39] been vacant since November 1916.[40] In well-informed circles in Munich and in the Vatican it was reckoned that Pacelli would be appointed. When the appointment was delayed, there were rumours that Pacelli was speculating on becoming the first nuncio in Berlin. Yet the Bavarian envoy to the Holy See, Otto Ritter zu Groenesteyn, held that reports of such personal aspirations on Pacelli's part were entirely groundless. In fact Benedict XV and Gasparri did not want to burn out their young, promising diplomat[41] in an initiative as unhopeful as the peace initiative. He should rather, unburdened by these circumstances, conduct the concordat negotiations in Germany after the war.[42] Instead Benedict XV sent Giuseppe Aversa to Munich. In January and February 1917 he sounded out the possibility of a separate peace between Germany and Belgium and created 'something like a centre of a movement for a Catholic peace'[43] in the nunciature; but it was all in vain, and at the beginning of April 1917 he died from the consequences of an appendix operation. Now Benedict XV had no option but rapidly to call his young, still untested, diplomat Pacelli to the nunciature which was the most important for the Central Powers. Ten days after the death of Aversa, King Ludwig III of Bavaria gave the *Agrément* for Pacelli. Groenesteyn gave a brilliant testimonial to the newcomer whom he had known since 1909. He had good manners, was unassuming and clever, and withal 'a strict champion of the canon law' and 'somewhat monastic in his bearing'.[44]

This impression could only be reinforced when Pacelli, barely arrived in Munich, wanted to insist on the reception of the new canon law. After consultation with the Pope, King Ludwig III on 12 April 1917 'nominated' Michael von Faulhaber to be Archbishop of Munich and Freising.[45] In accordance with the *Codex Juris Canonici*,[46] where an election was made by a local ruler, a 'request' (*postulatio*) had to be advised. Yet Minister of State Hertling refused Pacelli this wish because the kings of Bavaria had always spoken of '*nominatio*'.[47] As the Church historian Stefan Samerski rightly notes, from the beginning Pacelli pursued 'a concordat policy centred on the Curia and the Codex' coupled with a 'flexible and conciliatory cooperation' with the German authorities.[48] And as Fabrizio Rossi put it, perhaps somewhat too strongly: 'For Pius there were apparently no more than two instruments for dealing with the Church and the world – canon law and diplomacy'.[49] All this was supported by the 'strict hierarchical basic attitude characteristic of the period'.[50] With all personal modesty the young nuncio always represented the Church's claim to undivided leadership very selfconsciously.

Benedict XV personally consecrated Pacelli bishop in the Sistine Chapel on 13 May 1917. On the same day there also appeared for the first time to three shepherd children from the Portuguese village of Fátima, angels and members of the Holy Family. Mary's messages of peace, announced through the mouth of the children, had a profound influence on Pacelli. When in 1942 he dedicated the world to the immaculate heart of the Mother of God, he established the first Marian high point of his pontificate.[51]

On 26 May 1917 on the day before Whitsuntide Pacelli arrived in Munich.[52] At the end of June 1917 he began work as a peace-broker. Accompanied by the Archbishop of Cologne and Cardinal Felix von Hartmann, he made a journey to Berlin, emphasizing its private character in order to kill any fresh rumours of the establishment of a nunciature in the capital. He was received by (among others) the Reich Chancellor Bethmann-Hollweg, whom he informed of a letter of Benedict XV to Kaiser Wilhelm II.[53] Pacelli was subsequently to take the Pope's handwritten letter to the monarch at the General Headquarters at Bad Kreuznach. Although Bethmann-Hollweg wrongly supposed that the Papal Curia had previously taken soundings with Great Britain and wished now to damp down German claims, the conversation, in Pacelli's perception, went very satisfactorily. The parties to the conversation aimed at an understanding on arms limitation and arbitration courts to prevent future international conflicts. On the Belgian question the Chancellor declared that Germany wished to re-establish the full sovereignty of Belgium if it were guaranteed that that small country would not fall under the domination of the great powers of the West. When approached on Alsace-Lorraine, Bethmann-Hollweg showed a readiness to compromise and held that cessions of territory in return for rectifications of frontiers were entirely possible. Only in respect of German war aims in the East did the Chancellor remain vague, and referred to the revolution and the chaos prevailing there.

Pacelli did not know that Bethmann-Hollweg's confidential communications were expressions of personal opinion only and had been agreed with neither the army High Command nor with Wilhelm II. Highly delighted with (as he thought) the success of his mission,[54] he went three days later to Kreuznach, handed over the Pope's letter to the

Kaiser and advised him to seek peace even at the price of surrendering some German war aims.[55] Wilhelm expressed his regret that the Pope had not already supported the German peace offer of December 1916, and, while recommending a more powerful propagation of the idea of peace through the Catholic Church, warned against the peace activities of international socialism. According to the impression of the Kaiser's circle, the nuncio again left 'well satisfied with this reception'.[56] Yet the opposite was the case. To Gasparri he reported that the monarch was weary and distracted, spoke disconnectedly on various themes, and gave the effect of being 'quite fanatical and not altogether normal'.[57]

On 29 June Pacelli went back to Munich in order to meet the Austrian Emperor Charles I, who was staying with King Ludwig III of Bavaria. As he had done with the Germans, the nuncio sought to fathom the Austrian attitude towards the papal peace initiative. Since mid-June Gasparri had pressed the Austrian government, through a middleman, Provost Franz Segesser of Lucerne, to make concessions to Italy.[58] Now Pacelli received a positive answer. With the help of prior concessions from both the German empires, the Vatican wanted to set up a kind of working party to prepare for a peace settlement. However, the German government learned neither from the Curia nor from its Viennese allies that the Vatican had suggested concessions to Austria-Hungary too. Thus it was bound to gain the impression that concessions were expected from the German Reich alone. The success of the papal peace mission was further impeded by the resignation of Bethmann-Hollweg on 14 July 1917. Five days later the Reichstag adopted a peace resolution of its own.[59]

On 24 July Pacelli, again under conditions of strict secrecy, went to Berlin for a second time and made a formal offer of mediation to the Reich government under the new Chancellor, Georg Michaelis. As a basis of mediation he handed in a memorandum which, after a bilateral agreement, should be delivered to all the warring powers as an official papal peace note. That the Vatican had previously consulted the Reich and had submitted a preliminary text to it, should be subject to the strictest discretion.[60] This memorandum already included all the essential points of the papal peace note of 1 August 1917:[61] guarantees for the freedom of the seas; arms limitations all round; the establishment of an international court of arbitration; mutual refusal of reparations payments; and the military and political independence of Belgium. To avoid giving the impression that agreements had already been secured from the Reich government, rapid publication followed. Of course the moment could scarcely have been chosen more favourably for the Reich,[62] for in the east the Kerensky offensive ordered on 16 June collapsed hopelessly five days later,[63] so that once again the position of the Germans appeared very strong. On 9 August 1917 the envoys of Great Britain, Russia and Belgium received delivery of the papal peace note, and the Central Powers three days later.[64] France, Italy and the USA had no diplomatic representation at the Curia. Hence Gasparri begged the king of England to send on the papal note to the heads of state concerned.

Upon the memorandum, Michaelis, accompanied by Secretary of State Richard von Kühlmann, went to the General Headquarters near Kreuznach to discuss the Pope's peace proposals with Hindenburg and Ludendorff. The military took the view that the 'security' of Belgium should not be surrendered by a declaration, and hence rejected every prior concession. All the efforts of Gasparri and Pacelli to get another 'favourable answer on the Belgian question' foundered on the resistance of the military authorities and on the bilateral peace efforts with Great Britain, which appeared more hopeful than the papal initiative. The extraordinarily cautious formulations of Michaelis's reply on 24 September 1917 seemed to the Curia to mean the end of their mission. And Pacelli's argument that it was not only a matter of diplomatic success but of the moral outcome before world public opinion was absolutely fruitless.[65] Only in December 1917 did the Papal Secretariat of State learn of the Spanish initiative for a bilateral understanding between the German Reich and Great Britain. In disillusionment the Holy See had to take note how little its diplomacy was trusted.

The same was true of the other parties to the war. At the end of August 1917 the Emperor Charles informed the Apostolic Nuncio Teodoro Valfré di Bonzo who was accredited to Vienna between 1916 and 1919 that he could not entertain the proposal of the cession of Trent to Italy.[66] France[67] and Italy simply rejected the papal peace initiative, while President Wilson formulated his own peace demands; these, for example the abolition of monarchy, were equivalent to a rejection.

On the 24 October the successful offensive of the Central Powers against Italy began. Ten days previously, Winston Churchill, the Minister of Munitions, discussed in detail the peace conditions of Great Britain, demanding not only the reestablishment of Belgium, but also the 'liberation' of Alsace Lorraine.[68] Soon the entry of the USA into the war was to work to the disadvantage of the Central Powers. Nor did the Russian Revolution and the collapse of the Tsarist empire bring the hoped-for military relief. As Gasparri had foreseen, within a few months the constellations were to alter in such a way that 'no further peace proposals could be made' and the 'war [proceeded] to the bitter end'.[69] During the last months of the war Pacelli concentrated his concerns on charitable work for prisoners of war.[70] The support of the Holy See with food and wound-dressings, and their search-service for refugees and missing persons were widely and thankfully received.[71] These concerns enhanced the profile of the Vatican as a neutral power and earned worldwide diplomatic prestige.[72]

Pacelli's engagement with the papal peace offensive had become public, and he was bound to be affected by the defeat of the initiative. His reputation in Catholic circles remained undimmed; but on the side of the Protestant majority, with its overwhelmingly nationalist mood, a deeply rooted mistrust towards him persisted. In one respect the collapse of the Second Empire and the change of political elites in Germany to which it led favoured the progress of his career. During the peace initiative Pacelli had made use of the controversial Centre Party deputy, Matthias Erzberger,[73] as a middle man; he had had free access to the Munich nunciature, and had had the first sight of extremely confidential documents. This was not among the brightest diplomatic achievements of the young diplomat on the personal side.[74] Alternatively, Michael Feldkamp, a distinguished student of Vatican diplomacy, rightly endorses the view that such ' "collaborators" in the grey area between informer, spy or agent' were part of the stock-in-trade of every government.[75] Nevertheless, the Vatican was and is more than a political institution. It has also a moral role. This double viewpoint led and still leads repeatedly to critical enquiries on the relation of diplomacy and religion in the Papal State.[76] A little later the closeness of Erzberger to the Curia was to occasion great agitation in the Curia itself. In 1920 Erzberger had withdrawn to Biberach to write his memoirs. 'Knowing the nature of this man', wrote Pacelli on 15 July 1920 to Gasparri, 'I was immediately anxious that he might publish fantastic novelties compromising for the Holy See'.[77] He had Erzberger ordered by three different contacts that he should exercise the greatest caution in what he wrote, and gave notice that in certain circumstances the Holy See 'would see itself compelled, even though regretfully, to inflict a formal denial against him and publicly deplore his behaviour'.[78]

When Erzberger responded by giving him parts of the manuscript to read, Pacelli was dismayed. 'Much as I was prepared for his lack of caution, I admit that the reading exceeded my every expectation and anxiety; so compromising were they for the Holy See and especially for the person of the Holy Father himself, for example in the matter of Italy's entry into the war'.[79] Pacelli himself pointed to the omissions and alterations he regarded as necessary. Erzberger who thought he had written 'all these parts for the good name of the Holy See',[80] yielded at once and altered the passages concerned in his book. Pacelli, who again inspected the corrected chapter, was satisfied: 'I must acknowledge that when it [i.e. the chapter] appears in this form, it will not I think work to the damage of the Holy See'.[81] It was only the chapter on the papal peace mission that for safety's sake Pacelli sent once again to Rome.[82] Gasparri was worried: 'Especially the detailed account of the points regarded by the Holy See as possible bases for peace will certainly reawaken the impression that when the Holy See published the Papal note of 15 August 1917, it acted in agreement with Germany.'[83]

The papal peace initiative had repercussions in the Weimar National Assembly.[84] Primarily through Erzberger's reproach that the parties of the Right and the Army Supreme Command had torpedoed a possible peace understanding brokered by the Pope, and thus bore part responsibility for the fiasco of the German collapse, the National Assembly established a parliamentary committee of inquiry. A subcommittee of inquiry formed within this committee concerned itself also with the papal peace initiative. Although on principle as well as on diplomatic grounds the Vatican was not prepared to make its papers available,[85] the committee of inquiry obtained a knowledge of many papal documents. It was not only the Curia but also the German government that became alarmed that the publication of particular Vatican documents might give the impression that the Holy See had been altogether too pro-German. So the Centre politician Ludwig Kaas,[86] who was closely connected with Pacelli, was appointed *rapporteur*. Indeed, the work of the committee of inquiry never came to a conclusion, but the subcommittee declared that the German government 'had made mistakes in the formal handling of the Papal peace initiative'.[87]

Bethmann-Hollweg's memoirs confirm the essentials of this picture,[88] unlike the *Ereignisse und Gestalten*, written by Wilhelm II in exile in the Netherlands. There, the defeated monarch projected himself as the inspirer of the papal peace initiative.[89] After the vain attempts of Pacelli with the help of the Foreign Office and through the mediation of the Benedictine Abbot of Maria Laach, Ildefons Herwegen,[90] to stop the publication of Wilhelm II's memoirs in this form, Pacelli published a correction in the *Germania* and in the *Osservatore Romano*.[91]

1.3   The attitude of the Munich Nuncio towards the Bavarian revolution and the concerns of the Holy See for a just peace

After the end of the war Pacelli in Munich experienced the Bavarian revolution led by Kurt Eisner, a Prussian of Jewish descent.[92] On

8 November he sent a telegram to Gasparri: 'After yesterday's popular demonstration tonight a democratic-social republic is proclaimed. Provisional Council formed of workers, soldiers and peasants. Please inform families that we are well.'[93] Two days later he reported: 'Situation very bad. No serious guarantee [for the security] of papal representation. Request His Eminence to give me instructions or authority to take whatever means may possibly be advisable in unforeseeable new circumstances. My most heartfelt request is for broad powers for the whole of Germany, and also [possible] subordinate powers of attorney and to give ease to our families.'[94]

The following day he wrote a contrasting report:

> The Archbishop of Munich came to tell me that, should the clause in the armistice about the continuance [of] the blockade remain in force, in Bavaria alone several hundred thousands [will die] of hunger and there will be a frightful catastrophe. He begs His Holiness to intercede with President Wilson and the Entente Powers so that Germany may be spared this immense disaster. The Archbishop also foresees great and imminent danger [to] me personally, and advised me confidentially to go to Switzerland. Please send instructions for me and the staff.[95]

Gasparri informed Pacelli on 13 November that the telegrams and political reports had arrived. 'Your Honour has the full authorisations requested and *complete freedom to move elsewhere should you accept today's advice of the Archbishop*, whose warning was delivered.'[96] In a letter to Faulhaber of 9 December 1918 Gasparri showed his anxiety over the threat to religion posed by the revolution and praised Pacelli for his 'courageous decisiveness' in coming out for the freedom of religion.[97]

It is not possible to be absolutely clear about the reactions of the nuncio between November 1918 and May 1919, though there is a series of highly embroidered reports.[98] Their intention seems frequently to be to represent the revolutionary governments in the worst possible light so as to provide a personal motive for Pacelli's presumed anticommunism from this time.[99] The Archbishop of Munich, Michael von Faulhaber, avoided every contact with Eisner's revolutionary government,[100] and sought to put off taking up positions so as not to have to cooperate[101] with Johannes Hoffmann, the minister for public worship and 'an outspoken representative of the *Kulturkampf* and hater of the Church'.[102] Faulhaber wanted to move Pacelli too to this basic refusal of contact. The revolutionary government only sought a connexion with him, 'in order to create the impression among the Catholic people that the Apostolic Nuncio had recognized the Eisner government and legitimated the Revolution'.[103] Hence he had to leave Munich and go into Switzerland. Faulhaber does not mention that he twice urged the nuncio to follow the same course.[104]

Of the concerns of Eisner to establish relations with Pacelli almost no testimonies other than Faulhaber's have been taken into account. From a report of Pacelli to Gasparri of 20 November 1918, however, it transpires that the Provisional Government tried to arrange 'an accidental meeting' between Kurt Eisner and Pacelli. After brief reflection (according to Pacelli) he rejected the offer through the *Uditore* – the trainee lawyer at the nunciature, Monsignor Schioppa. Faulhaber, whom Pacelli would have liked to consult on this question, was not in Munich.

> The reasons for my answer were the following: 1) the present government (which moreover is only provisional) consists of atheists, Jews, Protestants, all revolutionary socialists, with whom an Apostolic Nuncio seems able to have no respectable connection. Particularly controversial is the person of the Foreign Minister, Kurt Eisner, a Galician Jew, often condemned to gaol for political offences. 2) The planned meeting would have made, I believe, a deplorable impression upon the Catholics and indeed on all supporters of order. 3) The government wishes now to create the appearance of being on good terms with the Apostolic Nunciature to pacify the Catholics and so weaken their opposition at the next elections. Afterwards, if they feel quite safe, they will put their anti-religious programme into action. That is why, while in Saxony and in Protestant Prussia the respective provisional governments have already declared the separation of the Church from the State, the Bavarian government has so far refrained from such a step in order not to goad the Catholic population. Had I agreed to that meeting, I would have played the game of the revolutionary and anti-religious government [...] 5) None of the other members of the *Corps Diplomatique* has made his way to the Foreign Minister. But it is indeed true that the monarchs by whom they were accredited have all lost their thrones. 6) The minister who has been in power for a fortnight has taken none of the usual steps to inform the *Corps Diplomatique* of his accession to office; he had indeed almost acted as if he were ignoring the nunciature to which at the beginning and only under difficulties he conceded the right to send telegrams in code (as I have already had the honour to report to Your Eminence). And I should have had to surrender

myself to a conversation with him in the rooms of a subordinate functionary – for the sole purpose of a subsequent public announcement that the Apostolic Nuncio had made a visit to Kurt Eisner, with whom he had good relations.[105]

Why Pacelli left Munich about 20 November[106] has been hitherto quite obscure. In the older literature his departure from Munich was attributed to his weakened state of health.[107] Vatican sources, however, suggest that it is more probable that, having informed Eisner of the above-mentioned political ground for a departure, he preferred to leave the revolutionary's sphere of influence. Whether he was in Munich again for the Landtag elections on 12 January 1919 is not known.[108] But shortly afterwards he reported from the Bavarian metropolis on the second revolution in Bavaria. Eisner's USPD had suffered a disastrous defeat in the Landtag elections in the middle of January 1919. On 21 February 1919 on his way to the Landtag, where he wished to announce his resignation as head of the government, Eisner, man of letters and pacifist, was gunned down by the law student Lieutenant Anton Count Arco auf Valley who was on leave.[109] After he had already reported on the political confusions immediately after the election,[110] Pacelli gave a detailed report on the situation on 23 February 1919:

On the 21st [February] when Parliament was to be opened, the streets leading to the Parliament building were occupied by troops from early morning. It seemed that every measure had been taken to ensure the best possible protection for the Landtag [...] All that was lacking was the Prime Minister Kurt Eisner. When finally Herr Fechenbach, Kurt Eisner's young secretary, appeared in the room deathly white and announced in broken tones that the Prime Minister had been murdered, an unheard-of din broke out in the room. Everywhere there were cries of terror, and only after many efforts did the President of the Assembly bring some calm to the tumult [...] In the adjoining rooms there was anger against the Interior Minister Auer, a well-known political critic of Eisner [...] After about an hour the sitting was reopened. Auer began to speak at once, and with touching and lively turns of phrase expressed his regrets at the murder of the Prime Minister, especially as Eisner had already resolved to hand in to the Landtag the resignation of the entire cabinet. The speech of the minister found general agreement and was interrupted by expressions of sympathy. Yet while the deputy Süssheim moved that the Landtag be postponed indefinitely, an individual broke into the room clad as a soldier but wearing a civilian hat, threw himself against the minister Auer, and discharged three revolver shots into his [...] breast. The minister was seen to lay his hands on his heart and collapse upon the chair. Someone went up to Auer to see whether he was still alive, and, since he was still breathing, he was taken to the hospital where he is still struggling between life and death. The general story is that the murder of Eisner took place as follows. He went alone and on foot from the Foreign Ministry to the Landtag, which is close nearby, when a young man who looked like a student fired three revolver shots into his neck; Eisner raised his arm, staggered, collapsed on the ground and died at once. The murderer is a Count Arco-Valley, who was at once attacked by a soldier and mortally wounded, though efforts were made to keep him alive. Since he is an aristocratic army officer and a Catholic, the Socialists could think of nothing better than to incite the people against the nobility, the officers and the church [...] For the moment no new government has been formed and the country is under the command of the soldiers' soviet [...] Meanwhile the war is beginning against members of the clergy. Clergy access to military hospitals has been strictly forbidden by a resolution of the soldiers' soviet. The priest can only do his work in cases of fatality or where the sick request him. Otherwise no Mass and no religious presence [...] All the efforts and the sacrifice made by the 'Bavarian People's Party' and the parties of order to get a parliament which should keep peace and order in the country have been destroyed by the thoughtless murder of Eisner [...][111]

When Eisner was buried at the beginning of March 1919, Pacelli reported that an impressive procession of about 50,000 people had formed, the revolutionary parties using the burial to stage a powerful demonstration. 'All the shops and public offices were obliged to close on that day. Every house had to hoist the black flag. Every church was forcibly compelled to ring its bells as a sign of mourning.'[112]

On 17 March 1919 the Landtag elected the minister for public worship, Johannes Hoffmann of the Majority Social Democrats, to be the new prime minister. At the same time there existed since 21 February 1919 a Central Committee of the Bavarian Republic led by the Augsburg teacher, Ernst Niekisch. Encouraged by the proclamation of a Hungarian Soviet Republic by the communist Béla Kun on 21 March 1919,[113] the Central Committee proclaimed the first Munich Soviet Republic, and announced the dismissal of the Hoffmann government. On 13 April the republican soldiers' army was defeated by the 'Red Army' of the soviet republic of the Hoffmann government which had retreated to Bamberg. Now the Bavarian Communists under Eugen Leviné seized the reins and founded the second Bavarian Soviet Republic. Yet the 'sun of world revolution' (Leviné) set rapidly again. The Bamberg government received military support from the Reich War Minister Noske, and from the Württemberg *Freikorps*, which on 3 May overthrew Leviné's soviet republic with bloodshed, and a month later executed its supreme People's Commissar.

Impressed by these struggles, Pacelli perceived the great danger of a spread of revolution with the development of conditions like those in Soviet Russia. Under such conditions Germany could no longer meet her reparation payments. The revolution could spread into France and Italy. 'If the Entente refuses or hesitates to send help, Bolshevism will triumph inexorably, and social destruction will be let loose in the whole world.'[114]

In the middle of April 1919 even the nunciature suffered detriment, although only on the 9th had Pacelli been given a safe pass.[115] Pacelli reported to Rome on how events were turning out.

> In consequence of these deplorable events it was thought opportune to hold a meeting of the *Corps Diplomatique* to arrive at some decisions relating to these events. After a long discussion it was resolved to speak directly with Levien, the supreme head of the Munich Soviet Republic, to press him to declare unmistakeably whether and how the present communist government intended to acknowledge and protect the immunity of diplomatic representatives. The negotiations were entrusted to the Nunciature and the Prussian delegation. Since it would have been absolutely inappropriate for me to present myself to the gentleman concerned, I commissioned the Monsignor *Uditore* [i.e. Schioppa] to go to him this morning together with the Prussian Chargé d'Affaires, Count von Zech. Levien had settled in with his staff – or if you prefer, with the council of the representatives of the people – in the old royal palace of the Wittelsbachs. The drama there is quite indescribable. The most chaotic muddle, the most offensive dirt, the continual coming and going of armed soldiers and workers, the obscene expressions, the resounding curses, make the former favourite seat of the King of Bavaria a veritable witches' cauldron. A host of employees come and go, pass on orders, circulate reports, and among them a series of unprepossessing young women, Jewesses foremost among them, who stand about provocatively in all the offices and laugh ambiguously. At the head of this group

of women is Levien's mistress: a young Russian, a Jewess, divorced into the bargain, who gives orders as head of house. And to her must the nunciature bow to gain access. Levien is a young man, a Russian and a Jew to boot, 30 or 35 years old. Pale, dirty, with impassive eyes, he talks himself hoarse: he is a truly offensive type, yet has intelligent and sly features. He condescended to encounter Monsignor *Uditore* on a walk, surrounded by an armed escort, among them an armed hunchback, his loyal bodyguard. With his hat on his head and smoking, he listened to what Monsignor Schioppa had to say, repeatedly and rudely interjecting that he was in a hurry for more important business. In a contemptuous tone he said that the soviet republic acknowledged the extra-territorial status of the foreign delegations just so long as the representatives of the powers, be they friendly or hostile (he made no distinction), did nothing against the republic.

When the *Uditore* pointed out to him that the position of the papal representative deserved special respect because of his mission, Levien laid it on ironically thick: 'Of course it is a question of protecting the Centre Party!' Monsignor Schioppa vigorously replied that it was a question of protecting the religious interests of the Catholics, not of Bavaria only, but of the whole of Germany!

The end of the conversation was that he sent the *Uditore* to Comrade Dietrich, the People's Commissar for Foreign Affairs. Then, all over again, a series of women, soldiers and workers; more shouting; more Babel [...] Essentially he repeated what Levien had said, adding in a way that permitted no discussion that, should the nuncio do anything against the soviet republic or other interests of the pro-letariat, he would be 'thrown out'. He repeated the principle already enunciated by Levien, that *they did not need the nunciature*, the more so as they were going to separate church and state.[116]

Shortly before the final triumph of the government troops, on 29 April, the extraterritorial status of the Munich nunciature was in fact infringed. According to the reports of Pacelli and Schioppa, the soviet government under threat of armed force required them to produce the official car of the nunciature.[117] Against the protest of Pacelli, based on a document of the People's Commissar for Foreign Affairs of the soviet republic of Bavaria, Hermann Dietrich,[118] the car was confis-cated; but it was returned when it was found that a skilful doctoring by Pacelli's chauffeur had rendered it immobile.[119] The next day the car was confiscated again. The city commandant, Josef Max Mehrer,[120] whom Pacelli had informed, sent his troops to protect the nuncio's car from confiscation by the 'Red Guard'.[121] Yet the 'Reds' won through, and the car was only returned through the intervention of an Italian officer of the Italian military mission in Berlin who had been detailed to Munich. In consequence, Pacelli preferred to spend several nights outside the nuncio's palace, fearing that the commandant of the Red Army, southern section, having been 'foiled twice'[122] would order a night attack on the building.

Pacelli and Schioppa could report yet another incident which took place on the evening of 3 May.[123] When indeed Schioppa put the light on in his bedroom, Prussian government troops shot at the nunciature; then 20 men and 3 officers searched the house in the belief that shots had been fired from the nunciature at their soldiers. Pacelli protested to the Prussian embassy in Munich at the breach in the law; and received a promise that such a mishap would not occur again. An apology from Prime Minister Hoffmann for this event was also handed in.[124]

Only after sticking out the revolutionary turbulence and on instructions from the Holy See did Pacelli leave Munich for the second time. The tense situation, especially the bloody terror perpetrated by the Freikorps and the actions of revenge against the 'Spartakists', made it impossible for the nuncio to conduct his office with dignity.[125] The immediate occasion for his departure was a telegram from Gasparri of 8 May 1919, which reached Pacelli via the nuncio in Vienna. It read: 'Inform Monsignor Pacelli that he is to secure the archive of the nunciature and then go with the *Uditore* into Switzerland where he will receive instructions'.[126] Pacelli at first hesitated to leave the nunciature in the lurch, and pointed to the apology of the Hoffmann government.[127] Only a second, very clear telegram from Gasparri on 10 May left him no choice.[128] In a letter to the Foreign Ministry of the Bavarian People's State he informed the government, however, that he would only go to Switzerland temporarily.[129] On 6 May, 21 Kolping apprentices had fallen victim to the excesses of a city in a state of siege,[130] and the usual Corpus Christi procession could not take place because of the unsafe conditions.

While the traditional church festivals were thus threatened, the secular state got down to establishing its own national celebrations. Erzberger advised Pacelli that the Vatican might establish 'the 1st May as a Marian festival' and 'give [it] thus a religious consecration'. They might thus 'remove from it the inconvenience which would otherwise attach to the day'.[131] Pacelli approved this proposal and passed it on to Gasparri.[132] Nine years later, Mothers' Day was introduced as a further secular festival. This day was also rejected by the Church which regarded it as competitive with its own religious interpretation. Referring to a sermon by Faulhaber of 31 May 1928, his canon wrote to the Bavarian Minister of State for Education and Public Worship: '[W]e Catholics need no new Mother's Days because we already have Mothers' Days in the Marian festivals of the Church year, and because this attempt to introduce a Mothers' Day is, in the eyes of his eminence, a quiet Protestant homesickness for the cult of Mary'.[133]

Again in the middle of June 1919 Pacelli – against the background of the draft constitution – showed himself deeply sceptical about political and religious development in Bavaria.

> The situation in Bavaria [...] is furthermore perilous, and the interests of the Church seem to be under great threat, so that there must be increasing fear that the prophecy of the Archbishop of Munich in his sermon of 31 December last will come true; he warned the faithful that if the separation of church and state were carried through in Bavaria it would follow not the American, but the French system.[134]

According to the draft constitution the Catholic Church enjoyed no privileges in relation to the other religious communities, in the schools question socialist doctrine was established, and there was no longer compulsory religious instruction.

The Catholic historian Stefan Samerski assumes that Pacelli's 'total [...] experiences and impressions [in revolutionary Munich] could not fail to affect his attitude to socialism' and to illuminate for him again 'the value of agreements by concordat for the relations of Church and State'.[135] The strength of this interpretation is that the people's representatives cherished no particular sympathies for the Church and moreover reproached the nuncio for protecting the Centre Party.[136] At the same time, the Bavarian envoys at the Holy See reported that Pacelli made light of the incursions and without more ado could understand 'why under present conditions diplomatic niceties did not receive due significance'.[137]

In contrast to this, in the wake of the Catholic press and the memoirs of Pacelli's housekeeper, Pascalina Lehnert,[138] numerous authors fashion the Nuncio's experiences of the Bavarian revolution into a key trauma for a deeply felt anticommunism which he never shook off. Moreover, events were so represented, as Heinz Hürten, the author of the standard work on *Deutsche Katholiken 1918–1945*,[139] worked out, that only the soviet republics were held responsible for the sensation, but not the troops of the Reich government. This early bias may be due to diplomatic considerations. Perhaps relations to a Reich government in the coalition cabinet in which there were three members of the Centre should not be held responsible.[140] In view of the alleged reservations of Pacelli towards 'godless Bolshevism', it must be said that these could not have had a powerful emotional colouring. Otherwise the Holy See would scarcely have drawn him into the secret negotiations with the Soviet ambassador in Berlin, Nikolai Krestinski, in 1925.[141] But Pacelli connected – at any rate for Germany – the danger of Bolshevism with the idea (also religious) of 'chaos'.[142] Another view tends to emphasize Pacelli's prejudices against 'Bolshevik Jews'.[143] On this the letter of the nuncio to Gasparri of 18 April 1919 quoted above should be useful. It describes the circumstances in which Schioppa, in the headquarters of the soviet republic, begged for guarantees for the extraterritorial status of the diplomatic representatives. Conceivably the situation must have been humiliating for the *Uditore*; he was dealt with in the corridor by the girlfriend of the revolutionary Max Levien. The reckoning that those present were untidy, of alien faith and indisposed to Church morality compensated for the insult he had received. As long as Jews did not convert to the true Catholic faith, they belonged in the Church's understanding to unbelievers and the stubbornly unrepentant. To support them in their false belief, as was requested in early autumn 1917, when a rabbi asked Pacelli to help him bring in palm leaves for the Jewish Feast of the Tabernacles, would have been a sacrilege from this religious point of view. What is more, Pacelli could call on the canon law which prohibited religious intercourse with unbelievers.[144] In this case it was not even a case of support 'within the scope of practical, arms' length, purely civil or natural rights common to all human beings'[145] but of assistance with the ritual of what in the Catholic understanding was a false religion. When it was a question of salvation, there was no room for diplomatic niceties.

In the last months of the war and after its end the principal anxiety of the Holy See was over the Central Powers. The Curia was less concerned about one-sided political relief for Germany, Austria[146] and Hungary,[147] and for the establishment of a secure and durable peace in Europe. First, Benedict applied himself to securing an easing of the Armistice conditions.[148] The Italian government immediately after the end of the war appealed to the secret article of the London agreement of 1915; by this the Holy See was not to be admitted to the peace negotiations, so the Holy See was refused immediate political intervention. The Italian fear was that papal diplomacy in the reordering of Europe would bring up the 'Roman Question' and get a favourable response. To the Curia it seemed that only the mediation of the American President could facilitate a compromise with the Italian government.

The Holy See recognized very early the future significant role of the USA.[149] Yet no arrangement was arrived at through these channels. Since the Pope could achieve a political result only through a well-functioning diplomatic network, it was important for the Curia to secure a rapid return of the German embassies to Rome – a point of difference with the Italian national state as also with France, which wanted to block the presence of the German representatives in the Holy City for as long as possible.[150]

In mid-September Diego von Bergen,[151] at that time director of Political Division II in the Foreign Office, travelled to Pacelli in Munich, to ascertain the possibilities of a mediation in the peace talks.[152] Pacelli saw no room for the Holy See to act, but gave von Bergen to understand that Germany must be ready to make concessions according to the state of affairs in the Alsace-Lorraine question. The note, with which Prince Max of Baden applied for an armistice on 4 October 1918, Erzberger leaked also to Pacelli; the latter passed it on to the papal Secretariat of State with the comment that he regretted the self-humiliation of the Germans and the fact that the hands of the Curia were tied.[153] Benedict XV thereupon turned on 11 October to President Wilson with the request that he use his influence in the interests of a just peace.[154] At the beginning of November, a few days before the armistice on the 11th Pacelli again sent an urgent report on the situation to Gasparri, in which he also mentioned the threat of chaos because of the Bolshevik revolution.[155]

Shortly after the armistice the Under-Secretary of State von dem Bussche sent an urgent appeal to Pacelli, vividly representing the catastrophic effects of the Allies' blockade of food and pointing to the threat of socialist revolution. Von Hartmann, Cardinal of Cologne, accompanied this request for intervention, and emphasized on his own account the necessity of a papal *démarche*.[156] After the beginning of the peace conference at Versailles, the special envoy of the Curia and Secretary of the Congregation for Extraordinary Church Affairs, Archbishop Bonaventura Cerretti, was able to make unobtrusive contact with President Wilson, but achieved no results of any kind.[157] At the beginning of April Cardinal von Hartmann proposed to the Curia that, as a first step towards the reconciliation of nations, they might foster contacts between the German clergy and those of the former enemy states.[158] On 8 May 1919, a day after the German delegation had received the complete peace treaty and it became clear that there was no more room for bargaining, Erzberger, a member of the German delegation, turned directly to Benedict XV and begged him to intervene.[159] The majority of the German episcopate also pressed for a papal intervention. On 11 May 1919 Pacelli sent on the vote of the bishops to Gasparri with the following comment:[160] 'I am asked by numerous German bishops, to beseech the Holy Father to intervene to obtain easier peace conditions for Germany, conditions which they think are not possible to realize and calculated to plunge the whole population into despair.' The next day the Dutch Internuncio Sebastiano Nicotra drew Gasparri's attention to the desperate state of Germany, and declared his anxiety about the possible Bolshevizing of the country.[161] Despite the scant prospect of success Benedict XV sent another note to President Wilson via his adviser, Colonel Edward Mandell House, seeking easier peace terms for the Germans.[162] Pacelli immediately informed the German episcopate of this step,[163] and even after the defeat of this intervention did not cease his efforts to move the Curia to fresh efforts.[164] Finally, though again in vain, the Vatican developed considerable diplomatic activity to stop the handing over and condemnation of the German Kaiser who was now in exile in the Netherlands.[165]

After the enforced signing of the peace treaties, it was Gasparri's opinion that they had created an intolerable situation in Europe.[166] Subsequently the Curia intensified its efforts to help the Germans, turning to the governments and to the episcopates of the Entente Powers with requests for deliveries of food for the hungry land.[167] Benedict XV and also Gasparri left no doubt that they considered the Versailles Treaty an unjust document, and a threat to peace.[168] In the encyclical *Pacem Dei munus* of 23 May 1920,[169] the Pope distanced himself from the Paris peace treaties.

The war and its consequences led to a considerable increase in the foreign-policy activities of the Holy See, and this left its mark in the founding of new embassies to the Vatican in Rome.[170] The Centre Party in particular favoured entry into the League of Nations to bring Germany out of her isolation; this of course did not succeed, the more so as no other state had a comparable interest in an integration of the Vatican into the international community.[171]

1.4 The establishment of an embassy of the German Reich to the Holy See and the Berlin Nunciature (1920)

Since the reopening of the Prussian embassy to the Vatican in 1882, which lasted till 1920, and the ending of the Kulturkampf,[172] the idea of creating a Reich nunciature in Berlin had been repeatedly considered.[173] During the First World War these views hardened. Plans of this kind were delayed by the worries of Bavaria that with a nunciature in Berlin the Catholic pre-eminence in South Germany would be relativized, and by the aversion of the Protestant north to a presence of the Curia in the capital. Again the Prince Bishop of Breslau, Georg von Kopp, would lose influence through a Reich nunciature, since diplomatic relations between Rome and Berlin would no longer have to go through him. Finally, the Centre Party also feared that it would lose independence if there was a representative of the Pope in Berlin.[174] After Italy came into the war, the Holy See signaled its readiness to accredit a *chargé d'affaires* in Berlin and later on to send a nuncio.[175]

The Pope showed not only a clear inclination to the Central Powers; he was also from interested motives – an international solution to the 'Roman Question' – concerned for a European balance of power, and within Italy found himself in a similar difficult situation to that of the Central powers in Europe.[176] These motives were strengthened as the war went on and peaked in the wish of Benedict XV to establish his most capable diplomat, Pacelli, as nuncio in Berlin.[177] When the *Germania*, the organ of the German Centre Party, openly brought up the question of a double accreditation in Munich and Berlin in the middle of February 1917,[178] Pacelli's predecessor in Munich, Aversa, at once spoke up for this solution to Cardinal Secretary of State Gasparri.[179] Hitherto the Roman Curia had made use, more often than not, of the Munich nunciature to forward its letters to the Reich government in Berlin.[180] Here it was of course important to have regard to Bavarian sensitivities and avoid everything which might be seen as a devaluation of the Munich nunciature.[181] Gasparri started from a stop-gap arrangement for the duration of the war, but expected, in view of the snubs they had so far received from Berlin, that the Reich government would have to take the initiative.[182]

Aversa got Erzberger to take soundings in Berlin and gave his negotiator the report on the way that 'the Holy See would give a sympathetic hearing to a request of this kind'.[183] The Reich government welcomed the sending of an Apostolic nuncio to Berlin, but saw difficulties on their side with 'additional accreditation' and were in any case afraid of the opposition of Wilhelm II.[184] Via Monsignor Rudolf von Gerlach, the former chamberlain of Benedict XV, the Reich government sounded out the attitude of the Curia to the establishment of a permanent nunciature in Berlin. To get a clear idea he wrote to the Vatican's German expert, Pacelli.[185] Pacelli replied to von Gerlach that the management of this very important question was in the hands of Aversa.[186] But at the same time he told him that the negotiations ought to be deferred to the end of the war.[187]

A fortnight later, on 17 April 1917, Aversa died suddenly. On 26 May 1917 Aversa's successor Pacelli paid his inaugural visit to the Bavarian President, Georg Count von Hertling, who openly expressed his opposition to the project of the Berlin nunciature.[188] Yet Pacelli held firm to the intention, and on his visit to Berlin in June 1917 certainly discussed it with the Kaiser, the Chancellor and the Foreign Secretary. On the strength of the reservations in Bavaria, no further steps were taken until 1919. But the project was kept in mind even in Berlin. Thus the Prussian envoy at the Vatican, Otto von Mühlberg, drew attention to the growing diplomatic significance of the Curia, at the end of July 1918, and expressed his fear that Germany might be at a disadvantage from its lack of foreign policy contacts.[189]

After the collapse of the Second Empire and the proclamation of the Republic, the social and political constellations in Germany had fundamentally changed. On this account and because of the *Codex Juris Canonici* (CIC), the *Zirkumskriptionsbullen* (the papal Church laws regulating the external relations of a diocese, which the Curia had concluded with the individual German states in the nineteenth century) now seemed outdated.[190] This breach with the past concerned the whole of Europe. The 3 great empires which had collapsed had alone given rise to 11 states.[191] In his Allocution of 21 November 1921 Benedict XV fundamentally ruled out a legal continuity and also a transfer of the old concordats to the successor states.[192] Thus for large parts of Europe relations of Church and State were no longer regulated by law.

An important presupposition of new regulation by law was the acceptance of diplomatic relations to the new states, which the Holy See wished to form on the broadest possible basis.[193] The new Prussian Vatican envoy to the Holy See reported to Berlin at the beginning of December 1919 that the Curia looked on the fact 'that [the] Reich maintained its own representatives everywhere abroad but not with the Papal See as degrading'.[194] On the German side too there was a powerful interest in taking up diplomatic relations with the Holy See: economically and politically the country was on its knees, and because of the provisions of the Versailles peace settlement was substantially isolated. They hoped that the Curia would provide mediation and contacts and at least in part overcome this marginalization, and they counted on support for the German population in the ceded areas – especially for the Catholic Germans in the new Polish territories. Reports coming from there of measures of Polonization and expropriation of churches of German Catholic congregations called for urgent diplomatic intervention, for which the Vatican was eminently suited.[195] Already in April 1919, after the Holy See had formally recognized the independent Republic of Poland, diplomatic relations with Poland were resumed[196] – a circumstance which was bound to put the Reich under powerful pressure.

A new impulse in favour of the resumption of plans for the nunciature was given by the fact that representatives of the German Centre Party sat in the coalition cabinet of the provisional Reich government of 13 February 1919. Again, in the same month, on 28 February the Centre deputy, Peter Spahn, took up the theme in the Reichstag, declaring it ludicrous that the Reich government had no representative with the Vatican.[197] The Vatican was informed of this venture by Pacelli.[198] After Friedrich Ebert had notified the Pope of his election as Reich president, Benedict XV used the opportunity in a personal letter to Ebert at the beginning of April to express his wish for closer relations with the Reich.[199] Of course there was also considerable resistance. When the plans became known France and Italy produced polemic against the rapprochement between Germany and the Vatican, in order to stop the latter supporting easier peace conditions. On the Bavarian side the old particularist reservations gained new weight from Article 78 of the Weimar Reich Constitution (WRV) of 11 August 1919, according to which the diplomatic representation of German interests lay with the Reich government alone.[200] The constitutional lawyers got round this trap by refusing to define the Holy See 'as a foreign state' (WRV Art. 78 s. 1) or 'foreign power' (WRV Art. 45 s. 1). Pacelli and the Holy See showed themselves in agreement with this legal position.[201] By this means the right of the German states remained untouched to establish diplomatic relations with the Holy See and to conclude concordats. The Bavarian government under Johannes Hoffmann vehemently championed the maintenance of the nunciature at Munich – even in the case that a second embassy be opened in Berlin.[202] This was entirely in Pacelli's interest; he indeed urgently approved the Berlin nunciature, but wanted to negotiate a comparable concordat for Germany in Munich.[203] So he tried to dispel Bavarian reservations against the Berlin project, making use of Bavarian Centre deputies for the purpose.[204]

On grounds of economy, the state budgetary committee of the Prussian legislative assembly resolved on 17 July 1919 to abolish Prussian embassies to individual German states; the Prussian embassy to the Vatican was to be taken over by the Reich on 1 April 1920.[205] Erzberger favoured Clemens von Brentano di Tremezzo for the new ambassadorial post; Pacelli brought his friend, the Prussian ambassador in

Munich, Julius Count von Zech-Bukersroda, into the discussion; both were respected Catholics.[206] Since the Vatican, the German bishops and the Centre Party raised no objection against a Protestant nominee, if at the same time a Catholic embassy consultant [*Botschaftskonsultor*] were nominated, and since the Protestant Diego von Bergen had earned Pacelli's confidence, the choice was finally to fall on the Prussian envoy.[207]

But getting to this point was still some way off. In September the Reich resolved to establish an embassy without including Bavaria in the process of decision.[208] The interest of Bavaria in the continuance of its own Vatican embassy and the Munich nunciature coincided exactly with that of Pacelli,[209] the more so as in view of the continued particularism of Bavarian policy Prussia was now also vacillating whether it should close its own embassy.[210] The Reich must – because of Rhenish separatism too – demonstrate its unity and could not on foreign-policy grounds reject the embassy; but it could not be blind to the particular interests of individual *Länder*. So the Reich cabinet proposed a bargain to the Bavarian government: the Bavarian embassy should be abolished, but in return they should receive the right of nomination of the German ambassador to the Holy See.[211] In contrast, Pacelli held firm to the Munich nunciature and was supported here by Faulhaber;[212] and he declared that the creation of a further nunciature in Berlin represented no problem. The Bavarian government and the Bavarian bishops were assured by the Holy See that the Munich nunciature would not be disbanded,[213] and the Bavarian ambassador Ritter zu Groenesteyn handed in new letters of accreditation at the Holy See.[214] This was not a favourable development for Berlin, but it was not to torpedo the plans of the Reich. Since Benedict XV wanted to escape the embrace of the Entente, he was urgently seeking diplomatic 'backing in Germany'[215] and hence would value the early dispatch of a German ambassador to the Vatican.[216]

The best possible solution sought by the Vatican fitted badly with political realities in Germany. In the middle of December 1919 the Landtag party of the Bavarian Centre (BVP) finally yielded and dropped their resistance to the dissolution of the Vatican embassy.[217] By mid-January the agreement of the cabinet for the dissolution was on the table.[218] In contrast, the Roman Curia continued to insist on the two diplomatic representations,[219] though Pacelli acknowledged that this solution was not attainable.[220] If the Reich government insisted on the dissolution of the Bavarian embassy, Gasparri declared at the end of January 1920, the *status quo ante* would be preferable.[221] The Reich Foreign Minister, Hermann Müller, declared just as unmistakably that three sets of German representatives in Rome were 'entirely out of the question'.[222]

Prussia finally saved the day. In mid-February 1920 Prime Minister Paul Hirsch announced his state's refusal of a Vatican embassy of its own, provided it was open to the Prussian Ministry of State and Ministry of Public Worship to do business with the nuncio.[223] The greatest haste was now required, for neither the Holy See nor of course the German Reich was willing for France to beat the Germans to it.[224] Nor was this a matter of trifles, for in the diplomatic order of rank the question of seniority played an important role.[225] On 10 March Gasparri informed von Bergen that the Holy See and France had reached an agreement for a resumption of diplomatic relations.[226] Barely a fortnight later Foreign Minister Müller informed the Curia of the setting up of an embassy of the German Reich at the Holy See, and requested the *Agrément* for the first ambassador, the former Prussian envoy von Bergen.[227] He arrived in Berlin a week later.[228] When letters of accreditation were submitted on 30 April 1920, the Pope gave notice of his intention to set up a nunciature of the first class in Berlin and to appoint Pacelli as the first nuncio.[229]

It was of course to be another five years, to 20 August 1925, before Pacelli finally moved to Berlin, although the Secretariat of State had announced the creation of the nunciature at the beginning of May 1920, and a month later the Reich government proclaimed that on its side there was no obstacle to the nomination of Pacelli.[230] There were several reasons for the delay in the complete change to Berlin. First, the Bavarian government sought to keep Pacelli in Munich as long as possible, justifying this primarily because of the concordat negotiations. Then Pacelli insisted on staying and sent the Bavarian bishops to the Curia to request that his stay in Munich be extended.[231] Von Bergen portrayed the Munich nuncio as 'very pro-German' and 'a highly-esteemed and influential man in the Vatican'.[232] How much this characterization related to the Catholic South-German circle in which Pacelli had so far moved, only now became really clear. Up to this time, he had no detailed knowledge of the other Germany, Protestant and Prussian.

His Bavarian confidants wanted to do their bit to discourage him from the change to Berlin. He found no embarrassment in inventing ever new excuses in order to put off the 'delicate and difficult' change.[233] The extent of his influence in Rome was revealed by the fact that the Curia, however unwillingly, let him stay, although it desired Pacelli's rapid move to Berlin as much as did the Reich government.[234] If Pacelli was to be doyen of the Berlin *corps diplomatique* the letters of accreditation from the Curia must get to Berlin rapidly because the allied powers had already agreed on the French ambassador, who, together with his British and Italian colleagues, had already given notice on 1 July 1920 of his inaugural visit.

After the nomination of Pacelli had been announced on 25 June both sides were anxious for the accreditation of the Berlin nuncio to take place as quickly as possible.[235] Early in the morning of 29 June Pacelli reached Berlin, to be received on the same day by the Foreign Minister. The following day the Weimar Republic began its first ceremony with the reception of the credentials by Reich President Ebert.[236] For him too an important step had been reached. 'With you, Herr Nuncio,' said Ebert on the occasion of the accreditation, 'I think of the mission before us, the regulation of relations between Church and State in Germany'.[237] Barely a year before he had met the nuncio in Munich and requested the moral and political help of the Holy See with the building of the new Germany.[238] In his address Pacelli referred to the consequences now that their relations were more firmly based; he was convinced 'that in this way the religious interests of the Catholic population [would remain] secure' and 'the welfare of the state [...] would be enhanced'.[239]

The Allied Powers, whose ambassador arrived on the following day, reacted to the *fait accompli*[240] with visible irritation, but took no measures to put the proceedings in doubt. On 6 July the new doyen gave a reception for the diplomatic corps, and after 20 days left Berlin again. In the following years too he continually stayed in Berlin for only a few days, although after the autumn of 1920 the nuncio premises in Rauchstrasse 20 and Corneliusstrasse 11/12 were ready for permanent residence, and he was under increasing pressure from Berlin as well as Rome to move.[241] On 18 November 1920 Gasparri presented the new Munich nuncio, Alberto Vassallo di Torregrossa, who was well known in the Bavarian capital from his service as *Auditor* between 1898 and 1905. The Bavarian *agrément* of mid-December 1920 was connected with advice that the change should follow only after the conclusion of the negotiations for the concordat.

It was Gasparri's wish that the conclusion of the concordat with Bavaria 'which might perhaps represent a useful precedent, might be accelerated as rapidly as possible. In the case, even in the possibility that negotiations for an agreement with the Reich should break down, it will always be better to have concluded a separate concordat with Bavaria.'[242] Until the Bavarian concordat had been concluded 'the negotiations begun with the Reich should be dragged out'.[243] From the beginning the Secretariat of State had expected greater concessions from the Catholic state government of Bavaria than from other German states.[244] Hence Gasparri and Pacelli wished to go into forseeably difficult negotiations with Prussia, Baden and the Reich with a Bavarian 'pattern concordat' already ratified. The negotiations with Bavaria dragged on till February 1924.[245] On 14 March 1924, Pacelli wrote to Cardinal Bertram:

> Today I am going again to Berlin for a few days. Complete agreement with the Bavarian government on the draft concordat has been finally reached. From now on only the Reich government has to make a negative examination of it to see whether there is anything in it which contradicts the Reich constitution. I hope this examination will go rapidly and smoothly. Specifically to push the business on, I am going to Berlin.[246]

The concordat was finally signed on 29 March 1924.[247] Pacelli's delight in this was disturbed only by his perception that 'in some of the regulations of the treaties with the Protestant establishments there are privileges not included in the concordat'.[248] That in Germany value was placed on a strict equality of treatment between the two confessions remained a thorn in the flesh for the Roman Church even in the negotiations with Prussia and Baden.

The concordat with Bavaria[249] followed that with Latvia[250] (3 November 1922), and in turn was followed by those with Poland[251] (10 February 1925), Romania[252] (10 May 1927), Lithuania[253] (27 September 1927), Danzig[254] (1928), Italy[255] (11 February 1929), Prussia[256] (14 June 1929), Baden[257] (12 October 1932) as well as Germany[258] (20 July 1933), and on all of them Pacelli left his mark more or less clearly.[259] The same is true of the concordat with the Kingdom of Yugoslavia of 1935, which was rejected in the Belgrade parliament at the demand of the Orthodox Church; and it is also true of the agreements with France[260] (1926), Czechoslovakia[261] (1927) and Portugal[262] (1928) as well as Ecuador (1937).[263]

1.5   The Hitler putsch and Pacelli's removal to Berlin

The Hitler putsch of 8 and 9 November 1923 seems to have made little impression on the nuncio, although he was staying in Munich.[264] But in his reports he kept Rome abreast of current events. Disquiet prevailed in the Vatican solely on the question of 'what would now become of the Bavarian concordat if it should really come to a dictatorship in Bavaria'.[265] On 9 November 1923 Pacelli telegraphed to

Gasparri: 'Last night Hitler with his armed bands declared that the Bavarian government had fallen, the prime minister and other ministers were imprisoned, and he proclaimed a new National-German government with Ludendorff as army chief [...] The belief is, to put it shortly, that order can be reestablished, but probably not without bloodshed.'[266]

On 10 November, after Hitler had already fled, Pacelli wrote to the Undersecretary of State Giuseppe Pizzardo:

> I could now see the Prime Minister [Eugen Ritter] von Knilling, who was imprisoned on Friday night by the revolutionaries, and then was able to get free. He was highly incensed. He told me that the ministerial council would now confer to come to very difficult decisions – everywhere the shout is 'Down with [*Generalstaatskommissar Gustav Ritter von*] Kahr!' The Reichswehr seems to want to back the National Socialists. Hitler is to march with his troops upon Munich. If this transpires, we can expect severe unrest.[267]

On 12 November he sent two telegrams to Gasparri: 'Situation still critical. The Nationalists rouse the people against the clergy, especially against [...] Faulhaber'.[268] And a little later: 'Hitler imprisoned. Peace seems to be reestablished.'[269] On 14 November he sent Gasparri a detailed report on the putsch, emphasizing the fundamentally 'anti-Catholic character' of the movement.[270]

Pacelli reported in detail on the anti-Catholic outbursts against the clergy, 'with which the followers of Hitler and Ludendorff [...] incite the people'; church people had thus been exposed to abuse and mockery. A central target for malice had been Archbishop Faulhaber, 'who in a sermon on 4 November and in a letter to the Reich Chancellor had criticized persecution of the Jews'. 'In addition there was the unfounded and absurd rumour, which was probably spread deliberately in the town, with which [Faulhaber] was burdened, that he had brought Herr von Kahr to alter his opinion; at the beginning while he was in the Bürgerbräukeller, apparently to escape from violence, he had joined the Hitler–Ludendorff *coup*, and had then pronounced himself against it.' Pacelli was particularly disappointed by the conduct of the Catholic associations in Munich – a passage in his report which he of course toned down again. Here he says: 'And in this whole muddle it was deplorable to see the lack of reaction (partly from weakness, partly from the confusion of ideas, which predominated at that moment) on the side of many of the Catholic associations [...] ; they failed to come to the defence of the Church against such attacks or of the Archbishop himself.'

Soon afterwards he informed the Cardinal Secretary of State of 'a "vulgar and violent campaign"' waged in the press by the Hitler party against Catholics and Jews.[271] Faulhaber too, with whom he was in close contact, condemned the National Socialist doctrine and agitation.[272]

The 7th Reichswehr Division had, by and large, refused action against the putschists; on 9 November Kahr had the putsch put down by the Bavarian units of the Reich army under Lieutenant General Otto von Lossow and the Bavarian police; and the day after that Hitler was imprisoned. Unwillingly Hitler with his uncoordinated proceedings had strengthened the republic. On 23 November General von Seeckt prohibited the NSDAP and the KPD. Pacelli gave a thoroughly relaxed impression. At any rate he did not experience the first revolt in Munich. After a short report on the situation, he went straight to the question of the concordat and the financial problems of the nunciature. But the theme of National Socialism was from now on always present in his reports to Rome. For in the Vatican they constantly harboured the fear 'that from this movement Christian doctrine in general and the Catholic Church in particular were threatened by growing dangers which should not be underestimated'.[273]

In the Spring of 1924 Pacelli condemned the 'vulgar and violent campaign' of the *völkisch* press against the Holy See, concluding that this movement regarded Catholics and Jews as their worst enemies.[274] There was a similar tenor to his draft report of 3 March 1924 on the Ludendorff trial; the accused in his defence speech portrayed the Roman Catholic Church and the Holy Father as Germany's worst enemies.[275] In this connection Pacelli also spoke of the 'blind fanaticism of intolerant Protestantism which is irritated by its own decadence and the growing prestige of the Pope'.[276] Incidentally in letters to Pacelli the Prussian prime minister and the Bavarian government also distanced themselves from this sort of language.[277]

But the continuing attacks against the Catholic Church, and especially the accusation that the Pope had been a partisan of France during the war, had their effect. Pacelli reported anxiously to the Cardinal Secretary of State that in Bavaria there is now a perceptible 'movement against the Holy See', which threatens the 'traditional veneration' for the Church in this country.[278] In his detailed report Pacelli again emphasized the danger which the 'ultra-nationalist press [has conjured up] for the veneration and respect for the Holy See in Germany',[279] and pleaded for the publication of the papal documents to put a stop to the campaign. 'What an echo such a publication might have in the Entente countries, especially in France, is not for me to judge.'[280] A fortnight later Pacelli reported in horror an article in the press, which put the Holy See along-side 'the Jews as the enemy of Germany'. 'We have ceased [so the article reads] to be a free people. Non-German powers, the Jew and Rome, shoot their mouth off in our country, and trample our rights under foot.'[281] As counter-measures to weaken the agitation of these 'fanatical Protest-ants or heathen of no religion at all', Pacelli recommended the beatific-ation and canonization of people whose 'reputation as saints in Bavaria is very strong. Although in matters of this kind every question of nation-ality must be disregarded, it seems that the rapid commencement of such proceedings would redound to the lively satisfaction of German Catholics and contribute to the strengthening of their attachment to the Apostolic See.'[282]

Repeatedly he notes with pain that 'many Catholics also are cheated and misled', which in respect to Germany confirms once more 'that nationalism is perhaps the most perilous heresy of our time'.[283] From his Munich experiences with communist and national-socialist move-ments it is unacceptable to suppose that Pacelli harboured any kind of sympathy with the one or the other extreme. If it did not exist previ-ously, the foundation was here laid for an absolute and irrevocable rejection of both political views in principle.

Pacelli's definitive transfer to Berlin on 20 August 1925 was 'like an act of state', indeed the Reich government sent him a saloon car to Munich.[284] Yet months later the Apostolic nuncio still wrestled with his fate. At the beginning of December 1925 he complained to Pizzardo:

> You know that I made myself available to go to Berlin with sacrificial readiness. As long as I was in Munich, although I had abundant reason to leave life in the nunciature behind me, I was restrained by the humanly pardonable wish (as I regard it) to conclude the Bavarian concordat into which I had already put so much work. Now in Berlin I have nothing but struggles and problems, and only from the love of God have I taken this heavy cross upon myself. Add to all this that the climate of this city is not the best for my health.[285]

To all this he joined bitter complaints that despite all the hardship the Curia had not even ensured the economic basis of his existence and he, as Pizzardo himself admitted, had 'the lowest stipend of all the nuncios in the world'.[286]

Yet (by a whisker) Pacelli might have been spared the translation to Berlin and the hard life of the nunciature in the Reich capital, for since 1924 he was reckoned – along with the Paris nuncio, Bonaventura

Cerretti, also a favourite of Gasparri – as the most promising candidate for the cardinalate. Largely on political grounds the Holy See preferred to elevate Cerretti, in order to give a positive signal to the French government and to counteract the impression that anti-French sentiment prevailed in the papal Curia.[287] Moreover, in von Bergen's view, the Berlin nunciature was much more important to the Pope than the position of a curial cardinal.[288] Pacelli indicated in a private letter to Pizzardo written in Rorschach that he thought little of the office of cardinal, and hence could hold on without difficulty in a 'state of holy indifference'.[289] But the 'comments and insinuations [...] and other similar humiliations' seem not to have left him entirely untouched. 'In any case when this is the situation I can not come to Rome.'[290] Even in Berlin he was 'besieged with questions about how and why &c' and hence was glad to be in Rorschach.[291] The Berlin government observed his failure to be nominated cardinal as an injustice towards the nunciatures in Paris and Brazil, the more so as, according to the newspapers, Cerretti would remain there as pro-nuncio.[292] To stop a complaint for the Reich government to the Holy See, Pacelli 'wrote to a trustworthy and influential person'.[293]

It was in the logic of his previous arguments in favour of remaining in Munich that the series of concordat negotiations with Prussia and the Reich[294] now required Pacelli's presence in Berlin. Moreover the Berlin government felt it 'inconvenient' that 'the papal representative accredited to them had not moved his permanent residence to Berlin'.[295] Thereupon he received the 'instruction' to stay 'longer than hitherto' in Berlin.[296] On the Prussian side after 1923 a fresh accreditation of Pacelli with the Prussian government was required.[297] Along with the setback in Bavaria it was established that Prussian church affairs would be dealt with by the Foreign Office on its own authority and unsatisfactorily.[298]

The Secretaries of State in the Prussian Ministry of Science and in the Ministry of State of the Prime Minister, respectively, Carl Heinrich Becker and Robert Weismann, pursued Pacelli's double accreditation with increasing intensity and stressed that this could only be advantageous for the negotiations. While they were supported in this by the Cardinals Adolf Bertram[299] (Breslau) and Carl Josef Schulte, the Curia, the Foreign Office and Pacelli himself were very critical of the notion. Gasparri described the 'Prussian idea [as] new to him and [as] unlogical and idiosyncratic'.[300] The Apostolic Nuncio was especially taken aback at the idea that he 'should virtually take over the initative in the affair'.[301] Prussia harboured the intention of reactivating its embassy in Rome, which seemed acceptable neither to the Foreign Office nor to von Bergen.[302] Yet the intervention of the two cardinals had its effect in Rome. The Pope finally gave in and gave his basic approval for the double accreditation.[303]

Although reservations continued on the side of the Reich government, it bowed to the coalition of Prussia and the Curia. Ambassador von Bergen was accredited also for Prussia on 12 June 1925. Pacelli presented his credentials to the Prussian Prime Minister on the 12 June 1925; he was now papal ambassador to the Prussian state government.[304] For the ambassador the double accreditation led to conflicts of loyalty for he was required to make no communication to the Foreign Office about the negotiations for the Prussian concordat, because in provincial [*Länder*] concordats the interests of province and Reich might collide.[305] On the basis of the law for the reconstruction of the Reich of 30 January 1934[306] the remaining rights of sovereignty of the provinces were handed over to the Reich and the *Länder* diplomatic representations were dissolved.

2
Vatican Foreign Policy 1920–29

Benedict XV was to experience no more of the modern concordats. A month before the conclusion of the concordat with Latvia, on 22 January 1922, he died. When the conclave met, Italy was in a political turmoil. The cult of Rome flourished among the nationalists, and Mussolini declared that politically the world was going to the right and turned against democracy and socialism.[1] In the conclave, the *zelanti* ('zealots') and the *liberali* confronted each other; Pius X's Cardinal Secretary of State was the favourite of the former, Benedict XV's Cardinal Secretary of State, Gasparri, was backed by the latter. At first noone thought of the Archbishop of Milan, Achille Ratti. When on 6 February he was finally chosen on the fourteenth ballot, he was accounted a compromise candidate. Ratti took the name Pius XI and made clear that he intended to continue the Church policy of Benedict XV, and especially his reconciliation with the Quirinal.[2] After his coronation he gave the apostolic blessing from the balcony of St Peter's for the first time since the fall of the Papal States; this was interpreted as a sign of a new openness to the world. At any rate Milan was the place from which after the First World War a militant Catholicism proceeded which was soon to spread over the whole country.[3]

2.1 Catholic nationalism in Poland and the role of Achille Ratti

Before his brief term of office in Milan, the new Pope had spent decades as the learned prefect of the Biblioteca Apostolica Vaticana, before the Curia entrusted him (at the age of 61) with a difficult diplomatic mission. On 25 April 1918 he was nominated Apostolic Visitor to the Polish State then in process of creation; four weeks later he took up his post in

Warsaw.[4] Ratti's appointment followed upon requests from the bishops of Poland and was thought of as an internal Church mission for the new regulation of ecclesiastical conditions in the new Poland.[5] But this was not the whole of his mission. At this eastern outpost of Latin Catholicism he was in charge not of Poles alone but also of areas like the Baltic which up to the Revolution had belonged to the Tsarist empire.[6] This double commission put Ratti between the upper and the nether millstones of national emotion. The Polish mood was dominated by hatred of everything Russian. To make it worse the Vatican had still in 1916 assessed the Polish independence movement as 'unrealistic'[7] and told one of its protagonists, Roman Dmowski, so.[8] It also took a dismissive attitude to the Versailles peace conditions. At the same time Ratti publicly welcomed the setting-up of the new Polish State, and in October 1918 Benedict XV expressed the wish to the Polish Primate, Archbishop Aleksander Kakowski, that the new Polish State might take its due place in the comity of European nations.[9] There had always been special relations between the Roman Catholic Church and the Polish people, though they had not been free of tension. Jan Ludwik Popławski, one of the founders of the Polish national movement, had written in 1897:

> We Poles are bound to Catholicism and to the Rome of the Pope not only by religious interest, but above all by political interest. In present-day conditions the Polish cause can only keep its international character through the mediation of Rome [...] Rome is for us the higher authority which is independent of foreign governments and to which in many cases we can appeal.[10]

The leaders of the national-democratic movement called for an understanding of the Church as a 'national institution' devoted entirely to the cause of national existence, a claim bound to be resisted by the Catholic Church with its universal orientation.[11] Nevertheless the pronouncements of the Polish clergy between 1863 and 1918 reflected the conviction that only loyal Roman Catholics could be really good Poles.[12]

After Polish independence in 1918 the controversial issues between Polish national ideology and universal Roman Catholicism gradually lost their significance. The leading personalities of the Second Polish Republic, intellectuals and politicians, came from the milieu of a newly revived Catholic religious practice. Thus the confessional element survived as part of the national destiny, but was increasingly able to establish itself against a merely 'national philosophy'. And it did this the more effectively as its opposite, the 'socialist philosophy' and its political representatives, lost ground. Already a few months after the consolidation of the young Polish Republic by the authoritarian regime of Józef Piłsudski[13] Poland and the Holy See established mutual diplomatic relations. The initiative for this came from Archbishop Aleksander Kakowski in November 1918. In the same month Cardinal Secretary of State Gasparri agreed to the wish of the Polish episcopate. On 19 July 1919, four months after the official recognition of the new Polish State, Achille Ratti, hitherto Apostolic Visitor, received his credentials as the new Apostolic Nuncio in Poland.[14] In the presence of Piłsudski and the diplomatic corps and 22 Polish bishops Ratti was consecrated bishop by Archbishop Kakowski in Warsaw cathedral on 28 October 1919. His correspondence with the Cracow cardinal Adam Sapieha illustrates the manifold difficulties in the early relations of Church and State. The composition of the Sejm and its religious policy did not please the Vatican, the Church's rights of possession had to be defended, and the representation of Poland with the Holy See was put on a lower rank than that of the Kingdom of Italy.[15]

Outwardly Ratti concentrated from the beginning upon inner-Church affairs, concerning himself with Church organization and the alignment of political and ecclesiastical boundaries. He tried to keep out of the processes of political decision in order to safeguard his diplomatic integrity and his neutrality in party politics; but, via the episcopate, he acquired an indirect influence.[16] Hence he participated covertly in the working out of the new Polish constitution and took pains to keep the Polish episcopate away from the exercise of political influence. When the Polish bishops on a motion from the Left were required to accept no senatorial posts, the first differences of opinion between them and Ratti arose.[17] The nuncio made extensive journeys through Poland and the Baltic, and on this occasion got to know the bishop of Riga, Edward Count O'Rourke, who was conducting the concordat negotiations with the Latvian government.[18] In this activity Ratti acquired great respect and also won the attention of the Polish people, persevering at the height of the Russo-Polish war in the summer of 1920 in beleaguered Warsaw;[19] but he was defeated as papal commissary for the plebiscitary areas of Upper Silesia, East- and West-Prussia. Against his will but at the express wish of Poland, he was as papal representative to guarantee the freedom of the vote in Upper Silesia.[20] The German government saw a difficulty in Ratti's dual function as nuncio in Poland and commissioner for the poll, and spoke out against his nomination.[21] Cardinal Bertram, the Archbishop of Breslau, to whose jurisdiction Upper Silesia belonged, in contrast supported the Polish proposal.[22] Subsequently the two governments tried to convince the nuncio who put in a long stay in Upper Silesia of their political view of the thing.[23] The Germans brought up the argument that, in the event of a Soviet victory in the Russo-Polish war, they would be sitting in Upper Silesia should that territory have previously become Polish.[24] In order to save Poland from apparently imminent defeat which would again have threatened its political existence, exploratory talks – mediated by the Vatican – took place between the German and the Polish governments.[25] The price for military help was to open discussion about the territories to be renounced by Germany. In this phase the basic object of the Vatican was to moderate Polish territorial claims on Germany. Pacelli thought primarily that the German Centre Party would be weakened by losses of territory, and hence, in relation to the Curia, took a rather pro-German attitude.[26]

When the Inter-allied Commission forbade Bertram to enter the plebiscite area, he at first received no support from Ratti. Only in the autumn of 1920 did the Warsaw nuncio, on the instructions of the Vatican, apply himself to preserve the rights of jurisdiction of the Breslau Cardinal.[27] The Holy See had never hesitated to reject any restriction of jurisdiction. In Paris and Warsaw this position, motivated purely by considerations of Church law, was assessed as a political option in favour of the Germans. In the following months Ratti visited the plebiscite areas and forbade the clergy – with the knowledge of Pacelli and Gasparri[28] – to undertake any propaganda for either side. During the most intense phase of the voting struggles he withdrew to Warsaw.[29] Yet both parties failed to detract from his neutrality. The Germans emphasized in their polemic his function as Polish nuncio, the Poles held it against him that he had intervened against the political agitations of the Polish clergy.[30] Already at the end of May 1919 Ratti wrote sadly to Sapieha, who had come straight back from Rome: 'I had hoped that he [i.e. Pope Benedict XV] would say something to you which would give me hope for a speedy recall to my library and my books [...] instead of this [...] all right, patience'.[31]

At the peak of the nationalist controversies Bertram finally turned to Pacelli and the Vatican. On 21 November 1920 with the approval of the Pope he made any political propaganda by any of the clergy of his diocese a punishable offence; those who did not comply were threatened with suspension.[32] The Polish side – government and bishops alike – erroneously held Ratti responsible for the decree, although in truth his sympathy lay rather with the Polish clergy.[33] Polish cardinals and bishops, some of whom had given their priests leave of absence to go canvassing for the political parties, signed a note of protest against Bertram's decree and sent it to Rome.[34] The Polish government demanded the separation of Upper Silesia from the Prince-bishopric of Breslau and the recall of the nuncio. Ratti had to leave Poland on 2 December 1920; in the same month Giovanni Ogno Serra was appointed as a voting commissioner. On 13 June 1921, Benedict XV nominated Ratti to be Archbishop of Milan, and at the same time raised him to the cardinalate.

In the Polish state constitution which was adopted in 1921 the Second Polish Republic defined itself in a high measure as national and Catholic; the latter increasingly gained the upper hand.[35] In no other country of Central and Eastern Europe did the Catholic Church possess the opportunities for influence it had in Poland. After the *coup d'état* of Józef Piłsudski in mid-May 1926 (the 'march on Warsaw') the ideological-political conception of national democracy got ever closer to the Catholic standpoint, and the affairs of the nation were increasingly subordinated to a Catholic ethic based on Thomism. Among the 'young' Catholic nationalists the slogan finally circulated at the beginning of the 1930s of the 'new Middle Ages', and it carried increasingly positive connotations, namely, the solution of the formation of a 'Catholic State of the Polish Nation'.[36]

Piłsudski himself, who between 1899 and 1916 had belonged to the Lutheran Church,[37] remained like most of the colonels rather indifferent in religion, even though he made a different public impression.[38] Yet the Catholic Church was not deceived by that. The question whether Piłsudski was really a Catholic led in connection with his funeral to conflicts with the Cracow Archbishop, Adam Sapieha.[39] The personal cult of Piłsudski, which yielded nothing to the later cults of Mussolini and Hitler, had its roots less in any Catholic convictions of the man than in his military and political deeds. Thus his followers ascribed the foundation of the state and the victory of Poland over the Red Army solely to the genius of their 'Leader' and reckoned the May Revolution of 1926 as another central basic date in the reestablishment of the fame, greatness and strength of the Polish State.[40] The reckless elimination of the parliamentary opposition in 1930 was also an integral part of the Piłsudski myth.

After the German-Polish agreement of 26 January 1934[41] the Nazi leadership latched on to the Polish image of Piłsudski. In the preface written by the Prussian Prime Minister Hermann Göring to the authorized

German edition of the Piłsudski biography, *Recollections and Documents*, it says:

> In selfless and extreme devotion Marshal Piłsudski worked for his fatherland. Already in his lifetime he entered the history of his fatherland in mythical greatness. Modern Poland would not have existed without Piłsudski [...] Josef Piłsudski was also the man who with our German Führer and Chancellor created the presuppositions and bases on which we can and will rebuild to the blessing of our nations and to maintain the peace of the world.[42]

The national-Catholic understanding of the Polish government and clergy as distinct from the Holy See came out also in the fact that the demands of the small minority of German Catholics in the province of Posen and in Middle Poland for the maintenance of their cultural peculiarities received almost no support.[43] In the area of Upper Silesia which was assigned to Poland there lived at least a quarter of a million German-speaking Roman Catholics.[44] The Lithuanian Catholics in the area around Wilna, where they represented a majority of the population, fared similarly.[45]

2.2   Vatican negotiations with Soviet Russia

On his journey to the new Polish capital in the spring of 1918 Ratti had stopped off with Pacelli in Munich, and subsequently acquainted himself in Vienna with the situation in Poland with Augustyn Hlond,[46] the abbot of the congregation of Salesians there, who devoted themselves to foreign missions and youth work. The journalist, Hansjakob Stehle, for years a correspondent of German papers and radio stations in Rome, describes Pacelli and Ratti as the two 'key diplomatic figures'[47] of the Vatican at this time. At all events they were both entrusted with delicate missions, among them the establishment of contact with the new rulers of Russia.[48]

Along with the comprehensive charitable assistance which the Vatican provided for the Russian people, there were various attempts to find a modus vivendi with the communist regime. Already in the spring of 1917 the Pope had welcomed the fall of the Tsarist government, hoping for a new era of freedom for the Roman Catholic Church in Russia.[49] At first the attitude prevailed in Soviet Russia that the Vatican was a political and historical anachronism which could be simply ignored. Trotsky never once mentions the existence of the Holy See. Only after

1920 are there regular files on the Vatican in the People's Commissariat for Foreign Affairs. The first official exchange of documents began with a telegram from the People's Commissariat of 5 December 1917 to the Russian representative at the Vatican, Aleksander L. Lysakowski, and to Nikolai Bok, the chargé d'affaires previously appointed by the Tsar, that they might endorse the foreign policy of the Soviet government. When the two Russian diplomats simply ignored the Bolshevik message, they were dismissed on 9 December 1917.[50] Up to the beginning of March 1922 Lysakowski was still there as conversation partner and mediator with the Holy See.

In the early summer of 1918, the Vatican commissioned Pacelli to go to Soviet Russia via the Prussian ambassador in Moscow, Count von Mirbach, and explain the readiness of the Holy See to preserve asylum for the Tsar Nicholas II and his family in Castel Gandolfo near Rome.[51] The Vatican was willing to bear all the costs of travel and board. But, like similar initiatives of other European states, those of the Holy See foundered on the unwillingness of the Bolsheviks to allow the Tsar's family to emigrate. In the night of 17 to 18 July 1918 they were shot in the cellar rooms of the Ipatiev house in Yektarinenburg, their corpses burnt and the ashes buried.[52]

Actual diplomatic contacts began with three telegrams in all which Benedict XV sent to Lenin in the spring of 1919 via Ratti.[53] In them the Pope requested that the Roman Catholic Archbishop of Mogilev, Monsignor Ropp, who was of Polish descent, be set free, and asked also for protection for Orthodox clergy who were persecuted by the Bolsheviks. Although – with the exception of Ropp who was set free on 17 November 1919 and expelled to Poland – these interventions finally bore no fruit, the Vatican held further contact and was concerned to obtain a privileged position for the Roman Catholic Church in Soviet Russia. At the beginning of July 1921 the Patriarch Tikhon turned to the Pope and begged his help for the persecuted Russian Orthodox Church.[54] When the Vatican offered the Soviet government a Caritas-aid mission, Kamenev, the chairman of the Pomogul, agreed. On 12 March 1922 the Vatican got involved in a 13-point secret agreement with the Soviet Union, which was confined to purely humanitarian questions, and on the Vatican side excluded from participation citizens of 'nations which are hostile to Soviet Russia', or, in plain language, citizens of France or Poland.[55]

The negotiator on the Soviet side was the head of the first Soviet Russian 'commercial commission' in Rome, Wacław Worowski; he had recognized the advantages, charitable economic and political, of a treaty with the Holy See.[56] As a middleman he used the German convert Wilhelm von Braun, who had a very close friendship with Pizzardo and also apparently very good connections with the clerical *Konsultor* at the German Vatican embassy, the *Prälat* Johannes Steinmann.[57] A native of Breslau, he occupied a key position among the Soviet contacts in the Vatican. On the side of the German government, the German ambassador in Moscow, Ulrich Count von Brockdorff-Rantzau, also supported the Vatican–Soviet rapprochement, and was of assistance to Pacelli in this affair. The German Reich was interested in better relations between Moscow and the Vatican because it wanted to break up the international isolation of the two defeated parties in the war – more exactly the Soviet Union and Germany – with the help of the Holy See.

For the Curia the Moscow mission was linked with religious and romantic ideas. There were dreams of a Catholic-Orthodox Union, or, at the least, since the former Orthodox state-church had lost its privileged position under the new regime, of an extended and unhindered mission for the Roman Catholic Church. The Curia was so avid for an arrangement that Gasparri signed the agreement between the Holy See and the Soviet government, although, apart from humanitarian assistance, it included nothing beyond previous promises. The Vatican was to send neither missionaries nor pastors to the USSR, and maintain no schools, but only papal charitable assistance to ease the famine in the pillaged land. Worowski's written assurances that the Roman Catholic Church might set up agricultural and artisan institutions for production and teaching were never realized. After Lenin's death at the beginning of 1924, even the charitable aid broke down.[58]

In mid-April 1922, also a month after the conclusion of the secret agreement, the Holy See – on the initiative of Steinmann – participated in the World Economic Conference in Genoa.[59] For the first time the two defeated powers in the First World War, Germany and the Soviet Union, were invited to an international conference.[60] In this constellation of powers the German Reich Chancellor, the left-Catholic Josef Wirth and also Pius XI perceived an opportunity to be used in various ways. During the conference the Holy See pleaded for the reduction of German reparation-payments and also for an end to the military occupation of parts of Germany.[61] On the conference fringe – it was written on 22 April 1922 and thus five days after the signing of the Russo-German Rapallo treaty – a meeting was arranged between Signori the Archbishop of Genoa and Georgi Chicherin,[62] who since May 1918 had been Trotsky's successor as Soviet Commissar for Foreign Affairs. Before the Genoa Conference Chicherin had stopped over in Berlin and got in touch with the Berlin government. During a dinner on the Italian cruiser *Dante Alighieri* before Genoa, the two men sat opposite each other quite 'by chance', and discussed a concordat and the possibility of the free practice of religion.[63] Chicherin put the case that in Soviet Russia all confessions were free and that a concordat with the Holy See would confer a one-sided privilege on the Roman Catholic Church.[64] A month later Pizzardo and Steinmann went to Santa Margherita near Rapallo in order to continue the conversations with Chicherin and Worowski begun during the dinner and also to conclude an agreement with the Soviets. In their bags they had a papal memorandum which demanded full religious freedom and the return of church property. At the intervention of Wirth, Pizzardo had of course dropped the last point already, respectively combined with humanitarian help, so that it was more a question of an exchange counter. Chicherin demanded a formal recognition of the USSR. To this the Vatican reacted cautiously for it already had information of a new wave of religious persecutions. On account of ideological misgivings within the Russian government, no Russo-Vatican agreement was reached in Rapallo. But the negotiations were continued. Brockdorff-Rantzau contrived a secret meeting between Pacelli and Maksim Litvinov in the Berlin villa of Brockdorff-Rantzau's twin brother, which took place on 4 July 1922.[65] This close diplomatic ensemble between Berlin, Moscow and the Vatican, basically similar to a new 'Triple Alliance',[66] was not without its problems – especially not when the political implications of the two temporal powers are recalled. A central common attitude of both the Germans and the Russians was indeed the weakening if not the liquidation of the Polish State.[67] A rapprochement of the Vatican with these two enemies of Poland was bound to be taken ill in Warsaw.

Notwithstanding continued brutalities against the Russian Orthodox and the Catholic clergy, the secret negotiations between the Vatican and the USSR proceeded. Along with the German Reich the Italian government under Benito Mussolini added a further connecting link to Russia from the end of October 1922. At the beginning of 1922 he had already made advances to the Vatican, and in March 1922 opened lines of communication to Wirth.[68] He claimed good relations with his 'revolutionary rival' Lenin,[69] and declared on 30 November 1923 that his fascist government[70] saw no difficulties in recognizing the Soviet Union. Nine weeks later, on 8 February 1924, the official recognition by Mussolini's government followed. They were among the first governments in western Europe to resolve on this step. But they were followed soon afterwards by Great Britain, Norway, Austria, Greece and Sweden, so that a diplomatic recognition by the Holy See was diminished in significance.[71] In the light of this development Chicherin wrote to Krasikov at the beginning of 1925: 'We now need nothing more from the Vatican, neither a recognition *de jure* nor the sending of a representative, a nuncio, and the Pope is for us only a spiritual office.'[72] Finally, by pressing ahead Mussolini had thwarted the Vatican's diplomatic Russian policy. Yet up to this moment negotiations had proceeded at a lively pace.

In May Pius XI took counsel with Gasparri, Pizzardo, the Jesuit general Wlodimierz Ledóchowski and Simonetti, how to proceed further with the Soviet Union. They were united in agreeing not to recall the mission, but also not to recognize the USSR before it showed some accommodation on the religious question.[73] On the Russian side they were agreed, as transpires from a letter of Litvinov to Worowski of February 1923, to make a formal recognition by the Vatican the presupposition of the conclusion of any agreements.[74] Hence in the summer of 1923 the Soviet government rejected the proposal of the leader of the aid mission, the American Jesuit Edmund Walsh, made on the instructions of the Vatican, to transform his institution into a permanent representation. Soon afterwards, on 18 July 1923, the Politburo confirmed a new instruction for dealings with the Vatican. Religious instruction should now be permitted, but they wished to make the condition that Polish clergy should be replaced by priests from Germany or Italy.[75]

At the beginning of December 1923 the successor of Worowski[76] and later ambassador at the Quirinal, Yurenev, presented the Vatican Secretaryship of State with a new proposal. The papal relief work was to be transformed into a nunciature and the Vatican should make new concrete proposals about aid to the USSR. In return the Soviet government would release the condemned clergy, allow freedom of Catholic worship, and permit religious instruction to be given. In the Sacred Congregation for Extraordinary Church Affairs which advised upon this offer in mid-December 1923, there were reservations. That in Poland especially this development was followed with suspicion could be no surprise.[77] Hence the counter-proposal of the Vatican turned out to be cautious. At first they wanted to send only a papal delegate to Moscow, but kept a diplomatic recognition in view in case the negotiations on the spot went satisfactorily.

On account of the unsettled 'Roman Question' Yurenev after his appointment as Soviet ambassador to the Quirinal turned out to be the conversation partner. The further negotiations were carried on via the Berlin nunciature. During his Berlin stay Pacelli met with the Soviet chargé d'affaires, Bratman-Brodowski, and soon with the Soviet ambassador in Berlin too, Nikolai Krestinski. The Soviets reacted with disappointment to the Vatican counter-proposal, the more so as about the same time the promised deliveries of aid fell far below expectations owing to the desolate financial state of the Holy See.

If Lenin's directives for the physical annihilation of Orthodox priests in 1922 were an unexampled cultural violation,[78] after his death a still more determined policy of religious persecution came into force. In order to forestall Soviet expulsion, the Vatican discontinued its Moscow relief-mission on 31 May 1924, but left open the prospect of its transformation into an Apostolic Delegation. On this question Pacelli negotiated up to the end of August 1924 in detail with Bratman-Brodowski; he also instructed the German ambassador Brockdorff-Rantzau over the current state of the affair and occasionally requested him to mediate.[79] On 18 September 1924 the relief mission ended its work.[80]

Four months later, on 8 January 1925, the Curia commissioned Pacelli to take up new secret negotiations with the Soviet ambassador in Berlin, Krestinski.[81] During the Berlin negotiations which lasted from 4 to 24 February 1925, the Soviet side required the diplomatic recognition of the Soviet Union by the Holy See and the recognition of the separation of State and Church as it was practised in the Soviet Union. This meant the authorization of every 'religious association' by the State, full control of its financial transactions, and also of the connections of the Catholic Church in the USSR with the Vatican. Moreover, the Soviets demanded that local priests and bishops should be chosen by their congregations.

Meanwhile the opposition in the college of cardinals to the Vatican's links with the atheistic regime hardened. In his Christmas address of 18 December 1924, Pius XI warned the statesmen of the world – at the end of October even France had recognized the USSR – of 'the extremely serious dangers, and the certain evil of Socialism and Communism';[82] they should keep themselves and their fellow citizens away from them. Although the negotiations continued, he had driven a philosophical stake through them. Not for the last time. A year later Pacelli wrote to Pizzardo that 'in Berlin they were very disturbed [...] because the Holy Father intended [...] in the next consistory to condemn Socialism again, and, by the same token, at least implicitly, the coalition with the Socialists'.[83]

The Christmas address of 1924 had been effective for the Centre Party, whose leader Wilhelm Marx was governing as Reich Chancellor with the support of the Social Democrats.[84] But not only for political Catholicism in Germany: after the murder of the moderate Socialist Giacomo

Matteotti by the Fascists,[85] the Italian Catholic People's Party (PPI) moved closer to the Socialists. The party leader, the priest Luigi Sturzo, had been provided by the Vatican at the beginning of October 1924 with an entry visa to Austria, so that the negotiations with Mussolini which began at the beginning of 1925 might not be burdened by the opposition of politically active priests.[86] On 25 October 1924 Sturzo went to London – originally to attend a congress.[87] More followed.[88] Whoever in Italy stood in the way of the rapprochement between the Vatican and the Fascist state, must like Sturzo go into exile at the instigation of the Holy See.[89] Moreover the *Popolari* had wished to oppose the Duce in alliance with the Socialists; but they, the Vatican was convinced, were not only an anticlerical but also an antichristian party with whom no cooperation was possible.[90] Also in exile Sturzo and others could scarcely count on Catholic support. The conservative Catholics in Great Britain and the USA received them coolly, and sought to minimize their influence as far as they could.[91] Only a small part of the Catholic press in Britain and the USA was open to their critical analyses.[92]

After the Italian recognition of Soviet Russia in public law, the diplomatic negotiations between the Holy See and Moscow were increasingly transferred to Berlin. In this phase Pacelli formed close connections with the current Soviet ambassador Nikolai Krestinski and his chargé d'affaires Bratman-Brodowski. The negotiating basis which Krestinski presented to the Berlin nunciature on 4 February 1925 offered, however, no starting point for a satisfactory agreement.[93] On 11 February Krestinski followed up with a 'concession' by which when the Russian government appointed bishops, and priests to parishes, the Vatican and the bishops respectively should have a 'say' and a right of confirmation.[94] These rather obvious things made the Russian proposals scarcely more acceptable, the more so as they were unwilling to make any written commitments. So on 24 February the negotiations had to be broken off without result. When it became known in mid-August 1925 that a Catholic priest of Polish descent was to be executed in Leningrad, Pius XI decided to procrastinate no further. He empowered Pacelli bluntly to reject the Soviet basis for negotiation as inadequate, without, of course, breaking off relations entirely. Rather, the Soviets should present new proposals for a realistic basis of negotiation.

To a corresponding letter of Pacelli of 7 September 1925, the Berlin nuncio received an official reply only 12 months later. At a dinner put on by the Reich Foreign Minister Stresemann for his colleague Chicherin as he travelled through he happened to meet Pacelli; the Soviet commissar confirmed that Pacelli's letter of September 1925 had been received. The two diplomats arranged a meeting for 6 October 1926 in the house of the Chamberlain, Ernst Count zu Rantzau. In the course of this meeting it became clear that in questions of politics and religion the Soviet government was also consulting the modernist Church of the Renewer, a split from the Russian Orthodox Church. This body was cooperating closely with the Soviet authorities, copied the Soviet system of councils in its organization, and up to 1925 enjoyed active encouragement.[95] Apparently the Roman Catholic Church in the USSR was to be constructed on this model of 'church bolshevism'.

Also in the delayed answer to Pacelli's letter, written on 11 September 1926 before the meeting at Rantzau's house, the Soviet government showed little desire for accommodation, and conceded to Catholics living in the Soviet Union only limited intercourse with the Holy See. A month later they informed Pacelli that foreign clergy would be forbidden entry to the Soviet Union till further notice.[96] A concrete occasion for this prohibition was the entry of two Jesuits, sent by the Vatican to the USSR, to build up a clerical seminary.[97] In mid-June 1927 the German ambassador von Brockdorff-Rantzau secured, as mediator, a further meeting between Chicherin and Pacelli.[98] These conversations too were a failure, because the Soviet side strictly rejected religious instruction because it was seen as indoctrination. A final initiative by Pacelli in October 1927, during which he conceded to the Soviets a right of objection when bishops were appointed, also ran into the sand.[99] Sergei Nosov sees a connection between the declaration signed by the Metropolitan Sergei, the administrator of the Patriarchate on 29 July 1927, and the end of the negotiations with the Vatican; for the declaration completed the final adaptation of the patriarchal church to the Soviet state.[100] In the spring of 1928, after Stalin had finally established himself, the Chicherin[101] era in foreign policy ended, and with it the interest in a modus vivendi with the Holy See.

After 1925 there were clashes and perhaps also impairments of the diplomatic activities of the Berlin nuncio through another initiative of the Vatican. In February 1926 the Secretariat of State had decided in all secrecy to send the French Jesuit Michel d'Herbigny to the USSR in order to reestablish the Apostolic Succession there by consecrating bishops.[102] On 29 March 1926 Pacelli consecrated d'Herbigny a bishop in the domestic chapel of the Berlin nunciature.[103] The Vatican kept d'Herbigny in ignorance of the diplomatic concerns to date, and sent him to Moscow at the beginning of April 1926, where he consecrated the Assumptionist father Pius Neveu bishop in the church of the French embassy. In May and June two further secret consecrations of bishops followed, the second in the French church Notre Dame de France in Leningrad.

At this point there was positive evidence of a clear improvement in relations with France. In the Encyclical *Maximam gravissimamque*[104] of 18 January 1924 Pius XI, despite his unaltered rejection of the law of 1905 separating Church and State in France,[105] accepted it as reality.[106] At the beginning of September 1926 good relations were again disturbed because Pius XI in a letter to Cardinal Paulin Andrieu of Bordeaux condemned the nationalist and monarchist philosophy of the *Action française* under the leadership of Charles Maurras[107] as basically atheistic and neo-heathenish.[108]

Under the protection of the French Embassy d'Herbigny then celebrated public services in Moscow, gave blessings, dedicated rosaries and candles, heard confessions, baptized and confirmed. Thousands of believers streamed to Moscow. The Soviet government regarded all this as a Vatican 'conspiracy' and expelled d'Herbigny on 6 September 1926. In 1931 as an expert on Russia he took over the leadership of the 'Papal Commission for Russia'. Two years later his office secretary, Edoardo Prettner-Cippico, came under suspicion (for which there were grounds but no proof) of having stolen and passed on secret documents.[109] The result of this affair was that d'Herbigny was dismissed and was permitted no longer to use his episcopal title.[110]

In diametrical opposition to the received view that the Vatican subscribed to an uncompromising anti-Bolshevism is the interpretation of Sergei Nosov, a writer extremely critical of the Vatican. He notes that the Vatican only turned against the Bolshevik crimes when its political and diplomatic defeat was unavoidable.[111] Previously it seems to have turned a blind eye to the grave abuses of the regime.

In fact the diplomatic maxim that doors are not shut for ever played a central role in the Vatican. On this basis, Cardinal Faulhaber in mid-November 1929 before the publication of a papal address had the section on Moscow struck out – among other reasons 'because it is not to be ruled out that in the foreseeable future the Holy Father himself form a connection with Russia on account of the Missions'.[112] The passage he purged read:

Before our eyes a tragedy will for a time be played out, and the attempt made to get a political order going without God. Contemporaries look on the rule of blood in Moscow with as much indifference as judicial murder in Mexico. We do not understand how a government which pays some respect to honour and other moral duties can give a handshake to another government through diplomatic relations and commercial treaties, when the hand of this other government is stained with blood. It counts in the life of nations too: what does it profit you if through economic treaties you gain the whole world, and lose your soul?[113]

After the peace initiative of Benedict XV it was the second time that a diplomatic mission in which Pacelli had taken a key role had foundered. After his departure from Berlin the Reich capital served the Holy See no more as a nerve centre for the Eastern policy of the Vatican. Pacelli's hesitating method of proceeding, always weighing up the possibilities, however, helped to prevent his practical failure adversely affecting his career. Even with little room to negotiate, Pacelli showed a striking flexibility and the readiness to go for what was politically impossible though the presuppositions offered few prospects. Ratti too counted as deliberate, as a *vas dilationis*.[114] But, unlike Pacelli, he was also decisive, less flexible, could even be stubborn, and was given to occasional choleric outbursts and coming to decisions on his own.[115] For both priest-diplomats concordats represented '*the* contemporary means by which the Church could maintain itself against the modern state of whatever stripe'.[116] And on this field both had so far been entirely successful. Hence it is clear that the complex of German concordats was closely bound with the negotiations for the acceptance of diplomatic relations between the Vatican and Germany, the question of jurisdiction over the areas separated from Germany, and with the relations of Germany's neighbouring states with the Vatican through either concordat or diplomacy.

2.3   The Holy See between Germany and Poland

For German foreign policy much depended on how the Vatican would put in hand the new ecclesiastical regulations for the separated areas in the East. Two-thirds of the territory of the former Prussian diocese of Kulm with its seat in the former Cistercian monastery of Pelplin had become territory of the Polish State.[117] The final third was divided among the Free City of Danzig, parts of East Prussia and western West Prussia. In 1920 the *Delegatur* of Tütz was set up for the parts of the Archbishopric of Gnesen-Posen which remained in the Reich. It also took charge over western West Prussia. The German bishop Augustinus Rosentreter could stay in Pelplin because he had spoken out for the reestablishment of the Republic of Poland. He submitted to political reserve on all sides and left even Pacelli's letters unanswered.[118] While the Vatican and Poland wanted Rosentreter's resignation, the interest of the German Reich lay in his staying put.

The Free City of Danzig[119] officially created in mid-November 1920 belonged ecclesiastically partly to the German see of Ermland and partly to the new Polish diocese of Kulm. The Foreign Office was in favour of incorporating for Church purposes the whole Free City in the German bishopric of Ermland. The outspokenly pro-German Dean, Franz Xaver Sander, who was delegated to the German embassy as embassy dean, succeeded in a personal conversation with Rosentreter in persuading him to back the separation of Danzig from his bishopric. At the same time he declared that the old bishop was fully equal to his job, so that his replacement by a Pole, as the Holy See had originally intended, could drop from the agenda.

Thus the Holy See had found ready made solutions corresponding entirely to German wishes. On 24 April 1922 Pius XI appointed Edward Count O'Rourke,[120] the strongly anti-communist Apostolic Legate for the Baltic States, to be Apostolic Administrator for Danzig. During his time as Apostolic Visitor, Ratti had cooperated closely with O'Rourke, who in 1917 had been appointed Apostolic Administrator of Minsk. At the end of September 1918 Benedict XV, at Ratti's suggestion, had nominated O'Rourke to be bishop of the re-established diocese of Riga. In this capacity, and in the closest understanding with Ratti, he pushed on the concordat negotiations with the Latvian government. On the basis of his preparatory work it was possible on 30 May 1922 to conclude the concordat with Latvia.[121] Whatever grounds Pius XI may have had to appoint O'Rourke as the first supreme pastor of Danzig when in April 1920 he had resigned his Latvian bishopric on grounds of ill-health and inability to assert himself, this personal decision of the Pope was widely regarded in Germany as the outcome of German diplomacy.[122] Although he described himself in 1922 as a supporter of 'Great Poland' and proclaimed his affinity to Polish culture,[123] both the Polish General Commissioner and the Polish ambassador lodged protests against the appointment of O'Rourke as Apostolic Administrator.

The decision of the Curia could hardly have surprised the governments of the Reich and of Prussia. At the end of February 1922 Pacelli had conferred on the Danzig question in Berlin with Ebert, Rathenau and the Prussian minister of public worship, Boelitz. During this he indicated 'that the future Apostolic Administrator will be of German nationality [...] The [...] gentlemen showed lively satisfaction over this solution and [...] Rathenau expressed to me the wish to learn in advance the name of the churchman whom the Holy See would designate for that office'.[124] To this Pacelli added 'that His Holiness expected as a return for such a proof of his goodwill that the [German] government on its side would show goodwill, and a mind to reconciliation and union in the question of the concordat'.[125] Thereupon Rathenau, 'although he is a Jew, [expressed] very eloquently the desire of the Reich government' that he would apply himself together with 'the Catholic [Reich] Chancellor Dr. Wirth' despite great difficulties 'with all zeal for this end', namely, 'to obtain the conclusion of a concordat satisfactory to both sides'.[126] A similar promise, 'albeit in a much more cautious and circumspect form', was also given him by the Prussian minister for public worship.[127]

Up to 1925 the Curia held firm to the provisional character of the Danzig Apostolic Administration, but at the end of the year the Holy See erected an exempt bishopric for the Free City assigned to no Church province; and on 2 January 1926 O'Rourke was nominated the first bishop. The concordat negotiations with Prussia and the Reich on the one side and with Poland on the other[128] formed the continuous background to Vatican diplomacy.[129] Pacelli encountered the integration struggles of Poland which wished to incorporate the Danzig question into the current concordat negotiations, when he threw German interests into the scales. Both states were bound to think that the Holy See observed their respective national interests. With respect to Poland the Vatican allowed the concordat negotiations which O'Rourke conducted with the Danzig Senate to fail,[130] while at the same time it kept the Free City substantially out of the Polish concordat. As an exempt bishopric Danzig was subject to no Metropolitan association, and the Bishop of Danzig was required to participate neither in the Fulda bishops' conference nor in the conference of Polish bishops.[131]

The third article of the Polish concordat, however, provoked among German Catholics and the clergy of Danzig violent indignation, because it said in the second section that the plenary authority of the Apostolic Nuncio in Warsaw extended also to the territory of the Free City. Of course the Foreign Office was not in agreement with this regulation, and ordered its ambassador in Rome to intervene. In the course of the negotiations to implement the concordat, a communiqué was issued which affirmed that the Polish nuncio should exercise no diplomatic functions in Danzig, but do internal Church business only.[132] O'Rourke sought to take a conciliatory position towards the Polish-Catholic minority. When in 1937, with the approval of the Vatican, he set up pastoral centres for Polish-speaking Catholics in the Free City, he came under such pressure from the side of the President of the Danzig Senate, Arthur Greiser, that in mid-June 1938 he resigned.

The question of Upper Silesia corresponded to that of Danzig. After this territory had definitively fallen to Poland, the Pope intended to appoint as Apostolic Administrator Teodor Kubina; he had been proposed by Poland and the Pope himself had got to know and esteem him during his time as nuncio in Warsaw.[133] Kubina, however, had emerged in the plebiscitary stage as a pro-Polish agitator, and so the German side – the Foreign Office and the episcopate alike – raised a powerful protest. Pacelli was afraid that the concordat negotiations would have a negative effect in Germany. Hence at the beginning of May 1922 the Curia favoured the Salesian Augustyn Hlond, who was then thought to be politically neutral.[134] At all events Pius XI reached the decision in favour of Hlond without previous consultation with Pacelli.[135]

The Germans regarded his nomination as a diplomatic victory. But Poland, supported in this by the French government and bishops,[136] did not give up. In connection with the conclusion of the Polish concordat in February 1925, the Holy See consented to the formal jurisdictional separation of Upper Silesia from the bishopric of Breslau. The separated area was raised to become the bishopric of Katowice, and ascribed to the church province of Cracow, without the latter receiving jurisdictional rights over the bishopric.[137]

A month after the conclusion of the Polish concordat,[138] the Reich Chancellor Wilhelm Marx turned to Pacelli, and drew his attention to the negative effects of the treaty in German domestic politics, and required financial compensation for the maintenance of the truncated diocese of Breslau. The German State could not take over the higher costs for the impoverished diocese.[139] Financial inroads were also the consequence of the fact that immediately after the establishment of the *Administratur* for Upper Silesia Czechoslovakia demanded a similar regulation for Teschen. This duchy, although up to 1919 part of Austria-Hungary, belonged ecclesiastically to the diocese of Breslau. Without informing Bertram, the Czech government had already in mid-March 1919 secularized Church property in Teschen. Because of this the Vatican refused to negotiate over the Czech request until the situation of Church property had been clarified.[140]

2.4 Pacelli, the Centre Party and the concordat policy towards Prussia and the Reich

The Holy See was not shy of tightrope-walking to unite its various treaty partners in compromises that did not result in political difficulties; and it became clear how advantageous it was to conclude one treaty before concluding the next. Despite this state of affairs, the Germans hesitated – to Pacelli's disappointment. He was convinced that this was because of the weak politicians of the Centre Party. At the beginning of December 1923 he wrote concerning Reich Chancellor Marx:

> He is without doubt a very good and well-deserving Catholic. Yet I must observe that it would be an illusion to expect of him at the present point of time a positive attitude towards the interests of the Church. Often I asked him whether it would not be reasonable to profit by the present situation rapidly to negotiate a concordat between the Holy See and the Reich, so that it could serve as a basis [...] for the one which should next be concluded with Bavaria [...] Herr Marx answered me ever more uncertainly and evasively, and yesterday he finally declared clearly to my repeated question that it was impossible. His reason was that the present Reichstag was drawing to a close.[141]

Marx did not understand that in the future Parliament, 'at any rate according to the general anticipation, the extreme right and left elements would come in in greater numbers, i.e. the Protestant nationalists and the Communists'. The new Parliament will be 'still less inclined [...] to accept a concordat advantageous for the Church'.[142]

This prognosis plunged Pacelli into gloom.[143] In the Reichstag elections on 4 May 1924, the radicals recorded strong gains; the moderate parties, with the exception of the Centre, had to accept great losses. Pacelli held that the Centre politicians, compared with those of the Bismarck era, were weaklings and pussy-footers; their predecessors had 'succeeded by courageous struggle' in 'maintaining their ground victoriously and breaking the resistance of the Iron Chancellor'.[144] When he expressed to Marx 'the firm expectation' that the Reich government would make 'no difficulties of any kind' in view of the Bavarian concordat and would declare that it did not contradict the German constitution, he reacted 'more hesitantly and less clearly' than his predecessor Stresemann.[145] A year and a half before the Catholic Centre politician and Reich Chancellor Wirth had told him that it was impossible to bring a concordat which the Vatican would like into Parliament.[146] Already in December 1919 Pacelli had opened the first round of negotiations with the Reich government.[147] He then asserted legal considerations against the relevant constitutional article of the Weimar constitution which had weighted the relation of Church and

State, especially in the area of schools, one-sidedly in favour of the prerogative of the State.[148]

The Apostolic Nuncio was aware throughout that the Bavarian bishops shared his reservations.[149] From that quarter came repeated criticism of the new order in the State and the demand for the restoration of the monarchy. But with this position the clergy could reckon on the support only of the right wing of the old Catholic party. At the Munich Katholikentag at the end of August 1922 it came to a notable row with those who supported the Weimar state. After Cardinal Faulhaber in his opening speech had criticized the revolution sharply as 'perjury and high treason',[150] the Oberbürgermeister of Cologne, Konrad Adenauer, answered in the concluding speech in his capacity as President of the Kirchentag: 'Our unity in the estimate and evaluation of many things is injured by the difference of our judgement of the present conditions of state [...] To make the present constitution responsible for present conditions betrays a serious failure in historical perspective.'[151] Since Faulhaber had previously asked the Catholic Reich Chancellor Joseph Wirth not to take part in the Munich Katholikentag,[152] the controversy acquired a political dimension, which was bound to bring the Holy See into the arena. Apparently at the request of the Curia, Faulhaber handed over to the Munich nuncio a legal document making a statement on the utterances in question.[153]

A month previously he had written to Pizzardo: 'Your excellency has written to the Apostolic Nunciature in Munich that our beloved Holy Father was satisfied with my speech at the Katholikentag in Munich. This was a great joy and comfort for me.'[154] Once again he repeated his intention: for him it was only a question of Catholic loyalty to principles, or a return to the principles of Catholic life and social order. Two years later the provincial of the Bavarian Volkspartei reproached Wirth's Centre Party, in a statment about elections,[155] with having 'sacrificed the principles of the great leaders of the Windthorst era for the flirtation with the Socialists'. The incident at the Munich Katholikentag in 1922 was to burden the relations between Faulhaber and Adenauer for the rest of their lives. When in 1949 the latter was elected federal chancellor, the cardinal was dismayed.[156] For him Adenauer simply supported the anti-clerical wing of the Christian parties. In mid-July in the Cologne Town Hall Adenauer received the delegates of the so-called 'White International', a gathering of European political Catholicism. Although the Italian Partito Popolare had already been dissolved, their representatives, among them Sturzo, took part in the meeting.[157]

In the concordat negotiations Pacelli followed from the beginning a two-track policy. Despite the 'pacemaker' role of the Bavarian concordat, he began from the summer of 1920 – partly via the Prussian chargé d'affaires in Munich, Julius Count von Zech – separate conversations with the new Vatican referent in the German Foreign Office, Richard Delbrueck.[158] In order to prevent the areas separated from Germany being also lost to the German Church, Delbrueck pressed for the 'rapid conclusion of a Reich concordat'.[159] The early concordat negotiations at the level of the Reich were also – unlike the *Länder* concordats – motivated entirely by foreign policy considerations. On 5 July 1920, Pacelli and Delbrueck in the presence of the Centre Party deputies, Ludwig Kaas and Georg Schreiber,[160] began conversations.[161] The written statement of principles, which had again been widened for the background of the conversations, made German citizenship and a specific academic training the precondition for the exercise of spiritual office in Germany.[162] Further points concerned the composition of cathedral chapters, the choice of bishops and the question of diocesan boundaries. The State guaranteed freedom for schools and the liberty of religious orders to open or to found subsidiaries in accordance with the constitution. Moreover both sides tried to achieve a basic theoretical agreement on the removal of State payments to the Catholic Church. Yet both the Bavarian and the Prussian governments put sand in the works, because as 'federal accomplices'[163] they wanted to give their own interests in the negotiation preference over those of the Reich.[164] Moreover, within the German Foreign Office there was an opposition group to Delbrueck, which gathered round Diego von Bergen[165] and resulted in a contest over the counsultant [*Konsultor*] at the German embassy in Rome.[166] During further negotiations in Munich with the nuncio and the Bavarian Minister of State in the middle of September 1920, Delbrueck contended for the putting aside of particular interests so that the Reich concordat could be shaped for more than religious agreements.[167] Alongside the tensions within the Foreign Office there emerged in 1921 other rivalries within the Reich Ministry of the Interior, which demanded a right to a voice of its own in questions of the concordat.[168]

In the spring of 1921 it became completely clear that Bavaria and Prussia would permit a Reich concordat only after the conclusion of their *Länder* concordats.[169] Through the change of government in Berlin and the Chancellorship of Wirth a new phase of the negotiations for a Reich concordat began in the autumn of 1921; but it was defeated by the resistance of Bavaria. Again Delbrueck had recommended that the school article required by the Vatican be accepted into the concordat in order to secure a rapid conclusion. The Curia, however, would not conclude a Reich concordat without a contractual protection of the confessional schools. On 14 November 1921 Wirth requested a list of Rome's wishes and promptly received from Pacelli a 20-point programme.[170] To the Chancellor as to the Holy See it was a question of concluding an outline concordat and of supporting the unity of the Reich,[171] but the Prussian ministry of public worship described the incorporation of the schools question as 'basically unacceptable'.[172]

At the beginning of January the Prussian government finally yielded to the pressure of the bishops of Cologne and Breslau and adopted a more cooperative attitude.[173] In a draft of his own of 18 January 1922,[174] von Bergen supported the policy of the Reich government in the schools question and tried to get a package deal: so far as German interests in the question of eastern jurisdiction were looked after they could meet the Vatican by accepting the school articles into the concordat. But since the Holy See in the spring and autumn of 1922 had supported the German interests in Danzig and Upper Silesia and had thus 'certainly furnished the advance payments for the acceptance of the school articles',[175] he took the pressure off the concordat negotiations. The reports of Pacelli to Gasparri from May 1922 to February 1923 reflect how arduously the negotiations especially with Prussia took shape from this time on. The nuncio feared on the part of Prussia 'an attitude of open opposition or at least passive resistance against the conclusion of a concordat with the Reich', and in May 1922 even saw in it yet another indirect danger to the Bavarian concordat.[176] Prussia expected the same treatment from the Vatican as Bavaria, and, especially in the school questions, was not prepared for any concession at all. The nuncio was especially alarmed by 'a new kind of Middle School called a construction [*Aufbau*] school'.[177] This new type of school was undenominational [*paritätisch*] and the timetable designated only two hours a week to religion. 'These are circumstances which occasion serious anxiety [...] since the schools concerned are especially to serve the training of future teachers [and hence] the future of the confessional elementary school would be irrevocably impaired'.[178] On another occasion there was the bitter remark that the Prussian minister of public worship, in the matter of the schools, was injuring 'the most sacred rights and central interests of the Catholic Church'.[179] Bavaria was, however, ready 'to incorporate the [...] school question in the concordat; so we cannot understand why Prussia cannot do the same'.[180] In other words: there were grounds to fear that through Prussian influence a Reich concordat would undermine the much more far-reaching agreements with Bavaria. Since 26 of the 66 votes in the

Reich council belonged to Prussia alone, there was no getting round her where a Reich concordat was concerned. 'There is no reckoning on the cooperation [. . .] of smaller states in favour of the concordat, like Saxony (with 7 votes), Thuringia (with 2 votes) etc. where there are purely socialist or majority Protestant governments. Without the support of Prussia, agreement on the Reich concordat is in practice impossible to obtain.'[181]

Especially in Saxony, where since November 1920 a left-republican cabinet (MSPD, USPD, toleration by the KPD) under Wilhelm Buck had counteracted the moderate social-democratic-bourgeois policy of the Reich, the Roman Catholic Church with barely 200,000 members was having a hard time.[182] The Saxon government more or less foiled Pacelli's concordat policy by seeking to regulate the situation of religious communities by unilateral State legislation which from a financial viewpoint was not even unfavourable to the Church. But 'such a proceeding [would] be exploited also in Prussia (not to mention Baden, Württemberg, and Hesse) and by many enemies of the concordat to show that an agreement with the Holy See was not necessary for the attainment of a new regulation of the relations of church and state'.[183] Against this Pacelli begged the bishop of Meissen, Msgr Christian Schreiber, 'to make clear to the Saxon government that the final conclusion and signing of the treaty in relation to the financial obligations of the state to the Catholic Church falls within the authority of the Holy See'.[184]

Since the Saxon government at first refused to deal with the Holy See or the nunciature, Schreiber, who did not want the treaty to fail on any account, proposed a kind of delegation proceeding as a result of which he would be empowered to act for the Holy See. Pacelli feared, however, that this would create a precedent, and rejected it on principle. It became very clear to him, nevertheless, that Saxony formed an exceptional case, since it had never in the nineteenth century concluded any kind of convention with the Holy See.

Without the wish of the Curia to take account of the Church further, the cabinet of Max Heldt finally ended the parliamentary controversy in the Saxon Landtag with two treaties and a draft law: in mid-January 1929 it proposed two parallel treaties with the bishopric of Meissen[185] and the Evangelical-Lutheran State Church of Saxony,[186] which reserved to itself alone the State support known as the 'lump-sum rents'. These two treaties were accompanied by a draft law on the public-law status of religious societies.[187] On 22 March 1929 the Reichstaatsgerichtshof declared the Saxon Landtag elections of 1926 invalid. This put an end to the attempt of the Heldt government to win a parliamentary majority for the Church package deal. Against an opposition majority of Left parties and the NSDAP the new cabinet of Wilhelm Bünger was not able to get the drafts through and finally on 14 January 1930 they were rejected in the Landtag.[188]

After this it seemed for a time as if Pacelli's perseverance would pay off. For on the night of 18 March Msgr Schreiber came into the Berlin nunciature and informed the representative chargé d'affaires, Luigi Centoz, that the Saxon government was now ready to deal with the nuncio. At once Dresden showed itself in a hurry and recommended a visit by Dr von Zimmermann of the ministry for public worship and education. Now of course the nunciature was embarrassed, because Pacelli was meanwhile in Rome, and the new nuncio had not yet arrived in Berlin,[189] and on 22 June 1930 fresh Landtag elections followed. From them the heterogeneous majority of left-wing parties on the one side and the NSDAP on the other emerged with fresh strength. The nature of the new parliamentary majority finally brought negotiations over the Church treaties and religion to a standstill.[190]

The situation in both domestic and foreign policy – especially after the conclusion of the new jurisdictional regulations in the east – entirely favoured the wishes of Bavaria and Rome. Unchecked by the interests of the Reich, the Bavarian concordat was signed on 29 March 1924 and was ratified by the Bavarian Landtag on 15 January 1925. A more favourable outcome Pacelli could hardly have imagined.[191] The basic principles of canon law came into full effect in appointments to bishoprics, canonries and other Church dignities. The comprehensive school articles assured the Church of a far-reaching influence upon the Bavarian education system. The State took on the perpetual obligations of protection, acknowledgement and support of the Catholic Church. Only in Article 13 did the Church concede to the State that it would employ essentially German clergy. The Bavarian concordat remained in force unaltered till 1966.

In October 1924 Pacelli again approached the Reich government under Wilhelm Marx and suggested that it should resume the concordat negotiations it had broken off. By mid-November the new draft was ready, but it was not pursued further. Only nine years later, in the spring of 1933 did Hitler's negotiator, Franz von Papen,[192] take this precise draft with him to Rome.

Already in 1921 the Vatican expressed doubt to Prussia whether in view of the teritorial changes the old agreements – especially the Bull *De salutate animarum*[193] – were still valid. A consultation therefore took place between Pacelli and the Prussian Minister for Education and the Arts, Otto Boelitz.[194] Since the Curia insisted on incorporating the schools question into the concordat negotiations, these first contacts ran into the sand. At the beginning of May 1924 Pacelli gave notice that the Vatican regarded the circumscription bulls of 1821 and 1824 as still in force.[195] On 27 November 1924 the Prussian government declared in a note to the government of the Reich that after the conclusion of the Bavarian concordat there would be only the question of a concordat of their own.[196] Thus the idea of a Reich concordat before the conclusion of a concordat with Prussia became unthinkable.

The negotiations which had begun under conditions of strict secrecy[197] in the spring of 1926 had proved extremely difficult, the more so as in the Protestant circles concerned a virtually *kulturkämpferische* mood against the whole treaty negotiation was widespread.[198] The general synod of the Old Prussian Landeskirche took up these misgivings and spoke in one of its resolutions of 'severe damage to the evangelical church, the national community and the state'.[199] To Pacelli's annoyance the Prussian ministry of public worship had sought 'to negotiate the long obsolete legislation of the *Kulturkampf* from the Bismarck era and to obtain a substitute for it'.[200] Owing much to the negotiating skill of Ludwig Kaas, provisional agreement was reached on most questions by the summer of 1927. Above all they succeeded in essentially undermining the mood of *Kulturkampf* which still persisted. But up to autumn 1928 three controversial themes remained unresolved: the erection of a bishopric of Berlin,[201] the regulation of episcopal elections and the schools question.

In the first two points the Prussian government ultimately gave way to the Vatican. The schools question was nowhere mentioned in the draft treaty. Nevertheless even before the exchange of ratification documents the Prussian government had to be ready for an exchange of notes with the Curia;[202] and, because of the continuance of confessional schools, expressly to confirm the status-quo guarantee of Article 174 of the Weimar Reich constitution. While the Curia observed this exchange of notes as part of the contract, the Prussian government refused an official publication of the text. On appointments to episcopal sees there was a compromise. Chapters retained the right to propose candidates, and the ultimate right to elect one of the three candidates chosen by the Holy See from those whose names had been proposed. The 'political proviso' ensured that the Holy See could appoint no bishop or archbishop against whom the Prussian State Government had successfully established reservations of a political nature.

On 14 June 1929 the agreement of the Free State of Prussia with the Holy See was signed, and on 9 July it passed through the Prussian

Landtag. The Prussian State Council also pronounced in favour of the treaty by a bare majority of 44 votes to 36. As in the case of Bavaria, the Reich government declared that it would not raise any legal difficulties relating to the Reich constitution. At the beginning of July 1929 the government brought the concordat into the Landtag. Central to the parliamentary negotiations was the question of confessional parity, and hence the demand to enter upon treaty negotiations with the Protestant Church too. When the third reading was concluded on 3 August 1929 an excellent majority for the concordat was secured of 243 votes to 172, the former from the economic party, the Centre, DDP and SPD, the latter from the NSDAP, DNVP and KPD.[203]

The Prussian concordat fell well short of the success of the Bavarian concordat, not to mention the triumph of the Lateran treaties.[204] It was merely a compromise. But Pacelli did not allow himself to be disconcerted by it, and sought further opportunities of concluding treaties with individual German *Länder*. At the end of June 1928 he took advantage of a journey to Rottenburg for the centenary celebrations of the diocese and a visit to the theological seminary at Tübingen for a confidential conversation with the Catholic President of State, Bolz, and his Minister of Justice, Beyerle, who was also a Catholic.[205] He 'discussed with them confidentially the possibility of eventual negotiations with Württemberg for a concordat [...] From this conversation it emerged that the conclusion of such an agreement – though doubtless very difficult because of the traditional anti-Catholic fanaticism of a great part of the Protestant population, [was] not impossible [...] especially if the current negotiations with Prussia were to reach a favourable outcome'.[206] This sounded only guardedly optimistic. In contrast, in the autumn of 1929 political conditions in Baden developed in an extremely favourable way. This had been long expected by Pacelli who had been paying careful attention to political development in the individual *Länder*, and repeatedly set up confidential conversations.[207] On the basis of a considerable gain in votes the Centre with the SPD were able to form a government, and in the coalition negotiations had secured a readiness to treat for a concordat.[208] Yet before negotiations could begin the nuncio left Berlin because greater missions awaited him in Rome.

2.5 The Church 'home policy' of the Vatican in Germany

The primacy of Vatican foreign policy had also determined the decisions of the Reich nuncio in German domestic affairs. Thus, for example, when the Catholic Women's League for the erection of the Peace Church in Frankfurt am Main begged for the verbal support of Pius XI for the collections, Pacelli advised against the Pope's participation.[209] More often than not Gasparri followed the advice of his nuncio.[210] He had written to the Catholic women:

> that the Holy Father despite his joy over the pious and generous work of the League of Catholic Women finds it inopportune to speak the word requested of him, because it says in the dedication of the new church that it has been erected *to the memory of the fallen heroes* and this circumstance prevents the intervention of the Holy Father; he has also not intervened in other lands whenever there has been a reference to those who have fallen in the war.

The reserve of the Curia in such cases rested on political and doctrinal, rather than upon ethical, considerations. When the Bingen priest and President of the Mens' and Workers' Associations of the Diocese of Mainz, Michael Eich, wished to put a resolution on the Catholic ideas of peace before the Holy Father, Pacelli recommended a rejection of the request.

> May I be permitted respectfully and confidentially to inform you that this resolution originates in circles which in my humble opinion represent an extreme and exaggerated pacifism […] which works entirely to the benefit of the Communists. For although the Church always rejects bloody conflicts and has furthered peace among the nations […] it has nevertheless always accepted, according to the general doctrine of the theologians, that there are cases *per se* of just war. It is a quite different question, especially in modern times, of the means used by parties at war, some of which may doubtless be impermissible and may be condemned.[211]

Gasparri adopted Pacelli's line, and simply added that an extreme and exaggerated pacifism worked to the advantage 'of communism and the extreme parties.[212] There has so far been scarcely any research into whatever role Pacelli played in the disciplining of German theologians and priests.[213] He seems to have acted in cases of pending doctrinal processes 'personally with the greatest caution'.[214] In this sector too he remained primarily the mediating diplomat, to whom nothing was less welcome than a sharpening of controversies. Even in cases which Pacelli judged unambiguously as false doctrine, he advised caution in the interests of concluding the concordats. This concerned even

Joseph Mayer, at that time an assistant at the Institute for the Study of Charity [*Institut für Caritaswissenschaft*] at the Theology Faculty of Freiburg University. In his book on *The Legal Sterilisation of the Mentally Ill*[215] he had attributed to the State the right of sterilizing all those from whom, so far as could foreseen, 'only low-grade descendants' were to be expected. Pacelli held the theses of the book as 'erroneous', as he explained in a report to Gasparri on 7 November 1928.[216] They stood 'in several points in contradiction to generally acknowledged principles of Catholic moral theology' and were 'objectively fitted to become an occasion to offence and immoral action'. Finally, he pointed to a decision of the Holy Office given on 22 May 1895, according to which the sterilization of women had been forbidden.[217]

Yet he advised caution: he thought 'that a condemnation of the book of a lecturer at a state university on the part of the Holy See at the present moment – when in anti-Catholic circles and their press the struggle against the concordat has so vigourously revived – would give fresh heart to the attacks of the enemies of the Holy See'. Instead he recommended pressing the German bishops publicly to oppose the view represented in Mayer's book. This stance gave preference to diplomatic over theological considerations. For the Holy Office had sought an opinion on Mayer's book from Franz Hürth, a theologian teaching at the Jesuit seminary at Valkenburg (Netherlands). In this he came to a simple condemnation of his young colleague's arguments. According to Catholic doctrine sterilization procedures were 'erroneous, mistaken, dangerous, and absolutely prohibited'.[218] As a result of this condemnation Mayer should withdraw his book and rewrite it. Otherwise it should be placed on the Index of forbidden books. Yet neither of these things happened. Despite the encyclical *Casti connubii* of 31 December 1930, which decisively rejected sterilization and of which Hürth took account in his opinion, Mayer was able to continue his university career in theology and in 1939 even wrote an opinion for the security service of the SS. In it he justified measures of euthanasia.[219]

Since already during the Weimar democracy diplomatic considerations occupied the foreground, it can be no surprise that this card really took the trick under the conditions of dictatorship. When the Nazis on 14 July 1933 passed the 'Law to prevent congenitally sick offspring' Bertram recognized that the law was diametrically opposed to Catholic doctrine. But the episcopate did not dare, 'on account of this matter's implications', to act themselves, and instead on 4 August 1933 requested the Holy See for an instruction.[220] Pius XI to be sure instructed the bishops to follow *Casti connubii*,[221] but gave no more concrete instructions; thus his feeble interventions could be comfortably ignored by the Nazi state.[222] Consequently, in fields relevant to politics there was despondency, much insecurity, even a recoil from the practical implementation of an ethical judgement which had formerly been properly recognized. But between 1930 and 1934 both the Secretariat of State and the Holy Office busied themselves intensively with the subject of nudism as 'an attack on Christian morality'.[223] The famous Enlightenment tract of the Netherlander Theodor Hendrik van de Velde on the subject of marriage also seemed to the Holy Office so dangerous that the clergy put it on the Index of forbidden books, and together with Mussolini put a stop to public discussion of it in Italy.[224] Peter Godman thinks he can establish a certain enthusiasm on the part of the upper clergy for such subjects. This may well be so. But more decisive is the perspective on society and politics which became obvious in it all. Here is once again expressed the determined defence of the Catholic Church against subcultures of a liberal or socialist stamp with a rather nonconformist lifestyle. For the free body culture – such as bobbed hair, shorter dresses, the concept of the family, new role models, the 'non-marriage question', modern marriage or a liberalizing of divorce laws – formed an important element in the framework of efforts for social emancipation – incidentally, especially of social democratic women.[225] In most of these areas an understanding with Fascism as with Nazism might be established with little difficulty, but not with social democracy.[226] Its emancipated model of the family – akin to the democracy it propagated – was contrary to the traditional model of the patriarchal Christian family.

From the middle to the end of the 1920s, Pacelli observed the internal politics of Germany entirely from the angle of his concordat plans. Hence his criticism was directed at the inclination of the Centre Party to form coalitions with the Socialists. At the end of May 1926, he wrote to Gasparri:

> If it is allowed that the parties of the Right, which consist largely of Protestants who are often very hostile to the Catholic Church, it must be allowed that the Socialists are no less so; for lately they have restrained their attacks solely on tactical and also temporary grounds. It seems moreover demonstrable from experience that a good concordat and a school law favourably framed for the confessional school, is probably more likely to be attained by an alliance with the German-national party than with the Socialists; that is, if considerations of [...] foreign policy and domestic social policy do not gain the upper hand in the Centre Party.[227]

From this assessment it arises that the nuncio in principle rejected a cooperation of the Centre with the Left as with the Right. But he presupposed in their view of the Church different motivational positions. His own experiences with the socialists and their ideology suggested to him that there were no grounds for cooperation with them. He suspected rather that the preference of the Centre for the socialists was due to other fields of politics – and especially foreign and social policy. In his critical undertones is a note of disappointment that, in Pacelli's perception, the Centre Party gave too little weight to his concordat policy.

His reservations against the Right were of a less basic nature. Here his thought moved entirely in the fields of conflict between Catholic and Protestant which were characteristic of Germany. Like the Jews the Protestants adhered to a false religion. In the eyes of the Curia they were 'heretic[s]',[228] who only a generation before in alliance with the State had given the Roman Catholic Church a hard time. The Evangelische Bund was always ready for a *Kulturkampf,* and there were always rumblings in these circles.[229] The great sin of the Right in his view was that it was dominated by this anti-Catholic confession. This apart, he held on philosophical grounds that there was more point in cooperation with the parties of the Right – if that was what there had to be – than with the atheistic Left.

2.6 The Lateran Treaty and the reestablishment of the Church-State

In Italy confessional antagonism did not apply, and no insuperable obstacles appeared. Thus the concordat negotiations with the Fascist state of Mussolini were bound to form an important milestone in Pacelli's estimate of the parties of the Right.[230] On this account – and not just because of his move to Rome but primarily because of the conclusion of the Lateran treaties – the year 1929 formed a decisive shift in the history of the Vatican. The comprehensive alliance with Mussolini ended its estrangement from the national state; this state had had a liberal and anticlerical stamp since 1861, but since 1923 had been gradually evolving in an authoritarian and nationalistic direction.[231]

Mussolini's fascist revolution did not lead to the disruption of traditional cultural lines. Rather the 'Duce' made compromises with the old elites and observed – on historical grounds – the cultural and social values of the Roman Catholic Church. 'In 1929 the state which had become authoritarian [...] and the Papal Church which had remained authoritarian and become increasingly centralized as a result of the dogma of infallibility (1870) and the new canon law (1917), came to a comprehensive mutual understanding';[232] this is the judgement of Rudolf Lill and his explanation of the relative harmony of the two authoritarian systems – at any rate up to 1936.[233] Pius XI entertained undoubted sympathies for the fascist movement – why otherwise would he as Archbishop of Milan have allowed fascist flags to be hoisted on his cathedral?[234] In the same year the Vatican let it be known that it would not oppose a Mussolini government which it prized especially for putting down the Left.[235]

Already Benedict XV had signalled to the Italian State that he was ready for a compromise settlement of the 'Roman Question'. Supported by Gasparri who represented the continuity of curial foreign policy, Pius XI needed only to continue the course adopted by his predecessors. From 1926/27 secret negotiations took place between the fascist state and the Holy See. Two aspects were important to the Pope: he promised himself first that, if Italy recognized the sovereignty of the Holy See, he would gain a confirmation of its international standing as a genuine small state 'Vatican city', with international, religiously based connections. Secondly, the treaties ought to strengthen the institutionalized, hierarchically framed churchmanship against 'modernists' of every kind.

In the negotiations Pius XI and Gasparri got to know an authoritarian regime, which accommodated the Church in almost every respect, and offered it more than the pluralistic constitutional states of the western stamp – one has only to think of Prussia. Certain sore points of contact with the fascist dictatorship, which regarded itself as 'totalitarian'[236] and in 1929 disabled the parliamentary system, did not at any rate exist on the side of the Holy See. This would also have been noteworthy, because the basic law of the Vatican city, a state of only 44 hectares in size, which Pius XI issued on 7 June 1929, established an absolute, if elective, monarchy. The Pope, a sovereign head of state over the *Stato della Città del Vaticano*, governed 'as an absolute monarch in a territory belonging to him personally'.[237]

The treaty signed in the Lateran on 11 February 1929 guaranteed the Pope full independent sovereignty and thus ended the period of the 'territorial imprisonment' of the Holy See by the national state. In return the Pope accepted the obligation of strict neutrality, declared the 'Roman Question' as finally ended, and confirmed on his side the Kingdom of Italy with Rome as its capital. The treaty went on to acknowledge the Roman Catholic Church as the sole religion of the Italian State. The concordat guaranteed the Catholic Church free exercise of its jurisdiction and preaching, and the protection of the 'holy character of Rome';

it promised that all spiritual offices should be freely occupied, and that a chaplaincy to the military forces should be established; moreover the militant lay association, Catholic Action[238] and its organizations, a work initiated by Pius XI himself with authoritarian and patriarchal intentions, received the attested right to free activity, so long as it kept out of politics. The clergy were barred from every kind of party politics. The concordat further ensured the unconditioned authority of the Church hierarchy over the clergy and the life style of the faithful. No priest might hold a public office without the agreement of his bishop; clergy who had fallen out with the hierarchy must be employed in no office which had any public connection. State legislation on marriage would be adapted to the canon law, thus excluding divorce. Catholic religious instruction formed the 'foundation and crown' of all the education in state schools. In the financial agreement the Holy See received a large compensation for the loss of the old Papal States: 750 million lire in cash, and a thousand millions in state securities.

The Lateran treaties were accepted by the fascist parliament and senate by an overwhelming majority, and were finally ratified in June 1929. With these treaties Mussolini had earned national and international respect, and the fascist system had acquired an acceptable face not only for the Church but also for democratic constitutional states. Unlike Bolshevism the fascist regime had imposed on itself by treaty a self-limitation of its totalitarian claims.[239] 'The official cult of the fascist organisations after the concordat of 1929 was Catholic.'[240]

The 'White International' of the Christian parties of Europe of course reacted in dismay to the Lateran treaties. In their eyes the Vatican had entered an alliance with the fascist government and betrayed the Catholic opposition to Mussolini. This development gave a new impulse to the latent anti-clericalism in the Italian People's Party (PPI). While Francesco Luigi Ferrari recognized the threatening isolation of the 'Popolari' in exile and launched numerous initiatives to maintain its power, Sturzo drew up a bitter balance sheet of the first five years of 'his' International.[241] In July 1929 at their congress in Brussels he reaffirmed once more that, in the interest of a united and peaceful Europe, 'the democratic polity was the best fitted' to overcome national egoisms. And 'Christian ethics' were those 'which corresponded best to the reconciliation of the peoples'.[242] This was poles apart from the perspective of the Vatican.

In his preface to the German-Italian edition of the text of the treaty, dated Easter 1929, Pacelli boasted of the alliance as an 'epochal turning point in contemporary history'.[243] He not only regarded it as the 'most far-reaching event in the history of Italy' but also underlined its 'timeless significance for the whole Catholic Church'. It was indeed a 'powerful work of peace [...] which rustles about us like the prevailing wind of Providence. Scarcely ever has a treaty been acclaimed with greater euphoria.'[244] In all this Pacelli spoke from the expectation that the peace concluded with the Italian State would lead 'in other lands too and with other peoples to tangible successes'.

As if to document the commencement of a new age and readiness to use modern methods, Pius XI, shortly after the signing of the Lateran treaties, gave instructions to found a radio station of his own. In the spring of 1931 it came to pass. Via Radio Vaticana the Pope addressed a call to peace to the people of the world: 'May the earth hear the words of my mouth. Oh hear all ye peoples.'[245]

The Lateran treaties formed the peak and also the summit of Gasparri's work as Cardinal Secretary of State. At his side Francesco Pacelli, the brother of the Reich nuncio, had cooperated in overall charge.[246] After ratification Gasparri had to retire,[247] and leave the field to the man whom he had supported for so many years: Francesco's brother, Eugenio Pacelli.[248] The power-conscious Gasparri, still of rustic aspect, had to give way so that Pius XI could exercise his sovereignty undisturbed. Pacelli, after 12 years' activity abroad and of aristocratic demeanour, had less good contacts in the Curia than his predecessor, and was therefore dependent upon the good will of Ratti.[249] At the end of 1929 Pius XI raised the Reich nuncio to the cardinalate as a grateful reward for his services,[250] and at the beginning of 1930 nominated him to be the new Cardinal Secretary of State. After almost 13 years of activity in Germany, Pacelli handed in his letters of recall to the Reich President Paul von Hindenburg at the beginning of December 1929.[251]

Even after he had entered upon his new office in Rome at the beginning of February 1930, German influence was sustained in the form of three very close colleagues: his housekeeper Pascalina Lehnert,[252] who had accompanied him since 1918, Robert Leiber, who stood beside him as private secretary since 1924, and finally Ludwig Kaas, who stayed in the Vatican from 1933 onwards. Also the German ambassador and Prussian envoy to the Vatican, Diego von Bergen, knew Pacelli from 1917, when he met with the ministerial officials at that time in the German Foreign Office in connection with the negotiations over the papal peace note.[253] Relations between the two were so familiar that von Bergen could give the new Cardinal Secretary of State immediate advice for 'modernising the conduct of the business' of the Curia and the 'establishment of a press department'.[254]

The most important adviser in Germany continued to be Cardinal Faulhaber. The close relationship between Pacelli and the Cardinal of Munich and Freising was based on shared experiences during the months of revolution. In negotiating the Bavarian concordat Pacelli took no step without having previously agreed it with Faulhaber.[255] The same was true for all the later concordat negotiations.[256] Even as Cardinal Secretary of State and Pope he continually sought the advice of his German friend whose influence upon the world Church in the Pacelli era can scarcely be overestimated. The informed gossip was that Pacelli took over the post of Cardinal Secretary of State only unwillingly. For a time rumours never ceased that he would soon give his office up. His critics in the Vatican were only now really disappointed because he could not assert himself against 'the authoritarian character [of the] Pope'.[257] Later the rapid conclusion of the Reich concordat troubled the relations between Pius XI and Pacelli.[258] Yet all these reports, if they possessed any substance at all, proved to be mere speculations.

2.7 Pacelli's judgement on the Catholic Church in Germany at the end of his nunciature

On the conclusion of his work in Germany Pacelli handed in his report on *The Situation of the Catholic Church in Germany*.[259] This had been requested already at the end of January 1929 by Cardinal Carlo Perosi, the Secretary of the Holy Consistorial Congregation. Yet Pacelli complained to Perosi on 18 November 1929 that the 'far from straightforward work of concluding and subsequently translating the concordat with Prussia' had 'hitherto hindered' him from doing the job.[260] This information comprised 45 pages, mostly statistical; but between the lines are Pacelli's interpretations which permit conclusions to be drawn as to his attitudes in secular as well as ecclesiastical politics. Thus he complained about the propaganda for people to leave the Church which was always effective, and 'which was pushed especially by the Communists; they have, for example, established central offices in Berlin, where, for a payment of two marks, all the necessary official steps for leaving the church will be undertaken'.[261]

In general, he seemed to regard the German clergy as 'too accommodating'[262] – for example, in granting dispensations in cases of confessionally mixed marriages – and wanted greater clerical application in other areas. The declining birth rate even in 'purely Catholic marriages' he attributed to the 'consequences of the unhappy war', which 'introduced the knowledge and also the use of unpermitted practices even into Catholic circles'.[263] A great danger for the public morality of the Catholic population arose from 'the perverse propaganda of nudism'[264] – and this, into the bargain, was a movement promoted by the social democrats.[265] In the Catholic Women's League 'not everything was done which might have been done, to keep the world of Catholic women from immoral fashions'.[266] The ideas which many Catholic intellectuals represented 'are from many points of view ambiguous or faulty: their philosophy is akin to that of the Protestants. Religion becomes an entirely subjective affair, an exclusively inner experience.'[267] Some, such as Ernst Michel (Frankfurt on Main), whose book *Politics from the Standpoint of Faith* [*Politik aus dem Glauben*][268] had been put on the Index, thought that in democratic times the Catholic Church must also become democratic. 'On this account Michel[269] [...] energetically attacks the concordat with Bavaria, which in his opinion represents a medieval conception of the relations of church and state'.[270] In Michel's view, the German Catholics must defend their rights to freedom before the demands and interests of the legal system of the Curia. And again the censure of the clergy follows: 'To prevent the evil, more watchfulness and courage on the part of the bishops are needed in the defence of sound doctrine, and ultimately by the censureship and prohibition of harmful books.'[271]

The seminaries in which Catholic teachers of religion were trained 'are generally imbued with a liberal spirit, and they themselves [i.e. the budding teachers] are under the influence of liberal, socialist, and masonic propaganda'.[272] Because of this development, only two and a half per cent of Catholic teachers in Bavaria, for example, belong to a Catholic association. In view of the regrettable predominance of undenominational [*simultan*] schools, 'the liberals were also supported by the Protestants who lack an authority like the Catholic Church, regard the state as the supreme governor of the school, and seek to minimize the influence of the bishops and the Holy See over them as far as they can'.[273] It seems that the socialists wanted to make common cause with the liberals, and promoted the undenominational school as the standard pattern.

Pacelli was massively critical of the post-war course of the Centre Party, 'the left-wing [of which] created extreme movements and perilous currents on its side'.[274] Thus there was a group labouring under the delusion 'that it was possible to be a socialist and a Catholic at the same time'. The threatening political division of the Catholics is damaging them severely. 'Certainly the Centre is not free of weaknesses and errors, yet it remains (in common with the Bavarian *Volkspartei* for Bavaria) the only party on whom we can rely to keep an eye on the interests of the Catholic religion in Parliament'.[275] The Catholic Caritas-Association 'is today in bitter and hard struggle in Germany with the liberal and socialist tendencies which [want] to replace it by public welfare on the part of the state and the community'.[276] The young clergy must be 'educated and challenged to cultivate a simple and modest, yet appropriate lifestyle [...] We must write prayer and obedience on the heart of the young clergy especially.'[277]

Pacelli was sharply critical of the cathedral chapters and the theological faculties. During the concordat negotiations with Prussia they had attacked the Holy See from behind. The cathedral chapters, 'up to the very end with ministers and deputies',[278] had pressed for the full right to elect bishops; the faculties had wanted to impede the broadening of the rights of the Church to appoint and dismiss university teachers [*Dozenten*]. By these tactics they had simply increased the difficulties which existed already. Pacelli also had some advice to the German episcopate. Thus his judgement upon Cardinal Bertram (Breslau) was that he was not likely to force through the necessary reforms in the Breslau theological faculty. In the case of Catholic Action, Bertram

> 'sabotaged' all the attempts and initiatives to set up an organisation or a central administrative committee like the one in Italy, or like the one the Polish episcopate had resolved to create in that land [...] Bertram has moreover a clear tendency to do everything himself, preferring, so far as he can, to leave the Holy See aside – except where he needs the Holy See to cover his responsibility.[279]

Cardinal Schulte (Cologne) earns a commendation for 'always showing himself respectful towards the Apostolic Nunciature'.[280] Of Archbishop Fritz (Freiburg) Pacelli says that he is 'of a rather cold and authoritarian character, perhaps exaggeratedly bureaucratic': he is 'in general rather feared than loved; he is conscientious, zealous and active; full of consideration and respect towards the representative of the Pope'.[281] The Bishop of Fulda, Josef Damian Schmitt, was a devout man, 'yet he cannot be said to be outstanding on account of his intellectual gifts or breadth of view'.[282] The Bishop of Ermland, Augustin Bludau, is reported as beloved by people and priests, but seems to remain 'inactive in the face of new religious and social needs' and also refuses to let 'others take the initiative'. Moreover, he does not distinguish himself 'by exaggerated respect and deference towards the decrees and decisions of the Sacred Congregations'.[283] The Bishop of Münster, Msgr Josef

Poggenburg, was a zealous pastor, but showed 'no especially remarkable qualities' and was 'weak and hesitant' when confronted by deviations of doctrine.[284] Augustin Kilian, the Bishop of Limburg, is reported to sustain 'particularly warm relations with the Apostolic Nunciature'.[285] Bishop Berning of Osnabrück confirmed to Pacelli his high intelligence and rhetorical gifts. But 'his speed in action and decision is perhaps the reason why in some particular cases the latter were not altogether cautious and opportune'.[286] Bishop Kaspar Klein of Paderborn takes no tricks in doctrine or special strength of faith, but he is a beloved, good-natured and energetic spiritual leader, who is 'extremely devoted to the Holy See and the Pope's representative, whose instructions he [implements] conscientiously and gladly'.[287]

So the report proceeds bishopric by bishopric. What is striking is not only Pacelli's occasionally sharp judgements, but also the criteria by which they are reached. Intelligence, piety, diplomatic skill and devotion to the Holy See seem to Pacelli to be the most important qualities of a bishop. It is striking that according to Pacelli's impression, the least important German bishops could unite all these qualities in themselves.

At the desire of the Curia, Pacelli was succeeded by Cesare Orsenigo, who from 1922 to 1925 had been internuncio in the Netherlands, and subsequently Apostolic nuncio in Budapest and Berlin.[288] There was a good deal of speculation about Cesare Orsenigo's appointment, since in comparison with Pacelli he was reckoned a second choice for the Berlin nunciature. Orsenigo came from a devout petty bourgeois family engaged in the silk trade in the countryside around Milan. Besides Cesare two cousins also took up the priestly vocation.[289] He lacked Pacelli's professional training in diplomacy. Only at the age of 49 did he exchange the vocation of a priest for a diplomatic career. But he was among those whom Pius XI protected energetically. When he objected that he was not qualified for such an office, Ratti, who had known him from Milan, replied that a good priest could also become a good diplomat. Had this not happened to the Pope himself?

Unlike Pacelli, Orsenigo acted in Berlin with caution and anxiety.[290] Because he was always concerned to avoid giving offence, noone took him quite seriously either in Berlin or in the Vatican. The British historian Owen Chadwick thinks that Orsenigo was weaker than the British ambassador Sir Neville Henderson in the last years of appeasement. Pacelli knew how weak the Berlin nuncio was. The Bishop of Berlin, Konrad von Preysing,[291] a friend of Pacelli, also had a very low estimate of Orsenigo's abilities. Yet Pacelli, even when he was later Pope, kept the nuncio in office. 'Was it that anybody in Berlin was better than nobody, and if he recalled Orsenigo he would never be allowed to send a replacement? Or did it suit his still nature to keep, as responsible for papal relations with Nazis, a clergyman so likely to put up with whatever happened?'[292]

Peter Godman sees in Orsenigo's style of reporting from Berlin a factor in the 'one-way-street' policy[293] of the Vatican towards the German dictator. But did it not imply a displacement of responsibilities if it was expected from Orsenigo to move Pius XI and his Cardinal Secretary of State to action through courageous reports to Rome? Finally the Berlin nuncio captured the political moods in Germany excellently, and hence advised caution and reconciliation. Noone in the Curia need follow instructions of this kind.

At first of course the signs in the Berlin nunciature all pointed to continuity. When Werner von Alvensleben,[294] an agent of Schleicher and president of an unconfessional league against the excesses of Russian religious persecution, informed the new nuncio in the spring of 1930 that in the view of Foreign Minister Curtius protests against the Soviet Union injured the interests of Germany in foreign and economic policy, Orsenigo was at once 'all ears'. Alvenseben reported further that when he objected that it was a question 'of the protection of religious, not political values', Curtius replied that the critics of the USSR also pursued political motives and ends 'under a religious and moral mask', and this included the Holy See.[295] The Vatican protested, it was true, against the closure of Catholic churches in the USSR, 'yet it did not protest some years ago when the Poles closed and suppressed Protestant churches'.

Orsenigo commented in his report to Pacelli that he ascribed these remarks to the 'anti-Catholic feelings of the Minister [...] He is in fact the son of a Protestant pastor.'[296] And again: 'the dangerous sympathy which the communists of Germany entertain for the atheistic education which was introduced in Russia, is no secret any more [...] The newspapers report a project to send 800 Berlin children to Russia in the holidays.'[297] Pacelli requested the Berlin nuncio to keep him posted.[298]

Two months later Orsenigo reported the conversation between Curtius and the Bishop of Berlin, Msgr Schreiber.[299] According to this, Curtius rejected Alvensleben's report as untrue, and described the informant as a political enemy. Yet Orsenigo remained distrustful: 'When I thanked the bishop of Berlin, I did not neglect to say to him that Soviet infiltration is so obvious here, that the minister is not short of opportunities to show even in practice how much his policy differs from every support of Bolshevism [...] The next political elections will tell us whether the Bolshevik flood can be dammed up by the usual means.'[300]

Was Orsenigo also thinking of 'unusual' means? To give emphasis to his judgement of the situation, the Berlin nuncio included a report on the Bolshevist campaigns in the previous months. In it he describes also the communist propaganda to persuade people to leave the Church[301] – together with the offer to undertake all the formalities:

> Happily this invitation does not much affect the Catholics; but by contrast there are many resignations among the Protestants. Would to God that these poor people may one day find the faith again and return to the Church, so that they may find the true Church. With this hope we may observe the present resignations with little fear: but alas! The hope is very weak.[302]

Again Pacelli showed himself extraordinarily interested. 'I am also glad that Your Excellency [i.e. Orsenigo] did not hesitate to have Mgr. Schreiber emphasize how great is the Bolshevik threat to Germany, and how very necessary it is to mount a rapid and energetic defence against it.'[303]

To the diplomat priests Bolshevism was the chief danger. To dam up and repel this movement was their prime political end. From this point of view it is not remarkable that in the spring of 1933 Pius XI at first spoke positively of Hitler's seizure of power.[304] That this view of things was always wrapped up with anti-Protestant emotion is obvious. The Protestants had not only fallen away from the Catholic faith, they were disloyal to their own community of faith and represented voting potential for the Left. On the other side Orsenigo also registered anxiously the meteoric development of the NSDAP into a popular party [*Volkspartei*].[305] Two days after the elections of September 1930 he commented on the earthquake victory of the NSDAP, which with 18.3 per cent of the votes and 107 seats had risen to be the second strongest party in Germany. That the KPD likewise, if not so spectacularly, had attracted 13.1 per cent of the votes cast, and disposed of 77 Reichstag seats, was of little comfort to the Berlin nuncio. Orsenigo transmitted the following picture to Rome: there is a 'great mistrust towards parliamentary life of the old stamp, which came out in a striking defeat of the liberal parties, which identified themselves with the old Parliamentarism'.

Further, there is an

> almost feverish desire for a new, even risky, solution for the economic situation, which has recently become very serious and is expressed

in six million new votes for the National Socialist Party (Hitler); this party in 1928 numbered only 809,000 adherents. Some regard it as only a passing phenomenon; but as they will still remain in opposition it is foreseeable that in an eventual new election they will capture more seats. Although the NSDAP numbers some Catholics among its members, their programme for the time being gives no ground for confidence. It deserves watching, however, because of its decided and often really violent opposition to the spread of Sovietism – but it is an opposition based not on religious principles, but only on nationalism.

Finally, Orsenigo took notice of the

conviction, taking root in increasing numbers of Germans, that only communism can present the poor with material well-being; this conviction underlies the notable growth which the Communist Party has experienced [...] This is perhaps the worst symptom of the political and religious situation in Germany, for it is not a question of opportunist adherents, but of those prepared by anti-religious propaganda. However there is comfort in the knowledge that the Centre Party with Catholics openly in the lead, despite momentary especial difficulties – it is at any rate identified with the government – has held its position exactly, since it won new seats in the proportion attributable to it by the increase in votes. In the context of the general collapse of the parties of the Right, the intact position of the Centre is equal to a brilliant victory. To this, even if with gnashing of teeth, not only democrats, but also the liberals, pay high respect. The situation arising from Sunday's elections offers little hope for durable political life: some reckon that these elections were a temporary stage; there are many who think a new dissolution of the Reichstag is unavoidable, and even alterations in the Weimar constitution. Among those elected on Sunday, is, for the first time, the famous cathedral preacher, the Protestant Doehring,[306] whose rejection of the Holy See is proverbial. In the Catholic ranks there are few changes. The election campaign in which not [a] few of the leading personalities among the clergy took part, remained calm and free from all political-religious confusion. Several bishops directed an inspiring word to believers, and challenged them to vote according to conscience, with a view to protecting Catholic principles and the rights of the Church. These data may help to complete the picture of the political and religious situation especially in Berlin: The Communists increased since 1928 by about 56,000 votes; the Centre by about 5,000. In 1929 6,570 persons separated from the Catholic Church and 50,170 from the Protestant church, and because in general the determining reason was to escape church tax, one can accept that these separations all work in favour of anti-religious communism. But the Catholics are exemplary in their piety: a very high level of participation in communion is calculated, about 3 million per year, or 6.7 per Catholic.[307]

The Berlin nuncio also saw the political problems very clearly. This was true even for National Socialism. Unlike Pacelli's earlier assessments, Orsenigo's optimism about political Catholicism is striking. And the loyalty of the Catholics filled him with pride and confidence.

3
The Foreign Policy of the Vatican under Cardinal Secretary of State Pacelli 1930–39

3.1 The first conflicts with Italian Fascism; development in the Catholic parties of Germany and Austria

Pacelli's style of government differed basically from that of his patron Gasparri. The latter had concerned himself only with really 'important questions',[1] but the former was inclined to have a finger in every pie, 'to concentrate affairs upon himself'.[2] The same was true of the *Osservatore Romano*, the semi-official organ run by the Jesuits, which reflected the viewpoint of the Pope and the Curia. Pacelli did not fail to subject its editions to a personal critical examination.[3] In the middle of 1931 the Italian fascist regime proceeded against the 'Vanguard Army'[4] of Catholic Action, fearing that the State would suffer competition from its social and cultural campaigns. The paper took up a clear position against leading Italian politicians.[5] Then followed the encyclical *Non abbiamo bisogno*. It sprang from the 'personal initiative and design'[6] of the Pope. In it he condemned the 'heathenish deification of the state' and rejected a revolution which 'tore young people from the Church and Jesus Christ, and nurtured their young vigour to hate, to violence and to irreverence'.[7] By contrast the Pope spoke of the youth organizations within Catholic Action as 'little crusaders of the sacrament'.[8] It was no accident that such sharp differences occurred precisely in the area of education, for this was the field of the Mussolini government's greatest efforts.[9] The leading philosopher of fascism and long-serving minister for education, Giovanni Gentile, wrote an answer to *Non abbiamo bisogno*; he set out once more the character of the Lateran treaties, the self-understanding of the fascist state and the conditions for peaceful cooperation. The agreement to set up the Stato della Città del Vaticano had been made possible by the Vatican's self-limitation of its state rights. He cited with agreement Pius XI's speech before the clergy on 11 February 1929:

> It will, we hope, be clear to all that the highest priest has nothing of his own except that little parcel of material ground, which is indispensable for the exercise of the spiritual power which is entrusted to men for the blessing of men [...] We rejoice to see the material ground reduced to such narrow limits, so that it too can be regarded as spiritual and must be the bearer and servant of the divine spirituality for which it is intended.[10]

While the treaty establishing the Vatican State related to its existence, the concordat was concerned with its work. 'The concordat [...] is a programme'.[11] But it could not be overlooked that it was agreed by the State. 'The Church got a treaty through the concordat, and the state got a concordat through the treaty'.[12] It was the mission of the State 'to give the clauses of the concordat a concrete content'.[13] The concordat was a 'transaction formula between the immediate demands of the Catholic Church in the political area, and the no less immediate demands of the state [...] But a transaction formula signifies an unstable balance or living formula which does not remain fixed, but moves in order to live.'[14] The decisive point of the agreement was the readiness of both sides to accept self-limitation.

To elucidate this relationship, Giovanni Gentile quoted from his Senate speech of 12 April 1930: 'State and Church are two totalitarian regimes. Their agreement can only arise from a self-delimitation; and whoever is disinclined to limit himself, whoever wants everything for himself and makes no concession to the right of the other, and wraps himself in stiff impatience, is asking for hard times for the concordat.'[15] The Church challenged the claim of the fascist state to be an 'ethical state'. Convinced of its ethical character, the fascist state claimed 'the unlimited right to educate the young'.[16] To this absolute right the ethical state would hold fast, 'even if it acknowledges the legitimacy of private forms of education (among them those exercised by the Church)'.[17]

The mediation of the Jesuit Pietro Tacchi Venturi, who possessed Mussolini's special confidence, made it possible to avoid conflict.[18] In an agreement of 2 September 1931,[19] the Vatican met most of the demands of the State; it decentralized Catholic Action, largely incorporated the Catholic youth organizations into the fascist organization of the State, and strictly confined Catholic activities to religious and educational missions.[20] It was especially the paramilitary deployment of Catholic

Action, its modern morphology, which must have irritated the State.[21] Mussolini's reception in the Vatican on 11 February 1932 marked the definitive end of the last great controversy between the regime and the Church in the area of education of youth.

At the moment of this early clash with Mussolini, the Holy See had also got through its first collisions with German National Socialism.[22] But other problems still loomed. Under the new conditions of the Weimar Republic, manifested in the positive separation of Church and State, the Roman Catholic Church had enjoyed a considerable upturn in its fortunes. This was not just a matter of organization – the Länder concordats and the creation of the bishoprics of Meissen, Berlin, Aachen and Danzig – but more especially of Catholic life.[23] Stirred by the general German youth movement, Catholic young people created for themselves in various youth associations a distinctive Catholic profile.[24] Pacelli[25] also took a very positive view of the flourishing 'Liturgical Movement',[26] and a new Church consciousness, a new desire to bring the Christian gospel to the world, made headway.[27] Not only at the spiritual but also at the political level, Catholicism gained rapidly in influence. The two parties close to the Church, the Centre and the Bavarian Volkspartei, as well as the large number of clerical mandate-holders, were evidence of the connection between the Catholic Church and politics, a connection not without its problems but close at times. At the end of 1928 the Prelate of Trier and adviser of Pacelli, Ludwig Kaas,[28] had to take over the leadership of the Centre Party, in order to save the party from break-up. Similar personal decisions at the provincial level – in Prussia as in Baden and Silesia, in Hanover as well as Saxony – produced an extensive 'clericalization' for political Catholicism. The bishops accompanied the frequent elections with the tunes of unambiguous pastoral letters.[29]

There was a corresponding development in Austria, independent of German circumstances. Here the university professor and Prelate Ignaz Seipel[30] had taken over the leadership of his Christian-Social Party already in 1921. He formed coalitions with the Great German and the German-National provincial league, and up to 1929 guided the destinies of his country, twice as federal chancellor; and he conducted an uncompromising anti-Marxist *Kulturkampf*.[31] Pius XI saw in him the powerful leadership personality which he missed in Germany. Like Mussolini, Seipel in the eyes of the Pope was 'one of those awakened characters, predestined [...] by Providence' to free their lands from an 'impotent parliamentary system'.[32]

Ratti was not to be disappointed in Seipel: in the course of controversies his antiparliamentary and antidemocratic ideas increasingly gained the upper hand. Seipel aimed to erect a one-party state under Catholic auspices.[33] Among other friends, Seipel received great sympathy from the home-defence units which had arisen from the associations of veterans of the front.[34] These units were supported by Mussolini, and also by Hungary,[35] with money and supplies of weapons.[36] In the confrontations between the home-defence members and the socialist Republican Protection League at the end of January 1927, an invalid and a child who were in the Protection League group were killed. When the responsible home-defence men were tried by jury they were released; the social-democratic *Arbeiterzeitung* summoned a demonstration before the Palace of Justice. On the command of Seipel, the police and army opened fire on the unarmed demonstrators. This incident was enough to force Seipel finally out of active politics in 1929, but in the background he continued to hold the threads. In the judgement of the Austrian historian Karl Vocelka, 'his thought prepared the way for Austrofascism';[37] he thus rejects the thesis that in Austria a 'defensive dictatorship' formed only as a result of the Nazi threat.[38] Already the constitutional reform of 1929 strengthened the position of the federal president to the disadvantage of parliament.[39]

At any rate there is no argument that, up to Hitler's seizure of power, a Great-German frame of mind predominated in Catholic Austria: an emphasis on the special character of the Austrian State developed only later.[40] After Seipel's death, a new generation of Christian-social politicians came forward, on his ideological basis; the most important being Engelbert Dollfuss[41] and Kurt Schuschnigg.[42] In May 1932 Dollfuss became federal Chancellor; he forcibly eliminated the social-democratic opposition;[43] and, governing by emergency order and martial law, constructed an authoritarian state which reached its peak in the oligarchic and elitist May constitution of 1934. In a speech on the two-hundred-and-fiftieth anniversary of the lifting of the Turkish siege of Vienna on 11 September, Dollfuss set forth all the elements of his programme: the establishment of a 'new Austrian identity' against the efforts of the 'Third Reich' to secure an *Anschluss* (union); the creation of a 'social, Christian, German state of Austria, upon a corporate basis, under strong, authoritarian leadership'.[44] At the same time he issued a programmatic rejection of parliamentary democracy: 'Parliament has eliminated itself, it has perished on its own demagogy and formalism ... such a representative system and such a leadership of our people will and must never return ... '.[45]

3.2 First conflicts with Nazism

In the predominantly Catholic countries such as Poland, Portugal and Spain, political constellations like those in Austria could take their place at the end of the 1920s or the beginning of the 1930s, and do so on the basis of corporative Catholic thought. In a confessionally divided country like Germany such a development to a Catholic corporative state was not to be expected. In the past the Vatican had noted the coalitions of the Centre with the socialists with anxiety.[46] Just as in Austria, the episcopate and the Catholic parties regarded the dramatic rise of the National Socialists as a serious threat to Catholic Christianity.[47] After the Reichstag elections of September 1930, the bishops finally reacted in the spring of 1931 with a rejection of the brown movement in principle.[48] Yet in between there was a phase of uncertain hesitation, a phase due in part to political calculation.

As a result of a report of the German embassy to the Holy See, Pacelli and Kaas met in Innsbruck on 26 September 1930. Great importance was attached to the meeting. 'For in the difficult situation in which the Centre [...] is placed after the last election, the enlightened advice of Pacelli might be of decisive influence, and that indeed in the direction of accepting relations with Hitler.'[49] Yet the German episcopate went another way.

There was a much-studied correspondence between the area leadership [Gauleitung] of the NSDAP in Hesse and the bishop's palace in Mainz. This was provoked by the press office of the Gauleitung at the end of September 1930, and it drove the Catholic Church into a process of formal clarification.[50] The General Vicar of Mainz, Jacob Philipp Mayer, had in a letter – without prior consultation with the other bishops – declared without compromise that Nazi cultural policy could not be reconciled with Catholic Christianity. This radical attitude was often unacceptable to the German episcopate, for the NSDAP was a party recruiting in Church circles. Orsenigo was also unhappy about the unnecessary haste of the Bishop of Mainz, Ludwig Maria Hugo. He wrote to Pacelli on 8 October 1930 that many young Catholics sympathized with the NSDAP, and moreover negotiations were taking place between Chancellor Brüning and the various parties. There were indeed Catholics who gave 'frenetic applause' to the letter of the Mainz General Vicar. But others criticized the 'exaggerated strictness' and thought that 'in any case there had been a failure of tact'.[51] A 'party of this kind had been made an enemy', a party which was 'not definitively hostile in intent' towards the Catholic Church and which might still learn to deal respectfully with it.[52] In a manuscript note to Orsenigo's report, Pacelli's Secretariat prompted the nuncio to give the Bishop of Mainz, to understand 'that he should enquire of the Holy See before making any more declarations of this kind'.[53] Finally it was a matter which concerned the whole nation and hence did not fall within the competence of any single bishop. About the same time as Orsenigo's report, the Holy See received a series of communications from Catholic believers, who were shocked by the Mainz decisions, inquired after the consequences or announced that they would leave the Church.[54] The letter of an adherent of the NSDAP concluded with the question: 'How was it yesterday in Italy, and how [is it] today?'[55] Subsequently Catholic Nazis repeatedly requested a dispensation from the Holy Father, often producing members of the Catholic high nobility as their supporters.[56] The episcopate, like the Curia, sought now to justify their standpoint in detail by writing letters. Pacelli obviously hoped that this controversy would bring the NSDAP to furnish of itself an official declaration of its attitude to the Church.[57] Yet this the party refrained from doing, and simply watched as the clergy in disarray either kept silent, or defended the NSDAP, or tried to evade the questionings of the faithful by excuses. Under these circumstances Bertram's concerns, to get a common declaration of all the bishops to back the push from Mainz, were bound to fail.

At the end of December 1930, 'the report seep[ed] through that the Catholic Centre, or rather Chancellor Brüning, were negotiating with the ring-leaders of this new party for an eventual participation in the new cabinet'.[58] Once again the situation for the clergy looked rather different: 'Of course this step of the Catholic Centre is made much more cautiously as regards statements against the National Socialists, and even the episcopate seems to want to put off a decision, which could now be over-hasty'; thus Orsenigo reported to Rome on 29 December 1930. Yet Brüning's conversations with the Nazis led neither to a covert form of cooperation nor even to a 'Brüning-Hitler synthesis'.[59] Until the spring of 1931 Göring maintained the connection, and repeatedly visited the Reich Chancellery. Pacelli, to whom the coalition of the Centre with the Social Democrats had long been a thorn in the flesh, had to be told by the Berlin nuncio 'that it would be a tactical mistake to separate from the Social Democrats at this moment, since Brüning's cabinet has to get agreement to the emergency orders, and everyone knows that without the coalition of the Centre and the Social Democrats that agreement could not be had'.[60]

Orsenigo summed up that the political situation had so far clarified that 'the Centre increasingly emphasized the impossibility of a politically motivated collaboration with the National Socialists'.[61] Moreover the NSDAP had done nothing to remove 'the anti-Catholic declarations for which they had been reproached' by the Mainz party.[62] An explicit condemnation by the episcopate did not, however, follow. 'The secret question put by the Breslau cardinal to individual bishops to learn whether they thought it opportune to publish a condemnation of the Nazi programme, was answered in the affirmative by only four bishops.'[63]

After the definitive defeat of all thoughts of a new-style coalition of the Right, the bishops needed to take no further heed of political considerations, but they had no option but to put on a united front. Already at the end of 1930, Bertram, in *An Open Word at a Serious Moment*, had given his warning against political radicalization, race mania and a national church.[64] Yet this declaration appeared to the Bavarian bishops insufficiently differentiated. Hence there appeared in February 1931 a Bavarian announcement entitled *National Socialism and Pastoral Care. Pastoral Instructions for the Clergy*. This avoided both the generality of Bertram and the uncompromising character of Mainz. It left the admission of National Socialists to the sacraments to individual examination and limited the rejection of Nazi doctrine both in time and in substance.[65] The Tübingen Church historian, Klaus Scholder, saw in this decision 'a notable example of ecclesiastical prudence'.[66] The Munich nuncio Vassallo paraphrased the pastoral instruction of the Bavarian bishops for Pacelli, and judged that it must 'have seemed bitter to that party, for [...] the *Völkische Beobachter* [...] sought to disseminate the belief that what the bishops condemned was not the official party programme. Yet that organ continued in a tone which makes it palpable how the freedom of the Church would look, were Nazism to come to power.'[67] The Vatican turned from an official statement of its own, 'to avoid reproach by not intervening in domestic political matters'.[68]

In the following month further official declarations followed from the Cologne, the Paderborn and the Upper Rhine Church provinces, which warned unambiguously against the errors of Nazism and its tendencies inimical to the faith, and strictly forbade the clergy any kind of cooperation 'with the National Socialist movement'.[69] In this pastoral advice as well as in a new Pastoral Instruction of August 1931 the bishops announced to the leading representatives of the anti-religious parties that they would refuse them admission to the sacraments.[70] Orsenigo regarded these declarations as very appropriate and expressed the hope that they might preserve the believers concerned 'from the danger of finally enrolling in the host of a party which is departing ever further from Catholic principles'.[71]

Among the principles incompatible with Christianity and the Church, the Bavarian bishops reckoned racism, 'the rejection of any concordat, the development of unconfessional schools', the 'radicalisation of the national idea' and 'opposition to the protection of the seeds of new life'.[72] Nazism, 'originally a political movement directed against Marxism', had increasingly 'veered off to the area of cultural politics, and in so doing had got into an attitude of *Kulturkampf* against the Church and its bishops'. Nazis were further forbidden to take part in church services 'in compact columns with uniform and flags'.[73]

The formula of the Bavarian episcopate unmistakably equated Liberalism, socialism and Nazism. 'The pastoral principles relating to National Socialism remain the same as were established by authority relating to Liberalism in former times, and relating to socialism in the last age.'[74] By this were meant recommendations for pastoral duties in respect of anti-Christian associations issued in 1921.[75] In the new draft of the Pastoral Instruction of August 1931, the bishops pointed expressly to the encyclical *Quadragesimo anno* of Pius XI of 15 May 1931. 'In every respect the [encyclical] of Pope Pius X as well as the Encyclical *Rerum novarum* of the great Pope Leo XIII already confirmed twice by Pope Benedict XV, and the Encyclical *Quadragesimo anno* of Pope Pius XI remain constantly exemplary in content and form, weight and expression.'[76]

3.3   'It is God's will!'[77] The ideal of the Catholic corporative state and the attempt to realize it in some European Catholic states

It was not just a question of the simple rejection of liberal, Marxist and Nazi concepts of the state. Rejection was completed by the outline of a 'Third Way' – of a state structure on the basis of Christian social doctrines proclaimed by Pope Leo XIII in 1891 in his encyclical *Rerum novarum* and taken up again by Pius XI in his encyclical *Quadragesimo anno* in 1931.[78] The first of these encyclicals recommended the creation of associations for 'raising and developing the physical and spiritual situation of the workers'[79] in order to keep them out of socialist organizations. 'Lack of knowledge in matters of faith, growing ignorance of duties towards God and the neighbour, should be combated through suitable instruction. There should be provision for basic enlightenment on the errors of the day and the fallacies of the enemies of the faith, for teaching and warning against the lures of temptation.'[80] Pius XI took the occasion of the fortieth anniversary of the encyclical of Leo XIII to set out the draft of a social order in an encyclical of his own to serve as the basis for the establishment of a Catholic state for a Catholic society. Central to this construct was the 'class-free' social order, organized on corporative lines by professions. There was no mistaking the claim of the Church to establish State and society on the basis of natural and moral law. On this pattern 'well-knit members of the social organism should be formed, also "orders" [*Stände*], to which men should belong not according to their respective place in the labour market, but according to their various social functions'.[81]

This concept of the ideal Catholic corporative state as a 'golden middle way'[82] between democracy and a totalitarian regime was no mere Utopia. It was realized at least in origin in the Catholic lands of Poland,[83] Portugal, Spain and Austria[84] and was among the developments welcomed and supported by the Church.

After the end of the monarchy and the formation of a republic in 1911 Portugal at first followed the laicizing example of France.[85] The Catholic Church was largely identified with the unpopular monarchy, and treated correspondingly badly by the republicans. It lost its privileged position, and felt – like Spain later during the Second Republic (1931–36) – truly persecuted through the effects of the law of 1911 separating Church and State. It came in Portugal to the confiscation of Church property by the State, the theological faculty at the University of Coimbra was closed, and many Church holy days were abolished. Divorce was introduced, church marriage lost its legally binding force and was replaced by civil marriage; processions and other expressions of Church life were limited by the State, religious instruction was forbidden in the schools. When these measures were enforced many bishops had to leave their sees and go into exile. In 1913 Portugal finally broke off diplomatic relations with the Vatican. From 1912 a Catholic student movement began at the University of Coimbra, the Centro Académico da Democracia Cristã (CADC) to oppose the laicizing efforts of republican secularism and champion Catholic interests in public life. António de Oliveira Salazar was one of the heads of this politically active student movement. Under the motto 'Piety, Study, Action' the CADC advocated a conservative unity movement, the moral regeneration of the country and the rechristianizing of Portugal. After a short Christian-democratic phase, Salazar, who had meanwhile become an economist at the University of Coimbra, declared that there were no satisfactory grounds for parliamentary democracy. After 1917 a Catholic party, the Centro Católico Português (CCP) took part in elections, and particularly in the north of the country had at their disposal a considerable reservoir of votes. As in other countries, the Catholic party of Portugal received various kinds of support from the Catholic Church. The election success and the entry of Portugal into the First World War in 1917 led to a cautious modus vivendi between State and Church. Through the appearances of Mary at Fatima between May and June 1917, there was a revival of popular piety.[86] In 1918 diplomatic relations with the Vatican were resumed. A further sign of the recovery of Catholic influence among the Portuguese people was the successful founding of the Catholic daily paper, *Novidades*, in 1923. In this paper and other Catholic regional sheets Salazar published his programmatic ideas for the economic and financial recovery of Portugal. At the end of May 1926 a military putsch toppled the First Republic. After an intermezzo as Finance Minister lasting only a few days in June 1926, Salazar took over this ministry once again at the end of April 1928. He rapidly got control of the economic and financial policy of the government, and by this means in practice directed the cabinet.[87] In 1929 his old friend from CADC days, Manuel Gonçalves Cerejeira, became Archbishop of Lisbon. Without allowing himself to be made a dogsbody of clerical interests, Salazar was able to work with him in tandem, for to Cerejeira too the independence of his Church from the regime mattered a great deal. In 1930 Salazar created a political instrument to gain power, the União Nacional; all other political movements, the CCP included, must be dissolved. Once in power, Salazar established his doctrine of 'balanced finances' [*Finanzausgleich*] and of the strong corporatively structured state. Economic success and the support of conservative circles led finally to his nomination as Prime Minister at the beginning of July 1932 – a position he was to occupy till his accident in 1968. Salazar called his regime Estado Novo (the New State) and in spring 1933 gave it a new constitution tailored entirely for himself. In a manipulated popular poll, 1.3 million votes were cast for his constitution. Alongside a strong President and a National Assembly greatly restricted in its authority, the constitution looked to a corporative chamber, in which sat 'orders' structured on professional lines, as a consultative body. The traditional means of labour struggle, the right to strike and freedom to associate, were forbidden. This corporative idea of the state was the actual centre of the system. Behind it stood the idea of 'a third way' and the rejection of a social conception of communist provenance based on the class struggle, and the rejection equally of the individualism of a liberal-capitalist system.

In the reshaping of his State Salazar called on the 'corporative' ideas of Catholic social doctrine. This was true also of his social legislation – authorized pay, hours of labour, and yearly holidays – on which he thought he could obtain express support from Church social doctrine. The 'unitary and corporative republic' wished to harmonize all the moral and social interests of the population. Apparently his translations into practice corresponded to Catholic self-understanding, for from this side he received the clearest support for his concept of the state. The formal separation of Church and State was never abolished, but the Roman Catholic confession counted as the traditional confession of the Portuguese nation. In 1940 a concordat and a mission agreement were concluded for the colonies. The latter obliged state schools to give instruction in Catholic religious and moral doctrine.

This body of thought also determined the policy of the Austrian priest-politician, Ignaz Seipel. He wanted to set up a 'Christian' regime with a 'leader-personality' at its head. To realize these ideas he needed only a pretext to permit him to disable the mechanisms of the democratic constitutional state. Such a situation – namely, the united resignation of the praesidium of the National Council in March 1933 – occurred only for his successor Engelbert Dollfuss, who used it to erect a clerical corporative state under authoritarian leadership. Austria's way into 'Austrofascism' was accompanied by the Roman Catholic Church with goodwill and support.[88] The positive attitude of the Vatican gave 'rise for broad Christian-social circles [... to] the fiction that a radical corporative rebuilding was on the pattern of the highest authority of political Catholicism, namely the Pope'.[89] The Austrian episcopate supported this view of the matter. A pastoral letter of the Austrian bishops of 21 December 1933 declared:

> If in this pastoral letter we have openly and unambiguously approved the basic ideas and efforts of our government, we may be subject to the not entirely unjustified reproach of taking a party-political attitude in the church. We stand fully and completely on the basis of those principles which Leo XIII in his encyclical of 10 January 1890 [...] put into words [...]; 'in matters of state which cannot be separated from the moral law and religion, we must continually and by preference keep an eye on whatever promotes the interests of Christianity' [...][90]

In the middle of April 1933 Dollfuss went to Rome;[91] the Austrian negotiating delegation under Schuschnigg followed soon after, to deal with Pacelli's 'personal representatives',[92] suffragan bishop Kamprath and Alois Hudal.[93] By Whitsuntide 1933 they had concluded a concordat.[94] For the part relating to the school question and the legal organization of worship, the concordats with Bavaria, Prussia, Baden and Italy served as models. The marriage regulations, for example, state recognition of marriages contracted in church, were central to the interests of the Vatican and followed the Lateran Treaty.[95] The Church was henceforth represented in the federal cultural council and in the provincial parliaments; resigning from the Church [*Kirchenaustritt*] was impeded by force of law.[96] On 1 May 1934, the day of the dissolution of the multiparty system in Austria, 'the concordat was also [ratified], which was not least the price of the church's support for the Austro-fascist system'.[97] In the mutual addresses of thanks given by Dollfuss and Pacelli on the occasion of the ratification of the treaty, not only the understanding but also the basis of the understanding was openly expressed. Dollfuss expressed his thanks to the Cardinal Secretary of State in the key phrases:

> At the moment when this concordat comes into force, a treaty the repercussions of which will be in the highest degree serviceable to the welfare of our country, I beg Your Eminence to accept my most respectful thanks for your understanding and active collaboration in the successful accomplishment of this work, a work very close to my heart.[98]

And Pacelli replied:

> The inner devotion and the truly statesmanlike wisdom with which Your Excellency devoted himself in these significant and troubled days to the realisation of this great work with which Austria consciously sets her political reconstruction on the basis of traditional loyalty to Christ and his Church, is sure of the joyful support of all those who see in the trusting and harmonious working of church and state the best guarantee for the true welfare of the peoples.[99]

Today Austrian Church historians mostly make a critical assessment of the affair. Ernst Hanisch points to the fact that the corporative state was based both upon fascist ideas and also upon the 'traditions of specifically Austrian authoritarianism'.[100] Wolfang Maderthaner sees an attempt to combine 'essential elements of fascist ideology with Catholic clericalism'.[101] Dieter A. Binder says 'that here an equating of "absolutism by the grace of God" and "bureaucracy representing the interests of the state" seems to have been intended as a *leitmotif* '.[102] The theologian Alois Hudal from Graz at the time linked the concordat with the Christian corporative state. In 1935 he wrote: 'This concordat is in some respects [...] completed and deepened through the reconstruction of the state on the ideal of Christian corporative organisation. In this the drawbacks of democracy and the exaggerations of the totalitarian state may be cleverly avoided by a golden middle way.'[103]

In the intention of the Vatican Austria was to become the starting point and centre of a Catholic restoration in central Europe, was, indeed, to introduce the recatholicization of the continent.[104] Even when the corporative reconstruction did not in truth go beyond marginal adaptations, it made transcendental claims: this model Catholic state derived its constitution from papal encyclicals. In actual fact it propagated a pre-modern Utopia with fascist features.

3.4 The visits of Göring and Brüning to the Vatican

The Brown House was clearly shocked by the harsh condemnation of National Socialism by the German episcopate. Hitler sent Hermann Göring, the leading NSDAP Reichstag deputy and 'one of the three General Secretaries' of the 'Führer', as a 'political commissioner' to Rome,[105] to calm the waves.[106] Since the 1920s Göring had good contacts in Italy, and applied himself early to secure a political rapprochement with Fascist Italy, a policy still contested in the Nazi Party. Several times he tried to organize journeys to Mussolini for himself and Hitler.[107] From then on he seemed to Hitler especially fitted to take up diplomatic relations also with the 'other' Roman ruler. In a letter of 30 April 1931, the leading German Nazi requested an audience with Pacelli. 'As party chairman as well as one of the responsible leaders of the NSDAP and quite special confidant of the head of this party – Adolf Hitler – I have a heart-felt concern to be able to speak with Your Eminence on the problems of our movement.'[108] Pius XI, however, decided that Göring should not be admitted first to see Pacelli,[109] but must content himself with an audience with Undersecretary of State Pizzardo. He prepared for Pacelli a memorandum of the conversation which took place on 3 May 1931.

> He [i.e. Göring] said that he came on the instructions of Hitler, in order to hand in to the Holy Father a complaint against the attitude of the German bishops against the National Socialist Party. He complained that the bishops had made doctrinal declarations

against the NSDAP, in order to favour the Centre. He disputed these doctrinal declarations as without foundation: He separated the responsibility of the party from that of some propagandists and writers, and especially from that of Rosenberg, for these views were out of date.

He regretted that the Centre had been pushed to the Left by Wirth, and that it was closely allied to the socialists, who are atheists and are driving Germany to ruin.

He regretted that the Holy See allows many priests to belong to the Centre and fight Hitler's party in encounters which are none of their business. The party possesses 2000 letters from Catholics complaining about clerical behaviour of this kind.

He regretted that Easter communion will be refused to Hitler's followers and that party colours and flags are not permitted at religious burials of party members.

He declared solemnly:

1. That it was not true that the party wished to set up a national church against the Catholic Church.
2. He declared that they would do nothing against dogma.
3. He declared that they recognized the authority of the Pope in religious and moral matters.

He explained that his party recognized the authority of God; and even in defending race they kept it in proper limits, since race was willed by God.

He said that his party will grow rapidly and that they will have to defend themselves; they will not attack the Church, but they will have to defend themselves against the attitude of the episcopate, the clergy and the Centre. The Lutheran Church has done nothing to them.

He said Kaas listened to him for three whole hours, but then made a speech against the NSDAP, in order to give an advantage to the Centre.

He had come to Rome to recuperate, but Hitler had told him he should take this step in the Vatican.[110]

The memorandum closes with the following notes upon the conversation:

Since it was a protest against the bishops and a kind of ultimatum, Msgr. Pizzardo did not tell him he was to put his complaints in writing. He [Pizzardo] answered only briefly, in order to refute some assertions against the bishops, and said he would report to his superiors.

Of Hitler's three secretaries, Strasser is a Catholic, but an invalid, Frick and he [Göring] are not Catholic. He is sympathetic.[111]

The *Demokratische Zeitungsdienst*, the organ of the German Democratic Party [DDP], called Göring's appearance in Italy a 'going to Canossa'; this was not strictly right. The self-conscious party leader of the NSDAP sought rather to correct the impression of the Catholic Church that his party was hostile to Catholic Christianity. At the same time, he pointed threateningly to the dynamism of his movement, and accused the Catholic clergy and the Centre of behaving purely with a view to power politics without respect to the spiritual needs of the faithful. What in the end he was demanding of the Curia was the separation of politics and religion.

Although the conversation was private and confidential, Göring's visit was soon the subject of gossip in Vatican diplomatic circles. The Bavarian ambassador, Ritter zu Groenesteyn, reported accurately that the Nazi had been 'very assured of victory', and he devalued Göring's explanation as the 'familiar general phrases'.[112] Whether the Curia assessed Göring's visit similarly is debatable.[113] Pizzardo stuck Göring's visiting card to his report and passed it on. Did everything really speak against the idea that the NSDAP might still develop in the direction of a fascism of the Italian pattern? At all events the Vatican acted more cautiously than the German episcopate, and were anxious to tone down the uncompromising attitude of certain bishops, for example, the Ordinary of Mainz, against National Socialism.[114] Göring himself portrayed his visit to the Vatican, like his meeting with Mussolini, as a great success, which, in view of the broad coverage in the German and Italian press, was not difficult.[115]

Yet the reactions in the press, so far as they were derisive commentaries, did not leave Göring unmoved. In a letter to Pizzardo of 26 May 1931, he made it clear that he had preserved the agreed discretion.

As Your Excellency will know, the whole German press carried the report that I had been with His Holiness to request Godspeed for my party. It was a question of a 'going to Canossa' etc. The version of this audience is given very variously. There is talk of a private audience and also of a mass pilgrim-reception. I would like to inform Your Excellency of my personal attitude to all this. So far I have made no communication to any paper, nor to anyone outside the circle, but have stuck strictly to the confidentiality of our conversation. Already in Rome I had to realise that the German press representatives knew something about my visit. I myself have reported our conversation only to the circle of our Führer, and only said to friends in Rome that I intended to be presented to the Pope [*sic*!]. This was, however, before our conversation. I have so far deliberately kept my distance from every statement in the press, and have left it to the imagination of the journalists to find their way. And I did not give the interview apparently given by me in the *Völkische Beobachter*.[116]

Pacelli said to the Bavarian ambassador to the Holy See, Ritter zu Groenesteyn, that he was 'glad not to have received Göring, because it would perhaps not have been possible for him in his position to have made no reply to the complaints made against the German bishops, and to have intentionally given himself to a discussion which ought not to take place if unpleasant tendentious explanations not desired by the Pope were to be avoided'.[117]

Of greater significance for the Vatican than the Göring visit was without question the visit of the German Reich Chancellor and Centre politician, Heinrich Brüning[118] at the beginning of August 1931. Brüning's memoirs give detailed information about this journey to Rome, though there is no agreement as to their value as a source.[119] Although in the judgement of the Stuttgart historian Andreas Rödder Brüning 'invented additional facts' and his memoirs have shown themselves in many respects 'not worthy of credence', their testimony cannot be ignored.[120] Subsequently Brüning recalled that his 'conversations with Mussolini and [his Foreign Minister] Grandi [were] among the less pleasant memories of this difficult time'.[121] He was completely won over by the political judgement, the cultural formation and human warmth of the 'Duce'. Entirely sympathetically he followed Mussolini's invitation to go to church together with the Order of Minorites, interpreting this as a possible 'demonstration against the Vatican'[122] and was not ashamed to lend it his support. He was well aware of Mussolini's contest with the Curia over Catholic Action, and during the church service he became 'conscious that I am on a state visit in the Vatican, and that if any suitable occasion arose, I must say a word upon the conflict'.[123] The meeting with Mussolini, who filled him with enthusiasm in every respect, was followed a day later by the 'inevitable state visit to the Vatican'.[124]

The conversation with Pacelli formed the mirror image of that with Mussolini. It began at first 'charmingly', but then went from one controversy to another. To Brüning's surprise, Pacelli did not enter upon the agenda apparently prepared by Kaas relating to an exempt army bishop,[125] but headed directly for the question of the Reich concordat. When Brüning on his part – like Wirth and Marx before him[126] – stressed the domestic political difficulties – namely, the 'furor protestanticus' and the 'lack of sympathy of the Left'[127] – the Cardinal Secretary of State pressed him 'to form a government of the Right with a view to a Reich concordat, and thus create the conditions in which a concordat could be concluded at once'.[128] If Pacelli in fact took this stance, it would have been in a certain continuity with his negotiating strategy in the 1920s.

The conversation between the two took an altogether unfortunate turn when Brüning confirmed his view that a Church treaty should be concluded with the Protestant Church of Prussia. According to Brüning's account, Pacelli held that it was 'impossible that a Catholic chancellor should conclude a Protestant church treaty',[129] subjected the policy of the Reich chancellor to sharp criticism, and declared that he would ask Kaas to resign his office as chairman of the Centre Party.

The ecumenically minded Brüning defended himself against Pacelli's cheeky suggestion that he wanted 'to take away the influence of the Vatican on the Centre Party',[130] and brought up the conflict between the State of Italy and the Vatican. As before when giving advice on alternative coalitions, Pacelli once more suggested a union with the National Socialists. To this Brüning replied, as he later answered Pope Pius XI, emphasizing the basic difference between National Socialism and Fascism. At all events the Pope seems to have taken a fundamentally different attitude towards the NSDAP than Pacelli. 'After the conversation with Pacelli I could hardly believe my ears when the Pope suddenly congratulated the German bishops on their clear and intrepid attitude towards the errors of National Socialism.'[131] Brüning dictated this chapter of his memoirs in 1934/35 when he was already in exile[132] – of course after the conclusion of the Reich concordat and the first frustrating experiences of negotiations over regulations to carry it out. Rudolf Morsey and Frank Müller have brought out Brüning's anticlerical attitude[133] and his criticism of the Catholicizing of the Centre by the election of Kaas as party chairman. This election led Brüning back at once to the good relations between Kaas and Pacelli. In the original draft of his memoirs he said that the Cardinal Secretary of State had 'never learned properly to understand the basic conditions of German politics and the especial position of the ZP [*Zentrumspartei*]', and his 'thought about concordats' had led him, as it had led Kaas, 'to despise the parliamentary system and democracy' and to toy with 'a system of hard authoritarianism in the state' and hence indirectly to give encouragement to National Socialism.[134]

It was Brüning's wish that this clear criticism of Pacelli should not go into his memoirs – any more than the controversial meeting in August 1931. In the latter case Brüning's editors, his former assistant Claire Nix[135] and the Munich theologian Theoderich Kampmann, did not obey his wishes.[136] The Protestant Foreign Minister Curtius (DVP), who accompanied Brüning on his journey to Italy, apparently noticed nothing of a disagreement between Pacelli and Brüning,[137] which may also be possibly connected with the fact that he did not attend the conversation between the two for the whole time.

In his memoirs Brüning gives the impression that he was a consistent critic of coalitions with the NSDAP, which is not correct. Thus between October 1930 and February 1931 and in September 1931 he himself considered a participation in the government by the NSDAP.[138] Rather, the case is that at this time all the participants – Pius XI included – were not yet completely clear about the character of the Nazis, and repeatedly succumbed to the illusion that contractual agreements could be made with them.

At any rate fear of communism was much more strongly expressed in Vatican circles than fear of National Socialism. On 11 October 1931, the day on which the 'national opposition' met in Bad Harzburg to demonstrate their unity in the struggle against the Weimar Republic,[139] Orsenigo sent a report on the political situation in Germany to Pacelli. In it the nuncio coolly calculated on the formation of a Nazi government and added the warning: 'If this experiment breaks down as well [...], then there could be a rise of communism [...] The economic relation of Germany to Russia is always very close – with the unavoidable if also regrettable consequence that Bolshevism is fostered especially in those souls who, lacking the Catholic faith, lack also the surest protection against this error'.[140] Ten days later, Orsenigo reported on the religious situation in Germany.

> The most awkward point [...] concerns the relations between Catholicism, Protestants and the NSDAP. So far as Protestantism is concerned, a certain revival of anti-Catholic hatred has become apparent in recent months, which perhaps stems from a certain jealousy at the deep respect which the Catholic religion has acquired in German public opinion; this has been brought about by certain happy events

and by the work of the clergy and shows itself even in social life. Some Protestant papers and circles, wishing to demonstrate total devotion to National Socialism, dare to accuse Catholicism of anti-patriotism, of eternally mystifying its dependence on Rome which is contrary to the interests of the nation [...] The Communists [...] on the basis of far-fetched conclusions about the wealth of monasteries, the exaggerated level of church taxes and colossal state subventions, all burdens on a proletariat hard pressed by unemployment, have led an attack against the Church. Clearly to be seen is the application of the well-known system, already employed in other nations, to inflame the masses and – at a suitable moment – to drive them to plunder churches and burn down monasteries. [...] Another source of insecurity is represented by the powerful advances of the phalanx of Hitlerites or National Socialists. From now on all assume that these young masses – with their feelings and yearnings for a rebirth of the national life, but without a regular party programme – will form an alliance and in the coming spring will represent the strongest party in Prussia. To be sure they will not be in a numerical position to govern alone, and hence will have to seek a coalition partner. It is foreseeable that with a firm grip on religious principles by the Catholics and with well-understood courtesy, it may be possible for this party so warmly courted by the Protestants, to rid their leadership of rabidly anti-Catholic elements, and to be capable of loyal cooperation [...] Hitherto the Centre has very powerfully fought the National Socialists, though always from political and never from religious grounds. This perhaps serves to distinguish the Centre from the Catholic people as a whole and religion from politics. The bishops helped to demonstrate the religious dangers of the NSDAP – some with clear declarations [...] others by equally clear silence [...] And so, as the episcopal harmony upon religious principles was useful, so also a certain differentiation as to the weapons of war will do no harm.[141]

Orsenigo was considering nothing less than cultivating the Nazis to make them potential coalition partners for the Centre!

3.5 Pius XI's understanding of the kingdom of Christ

Pius XI recognized in National Socialism a serious threat to Catholic authority in faith, but at the same time had 'little use'[142] for Weimar and other democracies, as Peter Godman put it mildly. When in 1932 Ratti spoke out for a 'Catholic totalitarianism',[143] a formula which in

Catholic historiography was repeatedly relativized, his inclination to an outspoken autocratic thought had long hardened. The Frankfurt historian, Patrizio Foresta, points to the roots of this thinking which go back to the first phase of Ratti's pontificate.[144] These are based on the further development of the idea of *Kingly rule of Christ*, as it was expressed[145] in the encyclicals *Ubi arcano*[146] and *Quas primas*.[147] The motive of this theologically understood offensive for recognition lies in the claim of modernity for an autonomy which had been almost realized even then; and against which Pius XI wished to contend again in 'holy struggle'. With the emphasis on the lordship of Christ – quite analogous to the development in Protestant theology in the 1920s[148] – went the denial in principle according to which the Christian faith and a morality stamped by it must remain limited to the area of private life, since the political, economic, social and cultural areas of life were determined by autonomous rules of their own.[149] On these 'unliturgical grounds',[150] the Feast of Christ the King was created in the Roman Catholic Church as the peak of this development in mid-December 1925.[151] As the opposite pole to the progressive secularization of public life, the festival was to confirm that the lordship of Christ was to be acknowledged in family, society and institutions.[152] These theocratic ideas, developed as a protection against modernity, were equated by Pius XI more or less conceptually with a 'Catholic totalitarianism'.[153] This, at any rate, is a second-hand, and not altogether reliable, tradition. Drawing the line at 'Fascist totalitarianism' Pius XI is said to have told Mussolini on the occasion of a papal audience at the beginning of February 1932 that this concept was entirely acceptable in the view of the Italian State, but for the salvation of souls 'Catholic totalitarianism' alone was competent.[154] However questionable it may be to apply the concept of totalitarianism to the theological concept of the kingly rule of Christ, there are clear convergences between Fascism and Catholicism at the level of political action. There were also divergences, which broke out for example in 1931, after 'Catholic Action'[155] as the 'army of occupation'[156] of the kingdom of Christ infiltrating the whole of society was to be rejected by the fascist state. Foresta rightly points out that the ideological controversy between the Catholic Church and the steady secularization of the West must not be narrowed to the historical situation of the 1920s and 1930s. To this of course it may be objected that Pius XI in appropriate doctrinal writings such as *Quadragesimo anno* of 15 May 1931[157] explicitly took up earlier interpretations and enforced them for the present day. Such ideas of the 'realisation of an effective hierocratic society'[158] are so far to be related to the historical situation. In countries such as Poland, Italy or Portugal, the totalitarian claims of political dictatorships and Roman Catholicism faced each other formally, and the Catholic Church sought to use this constellation for the restoration of Catholic states, and for a brief time seemed to have succeeded in doing so in Austria.[159]

In the description of the obstacles to the kingdom of Christ, Pius XI also made use of the negative phenomena of his age, as he saw them. In *Ubi arcano* he described the class struggle as 'the most deeply rooted and fatal sickness of society'; the party system served 'to satisfy the interests of individuals rather than to attain the common good'; finally, 'the gentle and peaceful sanctuary of the family will be destroyed'.[160] Churches and seminaries would be expropriated, priests murdered and the Church persecuted. Only the Church could wrest a victory over materialism and secularization, as it restored the lordship of Christ, whose law was to be obeyed in both private and public life. Catholic citizens and temporal authority are called to re-establish the kingdom of Christ in this sense. When Pius XI praised the advantages of acknowledging Christ's kingdom, the outlines of a Catholic corporative state appear:

> If men would have recognized in private and public life the sovereign power of Christ, unbelievable blessings would necessarily have flooded civil society, such as just liberty, quiet discipline and peaceful harmony. As the royal dignity of our Lord in a way sanctifies the authority of princes and heads of state, so it ennobles the duties of citizens and their obedience. This is what the Apostle Paul means when he requires women to venerate in their husbands the headship of Jesus Christ, to obey them not as men, but solely because they represent Christ as governor.
>
> When princes and legitimately elected magistrates are convinced that they give orders not by any right of their own, but much more by the commission and in the place of the king of heaven, they will all readily grasp what holy and wise use they will have to make of their authority, and what interest they will have in the general welfare and the dignity of their subjects when they create and operate legislation. If every cause of rebellion is thus removed, peace and order will soon flourish and consolidate themselves.[161]

Foresta draws attention to the fact that the choice of canonizations and beatifications between 1923 and 1931 seems to be supported by the viewpoint of interpreting symbolically the evil as well as the hopeful signs of the times. People who were sent by the Church to the apostates, or significant defenders of the Papacy like the Archbishop of Capua, Robert Bellarmine, received in these years the title of sanctity as a sign of the divine providence.[162]

In the historical reconstructions and attempts at interpretation the events of the Reformation appear as the initial kindling of the ever-present secular uprising against Church authority, a kindling to be snuffed out.[163] The regular clergy looked to a re-establishment of the authority of the Church hierarchy in the sense of medieval *christianitas* by the encyclical *Unigenitus Dei filius* of March 1924.[164] The calendar of the Church year also symbolized the sacred struggle, by which thanks to the Madonna for the Christian victory against the Turks in the sixteenth century could be transmuted into the victory of the Poles over the Bolsheviks.[165] Numerous circular letters [*Rundschreiben*] of Pius XI paying tribute to great churchmen who decades previously were canonized, or the anniversaries of whose death had been celebrated for many centuries, served the same end, to re-establish the medieval world order by modern means. Thus the circular letter on the sixth centenary of the canonization of Thomas Aquinas at the end of June 1923:

[Thomas] gives definite guide-lines and rules of life not only for individuals, but also for the common life in family and state. On these are based the moral science of economic life and the ethical doctrine of political science. To these belong those masterful sections in the second part of the *Summa* which treat of their paternal or domestic government of a family, of the lawful power of the state or nation, of the law of nature and of nations, war and peace, justice and property, of legislation and of obedience, of the duty to care for individuals and the prosperity of the whole body. And all this will be set in the context of the natural and supernatural order. If these principles are held sacred and preserved inviolable in private and public life, then there is no need to seek for any others to lead mankind to that 'peace of Christ in the kingdom of Christ' for which the whole world longs. Hence it is greatly to be wished that the doctrines of Aquinas on the law of nations and on the laws which claim validity for the mutual relations among peoples, develop into general intellectual property, for they alone form the bases of a true league of nations.[166]

Like Leo XIII in the encyclical *Annum sacrum* of 1899, it was a question with Pius XI of establishing the unconditional lordship of Christ not only over believers but also over mankind as a whole.[167] All peoples and governments should bow to his 'sovereign power' and bear witness to it.[168]

The encyclical *Quas primas* called for an 'active and militant religious observance'[169] in the good and holy struggle against the 'so-called laicism', the 'plague of our time',[170] and contrasted this with the ideal image of the Christian state.[171] The collective term of 'laicism' embraced all those modern phenomena which sought to deny God his authority over any area of individual and social life. To this extent Mussolini misunderstood the Pope in his audience of 3 February 1932, when he thought he remained within the framework of 'fascist totalitarianism'. On the contrary, the former ought to subordinate himself to the Church's claim to sovereignty, and cooperate actively in spreading the kingdom of Christ, that is, 'Catholic totalitarianism'.

This was why numerous Catholic clergy like Cardinal Ildefonso Schuster, Ratti's successor on the episcopal throne of Milan, could praise Mussolini's cruel Abyssinia campaign as opening the land for the Catholic faith and Roman civilization.[172] And the nuncio Angelo Roncalli, later Pope John XXIII, wrote from Athens: 'As the Duce has succeeded in everything, one point after another, one battle after another, without setback or interruption, one is almost led to believe that a heavenly power has guided and protected Italy. Perhaps it was the reward for his having made peace with the Church.'[173] Mussolini appears here as an obedient instrument of God and his Church, an understanding which did not differ from that of the Vatican. A little later Franco stylized his Putsch as a divinely-willed crusade against atheistic socialism in his country.[174]

The concordat policy of Pius X and his Cardinal Secretary of State formed – alongside Catholic Action – a decisive instrument for the planned establishment of 'Catholic totalitarianism'. Alongside the other countries already named, Germany as a 'concordat state' was a papal candidate to join in the political and cultural offensive of those confessional states which had the divine mission to reconquer for his representative on earth[175] the *Regnum Christi*. Such a 'vision' of Christian maximalism of course laid claim to the unconditional superiority of the one 'world-church'.

To determine relations between some elect European states and the Church in this way was bound to lead to a mutual preference between the Papacy and fascism, but was also the basis of dogged struggles in cases where spheres of power and influence clashed.[176] Such clashes arose especially when Mussolini sacralized contemporary politics[177] and in rivalries in the semantic, architectonic sacramental areas, and in folksy traditions.[178] Both sides used warlike and military metaphors, both worked with the triumphal form of collective mobilization, both preferred monumental buildings, and both played with concepts of ideological system which seemed capable of realization only in the European area; all these were circumstances explicable in the light of the much more relaxed relations between Rome and Washington during Pacelli's term of office.[179]

Repeatedly the Vatican proclaimed that the Catholic Church rejected no form of state. 'It lives in correct and good relations to states of the most various forms of government and the most different inner structure. It had concluded concordats with monarchies and with states of democratic and authoritarian leadership',[180] explained Pacelli at the end of January 1934. Decisive for the relations to these states was always whether they conceded to the Church the right to establish the kingdom of Christ and hence to witness to his sovereignty – a sovereignty of course which operated not in the vague realm of the spiritual but which was exercised representatively and quite concretely in this world by the Church. Since the acceptance of this basis for Church negotiations on the side of different states ran up against different forms of approval, the Holy See nevertheless had definite preferences.

3.6 'C'est mon concordat!'[181] – the origin of the Reich Concordat (1933)

For the time being the concordat negotiations with the Reich had stalled and those with Prussia had yielded results which were not altogether satisfactory; nevertheless Pacelli continued his concordat policy undeterred. Baden counted as the most important concordat area because the Upper Rhine metropolitan church was located in Freiburg. By the Prussian concordat the sees of Fulda and Limburg had been carved out of the metropolitan area of Freiburg, so that the old bull *Provida solersque* of 1821,[182] which had fixed its boundaries, and the regulations on the election of bishops of 1827 were in need of revision. The aftereffects of the *Kulturkampf* were still visible in 1918. The new constitution of 21 March 1919 guaranteed to recognized religious communities the right to regulate their internal affairs independently of the State; on this basis, thanks to the powerful influence of the Centre Party, the Baden Landtag and government refused to intervene in the internal affairs of the Church.

When Pacelli, still serving as nuncio, took up the negotiations, he and Gasparri made clear that because of the altered political conditions they were aiming at a completely new regulation. The Baden government in contrast pressed for the recognition of the old agreements as the basis for negotiation. A fortnight after Pacelli's letter of 2 June 1926, in which he reaffirmed the attitude of the Vatican,[183] the Bishop of Rottenburg, Paul Wilhelm von Keppler, died. The vacancy in the see thus created enabled Pacelli, as in similar previous cases in Bavaria and Prussia, to apply pressure and to question the cooperation of the State in the appointment of a successor. Only after long and dogged negotiations did Pacelli secure that the cathedral chapter of Rottenburg – like the Freiburg cathedral chapter in 1920 – should have the right of election without this decision prejudicing the later concordat negotiations.

Only after the conclusion of the concordat with Prussia and the Baden Landtag elections at the end of October 1929, in which the Centre received 38.66 per cent of the votes cast, were preliminary conversations on the concordat begun. Before he proposed to the government of Baden on 29 November 1929 that negotiations commence, Pacelli first consulted with the Centre politicians, Ludwig Kaas, Josef Schofer and Ernst Föhr.[184] Although the Baden President of State, Josef Schmitt, declared his basic readiness to conclude a concordat already at Christmas 1929, consultations were delayed because of Pacelli's move from Berlin to Rome. Despite his new office, Pacelli did not hand over the negotiations to his successor Orsenigo, but took advantage of a holiday in Switzerland to open conversations on October 1930. Finally in the spring of 1932 he took entire charge of the leadership of the negotiations. Again the Cardinal Secretary of State made clear that he regarded the Bavarian concordat as the pattern for the conclusion of a Baden treaty; and on 9 February 1932 he rejected the renewed proposal of the Baden Minister for Public Worship, Eugen Baumgartner, to let the earlier agreements continue in force. In the course of the negotiations the Archbishop of Freiburg, Carl Fritz, died, and for the third time the State declared itself ready to let the cathedral chapter elect the new archbishop. Despite the rather uncompromising position of the Curia, the State brought the concordat negotiations to a conclusion in the summer of 1932; this was due not least to considerations of parity between the denominations, because negotiations with the Baden Protestant Church were already far advanced.

On 12 October Pacelli and the Baden ministers Schmitt, Baumgartner and Wilhelm Mattes signed the Baden concordat together with a concluding protocol in Kloster Hegne near Konstanz. At the beginning of November 1932 another additional protocol followed. In place of State cooperation in appointments to the archiepiscopal see, there was now the 'political clause' by which the rights of the Church to the oversight of Catholic religious instruction were confirmed, but nothing was said about school organization in general. In contrast, the concordat refused any recognition of the Baden system of undenominational schools.[185]

When the Baden government brought both the treaties into the Landtag on 14 November 1932, they underlined the continuity of State-Church canon law in Baden. As the Social Democratic party was excluded from the government coalition at the beginning of the consultations, it appeared at first extremely questionable whether a majority for the laws could be put together. On the first reading the stalemate in the Landtag was removed by the deciding vote of the Landtag president in favour of the law; on the second reading the concordat was enabled to pass by a bare majority of 44 votes to 42 because two opposition members failed to turn up. On 10 March 1933, just before the Baden government was dismissed by the Nazi Reichskommissar, the concordat was ratified.[186]

As in the Prussian case, Pacelli had been unable to attain the object of his diplomacy, namely, to incorporate the school regulations similar to those of the Bavarian concordat into the concordat with Baden. What must have pained him even more was that his greatest objective, a concordat with the German Reich, had hitherto been beyond his reach. All his efforts up to the mid-1920s had foundered on the obstructiveness of Bavaria and Prussia, and above all on the constellations of parties in the Reichstag. Occasionally Pacelli could not fend off the impression that the Centre Party Chancellors had allowed their courage to fail.[187] The coalitions of the Centre with the Social Democrats had been observed by the Pope and his Cardinal Secretary of State with extreme regret, and they would have preferred an approach to the national-conservative parties.[188] Ludwig Kaas, who had been chairman of the Centre Party since the end of 1928, shared the reservations of the Vatican towards Social Democracy.[189]

Notwithstanding the distance the episcopate and the Curia had kept from Nazi ideology in 1930/31,[190] there were actually negotiations between the Centre and the NSDAP in May and June 1932 because members of the NSDAP had been taken into the Prussian cabinet. After the 'Prussian blow' of 20 July 1932 – the dismissal of the Prussian government and the nomination of the Reich Chancellor Franz von Papen to be Reichskommissar for Prussia – the conversations between the Centre and the NSDAP served the purpose of ending the Reichskommissariat by parliamentary means and bringing a new Prussian government into being.[191] The election victory of the NSDAP in the Reichstag elections of 31 July 1932 then made it appear that 'cooperation between the Centre and the Nazis' was 'the only conceivable possibility of forming a majority capable of governing'.[192]

Within the Centre as in the Bavarian Volkspartei a deep uncertainty of course prevailed as to a way out of the continuing crisis; and for that crisis the Centre renegade, Papen, was much at fault. Brüning and others, for example, the party chairman of the BVP, Johann Leicht, gave urgent warnings against an approach to the NSDAP. The former Reich Chancellor Brüning, who had fallen in May 1932, repeatedly pressed his party 'to defend and maintain the idea of law and of the constitutional state by all the means in their power'.[193] To solve the crisis Brüning's rival, Ludwig Kaas, without agreement with him,[194] and ultimately without any result at all, pushed the notion of a multiparty movement of 'positive' forces. His strategy ended in 1933 with the exclusion of both Catholic parties.

Before the November elections of 1932 Orsenigo gave the Cardinal Secretary of State an estimate of the political situation in Germany. He reckoned, accurately as it turned out,[195] with a small poll and a result which would again defeat the possibility of forming a stable government. The outcome would be that the government would carry through a reform of the Reich constitution which it had already prepared.

> In view of this probability it is in my opinion very important to maintain and cultivate – so far as possible – good relations with Papen; in the event of a revision of the constitution we may then exercise the greatest possible influence in the interests of the Catholic Church. Of course the most effective organ for all this is the Centre Party, and I hope that, when faced with a task of such momentous consequences for the Catholic Church, he [i.e. Papen] will be able to overlook his personal antipathies and develop all the collaboration needed to turn circumstances for the protection of Catholic interests.[196]

Things turned out otherwise. But these considerations were characteristic of the policy of the representatives of the Vatican. And in view of its underdeveloped inclination to think independently, we must accept that it thought on the prescribed lines. At the beginning of January 1933 – the Schleicher cabinet was foundering – Papen wanted to overthrow his successor in the office of Reich chancellor and with the help of the NSDAP return to power.[197] Several meetings between Papen and Hitler took place; the breakthrough came on 22 January 1933.[198] Papen seemed willing to be satisfied with the post of vice-chancellor in a Hitler cabinet, and Oskar von Hindenburg, the son of the President of the Reich, who was present at the conversation as well, and subsequently had a private conversation with Hitler, gave it out that the Führer of the NSDAP had made a powerful impression on him. The next day the Reich President showed himself not ready to accept Hitler as Chancellor, and pressed Papen to make himself available again.

Immediately after the conversation with Hindenburg, Papen hurried to Orsenigo. The latter got the impression that he 'entertained the hope of regaining power'.[199] Papen sought to use the nuncio as a mediator with the Centre. 'He [Papen] is [...] anxious about the hostility which the Centre will certainly evince towards him. He seems already to have tried in many ways to moderate the judgments of the Centre about him but I fear that it is futile.'[200] Orsenigo 'decisively' rejected the suggestion which Papen put to him, and was not even ready to give his personal 'opinion on the situation'.

Now Papen proposed to him that he would go to Rome to Pacelli and request his support.

> Then I ventured to say to him – solely with a view to saving your eminence a visit, which would probably call forth anxious commentaries: 'I have not the courage to recommend such a journey to Your Excellency. On the contrary I would think it opportune to reject the idea without more ado.' He asked me then whether the danger consisted in his not being received; I answered that His Eminence prefers not to be addressed for purely political ends and in times like these [...] He then offered me his excuses for having turned to me on such a side-issue, and with some formal words departed.[201]

Typical of the anxious nuncio was, on the one hand, his apprehension that 'it might leak into the press' that Papen had visited the nunciature. But, on the other hand, he was also afraid that he might have 'insulted' Papen with his unambiguous attitude, 'since it is not improbable that he will return to the Reich chancellorship'.[202]

On 4 March 1933, the day before the Reichstag elections, Pius XI spoke in the presence of his Cardinal Secretary of State: 'Hitler is the one and only statesman who speaks openly against the Bolsheviks. On this matter the Pope has so far stood alone.'[203] There are testimonies to similar utterances of the Pope from one of his privy chamberlains – Franz von Papen. Following him, the Pope showed himself happy 'to see in Hitler a personality at the head of the German government who has inscribed upon his banners the uncompromising struggle against communism and nihilism'.[204] Faulhaber too must have perceived this mood in the Vatican, for a month later he put the thought to his bishops' conference that the Holy See sees 'National Socialism like Fascism as the sole saviour from Communism and Bolshevism'.[205]

The Reichstag election of 5 March 1933 was held already under the shadow of terror and of a gross preponderance of Nazi propaganda; from it the government of Hitler emerged as the unambiguous victor. The NSDAP won 43.9 per cent of the votes cast, an increase of over 10 per cent compared with the elections of November 1932; the Black-White-Red Battle Front, which consisted of the DNVP, Stahlhelm and conservative politicians like Papen, gathered 8 per cent of the votes. The Social Democrats with 18.3 per cent had to swallow small losses, the KPD with 12.3 per cent much larger ones.[206] The Centre barely maintained its position with 11.2 per cent; the BVP received 2.7 per cent.

Immediately after the election victory, 'national revolution' followed, with the forcible bringing into line [*Gleichschaltung*] of provinces and communes. In March the first concentration camps were established, beginning with Dachau, and numerous pogroms were begun. On 21 March the victorious party staged the solemn opening of the Reichstag in the Potsdam Garrison Church, thus linking the brown revolution to the old Prussian-German traditions. Only the Social Democrats demonstratively kept their distance from the spectacle; the churches cooperated vigourously. Two days later the National Socialists and the DNVP introduced a bill for the abolition of poverty in the people and empire into the Reichstag. As a result of this 'Enabling Act' the government was able, for a period of four years, to pass laws deviating from the constitution of the Reich without participation of the Reichstag and Reichsrat.

Already before the law was passed, the government began to breach the constitution to ensure the necessary majority for altering it. It declared the communists' mandate non-existent, and thus reduced the number of Reichstag seats by about 81. The standing orders were altered, so that deputies absent without leave could be excluded from the business for up to 60 days' sittings, but yet be counted as 'present'. In this way it was made easier to attain the required quorum of two-thirds of the 'legal members'. The 'No' of the 93 Social Democrats present – the rest were in 'protective custody' – was reckoned on by the Nazi government, but that of the Catholic parties was not. In order to put together 378 votes for a two-thirds majority, Hitler needed another 25 to 30 'Yes' votes from the Catholic camp. In a test vote a minority of from 12 to 14 Centre and BVP deputies voted against. In the vote in the full assembly, the opposing deputies are known to have bowed to party discipline and voted unanimously – the Centre with 72 and the BVP with 19 deputies – for the Enabling Law. Brüning had had Kaas authorized by the country representatives of the Centre to punish any deputies voting against the bill with expulsion.[207]

It appears entirely credible that Kaas, who in these weeks 'played a truly inglorious role',[208] allowed himself to be intimidated by the violence of the previous weeks and Hitler's renewed threats in the conversation of 22 March.[209] The French ambassador André François-Poncet observed that the leader of the Centre Party spoke 'humbly and deferentially' and 'moved with the greatest caution'.[210] In contrast, a Yes vote was consistent with 'the line of that development to the right which the party had pursued since the election of the Prelate [Kaas] in December 1928'.[211] On the one hand, Kaas was afraid, in the case of a No vote, of 'unpleasant consequences for the party in parliament and in the country'[212] but, on the other hand, was inclined to accept the authoritarian state; there was here only an apparent contradiction. For in the past he had consistently believed he could recognize rational features even in the politics of the NSDAP.[213] Throughout, he thought that something positive could be gained from Hitler and his policy, and he had a specially high opinion of Mussolini.[214] The authoritarian state certainly did not frighten him, the more so when in 1932 he thought he had perceived that it was easier for the Church to conclude concordats with an authoritarian than with a democratic state.[215] Moreover, he believed the assurances of the present head of government, who took up some of Kaas's formulations into his government declaration[216] and in addition made oral promises.

A package deal between the consent of the Centre to the 'Enabling Act' and an offer of a concordat was contested by all the Centre deputies.[217] Yet again: the notes of the former Freiburg Reichstag deputy Prelate Ernst Föhr, on the party meeting on the afternoon of 23 March, recount with reference to the report of Kaas on the conversation with Hitler and Frick the previous day: 'Concordats etc. assured. Reich Concordat not mentioned.'[218]

Considerable controversies broke out in German historiography, especially in the 1960s and 1970s, over the interpretation of the events of 22/23 March 1933. It is unmistakeable that the different lines of argument reveal striking parallels to the confessional connection or orientation of the groups of historians who took part. Supported primarily by Brüning's account[219] the overwhelmingly 'Protestant' group of historians sees a causal connection between the agreement to the Enabling Act and the conclusion of the Reich concordat on 20 July 1933.[220]

Against this, the predominantly 'Catholic' historians think that no kind of concordat offers or a 'government concordat plan'[221] motivated the Yes of the Centre to the Enabling Act.[222] Those who suppose that there is a connection blame Kaas; he, under the influence of Pacelli, surrendered German political Catholicism, in order to get a concordat[223] of the fascist pattern.[224] Karl Otmar von Aretin summed up the controversy in 1988 as it then stood,[225] and Heinz Hürten devoted two important chapters to the objects of the Centre and the Reich concordat in his work *Deutsche Katholiken 1918–1945* (1992).[226]

It appears improbable that to the concordat lawyer Kaas, at the very least a close adviser of Pacelli, it should have become clear only on 8 April 1933, on a chance meeting with Papen on a fast train to Rome,[227] 'that the view often mooted in public of a possible conclusion of a concordat was now a fact',[228] while the President of the German Protestant Church Federation [DEK], Hermann Kapler, learned of the corresponding plans of the Reich government already on 23 March.[229] In any case, Kaas's sentence can hardly bear the interpretation that on this occasion he heard for the first time of the intentions of the Hitler government, for what had previously been announced 'in public' must not only have come to his hearing but also have aroused his burning interest. According to Brüning, Kaas should already have known of Papen's views on the concordat 'after Hitler's seizure of power',[230] and was indeed well informed on earlier concordat considerations.[231]

It is no surprise that Kaas of all people showed himself alarmed[232] by the passage in Hitler's declaration of 23 March that the Reich government 'attached the greatest value to cultivating and reshaping friendly relations to the Holy See'.[233] Although this sentence, which is said to have impressed even Pacelli,[234] was not part of the arrangements which he negotiated with Hitler, it corresponds entirely to the tenor of the desired de-escalation. Did Kaas suspect that the Vatican was negotiating directly with Hitler without consulting him, the adviser of Pacelli? At any rate, the next day he went surprisingly to Rome, then very shortly came back to Berlin again, in order to set out once more to the holy city on 7 April. The Passau historian, Winfried Becker puts it rightly: 'Through the journeys to Rome Kaas left his party in the lurch.'[235]

With the events of 23 March the last bridges between Kaas and Brüning were broken down; and so were the connections to the other dissidents. The conflict within the Centre had at bottom its origins in ideas; personal differences might reinforce it, but were certainly not decisive. Johannes Schauff, one of those who had voted 'No' in the test vote, clarified the whole conflict in retrospect:

> He [i.e. Kaas] appeared to me always as an ecclesiastical diplomat, the adviser of the nuncio, who saw in the Centre Party the political instrument of Church policy, and acted not with the methods of a politician but with those of a clever leader who was legally expert in negotiations. For him the Centre Party was thus not so much an integral part of the German nation, bound up with its fate, and based on a rich tradition; he looked on it as does a prelate. Thus for him its task could only be a tactical question, required by the circumstances of the time and signifying little to the eternal church in the rapid change of front.[236]

According to everything we know, Kaas was ready to surrender the Centre and support the 'great National Socialist movement',[237] provided only that the new authoritarian state showed itself ready to give certain 'cultural-political' guarantees. Of course it must not be overlooked that the Centre deputies were finally moved by a tangle of reasons and motives to vote unanimously for the Enabling Act.[238] Fascination and anxiety may have played an important role in it. Moreover at this point of time scarcely anyone could be clear about the catastrophic consequences of this step – with the exception perhaps of some Social Democrats, above all the leader of the parliamentary party, Otto Wels. But in the spring of 1933, for the Centre, which had long since veered to the right – not merely on account of the arithmetic of votes – a coalition with the left was not even open to discussion. This becomes especially clear, when one follows the reports of Orsenigo to Pacelli.

On 7 February 1933 the nuncio recalled the condemnations of Nazi ideology by the German episcopate, and the prohibition of Catholics to belong to the NSDAP.[239] 'Unfortunately I must tell you', Orsenigo continued, 'although they were accepted obediently by the clergy, and also applied with cautious strictness, they did not attain the whole result expected; especially the young students were among the most refractory. Meanwhile the NSDAP continually strengthened their ranks, until with the last political manoeuvre – with Papen as its promoter – they obtained power.'[240]

After the Centre came out against the Papen cabinet, called for the taking over of power by the NSDAP, and Papen gave up this position when he left the party,[241] there was a tense relationship between the Reich chancellor and the Catholic party. Against the will of the Centre

and in competition with it Papen sought to create a new political and
religious formation upon the right wing of political Catholicism; this
oriented itself to the idea of a national Reich, to ideas of an authoritarian
state, and to a corporatively structured social model.[242] At the beginning
of April 1933 the formal foundation took place of the right Catholic
'League of Catholic Germans "Cross and Eagle" ',[243] which was to oppose
a Centre party which had apparently become too liberal, and which
enthusiastically welcomed its own self-dissolution a little later.[244] And
even if the 'Cross and Eagle' project turned out rather unsuccessful, it
still connected intellectual powers with its Catholic-national 'empire-
theology' [*Reichstheologie*] which the Centre lacked. With a view to the
concordat Papen had in mind a reorganization of the Roman Catholic
Church in Germany, headed by a Primus Germaniae.[245]

On all these grounds the Hitler-Papen cabinet was regarded by both
the Centre and the Vatican with the utmost distrust, and they refused
cooperation unless there were guarantees for the constitution. At a great
festival banquet on 11 February 1933, given annually by the nuncio
and attended by Hindenburg, Hitler sent his apologies.[246] During the
election contest the Catholic associations published an appeal against
the dictatorship, in which they declared their wish to fight 'against
the unchristian absolutism of the state in the spirit of the great papal
encyclicals'.[247] The NSDAP asserted in reply that they were no enemies
to religion, only to its political abuse. Hence they participated in demonstrative and prominent roles in the religious celebration of the jubilee
of the coronation of the Holy Father, but at the same time 'cleansed'
public offices of democrats and representatives of political Catholicism.
Thus, for example, the president of Catholic Action in Berlin, the former
ministerial director Erich Klausener,[248] was dismissed from his office.
Orsenigo's judgement was that:

> To support the National Socialist government would be naïve and illo-
> gical. They have given no assurances to quieten our doubts as distinct
> from the conduct by which they formerly earned the condemnation
> of the episcopate. Yet to fight openly in the name of religion for
> an obviously electoral object, may also lead to a hardening, indeed
> let loose a genuine *Kulturkampf* [...] To give a prophecy for 5 March
> would be premature. There will certainly be a high poll, and, should
> there be good results, so that a parliamentary majority with a coali-
> tion of only two or three parties becomes possible, parties which fight
> against the left (National Socialists, German-National, Centre), then it
> would be not improbable that a coalition would be concluded rather

with the Centre than with the German-Nationals. Everything turns on not ruining everything in advance.[249]

Despite his reservations against the NSDAP Orsenigo also speculated upon a possible coalition with the Centre, advocating a rather moderate election campaign to keep this route open! At the same time, he reported soon afterwards on the growing tension between the Centre and the Nazis. 'The presumptuousness of the latter is now unbounded.' They kept on terrorizing the representatives of the opposing parties.

> How we are to get to and carry out the elections in so emotional an atmosphere, I do not know [...] The opposition between the Centre and the National Socialists is now so open and acute that it seems to me no longer possible to hope for that dignified, but also reserved, attitude, which might later have offered the Centre the possibility of becoming an element of compromise and peace [...] Von Papen alas! continues his sad performance, cultivating confusion, and trying to make out that the 'good Catholics' are those who will vote for the Hugenberg coalition.[250]

After the elections Orsenigo gave the Cardinal Secretary of State an analysis of political conditions which was not without admiration for the 'remarkable success of the government'.[251] The decline in the Communist poll he attributed chiefly to a broad consensus 'that the progress of Bolshevism [...] seriously threatened to drive the nation into the abyss'.[252] On his own camp he reports:

> A deplorable conclusion for the clergy is that beyond the roughly 6 million Catholics who voted for the Centre and the BVP, there are certainly another 6 or 7 million Catholics who took part in the election. There are actually 39 million voters, so that, reckoning on a proportion of one-third of the Catholic population in Germany, we must start from 13 million Catholic voters. Now it is accepted that these 6 or 7 million Catholic electors mostly voted for Nazism, despite the standards of discipline which the episcopate issued against this party. This considerable number of refractory voters supplies much food for thought about the practical effectiveness of the instructions of bishops in a people made so rabid by new ideas.[253]

Orsenigo was also deeply disappointed by the electoral behaviour of the Catholic people, and spoke often of the 'fascination' exercised on

Catholics by National Socialism. Impressed by the conviction that the political dam was about to burst, he threw sober analysis to the winds and calculated unrealistically high numbers of Catholic voters who had apparently voted for Hitler.[254] In this respect he contributed to a kind of panic which in these weeks was to seize the episcopate, and even make inroads into Vatican diplomacy. In view of the mass enthusiasm in the German people, it was held quite pointless to try to stem the brown flood; what was left was compromise.

On 9 March the nuncio at Berlin informed the Cardinal Secretary of State that he intended to take part in the ceremonial opening of the Reichstag in the Potsdam Garrison Church. Probably the whole diplomatic corps would take part.

> I do not know [...] whether the fact that the Parliamentary sitting takes place in a Protestant church, creates any difficulty. Certainly all the Catholic deputies including the priests will be there; my absence could therefore give rise to the interpretation of hostility or disrespect towards the new government; moreover because of the dominant tension between the various parties, it could perhaps injure the good relations between the government and the nunciature.[255]

On the 22 March the nuncio cabled his boss in Rome that because of the condemnation of the NSDAP by the German episcopate Hitler had absented himself from High Mass. 'Eighty Nazi deputies were present.'[256] In a detailed report to the Curia, Orsenigo, obviously deeply impressed, described the solemn act in Potsdam.

> The ceremony [...] unfolded with an unexampled splendour and solemnity, and with so broad and enthusiastic participation of every rank of citizens that even the hopes of the most optimistic National Socialists were exceeded. In the religious ceremony which followed in the Catholic Church Vice-Chancellor von Papen and the minister Eltz von Rübenach took part, several diplomats, [...] all the Centre deputies and, besides them, a group of about 80 'Catholic' Nazi deputies in uniform. [...] About 5 p.m. a sitting of the Reichstag followed in Berlin in the Great Hall of the Kroll Opera; voting for the office of Reichstag president followed, so that there was a previous agreement between the Centre and the National Socialists. Choice fell upon a Nazi as president and a deputy of the Centre as Vice-president. The most regrettable aspect of the day was the official explanation given by the Reich Chancellor for his absence and that of minister

Goebbels from the Catholic religious ceremony. It is alas! undeniable that the Catholic people with few exceptions have turned to the new regime with enthusiasm and have forgotten the disciplinary standards published by the episcopate at Fulda under the leadership of His Eminence Cardinal Bertram; standards which in truth concern the ideological or religious content of the National Socialist movement, and certainly not their political behaviour. The people were entirely fascinated by this political conduct and sought to separate themselves from its ideological and religious content. In truth the new government has given no ground for religious anxiety; indeed it seems to have good intentions even towards the Catholics: It should also not be difficult with some good will to reach those mutual declarations which will settle this unhappy contest with the episcopate [...] If it is not settled, it could explode in a very dangerous spark, since there is no lack of pamphlets and papers which gather inflammable material by means of old insinuations that Catholicism abroad has an exaggeratedly Roman note, so that it stifles the character of every individual people, and that there is a slavonic and oriental church which is Catholic as well (its own liturgical language, abolition of celibacy). Thus they say they cannot understand why a Catholic Church should not be possible in Germany too, the better to preserve the character of the German people.[257]

Two days later Orsenigo telegraphed to Pacelli that Hitler had declared in the Reichstag that he wished to maintain and build up a friendly relationship with the Vatican, and would respect agreements between Church and State.[258] Already 48 hours afterward, this report followed:

I accept that Your Eminence will be pleased to learn that the German episcopate upon the initiative of the Rev. Cardinal Bertra[m] from Breslau is just preparing a collective declaration modifying the earlier disciplinary norms concerning the attitude of the Catholic Church in relation to National Socialism. The occasion for this revision was offered by the conciliatory speech given last Thursday by the head of the government in the Reichstag; yet the true, decisive ground must be sought in the attitude of growing sympathy among the young and not-so-young masses of Catholics for the new regime. Already today it is very difficult to restrain this mass of sympathizers who clamour to enrol in the ranks of National Socialism. Indeed there is a danger that the Catholic associations even apply 'as a body' for the National Socialist membership card: a thing which, in my humble opinion, would work out very harmfully for the social structure of the Catholics, especially in a confessionally divided land such as Germany. At present Cardinal Bertra[m] is working out the final text of the declaration on the basis of notes which invited all the bishops concerned to address him on the pattern of a draft of the declaration circulated by him. Bavaria too was informed of what was happening. These instructions seem to me to have been drawn up with much prudence and in a broad conciliatory spirit; given the unbending inclinations of some of the young clergy this was unavoidable. In the declaration there is almost no reference to the famous Article 24 of the National Socialist programme which at that time was one of the chief motives for the condemnation issued by the bishops. Perhaps a new interpretation of the article might have been developed, and in my opinion it must be; and the same time many a precise obligation to the freedom of Catholic organisations might have been received. Yet the episcopate has preferred to formulate its declaration – which is full of hopes – without taking up any contact, not even in secret, with the government. Since there was no negotiation of this kind at all, it was not possible to think of concessions as services in return. I think that the declaration of the bishops will be printed on Thursday afternoon or Friday morning. I will not delay to send Your Eminence the final and complete text. The government continues meanwhile on every occasion to express its burning wish that the bishops' outspoken condemnation of National Socialism be revoked. Whether this wish is only the expression of a love of peace, or points to the opening of a mass accession of Catholics to the ranks of Hitlerism is at present difficult to say![259]

Within three weeks the Apostolic Nuncio conceded the basic positions of the Catholic Church under the impact of the victory of the NSDAP and recommended – in all scepticism – cooperation with Hitler by the Holy See and the withdrawal of the condemnations by the German episcopate. Decisive for this revision seems – in Orsenigo's perception – the frenetic enthusiasm of the Catholic part of the population for the Nazi movement. Pacelli agreed with the opinion of his Berlin nuncio. On 29 March under reference to the declaration of the Reich Chancellor, he instructed the Munich nuncio, Vassallo di Torregrossa, to inform Faulhaber, 'confidentially and by word of mouth', 'that it could be appropriate [to formulate] for clergy and the faithful new guidelines on the attitude of Catholics towards the National Socialists [...] naturally with the necessary caution and reserve for the future'.[260] Orsenigo received an order to similar effect.[261]

At the end of March the Berlin nuncio could of course report to Rome: 'My work was unnecessary.'[262] And a day later he telegraphed: 'Bishops yesterday published new directives [...] well received by the public [...] government also very satisfied.'[263] Orsenigo had previously, in a confidential letter to Bertram, inquired after the new attitude of the episcopate to National Socialism as a reaction to the explanations of the Reich Chancellor. But Bertram had already been able to send him the draft of a declaration and a secret instruction, and asked for eventual modifications. A few days after Hitler's government declaration, on 28 March 1933, the German episcopate formally withdrew its prohibitions and warnings against Nazism.[264] On the following day the Fulda bishops' conference published an instruction for the Catholic clergy, from which it emerged unambiguously that henceforth all Church penalties against adherents of the National Socialist movement were invalid, and that participation in church services by uniformed National Socialist formations was immediately permitted[265] – an innovation which the Nazi Reichstag deputies had already practised a week previously. Pacelli noted with satisfaction, 'that the press in general has given a good reception to the declarations of the episcopate'.[266] At any rate he showed himself remarkably touched by a commentary in the *Germania* of 29 March that, recognizing the fact that the Vatican had officially kept out of it, emphasized the sole responsibility of the bishops. Since (according to Pacelli) it was a question of the doctrines of the faith and the essence of the Church, this interpretation might 'create confusion and errors among readers'.[267] And in fact the rapid change of course gave rise to many irritations, not least because the bishop of Linz (Austria) at the same time confirmed once again all the prohibitions against Nazism. Faulhaber wrote justly to Pacelli that the people did not understand 'the different statements of the bishops about National Socialism'.[268]

Again on 10 March the chairman of the Fulda Conference of Bishops, Cardinal Bertram, in a letter to Hindenburg expressed his fears that the government of the 'national coalition'[269] might use its absolute majority to hollow out 'the security of law and justice and of legally guaranteed freedom' and to attack the position of the churches. At the same time the Archbishop of Freiburg, Gröber – the Baden concordat had just been ratified[270] – advised Pacelli to a 'certain elasticity' towards 'the new conditions', 'without surrendering any Catholic outlooks and political connections by it'.[271] Every provocation must be avoided and a modus vivendi sought. Nazism would establish 'a durable rule by every means in its power',[272] and many Catholics would have turned to the movement or anxiously withdrawn from Catholic organizations. With a view to a possible defeat of the NSDAP he of course also recommended keeping a distance, 'so that the Church does not again have to pay for its fraternizing with National Socialism by a counterblow'.[273] He sees the decisive difference from Italian fascism in the radical forces in National Socialism hoping for a *Kulturkampf*, and links this observation with the biconfessional character of Germany. 'Italy, praise be, is still a country united in the faith, while Protestantism used every political opportunity to vent its hate and will to annihilation against the Catholic Church.'[274]

Pacelli had also, according to a conversation with Brüning in August 1931,[275] not given up his plans for a concordat. The connection of the question of an army chaplaincy with the project of a Reich concordat was indeed defeated, after the Reich Minister for Defence, Kurt von Schleicher, insisted to the German bishops in mid-July upon an exempt military pastoral care and obstructed the interim appointment of a Catholic forces' chaplain [Feldpropst]. The bishops had thereupon given up their resistance to an exempt Catholic chaplaincy, so that a regulation of the matter was no longer an obstacle. At the end of October 1932 Pacelli agreed to this solution, but linked with it the recollection of broader questions which must 'at the same time be brought to a satisfactory regulation'.[276] However, in the face of the escalating crisis of the last months of the Weimar Republic, his negotiating proposal did not emerge from examination in the ministries concerned.

At the end of March or the beginning of April 1933 it was again on the political agenda. Despite the still 'unconcluded discussion',[277] whether the Reich concordat was the object of negotiations from 23 March or only from 8 April, there can be no doubt of the determination of Kaas and Pacelli that, even against sceptical voices in Vatican circles,[278] they would ensure the rights of the Church by a treaty of this kind. It must also be reckoned as certain that even before his journey to Rome on 24 March, Kaas agreed with Papen in the intention to conclude a concordat.[279] A guarantee in favour of the Church's facilities for action was valued more highly by both the leader of the Centre and the Cardinal Secretary of State than the continuance of a divided political Catholicism, which had revealed its weakness only too obviously in the recently concluded election controversies. Both sides were well aware of the example of the Lateran Treaties of 1929, including their pre-history and subsequent fortunes.[280] This meant for the State that both clergy and the Catholic organizations be excluded from politics. Luigi Sturzo's emigration, the self-dissolution of the Partito Popolare

Italiano (PPI) in 1927, the way in which the party had approved the giving of exceptional powers to Mussolini's government in 1922 and in 1925 had lost its resources,[281] the suppression and the persecution of the Opposition, not to mention the struggle over the Italian Catholic Action, formed for both Church and State the pattern of their hopes and fears. Astonishing parallels may be drawn even between the PPI leader Alcide De Gasperi and Kaas, who led the Centre up to May 1933, for both fled to the protection of the Vatican.[282]

Already at the beginning of April 1933 negotiations on the Reich concordat began, and already on 20 April Kaas was able to produce the first thoroughly organized draft.[283] In it he was concerned to weaken the depoliticization of the clergy demanded by the State.[284] The resistance of the Church negotiating partners to the unreasonable depoliticization demands of the State of course declined in proportion to the liquidation of the parliamentary system.[285] But at the same time measures of persecution and the dismissal of civil servants who belonged to the Centre set in, and information constantly reached the Vatican of Jewish citizens and of civil servants begging the help of the Holy See. The chairman of the Fulda bishops' conference, Bertram, reacted quickly. Already in the first half of April he sent letters to the President and Chancellor of the Reich battling for Catholic civil servants and associations.[286] In this first correspondence between the episcopate and Hitler, the 'anti-bolshevism' of both was confirmed as the incantation for a possible cooperation. Hitler ascribed the dismissal of state servants on the overblown administrative apparatus, and assured the Breslau Cardinal that there was no intention of proceeding against Catholic associations, provided they 'harboured no party-political tendencies hostile to the present regime'.[287] Moreover he pointed to the difficult transitional phase of the 'national elevation', and to his efforts 'to reestablish perfect peace and order in Germany' as quickly as possible. None of this sounded incredible, and part of the episcopate had already heard a pacifying message at a meeting with Hitler in Berlin on 25 April.[288] Nevertheless the chairman of the Fulda Bishops' Conference remained watchful, and in further letters of the beginning of May, the end of June and the beginning of July 1933 put before the Reich Chancellor his anxieties about the continuance of confessional schools, the unimpeded influence of the Catholic Church on the education of young people, and the further existence of Catholic workers' associations and youth movements.[289]

In a common pastoral letter on 3 June 1933, the bishops welcomed the 'new state' and the 'national elevation', approved the relentless struggle against Bolshevism, and on this basis desired promises of freedom for church activities and for the continuance of Catholic associations and press.[290] These episcopal statements, even before the conclusion of the concordat, support the view that the bishops felt, on the one side, forced onto the defensive against the early measures of coordination [*Gleichschaltung*], and, on the other, offered the regime a common political platform to attain the modus vivendi for which they still hoped.

The Cologne Cardinal, Schulte, be it noted, held that this modus vivendi was not possible. 'The government is a revolutionary government', he remarked at the end of May 1933. 'Law and justice at the moment do not exist. With such a government' no concordat could be concluded.[291] From the viewpoint of Vatican diplomacy the alarming reports from Germany undermined the negotiating position of the Holy See, the more so as Orsenigo reported of various plans for the erection of a German 'National Church'[292] and the appointment of a commissioner for the Catholic Church by the Prussian government.[293]

This background forced Pacelli to move faster.[294] In addition to the school problem, the negotiator had to create the depoliticization article. After the end of the trade unions, social democracy and finally the DNVP, it was only a question of time when the Centre would follow. But then, and this was the view of Pacelli's Secretary, Robert Leiber, 'Article 31 [of the draft concordat] by which the government alone makes the concordat, would be no concession by the Church any more'.[295] At this stage the Catholic party was not a bargaining counter. Hence it appeared particularly important to negotiate for the continuation of the Catholic associations and a guarantee of their free development. It was thus the more problematic that the Curia did not succeed in integrating the list of protected associations into the text of the concordat.[296]

The Holy See made no attempt to save the Centre Party, although among Catholic politicians the view prevailed that in a Germany of mixed confessions Catholic parties were needed very much more than in Italy.[297] A motive for this indifferent attitude to the Catholic parties[298] may have been the desire to put the work of the Catholic associations under Church control, and less happy experiences with the Centre, the last president of which, Brüning, indeed fought to the end for a reorganization of his party and – just like Alois Dempf[299] and Hermann Joseph Schmidt – warned against the conclusion of the concordat.[300]

At the end of April Orsenigo had written to Pacelli: 'Unhappily the most flourishing and important Catholic associations are presided over solely by outstanding personalities of the Centre Party, and so, if Catholics join, this is, if not undesirable, certainly very suspect.'[301] The broad emigration of parts of the Centre into the 'national camp' after March 1933 often took place under the popular slogan that it was necessary to put an end to the mixing of the interests of the Church and party politics. All this was topped off with accusations against Centre politicians from Cologne of financial irregularities and the waste of public funds. 'This whole avalanche of mishaps brings of course a kind of disorganisation into the ranks of the Catholics and especially of the Centre', reported Orsenigo to Pacelli in this connection.[302] The Centre must see 'how its adherents – especially the young – are falling away to enrol in other parties'.[303]

A possible component in the Vatican decision process in these weeks was constituted by a note of Gasparri of 30 June 1933. In it Pacelli's still very influential predecessor in the office of Cardinal Secretary of State recommended avoiding every controversy with the Nazi regime. Neither the Vatican nor the German bishops were to condemn the NSDAP. If Hitler wished to dissolve the Centre Party, it would be preferable for him to 'be obeyed without fuss'.[304] Like the Catholics in Italy, he emphasized several times, German Catholics should also be able to join the NSDAP. The motive for this totally defensive style of policy lay in his estimate of the German mentality and seemed to confirm what Orsenigo had also reported. The substance of Gasparri's key sentence was: 'I am of the opinion that Hitler's party is in harmony with nationalist feeling in Germany. For this reason a political and religious struggle with Hitlerism [...] in Germany must be avoided at whatever the cost, especially while [...] Pacelli is Secretary of State.'[305]

To whom this note was addressed is not known, but it clearly embodies a change of opinion by Gasparri, and one to which he was not committed. We know from the manuscript's date-mark with the addition 'Emo. Card. Gasparri' on that it got into Pacelli's hands. In terms of content the note only shows that Gasparri naively transferred Italian conditions to Germany. But were his position to have been representative of the mood in the Vatican, it of course appears as more than a matter of chance that the Reich government, negotiating with a view to excluding Catholic clergy from party politics, was completely successful.[306]

In the final phase the Curia consulted with Gröber as representative of the German episcopate and, with regard to the State, the director of the cultural-political department in the Reich Ministry of the Interior, Rudolf Buttmann, in order to add more vigour to the demands of the respective sides. Despite much scepticism it was possible to initial the text of the treaty on 8 July. At any rate the head of the State negotiating party, Papen, had to give an explanation beforehand that the decrees of dissolution against Catholic organizations and measures of compulsion against Catholic clergy would be cancelled.[307] This declaration was expressly noted by Pacelli.[308] Moreover, Hitler reinforced his Vice-Chancellor's assurances with an instruction of his own.[309]

The existing Länder concordats remained in full force, and were modified by the Reich concordat only in respect of a few completions, where corresponding individual provisions were lacking. For the rest of the Reich territory the new treaty came into unrestricted operation. In a secret appendix it was further established that in the event of general military service being introduced the clergy would remain exempt; in the event of war, a group of clergy would be free of military service, and others would be taken in as army chaplains or medical orderlies.[310] On 5 July, three days before the initialling of the concordat, the Centre Party dissolved itself. According to the testimony of his closest colleague, Leiber, Pacelli was really unhappy at this moment, because he had promised himself that the Catholic party would continue to exist as a 'backing' for the concordat.[311]

In mid-July 1933, in a letter to Schioppa, Pacelli took up a position towards the self-dissolution of the Centre and the Bavarian Volkspartei. The occasion of the letter was a report in the *Uditore* that the Dutch Catholics did not understand the conclusion of the concordat, and looked upon it as a kind of alliance between the Church and the National Socialist State. Even at this early moment critics in the Catholic camp suspected a connection between the conclusion of the treaty and the end of the Christian parties. This was denied by the Cardinal Secretary of State:

> Above all it must be remembered that the Centre and the Bavarian Volkspartei have dissolved themselves on the basis of a decision entirely independent of the Holy See. The latter [i.e. the Holy See] accepted on the contrary that before they dissolved they would at least await the ratification of the concordat. Instead of this they spontaneously (as I said) dissolved themselves – without informing the Holy See, which first learned of it from the newspapers. It bears no responsibility for the dissolution of these parties.
>
> But, given the new political situation which has taken shape in Germany, in which the Holy See has not had the smallest part, there remains no other way to ensure the rights and privilege of the Catholic Church in so important a nation as Germany, than that of a concordat. Before the conclusion the Holy See requested the whole

German episcopate, including that of Bavaria, to meet in Fulda and to state their wishes in this respect. Msgr. the Archbishop of Freiburg [Gröber] who was at the meeting came on his own to Rome, to take part in the concordat negotiations. He reported that the bishops were unanimous that it [the concordat] was 'the last hope' of avoiding a much worse *Kulturkampf* in Germany than the one in Bismark's [*sic!*] time. On the other side, the concordat assists the Church to great advantages with the Catholic schools, for the school question is included in it, as all will be able to see as soon as the concordat becomes generally known.

[...] Please also consider that in order to obtain the concordat in question, which is certainly not less favourable for the Church than the three concordats already concluded with the German Länder, long and hard discussions had to be conducted, and very great difficulties overcome.[312]

On 17 September, two days before the ratification of the Reich concordat in Rome, Orsenigo celebrated a Thanksgiving Mass in the Hedwigs Cathedral in Berlin, attended by numerous Nazi organizations. Also thankful for the outcome of the negotiations were Faulhaber[313] and Bertram, who on 2 September 1933 had pressed Pacelli to ratify the concordat because the position of the German episcopate was becoming noticeably weaker.[314] Many Catholics felt that the Nazi State, like fascist Italy in 1929, had set limits to its totalitarian claim; the latter ceased at the point where the Church made good its authoritarian claim to the religious thought, feeling and behaviour of mankind. So many people thought before they realized their mistake.

On 2 June 1945, in an address to the college of cardinals, Pacelli spoke, despite all his reservations, in general positively about the effects of 'his' concordat: 'At any rate one must admit that in the following years the concordat brought various advantages or at least protected from worse harm. Despite all the injuries to which it was exposed, the concordat gave the Catholics a legal ground of defence, a position in which they could entrench themselves, in order, so long as was possible for them, to defend themselves against the constantly rising flood of religious persecution.'[315]

An important, if certainly not the central aspect of the concordat dealings, was the biconfessional situation in Germany and the inner condition of German Protestantism. Already at the beginning of April 1933 Orsenigo had reported to his Cardinal Secretary of State on plans to erect a 'national church'.[316] What he had to report to Rome on the development of the 'new German Protestant Church' seemed fully to confirm the insurance policy of the Curia in Church and State.

> This entire reform has the object [...] of replacing the whole church personnel by new elements, [wrote Orsenigo]. Everywhere the young followed, or the sympathizers of the young – at the head, as Reich bishop, Dr. [*sic*] Müller, the confidant of the Chancellor. It is obvious that all this imposes an impressive appearance of unity on this giant mass of about 40 million Protestants (today it is no longer officially acceptable to be an atheist) a certain impressive unification of the outward movement; noone cares a fig for the true inner unity, that is, a unity of the faith: the few dissidents who remain true to the old individualistic principle of Protestantism are silent and suffer in the shadows.[317]

3.7   Persecution of Jews and Catholics

While the Centre Party was being dissolved and during the desperate efforts to conclude a favourable concordat, the first wave of persecution fell upon the Jews.[318] It began with the boycott of Jewish businesses throughout the Reich provoked by Nazi propaganda round about 1 April 1933. The spreading anti-Semitism, terrorism and exclusion of Jewish citizens were supported by a bundle of legislative measures.[319] Already on 31 March upon the suggestion of the Berlin clergy Bernhard Lichtenberg, the director of the Deutsche Bank in Berlin, and president of the Committee for Inter-Confessional Peace, Oskar Wassermann, had asked the chairman of the Fulda Bishops' Conference to raise an objection to the boycott.[320] Bertram hesitated and sought the advice of his episcopal colleagues. His own advice was that it was a question of an 'economic struggle in a circle of interests not near to us ecclesiastically'.[321] Faulhaber held that a protest was 'pointless', indeed counter-productive, and thought he could also perceive a decline in measures of force.[322] Gröber put into words what was to remain henceforth a central anxiety of the Catholic Church: that even Jews converted to Catholicism were affected by the boycott measures.[323]

On 7 April 1933 what was popularly known as the 'Aryan paragraph' was issued: the 'law to re-establish the professional civil service'. This law permitted political critics of the regime and officials of Jewish descent to be dismissed from the public service. This was the background to a letter from Faulhaber to Pacelli of 10 April 1933, arguing in similar terms as Gröber had done before. He held it as 'unjust' and 'painful' that even those should 'lose their places' who for decades or even generations had been Catholic Christians.[324]

On 4 April 1933 Pacelli informed Orsenigo that highly placed Jewish dignitaries had turned to the Pope to 'request his intervention against the danger of anti-Semitic excesses in Germany'. It was in the tradition of the Holy See, 'to exercise its universal mission of peace and love among all men, without respect to their social circumstances or the religion' to which they adhered. Hence Pius XI commissioned the nuncio 'to see whether and how it is possible to take up the matter in the sense they wish'.[325]

Orsenigo replied five days later, and thus after the adoption of the 'Aryan paragraph',[326] that the anti-Semitic struggle had 'taken on a government character'; hence an 'intervention of the representative of the Holy See' would be the equivalent of a protest against a government measure.[327] Without mentioning the Vatican initiative he had reminded the episcopate of their mission of universal love to their neighbour. The 'situation was the more difficult as [the] episcopate – apart from the Archbishop of Paderborn[328] – did not protest earlier against [the] anti-German propaganda from abroad'.[329] Two days later the nuncio completed his information by sending an announcement of Archbishops Schulte (Cologne), Klein (Paderborn) and Bishop Berning (Osnabrück), which had appeared in the Catholic press. These chief pastors had written:

> Filled with the warmest love to their Fatherland, the national rise of which they continually further with all their powers, the bishops see with deepest worry and anxiety, how the days of national elevation have become for many loyal citizens and among them many conscientious officials undeserved days of the most severe and bitter suffering.[330]

A relieved Orsenigo commented in his accompanying letter: 'In the expression "loyal citizens" I think I can read an allusion to the Jews.'[331] Reassuringly, he added that by special decrees many exceptions were being made, 'in order to soften the law. But unfortunately the anti-semitic principle is accepted and sanctioned by the whole government, and alas! this fact will become an unworthy and permanent blot upon the first pages of the history which German National Socialism is writing, and is not without merit.'[332] It is quite clear from this how Orsenigo assessed the Jewish boycott: as a shameful blot. But it also becomes clear that these proceedings were for him a hateful episode, something accidental, which in his eyes was in no way characteristic of National Socialism.

Moreover, the nuncio was able to send his Cardinal Secretary of State a message in code, to calm Pacelli down: the 'Duce' had taken up the matter and sent Hitler 'first a verbal warning and then a secret communication in which he besought him not to let himself be dragged into an anti-Semitic campaign'.[333] The cabinet had indeed adopted the 'Aryan paragraph'. But at this point of time there was still a widespread conviction that Hitler was the 'junior partner' of Mussolini, that he admired him, and allowed himself to be led by his 'mentor'. At any rate after taking power Hitler had praised Mussolini's movement in the highest terms: 'I can safely thank Fascism that I myself have succeeded to this point.'[334] Despite this early admiration for the Italian head of state, in the matter of anti-Semitism Hitler threw all Mussolini's well-meant advice to the winds, and told him through the Italian ambassador, Vittorio Cerruti, that he understood nothing of the question: 'I do not know whether in two or three centuries my name will still be highly honoured in Germany, such great things I hope to achieve for my people', he blustered to the diplomat, 'but of this I am absolutely certain, that in five or six centuries the name of Hitler will be everywhere venerated as the name of the man who rooted out the universal plague of Judaism once and for all'.[335] Yet Pacelli intended, upon a suggestion of Faulhaber,[336] to take advantage of a dinner given by the ambassador von Bergen to speak with Papen about the 'converted Jews'.[337] Because of a cold, however, he had to decline the meeting, and passed on the job to Pizzardo. 'Monsignor Pizzardo complied with his wish, and was well received by Herr von Papen.' He is in hopes (he continued to Faulhaber) 'that corresponding practical measures will follow very soon'.[338] But nothing happened. Even the newly accessible documents give no cause to revise the basic conclusion of Saul Friedländer that, on the Catholic side, 'Nothing was done.'[339] Among the Catholics of Jewish descent who in these days turned to the Pope with desperate letters was Edith Stein, at that time 42 years old, and a *dozentin* in philosophy.[340] Because of the 'Aryan paragraph' of 7 April 1933, she had had to give up her appointment at the Deutsche Institut für wissenschaftliche Pädagogik, and was on the point of entering the Carmelite order at Cologne.[341] In her letter to the Holy Father of 12 April 1933, she indicated briefly the measures of persecution inflicted by the regime, and then put into words what she and many other Catholics expected of the Holy See:

Not only the Jews, but also thousands of loyal Catholics in Germany – and, I may say, throughout the world – have been waiting and hoping for weeks for the Church of Christ to raise its voice to put a stop to this abuse of Christ's name. [...] All of us who are loyal Catholics and observe conditions in Germany with open eyes fear the worst for the reputation of the Church if this silence goes on much longer. We are also convinced that this silence is incapable of buying peace with the present German government in the long run.[342]

On 20 April 1933 Pacelli answered the Archabbot Raphael Walzer OSB of Beuron monastery, where Edith Stein was performing her Easter devotions:

May I thank your Grace especially for the safe arrival of the kind letter of the 12th inst. and the attachment which came with it. I leave to your discretion to let the sender know in a suitable way that her message has been duly put before His Holiness. With you I pray God to take his holy church into his especial protection in these difficult times, and grant all the children of the Church the grace of courage and splendour of mind which are the presuppositions of ultimate victory.[343]

Konrad Repgen represents the view that Stein's letter was taken very seriously in the Vatican, and is to be reckoned an important impulse for the corresponding counter-measures of the Holy Office.[344]

Three days before Stein's letter, the Vienna rabbi, Dr Arthur Zacharias Schwarz, turned to Pope Pius XI whom he knew well from his time as Prefect of the Bibliotheca Ambrosiana in Milan. In it he begged Ratti for a personal word.

High dignitaries of the Church have protested against the persecution of Jews in Germany. Your Holiness will scarcely be aware of the effect which a word from the highest personality of all would have upon practising Jews who like me reject radicalism entirely. If it were possible for Your Holiness to speak out that injustice even against Jews remains injustice, such a word would raise the courage and morale of millions of my Jewish brethren. It would especially calm the situation where, as here in Austria, anxieties have not disappeared despite the efforts of the government.[345]

Under the date of 26 April 1933 there is a note of a colleague from the Secretary of State's Office: 'Dr. Arthur Zacharias Schwarz (Rabbi) requests the Holy Father to intervene against the persecution of the Jews in Germany. It seems to me to require a very delicate answer. Would it not be better if the bishops of Germany took this step first? Perhaps then on the indirect route via the nunciature?'[346] No answer followed; nor was there an answer to the telegram of the New York rabbi William Margolis of 22 April 1933: 'In the name of everything which Christendom holds sacred! I implore you to raise your voice to condemn the Hitlerite persecutions without reservation. Your disapproval will have a far-reaching influence upon the German government [...] especially among Catholic office-holders [...] and bring about the reversal of the policy.'[347]

The German episcopate knew at the latest from 26 April 1933 of Hitler's attitude to the 'Jewish Question' from his own mouth.[348] Under the leadership of Bishop Berning some prominent clergy sought on this day and the one before to call on Papen, Göring[349] and Hitler, as well as the Prussian minister of public worship, Rust, in order to discuss the problems which were arising. During the meeting of Berning and Prelate Steinmann with Hitler, the dictator explained (according to Orsenigo's report) that

he was convinced that without Christianity neither private nor public life could be built up. [...] On the Jewish question he emphasized that he regarded the Jews as damaging; he recalled the attitude of the Catholic Church up to the 15th century and regretted that liberalism had not seen this danger; he concluded that he sees in the representatives of this race a danger for both state and church, and hence he thinks that when he acts thus he does the Church a very great service.[350]

Rosenberg's *Myth of the Twentieth Century* Hitler described as a private work; it had not been 'written as a party manifesto'. Craftily he exploited confessional opposition, describing himself as a Catholic 'who would never understand the Protestant Church and its structure'.[351] He further spoke against secular [*laizistische*] schools and in favour of confessional schools. 'When I look at the matter as a statesman, I need men of faith. Dark clouds are approaching from Poland. We need soldiers of faith because they are excellent soldiers [...] and so we will keep the confessional school [...] but of course it is important that there should also be *believing* teachers there'.[352] Orsenigo's report is in essential agreement with that of the official minutes,[353] which is not surprising since the nuncio himself did not take part in the conversation.[354] Hence his account must rest on the reports of Berning and Steinmann after the meeting.

On 28 April 1933, Orsenigo received a visit from a significant Jewish personality. The meeting had been arranged by Pacelli and notified to the nuncio in Berlin. Orsenigo reported the substance of the conversation to Pacelli thus:

> On the question of taking the opportunity to do something to ease the persecution of the Jews, I assured my conversation partner that everything possible had already been done, and that – in harmony with the principles of Christian and universal neighbourly love, of which the Catholic church was always the great teacher – nor would we forget in future to apply our feelings for peace. To a second question of our willingness to permit Jewish pupils who have today been expelled from state schools to be received in private Catholic schools, I replied that this was contrary to the educational principle which the confessional school still represented. The Church – I added – stands by this point of view and is quite certain that noone would see an antisemitic weakness in this refusal.[355]

That the first principle of love to the neighbour and the second – the refusal to accept Jewish children into Catholic private schools, in order to preserve their Christian identity – stood in a certain tension to each other seemed not to strike the Reich nuncio. Only in the third conversational complex, charitable work did Orsenigo see possibilities of cooperation:

> To the question whether Jewish hospitals, which are now in danger of being closed because state support will be withdrawn from them, could be taken under Catholic management, I replied that in this matter I believed two things opportune: 1. that the transfer, if made at all, should proceed with the prior agreement of the government in order to ensure the subsidy which today will be refused; 2. that I think it right that so far as the implementation of such a transfer is concerned, he should turn to the Order of Malta or the League of Charity [Caritasverband]. He went away satisfied, and I accept that, so far as he can, he will try to act in the direction indicated.[356]

Why Orsenigo's guest should have been 'satisfied' with the conversation does not emerge from the nuncio's report. The final sentence reflects rather a certain resignation in Orsenigo, but also a faint hope that foreign visitors might have an effect upon the German government. 'Here the social liquidation of the semitic element is proceeding in a big way; at the same time, there is certainly no lack of persuasion which is being addressed to the government asking for it to let gentleness prevail – even from the highest personalities. Today even the king of Sweden came to Berlin.'[357]

Along with personalities from abroad who intervened in Berlin, German politicians also received similar reproaches upon the racial policy of the Hitler government on the occasion of state visits. In April 1933 two Nazi grandees were also to visit the Eternal City: Hermann Göring and Joseph Goebbels. Göring, who regarded Italy as his 'special territory',[358] stayed from 10 to 20 April in Rome – at the same time as Papen who together with Kaas was preparing for the conclusion of the Reich concordat.[359] On 12 April Göring, together with Papen, was received by Pius XI and Pacelli, before he had spoken with Mussolini; on 13 April he met the Italian Air Minister, Italo Balbo, and on 18 April he had an audience with King Victor Emmanuel III. There are only suppositions as to the background and objects of Göring's visit. British diplomats at any rate accepted that the Italian government would use the opportunity to give Göring the good advice that his government should moderate its excesses against the Jews and other critics of the regime.[360]

Certainly Austria and, in this connection, still vague considerations about an *Anschluss* (union) formed one theme, which was particularly unfortunate because Dollfuss was also staying in the city. Mussolini informed the Austrian federal chancellor on the same evening about the conversation with Göring. As a result Dollfuss had a meeting the next day with Papen, but avoided a meeting with Göring.[361] From Mussolini Dollfuss received the assurance 'that an authoritarian regime in Austria, which set out to maintain an independent Austria' 'will always be able to reckon' on his friendship and help.[362] Again the fascist and the 'austro-fascist' systems – both accompanied by the goodwill of the Catholic Church – stood together against Nazism. Yet Mussolini could not stop the Hitler government – as an answer to the expulsion of Minister of the Reich Hans Frank, who in a radio address had openly threatened the occupation of Austria – damaging the tourist trade of the Alpine Republic by economic measures. From May 1933 every Reich German travelling into Austria had to pay 1000 marks – a sum beyond the capacity of almost every German.[363]

To prepare Pacelli for Goebbels, Orsenigo sent him a brief character study of the propaganda minister:

> Goebbels is one of the best educated and most active of the ministers. He is a Catholic by religion, and his past years, especially his

youth, were spent in a Catholic atmosphere. He completed his studies with the help of a scholarship from the Albertus-Magnus-Society, and in his early years his piety was considerable, and stamped its mark upon him. Before long he joined the National Socialist movement and took a higher position in it. Last year he married a Protestant without making any attempt to follow the canon law rules governing mixed marriages. On the contrary – to the great pain of Catholics, he celebrated the rite in Berlin before a Protestant pastor. Given such a previous life, I do not accept that, even on a visit to Rome, he plans any visits to the Vatican.[364]

Goebbels's visit to the Holy City took place not at the end of April, as Orsenigo at first supposed, but only at the end of May.[365] It was the first time that he and his wife, Magda, had been to Rome. The object of his journey was primarily 'to take up personal connections with the Italian government and party and to enhance links of friendship'.[366] Unlike Göring and Papen, Goebbels wished to avoid a visit to the Vatican. Hence the German Foreign Office looked for means of avoiding a visit which, according to protocol, was usual.[367] In fact the Propaganda Minister did not have to visit the head of the Church (whom he hated), but was not able entirely to escape the ecclesiastical aura of Rome. 'Journey through Rome. Eternal Rome. Roman forum. S. Peter's Church in the distance. Via Appia. Got quite hot with sight-seeing.'[368] During his audience with the king Goebbels spoke appropriately, showing emphatic enthusiasm for Mussolini and Fascism. 'Fascism is at work. There is no limit to its creative power. Mussolini is its motor. [...] Fascism is modern and bound to the people. There we shall learn.'[369] At breakfast with the German ambassador to the Vatican, von Bergen, he met 'with patriarchs and other noble beasts'. 'I spoke sharply against Cardinal Bertram. The soutane-wearers are very small and they grovel.'[370] Astonishingly, Mussolini appears not to have spoken to his German guest about the persecutions in Germany.

The violent measures against Jews and critics of the regime had forced the Vatican to accelerate the conclusion of the concordat. But even after the treaty was concluded the complaints from the Catholic Church about the persecution of Christians of Jewish heritage and other parties did not diminish. Understandably those concerned now expected that a Vatican, supposedly strengthened by the concordat, would intervene for them. On 23 July Cardinal Bertram had requested an intervention from the Holy See in favour of Catholic civil servants who had been dismissed by the Hitler government.[371] Thereupon Pacelli asked the Berlin nuncio, 'to apply himself in the [...] desired direction' and to send 'a kind communication upon the results of what he had done'.[372]

On 23 August 1933 Orsenigo answered:

> Unfortunately all the heads of government are on holiday; but since I was not willing to wait too long, I have spoken with those who represent them in the Foreign Ministry. I was heard very kindly, and also received many promises that they will interest themselves in the difficulty complained of, but at the same time they suggested to me that a word from me to the heads of the department would be much more effective. If as I hope I will soon have an opportunity to have a conversation with the heads, I will certainly raise this matter again. But I do not think I can get far, since I already know the justification they will make, namely the excessive numbers of Catholic civil servants, which – thanks to the long period of Centre government – have parked themselves in the offices of state, or the weak performance of some whose political mentality is too remote from that of the directives of the new government. Perhaps my position would be strengthened if the bishops sent me some documents which proved incontestably many irregular dismissals, or if they themselves put these before the government in the best way: I accept that some cases are exclusively the work of subordinates, that the government has no knowledge of these, that one must accept that the latter, when they do learn of them, would not approve of these dismissals. If Your Eminence thinks it opportune that I inform the Very Reverend Cardinal of Breslau, please be good enough to let me know at once so that I can do as much as possible before the Fulda bishops' conference.[373]

Orsenigo was resigned to the fact that Catholic civil servants were being systematically driven out of employment, but tended to blame subordinate Nazis for these actions, since he did not want to believe that the orders came from further up the hierarchy. He delegated German bishops and clerics to ask for clarification of such events (instead of doing so himself, probably out of fear that, if he did so, this might harm Vatican-German relations). Pacelli allowed him to pass on his (Orsenigo's) point of view to the German episcopate, but noted 'that the number of Catholic officers brought into the ministries of state by the Centre was always less than what would have been required by the so-called parity'.[374] Parity meant that, since the German population consisted of about two-thirds Protestant and about one-third Catholic inhabitants, a third of civil service employees were supposed to be

Catholic. The parity was a quota that should have ensured Catholics were not disadvantaged.

At the beginning of September 1933 the editor of the London journal, the *Jewish Chronicle*, asked whether it was true that the Pope had spoken publicly against the continuing anti-Semitic persecutions in Germany.[375] No answer from the Vatican is to be found in the documents.

In mid-November 1933 Maria Pfannenstiel of Speyer sent a petition to Rome which reached the Vatican via the nunciature at Munich. The 'Aryan paragraph' threatened the entire Catholic family. Because the father of the petitioner was of Jewish descent, her son lost his job as a qualified librarian at the university of Freiburg, and her daughter could not marry her bridegroom, since the latter would otherwise have to leave the State service. 'Now if a law should come out in Germany forbidding marriages between Aryans and non-Aryans, whom then should our Catholic children marry?'[376] In the first and last paragraphs Maria Pfannenstiel put into words her understanding of the Catholic Church and her request based on it. She turned 'with trust' to her church, 'that if all the world leaves me in the lurch, our holy mother, the Catholic Church, will have mercy upon us. [...] Would it not be possible that from the side of the Church a relaxation in this frightful severity may soon be brought about.'[377]

Pizzardo instructed the Munich nuncio Vassallo di Torregrossa 'to inquire into the case, and if there is no impediment, will you ask for intervention in the case'.[378] Vassallo confirmed, in a letter to Pizzardo of 7 February 1934, all the details of Maria Pfannenstiel, but thought that a marriage dispensation 'in the present acuteness of the Aryan question [...] was unthinkable'.[379] He told the Undersecretary of State that he had sent a letter of recommendation for the son to Archbishop Gröber of Freiburg. 'Yet I doubt if it will be of any help.'[380] From the letter of Pizardo to Vassallo of 18 February 1934, it emerges that the interventions 'have regrettably not brought the desired result'.[381] He requested the Munich nuncio to let Maria Pfannenstiel know through Bishop Sebastian of Speyer 'what the Holy See has done'[382] and make her aware of the negative answer. Cases of this kind cut to the marrow of the Church, for a Jew converted to Catholicism was no different in the Catholic view from other believers. Hence Pacelli handed in to the German embassy to the Holy See in September 1933 a memorandum of the German bishops in which a protest was lodged against the persecution of Catholics of Jewish descent.[383]

A contemporary key scene for the engagement of, on the one side, Jews converted to the 'true faith' and, on the other, for the clear distance from the 'people of Israel' has been described by the Münster Church historian Hubert Wolf.[384] At the beginning of 1928, that is, five years before Hitler's seizure of power, the prayer brotherhood, Amici Israel, a Catholic priests' association for the promotion of mission among the Jews which was active throughout the world proposed to the Vatican Congregation of Rites to alter the Great Intercession of the Good Friday liturgy. In this intercession it says, 'Let us pray for the faithless Jews', and in another passage, 'Almighty, eternal God, who dost not exclude even the faithless Jews from your mercy, hear our plea which we put before you because of the blinding of that people: in order that they may acknowledge the light of thy truth which is Christ, and be snatched from their darkness.'[385] The motive of the President of Amici Israel, Abbot Benedikt Gariador OSB, for the elimination of the concept 'faithless' and an alteration of other phrases which sounded anti-Jewish was to give more space to the actual concern for salvation of the original Christian intercession and to ease transition to the Catholic Church for Jews disposed to conversion. Abbot Ildefons Schuster OSB requested a report from the Congregation of Rites and supported the petition of the Amici Israel.

Yet in the Holy Office, to which the Congregation of Rites had directed their recommendation, nothing positive could be made of the reform proposal. The papal theologian Marco Sales OP rather reinforced the view that the Jews themselves had taken responsibility for the crucifixion of Christ, referring to Matthew 27: 25 ('May his blood be upon us and our children'). At the same time the Holy Office condemned the pamphlet *Pax super Israel* published by Amici Israel (1927/28); the consultants saw in the association of priests the spread of dangerous tendencies, advocated the abolition of the association, and pressed for a warning to Schuster who had given his opinion.

Cardinal Rafael Merry del Val, under Pius X a leading anti-modernist, and under Benedict XV put out of harm's way, regained greater influence under the conservative Pius XI as the leading cardinal of the Holy Office. In the College of Cardinals he rejected the reform proposal as 'entirely unacceptable, indeed nonsensical' and emphasized the meaning in the liturgical prayer – namely, expressing 'the abhorrence of the rebellion and betrayal of the Chosen People' – and stressed at the same time that these turns of phrase applied self-evidently not to individual Jews willing to undergo conversion but to the Jewish people as such, which had continuously behaved 'faithlessly' towards Christendom. At the same time he also condemned the Zionist movement, which wished to restore the kingdom of Israel in opposition to Christ and his Church. The cardinals followed the votes of Marco Sales and Merry del Val. When Pius XI concerned himself with the case at the beginning of March 1928, he not only confirmed the resolution of the cardinals but also sharpened it further. The suggestion of Amici Israel should be expressly rebuffed and every alteration of liturgical practice expressly rejected. Ratti also shared the conviction of the Amici-critics that the association had committed serious mistakes, and sanctioned its abolition. In the corresponding decree, which appeared on 25 March 1928,[386] tribute was paid to the ideals of the brotherhood of prayer, but their deviation from the Holy Liturgy was condemned. At the same time every form of anti-Semitism was condemned as hate against the formerly elect people of God and – just like Orsenigo five years later – it was once again said that Israel was expressly included in the general Church commandment of love. Gariador, the Amici secretary, Anton van Asseldonk and Schuster had to distance themselves from their erroneous views in letters of submission. In the following year Schuster at any rate was nominated to be Archbishop of Milan, personally consecrated by his predecessor, currently Pope Pius XI, and raised to the cardinalate.

Whether Pius XI, as Hubert Wolf thought, wanted the decree on Amici Israel to be very carefully worded, because he was afraid of negative reactions among the public, appears rather questionable in view of the anti-Judaism widespread in Europe. Saul Friedländer has pointed to a number of European centres of hostility to Jews.[387] The list of places named by him could be readily extended.[388] In Europe at least Pius XI had got to know the anti-Semitic climate in Warsaw, and had no reason to fear powerful philo-Semitic protests.[389] The real difficulty for the Catholic clergy subsisted in distinguishing the religiously motivated anti-Judaism they intended from a racially based anti-Semitism. As pastors of souls they had of course to know that, in the broad mass of the population, such a power to differentiate was hardly to be reckoned on.

When the Polish Primate Augustyn Cardinal Hlond referred, on the one hand, to a 'Jewish problem' and stigmatized the Jews as 'the vanguard of godlessness, of the Bolshevik movement, and of subversive action',[390] he could, on the other hand, scarcely expect the faithful to follow him when he summoned them not to hate the Jews, not to strike or slander them. His recommendation to make Jews 'harmless' by social exclusion could serve as a classic example for the rise of prejudice and hostile images: 'It is necessary to find protection from the harmful moral influence of the Jews, to keep away from their anti-Christian culture, and in particular to boycott the Jewish press and demoralising Jewish publications.'[391]

Unlike Nazi anti-Semitism there was a means of being accepted into the Christian cultural circle: conversion. In this respect too, the formula of Pius XI protected Hlond with crystal clarity: 'When God's grace enlightens the Jew, and when he honestly joins the ranks of his and our Messiah, then we will gladly welcome him into the Christian host.'[392] It was just this principle that the Hitler regime undermined – first in Germany, then in the Europe it dominated.[393] At any rate it is fair to ask whether a clear separation of traditional religious anti-Judaism and modern, racially based and politically motivated anti-Semitism could be sustained in the Catholic Church itself. The Catholic societies of Europe could scarcely escape completely from the modernizing processes even in this field. In the interests of an ideology directed against modernity, modern racial patterns of argument – for example, in connection with the stereotype of the moral 'destroyer'-motif – seep into the inherited apologetic polemic.[394]

There were of course other voices. Along with the bishops, the nuncio and those personally concerned, Catholic laity and theologians also wrote to the Vatican begging for a simple message against Hitlerite racism, or supplying the diplomatic service of the Curia with information. One of this circle of personalities was the Jesuit Friedrich Muckermann, now a refugee in the Netherlands; he was one of the sharpest critics of National Socialism.[395] In his newspaper in exile, *Der deutsche Weg*, he attacked the Nazis, and in mid-November 1934 he ventured incognito into the Bavarian nunciature to hand in his report.[396] In it he defined blood and race as the pillars of the new religion, was critical of the hesitant attitude of the German episcopate, and demanded that the Church be as resolute against Nazism as against Bolshevism. But Muckermann was too radical for the papal diplomats, who could not expect him to support their analyses and decisions on his insights or ask him for an official opinion.[397] The German embassy to the Holy See described Muckermann in mid-June 1937 as one of the 'most dangerous and active opponents of National Socialism'.[398]

From 1935 the Roman Catholic Church concerned itself in various ways by facilitating emigration from Germany for Catholic Christians of Jewish descent.[399] The Holy See had precise information about these activities, as the documents show.[400] The Curia was apparently especially interested in the picture of the activity of the American Christian Committee for German Refugees (Catholic group). On their behalf, the Revd Hans Ansgar Reinhold,[401] the former General Secretary of the

German Catholic Seamen's Mission in Hamburg and himself a refugee, brought a memorandum to the Holy See at the beginning of June 1936. In it proposals were sketched out 'how such Catholics who because of their faith, their former political activity, or their belonging to the Jewish race (non-Aryan) must leave Germany, could be helped from the Catholic side'.[402] Helene E. Froelicher, envoy of the American Christian Committee for German Refugees, undertook a journey of enquiry through Germany, which led her among other things to the Archbishops Gröber and Faulhaber. 'Dr Gröber intended [...] in order to give the work a powerful international shape, to choose a head office in Rome. He proposed Bishop Hudal in Rome for this,[403] which was subseqently supported[404] also by Cardinal Fauhaber'.[405] Through the Swiss chargé d'affaires at the Vatican, Aldo Laghi, the Holy See also received reports on the refugee conference at Evian in the summer of 1938.[406] Laghi emphasized in his report the criticism from the Jewish side of the results of the conference. They would have 'liked to see [...] the conference concern itself with them more clearly [...] and complained that the European nations had shown themselves disinclined to receive them in their territories'.[407] Laghi reported very positively on Myron C. Taylor, the chairman of the Inter-Governmental Committee on Political Refugees. The 66-year old Protestant was a close friend of President Roosevelt, who in the following year was to call him to be his personal representative at the Vatican.[408]

Pacelli showed himself very interested in the question of emigration. The Parisian lawyer Jacques N. Politis thanked him at the beginning of August 1938 for the kindly reception he afforded him in March, 'when I came to put before him the project of our Jewish association',[409] and sent him some articles on the Conference in Evian. In the framework of the refugee conference Brazil had promised 3000 visas for the persecuted, but afterwards kept raising new hurdles. Max Joseph Grösser of the Special Aid of the St Raphael Association[410] then wrote to Faulhaber that both countries – that is, Brazil and Argentina – wished 'to avoid a Mosaic flooding of their countries'.[411] Yet the Archbishop of Munich and Freising did not let go.[412] He was anxious that Pacelli should use every diplomatic and inner-Church lever to move the Brazilian President Getulio Vargas to redeem his promise. This procedure illustrates that the alleged power of the Vatican was a mere myth. For neither Pacelli's letters to Vargas nor his letter to all the bishops on earth, the interventions of his nuncios or those of the Brazilian episcopate led to a positive result. The Holy See had to recognize the narrow limits of its influence and manage within them in future.

3.8 The end of the Munich nunciature

With the law on the reconstruction of the Reich of 30 January 1934, the diplomatic representative bodies and accrediting of foreign ambassadors to the respective Land governments lapsed, because the latter's rights of sovereignty were transferred to the Reich.[413] This meant the end of the Munich nunciature, for the continuance of which Pacelli had applied such persistent pressure in the mid-1920s. At that time he had even spoken out for leaving the Munich nunciature in existence even should the Bavarian embassy to the Holy See be dissolved under pressure from the Reich government.

Cardinal Secretary of State Gasparri had presented as Pacelli's successor in Munich in mid-November 1920 Alberto Vassallo di Torregrossa, who had already worked in Munich from 1898 to 1902 and from 1903 to 1905 as Auditor or business manager, and since 1915 had been active as nuncio in Buenos Aires. In mid-December 1920 the Bavarian government declared its agreement to the candidate – with, of course, the reservation that the change should follow only after the conclusion of the concordat negotiations. Pacelli and others would rather have seen Pizzardo as nuncio, and sought to get their way both before and after the nomination of Vassallo. Yet once the decision in favour of Vassallo had been made, it stuck; and in 1925 as planned after the conclusion of the Bavarian concordat, and the final transfer of Pacelli to Berlin, he took over the nunciature at Munich. Very soon it seemed to prove that Vassallo's critics, who held that he was lifeless and without backbone, were right.[414] The Munich nunciature sank into increasing insignificance, and the Curia complained that the new nuncio 'does not bother about anything'.[415] Yet it was not this cheerless development but Nazi legislation that put an end to the nunciature. To Pacelli's consternation the new legal situation also meant *finis* for the Bavarian embassy to the Holy See – a report which the Cardinal Secretary of State received in December 1933 through the Bavarian ambassador Ritter zu Groenesteyn. The ambassador also foresaw that the withdrawal of the two diplomatic representations 'would make it much harder to overcome differences of opinion between State and Church over the execution and exposition of the provisions of the concordat'.[416]

At the level of the Reich there was no understanding for considerations of this kind, and it was proposed that the extreme limit for the abolition of the Bavarian embassy should be 30 April 1934. Ritter zu Groenesteyn recommended that the embassy be not recalled till the canonization proceedings of the Bavarian capuchin, Konrad von Parzheim, were complete – a proposal which Foreign Minister von Neurath accepted, and appointed 31 May as the new terminal date for the abolition of the diplomatic representation. Pacelli's idea of leaving at least an Apostolic Delegate without diplomatic status in Munich after the dissolution of the Munich nunciature encountered consternation in Berlin. For the recent establishment of Apostolic Delegations had otherwise only taken place in countries with which the Holy See maintained no diplomatic representation.

And the argument that the Bavarian embassy in Rome and the papal nunciature in Munich should be allowed to subsist as long as the Bavarian concordat was valid cut no ice. Neurath replied to a similar attempt by Orsenigo that the insistence by the Holy See upon such a regulation could only occasion the Reich government 'to cancel the Bavarian concordat at once'.[417] At the end of May 1934 the embassy and the nunciature were abolished; on 20 June 1934 Pope Pius XI received the Bavarian ambassador in a farewell audience; five days later Ritter zu Groenesteyn left Rome. The papal nuncio by contrast remained as a private person in Munich, without his status – for example, the question of the continued validity of extraterritorial rights – becoming quite clear. In September 1936 Vassallo was sucked into the currency trials staged by the Nazi State against Catholic clergy, regular and secular.[418] When the Reich Office for Procuring Currency ordered a search in the former nunciature in the Kaulbachstrasse, Vassallo opposed a house search and reported to a colleague in the Bavarian Ministry of State. They informed the Foreign Office that Vassallo no longer had extraterritorial rights, but that the documents of the former Munich nunciature now belonged to the Reich nunciature in Berlin. Against the advice of the Foreign Office, the Reich Ministry of Justice carried through a house search which was executed by the Sonderstaatsanwaltschaft [Special state attorney's office] in Berlin with the cooperation of the Gestapo. According to the information of the judicial authorities Vassallo, during his time as an active nuncio, was said to have illegally transferred 44,000 Reichmarks to Rome, and there was the suspicion of further currency offences down to the present time. And in fact Italian lire were found in the house, which confirmed the suspicion of currency offences. In addition a ciphering machine for coding and decoding was confiscated as well as some documents in Italian. A nun who worked in the house and who had tried to burn documents in an open fire was arrested.

On 5 October 1936 Orsenigo protested about this incident to Legationsrat Karl Dumont[419] in the Foreign Office and classified the proceedings of the German authorities as a serious incident at the diplomatic level. At the same time Pizzardo complained to the German ambassador von Bergen about the 'brusque style of the proceeding'.[420] On the German side there was union in the euphemism that it was a question of 'an investigation into currency matters'.[421] Pius XI showed himself extremely put out by the proceedings of the criminal prosecution authorities, and considered breaking off diplomatic relations with the German Reich. In a feverish diplomatic action, in which Orsenigo and the head of the political division in the Foreign Office, ambassador Ernst Baron von Weizsäcker,[422] played the leading parts, Vassallo had finally to leave for Rome on 23 October 1936. The press was not informed of the proceedings.

According to the information of the criminal prosecution authorities Vassallo during his time as former nuncio was supposed to have got another 100,000 Reichmarks out of the country. Moreover he had to reckon with a charge of treason because among the confiscated nunciature documents were also five volumes of documents from the holdings of the Foreign Office and the former Bavarian Foreign Ministry. If Vassallo wished to avoid the danger of imprisonment, he could not return to Germany. Ambassador von Bergen had the charges of the customs authorities served to the former Munich nuncio; Vassallo answered them in a detailed memorandum.[423] This the ambassador did not transmit to the Berlin government. On 5 November 1936 Orsenigo informed the German Foreign Office that the archive of the Munich nunciature had been moved to Berlin.

3.9 The struggle over the resolutions to carry out Article 31 of the Reich Concordat relating to associations

As was soon to become clear the Curia had delayed, before signing the concordat, to reach an agreement with the State over a list of organizations approved by the concordat. Instead of immediately presenting a list, the bishops acceded to a demand of Minstererialdirektor Buttmann to work out 'expository principles' to article 31 of the Reich concordat. On the Church side the Bishop of Osnabrück, Wilhelm Berning, was commissioned to manage the conversation. During an audience with the Reich Chancellor on 26 April 1933 he had presented the demands of the episcopate in Church policy and listened to Hitler's tirades against the Jews as enemies of State and Church without contradiction.[424] Hitler's account, according to which Catholic Christianity was to form an important basis for the new state, made an impression on the bishop; the Chancellor expressly distanced himself from Protestantism.[425] He revised his originally hostile attitude towards the NSDAP and, trusting in Hitler's words, wished to attempt bridge-building between the Nazi regime and the Church.

In mid-July 1933 Berning was nominated by the Prussian Prime Minister Göring to the Prussian State Council – an honorary office without political influence, but signalling a certain closeness between State and Church and thought of by Göring as a way into the German episcopate.[426] Both Bertram and Orsenigo agreed to the acceptance of the office. On the occasion of an audience with Pius XI on 3 September 1933 Berning moreover asked the Pope whether he should continue in the honorary office, and did not receive a negative answer.[427] It is entirely reasonable to accept that on the side of the Church there were hopes of deriving advantage from this direct wire to the centres of political authority. During the year 1933 Berning several times required pledges of loyalty to the State and support of the new order – among them, certainly, the usual formulations, but still more than other bishops were prepared to say. Despite disillusioning experiences, all these utterances were borne by the faith that this new state would favour the Christian Church and struggle with it against unbelief and immorality. Such motives might have determined Berning when on the occasion of the ratification of the Reich concordat he held a service of thanksgiving. At the Bremen Katholikentag (Catholic Church conference) on 24 September 1933 the bishop of Osnabrück even drew parallels between the Nazi and the Church 'leadership principle': 'In our new German Reich we have the *Führerprinzip* [leadership principle]. There is one leader and the whole people must and will perform allegiance. In our holy Catholic Church we have already received the leadership principle from the founder of our Church Jesus Christ.'[428]

In his euphoria Berning thought to see Hitler in the service of a corporative order of Catholic provenance. 'Leaders here upon earth have no other mission than to lead you and your souls to the supreme bishop and shepherd of your souls, Jesus Christ.'[429] He had the same view when he pressed his hearers among the faithful to join with him in the cheer: 'Our Holy Father, Pope Pius XI, the leader of our Church, and the leaders of our government, Reich President von Hindenburg and Reich Chancellor Hitler, three cheers.' Then the entire company stood and 'with raised right arm'[430] sang the papal hymn and the national anthem.

Repeatedly Berning went back to the leadership idea in Church and State; at the beginning of August 1933 he recommended his clergy 'in official business with the authorities to use the Hitler salute';[431] he legitimated the struggle of the new state against 'the Godlessness of Bolshevism' and public immorality. Whoever contended against the Church and her doctrine did not deserve the protection of the State. By contrast the NSDAP must bring their flags and insignia into the churches of his diocese and set them up in the nave. In public he maintained this attitude up to the end of January 1934.

Impressed by the grave derelictions to the promises given by Hitler, Berning of course gave vent to ever more frequent criticism out of the public eye, and thus marked the 'limits of accommodation'[432] to the Nazi regime. Before the background of the efforts of the regime to force everything Catholic out of German society, the bishop spoke of a 'second secularisation'.[433] This bishop of all bishops, who perhaps more than any other was ready for cooperation with the Nazi state, had, in connection with the putting into effect of agreements to Article 31 of the Reich concordat, to accept one disappointment after another and many a severe humiliation.[434] Step by step he had to take leave of the illusion of a relationship of State and Church acceptable to the Catholic Church. The increasing unwillingness of the clergy to cooperate with the Nazi regime is not the only thing which can be followed in the example of this bishop; it also shows the necessity of taking seriously the small steps in the developing relationship of State and Church. From year to year, often from month to month, or even week to week, the relationship of State and Church was altering.

At the end of August 1933 the bishops' conference issued its list of associations, and encountered massive criticism at the level of the Länder. And the negotiations between Buttmann and Pacelli begun in autumn 1934 did not turn out successfully. All Catholic associations should either be tightly 'clericalized' or, so far as they also served cultural, charitable or sporting ends, 'integrated' into the corresponding formations of the State party. A deep break was brought about by the 'Röhm putsch' at the end of June 1934, in which a series of Catholic critics of the regime, for example, the president of Catholic Action in Berlin, Erich Klausener, were murdered.[435]

As the negotiations dragged on, there were errors in coordination between the Curia and the German episcopate and inconsistencies conditioned by them; these were recognized by the Nazi side and exploited. In mid-August 1934 the bishop of Osnabrück became conspicuous because the *Hannoversche Kurier* printed a declaration by Berning on the popular vote on the union of the offices of Reich Chancellor and Reich President. On this he was said to have held it to be the 'self-evident duty of every German' to give a joyful 'Yes' to the Führer's question. In a letter to his episcopal colleagues and to the Berlin nuncio,

Berning sought to make clear that he had been betrayed by the press and had made no such declaration directly. The letter ends with lively regrets for the disquiet in Catholic circles which the publication had occasioned and for the distress of conscience it had caused for many Catholics.[436]

Even detailed conversations between Berning and Orsenigo at the end of August/beginning of September could not completely re-establish in the Vatican their old relations of trust with Berning, their German business manager.

In comparison with the popular vote of 12 November 1933, the acclamation of 19 August 1934 showed very clearly that the number of 'Yes' votes had fallen from 89.9 per cent to 84.3 per cent[437] – a circumstance which the nuncios both of Berlin and Munich immediately reported to Rome.[438] Orsenigo informed Pacelli that the proportion of 'No' votes in Catholic constituencies was no higher than in the others, and thus strengthened the Vatican in its fear that the power of resistance even in the Catholic population had ebbed.

Orsenigo took no part in the funeral of Hindenburg on 7 August 1934, because three days previously the following telegram had reached him from Rome:

> The Holy Father thinks that you may, if you wish, take part in the civil ceremonies in the presence of the Diplomatic Corps – up to the moment in which the rite or prayer by the Reich bishop or some other pastor begins. You must leave from the moment when mixed civil or religious ceremonies are appointed. If it should be difficult to absent yourself at that moment, prefer not to go, and limit yourself to attending the memorial service in the Reichstag.[439]

Orsenigo repeatedly drew hope from Hitler's vague hints and promises. Thus he reported to Pacelli a reception of the Diplomatic Corps on 12 September 1934 with the Reich Chancellor. Hitler indicated 'his lively wish' 'to attain full peace with the two confessions'.[440] Yet at the same time the dictator went on persecuting the Church.

A new escalation in the relations of Church and State began with the announcement of the Reich Minister of the Interior, Wilhelm Frick, on 7 July 1935, that he wished to 'deconfessionalize' public life.[441] On the basis of similar decrees, the Catholic youth associations were to be strictly limited to the area of worship, and furthermore the young people should be required to join the Hitler Youth. Then the Reich Church minister Hanns Kerrl at the beginning of September 1935 wished to examine Catholic associations via registers at the diocesan level, but the bishops agreed to put a single list before the minister, to hinder their being played off one against another.

The negotiations dragged on without result, the Nazi State being unashamed repeatedly to dupe both episcopate and Vatican. Memoranda lay unanswered for months, telephone calls by Berning to the Reich Church ministry were rudely blocked.[442] The printing of translated articles from the *Osservatore Romano* in the German diocesan magazines was forbidden.[443] In the period between the ratification of the Reich concordat (September 1933) and the enactment of the encyclical *Mit brennender Sorge* (March 1937) the Holy See directed over seventy notes and memoranda to the government of the German Reich.[444] About 12,000 secular and regular priests from all German dioceses were affected by measures of persecution, which began after Hitler's seizure of power and constantly increased in scale.[445]

At the same time, Orsenigo repeatedly reported to Rome how Hitler was adored by the German people. In connection with the celebrations on the occasion of the Führer's forty-seventh birthday, for example, his report says: 'The diplomats are united in recognizing that the German people – despite differences in judgement and in judgements in respect of party – are completely united in attachment to the Führer, and esteem him highly'.[446]

In May 1936, morality trials against Catholic regulars and secular priests began, and the controversies entered a new stage.[447] On the basis of the negotiating situation which from now on was hopeless, the resolution gradually ripened in the Holy See in the second half of the decade to draw attention to the desperate situation of the Roman Catholic Church in Germany with the aid of an encyclical. But even this process of decision was interrupted by an episode which occasioned new speculation about cooperation of State and Church: the three-hour conversation between Hitler and Faulhaber on the Obersalzberg on 4 November 1936.[448] For a few weeks it looked as if the anti-communism common to the two parties might become the enzyme for an alliance.[449] After this conversation Faulhaber named as the basis for an understanding the concept devised by Alois Hudal, the suffragan bishop who came from southern Styria, now rector of Santa Maria dell'Anima in Rome.[450] The occasion for this was offered by Hudal's book which appeared in October 1936, *Die Grundlagen des Nationalsozialismus* [*The Bases of National Socialism*]. Hudal had sent Faulhaber a copy,[451] and dedicated the first copy to Hitler.[452] One section on 'The Race Problem' Hudal had previously published as a pamphlet.[453] Pius XI, however, was not impressed by the *Bases*, and even wanted the pamphlet of the consultant of the Holy Office on the Index,[454] which would have created an immense furore. Instead of this Pacelli had a piece published in the *Osservatore Romano* of 13 November 1936, discreetly distancing the Curia.[455] Three days later he informed Faulhaber that the Holy See 'throughout had no connection, with certain publications of Hudal'.[456] Although the Innsbruck cardinal Theodor Innitzer did not take this view of the matter and finally gave the book the Church imprimatur, this proved to be no turning point.

3.10 The Catholicizing of National Socialism? Alois Hudal's attempt at bridge-building

Along with Hitler's *Mein Kampf*, Alfred Rosenberg's *Mythus des 20. Jahrhunderts: Eine Wertung der seelisch-geistigen Gestaltungskämpfe unserer Zeit* [*The Myth of the 20th Century: An Assessment of the Spiritual and Intellectual Formative Struggles of Our Day*] belonged to the ideological foundation literature of Nazism.[457] This book, first published in 1930, and difficult to understand, attracted no attention. Only after Hitler had handed over to the old party comrades, who were always treated in a somewhat step-motherly fashion, on 24 January 1934 the duty of 'Watching over the general intellectual and philosophical training and education of the NSDAP' was there a rapid increase of interest in the programmatic work of philosophical National Socialism. In his book, Rosenberg expressed his conviction that Nordic blood represented that mystery which constituted the essence of mankind and replaced and overcame the 'old' sacraments.

On 7 February 1934, immediately after his official promotion to be the party's ideological boss, the Holy Office put Rosenberg's *Myth* and Ernst Bergmann's *Deutsche Nationalkirche* on the *Index librorum prohibitorum*.[458] By this means practising Catholics were forbidden to acquire, possess or read unambiguously anti-Christian books. By this decision the Church plunged the faithful into severe conflicts of conscience, for in any aspect of German education or examinations Rosenberg's sorry effort was obligatory reading.[459]

Alois Hudal, since 1923 Rector of the German national foundation Santa Maria dell'Anima and from 1930 onwards Konsultor to the Holy Office, maintained in his posthumously published *Römische Tagebücher* (1976) that he had also contributed an opinion on the *Myth*.[460] And even if in the Vatican Index files only one of Hudal's opinons is to be found, that on Bergmann's book,[461] his version appears not improbable, the more so as his papers include the draft of an opinion on Rosenberg's *Myth*.[462] In his opinion, Hudal criticized Bergmann's German Church movement, which emphasized ideas of biological and racial superiority and embraced all religious errors since Nietzsche, and also mentioned Rosenberg. In the result the Konsultors of the Congregation at their meeting on 29 January 1934 came out in favour of inquiring into other books of the National Socialist movement, and especially Rosenberg's *Myth*.

On 7 February 1934, the day of the condemnation of the *Myth*, there appeared in the *Osservatore Romano* a detailed article with the title: 'Book for German youth with hateful falsities'.[463] The book was described as 'fanatical' and 'violent', 'anticultural, anti-Christian [...] and misanthropic'.[464] But the official Vatican paper also underlined that, in the case of the *Myth*, it was a question of a private work of Rosenberg. Although the Curia could not ignore the official promotion of the book by the Nazi State, they thus took up the continually repeated version of Hitler and his henchmen. In this way Rome could not be reproached with attacking the party of state and its ideology. Moreover this strategy permitted a distinction between moderate and radical forces in the Nazi movement. At any rate this view of things made it impossible to examine even Hitler's *Mein Kampf* and if need be to put it on the Index.[465]

Putting the *Myth* on the Index had in any case refuelled the 'Church struggle'. The party and government machine set in motion a widespread campaign of defamation against Catholicism; obstacles were placed in the way of replies to the *Myth* such as the *Studies on the Myth of the 20th Century*.[466] The faithful were ground between the upper millstone of social disadvantage and exclusion and the lower millstone of religious and sacramental penalties.

Under pressure from Hudal and the advice of the other Konsultors, Pius XI wanted to have a 'syllabus' of Nazi heresies worked out. In his *Römische Tagebücher* (concluded in 1962) the Rector of Santa Maria dell'Anima recalls:

I used [...the] audience in October 1934 [...] in order to present to the Pope the following petition, in which I proposed the solemn condemnation in the form of an encyclical or a new Syllabus of the three following errors of the day: [...] 1. The totalitarian concept of the state which oppresses the personal value of the individual man, 2. the radical concept of race which dissolves the unity of humankind, 3. radical nationalism with the surrender of natural law, in consequence of the exclusive validity of the positive law decreed by nation and state.[467]

Hudal was no longer satisfied with preachers of the second rank. He wanted to bring the 'arch-fathers of the great modern ideologies, Lenin, Stalin, Mussolini and above all Hitler [...] before the tribunal of the Roman Inquisition'.[468] Pope Pius XI was said to be 'very impressed' by his suggestions and was ready 'to have these questions examined by the highest Congregation'.[469] 'Perhaps the German and the Austrian people would have been spared a great deal [continued Hudal] if in 1934 at the right time excommunication had been hurled against these errors, which were to bring so much misery upon Europe'.[470]

On 7 October 1934, Hudal wrote to the Cardinal Secretary of the Holy Office, Donato Sbarretti, requesting the teaching office of the Church to concern itself with the dangers of modern racial doctrine in Germany. The young people in particular were in extreme danger from the ideology of blood and race represented by the Nazis. The foundations of the Christian religion were destroyed through this new 'Aryan-nordic' religion which was more than a political party.[471] The 'national mysticism' of National Socialism seemed to Hudal so heretical that he thought it was not enough to put the corresponding books on the Index. Rather he pressed for an encyclopaedia or a Syllabus of Errors. On 25 October 1934 the cardinals of the Holy Office under the presidency of Pius XI granted his request. After consultations with the Jesuit General Ledóchowski the Pope commissioned two professors at the Papal Gregorian University, Franz Hürth SJ and Johannes Baptista Rabeneck SJ, to prepare the appropriate opinions.[472]

Was Hudal really a key figure – that wise priest who warned at the right time but whose logical analyses and policy recommendations had tragically to fall foul of contradictory relations in the Vatican? Peter Godman emphasizes powerfully in his account of Hudal the psychological side in the behaviour of the shoemaker's son from Graz, and describes him as an 'outsider on the make',[473] who wished to have a prominent role to play at almost any price. '[A]ll of his activities were aimed at securing influence' for himself.[474] Hudal's double game towards Nazism – the public emphasis on his political nearness to the movement while at the same time fighting the National Socialist ideology in the secret chambers of the Vatican – Godman apparently finds so repulsive that he speaks indeed of 'denunciation'.[475] The objection to this is that Hudal in many of his writings never disguised his rejection of the philosophical side of National Socialism. Dominik Burkard takes him indeed for 'the decisive force [...] which repeatedly pressed the Curia to distance itself clearly from (philosophical) National Socialism'.[476] And the fact that Hudal in October 1943 played a decisive role in the termination of the deportation of Jews from Rome[477] is not sufficiently taken into account in the one-sided picture which Godman draws of the Rector of the Anima.[478] In contrast, Philippe Chenaux emphasizes that Hudal's basic position, that the Vatican must arrive at a modus vivendi with the German government, was shared by wide circles in the Curia – not least by Pacelli and his German adviser Kaas.[479]

Already at the end of 1927 Hudal had sent a memorandum to the Pope in which he pointed to the negative consequences of the German 'cultural crisis' among budding priests and recommended as a tried and tested antidote an introductory course in the doctrines of the faith. This of course could best take place in the Anima in Rome.[480]

In 1935 Hudal emerged with two works at the same time: *Deutsches Volk und Christliches Abendland*[481] [*The German Nation and the Christian West*] and *Der Vatikan und die modernen Staaten*[482] [*The Vatican and the Modern States*]. In the first book he hoped to save the threatened unity of the West, pleading – after the Italian model – for a harmonious cooperation between the Führer and the Pope. By this means Hitler, supported by the Papacy, was to cut out the extremists in his own camp. What Germany lacked was the spiritual leadership of Christ; he and none other must be the lord of the whole life of culture. Should Hitler calm down and acknowledge the spiritual leadership of the Church, a powerful alliance could develop. Rome, so he argued in his second tract, was ready to cooperate with the true, more conservatively minded wing of the dictator, and on this basis to establish 'modern conditions'. The common enemy, he repeatedly emphasized, was Bolshevism; in Hudal's view Protestantism had no future. With his anti-Bolshevism he linked an anti-Judaism with clear racial accents; he spoke of the

> religious and moral dregs of Judaism [...] which from its centre in Moscow keeps the Christian peoples of Europe in constant unrest, in order to prepare the way for the world domination of a race which has given mankind valuable cultural goods and outstanding personalities, but which, as soon as it loses its religious roots, has to destroy every other cultural milieu.[483]

Theses of this kind betray how far Hudal had gone towards the Nazis in order to be able to cement his alliance.

Among Hudal's supporters in Rome was the arch-conservative ultramontanist Rafael Merry Del Val, who had also called him in 1930 to be a Konsultor of the Holy Office. After his death Pacelli became protector of the Anima.[484] Franz von Papen,[485] since 1934 special ambassador in Vienna, saw to it that Hudal's book, *The Bases of National Socialism*, reached the hands of Hitler, and, although a prohibition of the importing of Austrian literature was in force, enabled 2000 copies of the work to be sold in Germany.[486] Papen sheltered Hudal, because, as he wrote to Hitler immediately after the agreement of the Reich with Austria on 11 July 1936,[487] it was important for future development that 'this man be kept fighting fit for us'.[488] In almost identical terms the ambassador von Bergen also recommended that Hudal's abilities 'must be put to use at the given time', and reported on the current rumours in Rome, according to which the bishop maintained good relations with Göring, General von Fritsch and Papen, while Goebbels and Faulhaber took up a rather reserved attitude towards him.[489] Although his views were rejected by Pius XI, Hudal criticized three heresies of Nazi philosophy in his book,[490] *The Bases of National Socialism*: the idolization of blood and race, which leads to a 'pseudo-religious, anthropological materialism' and creates anti-Jewish and anti-Christian exaggerated self-esteem; the totalitarianism of the Nazi world-outlook, which stylizes the State to be a church and the Führer to be a saint; and the entirely exaggerated understanding of Nation and *Volk*, which flowed over into the sphere of the religious.

Hudal wanted to keep and strengthen National Socialism as a political movement, even while he separated himself from its philosophical wing. As an example, he took the fascist movement which had broken free from its philosopher, Giovanni Gentile, who was also on the Index.[491] He represented the thesis that within National Socialism two parties contended with each other – a left socialist, anti-Christian wing, and a right conservative-reforming wing. The conclusion he drew was to strengthen the latter, indeed to ally himself with it, against the growing threat of Bolshevism in Europe.[492]

Hudal mostly proceeded in such a way as to perceive the 'exaggerations' in Nazi ideology and – in controversy with Rosenberg – to begin to soften them. On the 'modern race question' he says for example:

> Noone can deny that since the French Revolution with its principles on the rights of nations and men in Europe a mixture of races and nationalities has grown up in which the consciousness of nationality, race and its high cultural values has often lost all significance. [...] The race question and Christianity must [...] not be opposed. It is only where radicalisms begin and generate struggles, oppositions and difficulties, because Christianity consists essentially of harmonising, compromise, and the union of the natural and the supernatural.[493]

Rosenberg was willing to carry out Papen's demand that from the side of the 'party every polemic [against the book] should stop' only if Hudal altered the title.[494] He directed a similar petition to forbid this use of the title to the Reich Propaganda Ministry.[495] After the book came out in Austria, the Reich Director 'for the whole intellectual and philosophical education of the NSDAP' submitted to Hitler an annihilating opinion. Hudal had produced 'a critique of the essence of the NS-philosophy', the 'sole achievement' of which, flattened by false historical categories, required, with the exception of the political, a 'complete abdication of the philosophical area to the Church' and rejected the racial thought of National Socialism as its philosophical basis.[496]

With this assessment Rosenberg hit the mark, for in practice Hudal intended nothing less than a Catholicization of Nazism. In this the Rector of the Anima was well wide of the object of his demands – as, for example, when he denounced 'the semitic race' as upholders of democracy and cosmopolitanism and reproached Judaism with isolation and the desire to dominate.[497] Just like his Osnabrück colleague Berning, Hudal thought that Rome represented the true 'Führer principle',[498] and hence perceived also numerous possibilities of mediation between Roman Catholicism and National Socialism.

Hudal was perhaps the most popular, but not the only, Catholic looking for syntheses between Roman Catholicism and Nazism. Most of them belonged to the intellectual sphere of Franz von Papen's national Catholic initiative;[499] Hudal was closely connected with him. Also the less well-known priest Wilhelm Maria Senn of Sickingen attempted, for example, in his work, *Katholizismus und Nationalsozialismus*, to show the compatability of the two. The author desired the 'reconciliation of Catholicism with Nationalsocialism' and left no doubt that he expected a kind of expiatory offering on the side of his Church. Archbishop Fritz of Freiburg prohibited the pamphlet and for this he received the full support of the Holy Office.[500]

3.11 Drafts of the Holy Office against the totalitarian systems (1935/36)

On 14 March 1935, the Jesuit General Ledóchowski put before the Holy Office the work of his two scholars, Hürth and Rabeneck.[501] Like Hudal, Hürth also came to the conclusion that the Nazi theory of race was fundamentally opposed to the Christian image of man. The Jesuits took as a chief source for the analysis of the Nazi doctrine of race Hitler's *Mein Kampf*. Systematically they went over the political religion of National

Socialism. 'Racial mixture' was for Hitler 'the original sin of the world'; he demonized the Jews, in order to present himself as the redeemer of the 'Aryan blood'. The cult of good blood gave rise to the idea of sterilization. The education of the master race contradicted every thing taught by the Christian religion; the absolute position of the racially pure national community gave no heed to the individual and his wishes on the one side, and on the other destroyed the unity of mankind.

After detailed enquiry, the opinions and the theses taken from them gave rise to a list of *47 Propositions* – statements which were to be condemned in the ancient style. They were written by Hürth and the Canadian sociologist Louis Chagnon. These propositions went for comment to the three Konsultors of the Supreme Congregation.[502] The sentences are clear and simple, with no diplomatic ornamentation. On the relation of 'Church and totalitarian State', for example, the following theses were styled as worthy of condemnation:

37. The Church too is subject to the totalitarian state both as a matter of fact and as a matter of law.
38. The Church has not natural or divine right to full independence from civil society, nor does it have full sovereignty as regards its own aims.

    The Church has only that permission to teach, organize, and practise worship in civil society that the totaltaran state concedes to it and for the period during which that permission is granted.
39. In particular, the Church has neither the duty nor the right to teach and insist on moral principles upon which civil – and especially – political and economic life is based.

    By behaving in this manner the Church exceeds the limits of its competence and invades the competence of the State. It is the right of the State alone, from the fullness of its power, even in regard to the conscience, to determine political ethics and make decisions about them.[503]

This was unambiguous. Yet theses like these will not surprise the attentive reader of what the Vatican demanded from the German Foreign Office. In the controversial exchange of notes between the Holy See and the Nazi State, the self-understanding of the total state repeatedly plays a part. One must not be taken in by the characteristic analytical style and the diplomatic language which Pacelli mostly used. In substance he was quite clear. Thus in his memorandum of 14 May 1934, Pius XI holds it to be necessary in respect of the concept of the 'total power' of the State to draw an essential distinction between total power rightly and wrongly understood, if a dangerous confusion of concepts is to be avoided. If the total power is so understood that, in everything which according to the actual purpose of the State belongs to State's responsibility, the entire body of citizens is subject to the State without exception and to the legal government guiding it (subjective totality = totality of the group of persons subject to the State), this is doubtless to be agreed. However, nothing of the kind is to be said if, under this heading, there is included a so-called objective totality (totality of the subject area) and it is maintained that the whole body of citizens is subject to the State also in the totality of that which includes their personal, family, spiritual and supernatural life, or – which would be still more false – to the State alone or preeminently. [... It can] only be emphatically pointed out that 'a totality of the regime and of the State, which also wished to embrace the supernatural area of life would be already in the idea obviously meaningless [...] and – translated into action – a real monstrosity [...]'. The claim to educational totality is accordingly not only *in thesi* false but also *in praxi* suicidal in the long run. Minds that it brings up in the ways of a confession-free and anticonfessional state education will, in their lack of religious connection, be its enemies tomorrow. There is no true welfare of nation or state without religion. [...] The norm of humanity is unthinkable without anchorage in the divine. This ultimate anchorage cannot lie in an arbitrary 'divinity' of the race. [...] Such a 'God' of blood and race would be nothing more than a self-created image of the world with its own peculiar limits and narrowness. [...] The return to a 'national religion' preached in many quarters would be not only a 'fall of man' in the supernatural sense but also a relapse in the natural and cultural sense. The Church as the guardian of the heritage of faith in Christ cannot look on without resistance, if to the youth, the bearer of the coming generations, is preached, not the good news of the doctrine of Christ but the protective and lying gospel of a new materialism of race, and state institutions are abused to this purpose.[504]

Although he was kept informed in detail by Orsenigo's reports on breaches of the concordat,[505] Pacelli rejected a continual demonstrative rebuffing of the philosophy of National Socialism – presumably because he feared the repercussions of such a confrontation upon German Catholics. From the beginning he as a *Realpolitiker* doubted their powers of resistance.[506] He had to take note that the Germans stood behind Hitler almost to a man. This was true also in respect of the 'Jewish question' as Orsenigo could report in connection with the 'Nuremberg laws' in mid-September 1935.[507] It was his impression that there were scarcely any German non-Jews who disapproved of the measures. 'I do not know', wrote the nuncio, 'whether Bolshevism is an exclusive work of the Jews, but here they have found the means to establish this idea and proceed against Judaism accordingly. If, as looks likely, the Nazi government is going to last, then the Jews are bound to disappear from the nation.'[508] But the Church had a still greater stamina and an experience of 2000 years, as Pacelli constantly repeated.[509] In such a situation it made no sense to go in for confrontation. The time was not even suitable for it. They had to be able to wait. But as soon as the opportunity arose – for example, at the end of April 1935 in Lourdes – Pacelli raised his voice against the 'superstition of race and blood'. Those who thought thus lived according to principles 'fundamentally opposed to those of the Christian faith and the Church will never, at any price, have dealings with them'.[510]

During his time as Cardinal Secretary of State Pacelli stuck to this strategy and repeatedly tried with his Nazi 'partners' to sue for contractual loyalty towards the concordat. Here he saw himself up to 1939 in the first place as a loyal executive assistant to his pope, and hence did not develop any independent initiatives.

The Konsultors of the Holy Office did not have to take any such considerations into account. Their research results were peak achievements. Without relating themselves to the work of other scholars, they affirmed – along with Eric Voegelin, Raymond Aron and many others[511] – that National Socialism had created a 'political religion'. The religious nationalism promoted in Germany by the State (so they explained) was an heretical State-cult, which stood in direct competition with Christianity.[512] They condemned the aggressive policy of *Lebensraum* and the militarism which endangered peace, and they defended the 'unity of mankind' – a formula which was against every kind of racial discrimination. The 'race instinct' and decisive measure for the judgement of universal principles like revealed truths was strictly rejected.

Between Pacelli and the Jesuits who had been acting for the Holy Office there were no differences of substance in their judgement of Nazism. But they had no doubt different functions, and this circumstance left its mark on their forms of public utterance. How Pacelli thought emerges among other things from the fact that Alfredo Ottaviani, who as Undersecretary of State was his closest colleague, brought out a textbook on canon law in 1935, in which – at any rate in Latin – he named and shamed the Fascist and National Socialist theoreticians.[513]

The three Konsultors, to whom the propositions were handed over for comment, did not belong to the Society of Jesus. Martin-Stanislaus Gillet, Master General of the Dominicans, concluded in his opinion of 20 April 1936 that nationalism, totalitarianism and racism were the common products of a *single* 'new idol' which he described as 'social modernism'. Here he linked up with the 'heresy of modernism' against which Pius X had already fought. For Ernesto Ruffini, Secretary of the Congregation for Universities and Faculties and also Konsultor of the Congregation for Extraordinary Church Affairs, 'hypernationalism' formed the 'heresy of our time'. Domenico Tardini,[514] who had succeeded Ottaviani as Undersecretary of State in 1936, pleaded at any rate for an encyclical and for a decree of the Holy Office for a solemn condemnation of the oppressive errors of the age. But he advocated the condemnation of communism and nationalism equally as 'extremely damaging errors'. If the Church took up a position against both extremes from a pastoral perspective it could 'once again show that it followed the golden mean of truth and virtue'.[515]

All three were of the conviction that the propositions were too academic and differentiated, and hence must be shortened and simplified. Its proposal made it necessary to appoint a new commission of 29 April 1936 which should pursue similar inquiries on communism. Although Friedrich Muckermann was meanwhile working as a professor of Russian Literature at the Oriental Institute in Rome, he was again not asked, although Joseph Ledit SJ, who edited the *Letters from Rome*, a publication which sought to document the essence of communism, was.[516] Godman believes that this decision on personnel was not a matter of chance. Rome shunned the spotlight, and hence decided for people who planned the Vatican 'offensive in [...] secrecy'.[517]

The new commission looked for common ground between Nazism and Communism. They found, especially in the ideas of totalitarianism, parallels which led them to similar formulations, as Hürth and Chagnon had used in relation to Nazi racism.[518] Ledit laid especial emphasis on materialism as the determining principle of communism and created practical references to the altered lifestyle of the men concerned, in which he included the emancipation of women from their traditional functions in marriage and the family, and the education of young people in communist collectives.

All that was lacking now was fascist totalitarianism.[519] Angelo Perugini was commissioned to inquire into it; otherwise he wrote Latin letters for the Secretariat of State. Perugini analysed primarily the writings and speeches of Mussolini which were published in Milan in 1934/35.[520] Here he could gain support from the book of the journalist, Mario Missiroli,[521] who had quoted passages from Mussolini's speeches with positive intentions, which had now been condemned by the Church as heresies. For this reason the book had been put on the Index on 30 June 1930.[522]

Many of the reports drawn from Mussolini came from his early 'socialist' period, in which he often spoke disrespectfully or even heretically about the Catholic Church. The chief points of complaint concerned the claim of the State to a monopoly of power and education, which injured the rights of the Church, the glorification of military and other force, the cult of the dead built up around the fallen heroes, and the drive for empire. Perugini used the Abysinnian War[523] as a support for the totalitarianism of the fascist system quite differently from Schuster.[524] On 12 July 1936 a three-part draft went to press which condemned all three totalitarian systems. The first part sketched as a positive standard the Christian anthropology, the second set out the appropriate positions derived from it on race, nation and proletariat, and the third confronted 'the erroneous doctrines of racism, hyper-nationalism, communism'.[525] In view of the third part it was immediately considered that it could lead to difficulties with the governments concerned and hence that it would be better if it were dropped.[526] But such tactical considerations were contrary to the peculiar understanding of the Church, the scope of which the authors had formulated very comprehensively. 'The Church is not only a perfect but also a universal and total society in the sense that it embraces the whole of mankind and all its conceivable dealings insofar as they concern an ultimate purpose and are subject to the laws of faith and morality.'[527] The Catholic Church limited itself not to particular claims affecting only its members. It saw itself rather as commissioned by God, to set up its universal morality as a standard for all peoples, and to champion for them certainly not the modern, but the Catholic, rights of men duly baptized. Thus it says in relation to racism that the revealed unity of humanity 'under no circumstances' permits the exclusion of the 'semitic race'.[528] Against all the sentiments in the Catholic Church itself the claim to universal representation was extended even to 'unbelievers' – a form of self-mastery through the power of the word of God if it could be theologically formulated.

However, this testimony to theological incorruptibility was never published. The theses on racism, nationalism, communism and total-itarianism had now been edited to the point where they could be presented to the Holy Office on 13 October 1936.[529] In them racism, hypernationalism and communism were unmistakably condemned. The following understanding of 'totalitarianism' was rejected as heretical:

> 22. The State has absolute, direct, and immediate rights over every-one and everything that has to do with civil society in any way. [...]
> 24. Education is the unique and complete preserve of the State. 25.
> Even the Catholic Church is subject to the State and has no rights except those granted by the State. That is why the Church has no innate right to teach and to urge ethical principles by which the political and economic life of civil society is ruled.[530]

But even this paper was not to see the light of publication. Under the pressure of the Spanish Civil War, attention had shifted to seemingly more important matters. Atheistic socialism and communism and their anti-Church measures on which day in day out there were reports of abominations[531] were in the foreground. Racism and totalitarianism by contrast appeared eminently forgettable. Moreover, on 18 November 1936, some of the cardinals within the Holy Office, out of political opportunism, attempted to stifle the report. Others agreed to support a 'brief instruction to warn the faithful against such erroneous theories and especially against the errors of Communism'.[532] The next day Pius XI declared that the decision on the condemnation had been postponed indefinitely.[533]

A few days afterwards, namely, on 25/26 November 1936, and thus three weeks after the meeting between Hitler and Faulhaber, the Bavarian bishops condemned Bolshevism, and confirmed their 'loyal and positive attitude towards the present form of state and towards the Führer'.[534] But even this pastoral word contained so much that was offensive to the Nazi State that the Reich church minister Kerrl had it confiscated and forbidden.[535]

3.12 The Spanish Civil War

On 13 September 1923 Miguel Primo de Rivera, Captain General of Cata-lonia, seized power by a coup.[536] Like the Italian king Victor Emmanuel III in the case of Mussolini, King Alphonse XIII legitimated the revolt when he nominated Primo de Rivera to be President of a military directory. The constitutional system of 1876 thus came to an end and a dictatorship began which was to last from 1923 to 1930. Cardinal Secretary of State Gasparri was confident that the military government of Primo de Rivera 'might very well introduce a healthier atmosphere'.[537] Like the governments at the beginning of the Restoration period the dictator was able to find support from (on the one side) the agricultural oligarchy in the centre of the country and (on the other) from the industrial bourgeoisie on the periphery. The third pillar of the State was the Roman Catholic Church, which received numerous privileges in the education and training sector.

This was the time when Opus Dei was founded in the year 1928. Its founder, the Spanish priest Josemaría Escrivá de Balaguer, aimed with this 'work of God' to enable men and women in a strictly organized society to live according to the guidelines of faith and morality preserved in the Church for centuries, and to do so in their personal, professional and social lives. From these initial conditions, and on the basis of internal structures demanding unconditional obedience, Opus Dei developed into a pillar of the Spanish dictatorship.[538]

The fourth pillar of the Rivera dictatorship was formed by the socialists. On the basis of Catholic social doctrine Primo de Rivera succeeded, as Piłsudski had succeeded in Poland, in integrating nationalism and socialism. Central to these concerns was a paternalistic harmonization of capital and labour. A draft constitution made public in July 1929 encountered harsh criticism from liberals and republicans because of its absolutist features. Under Mussolini's influence royal prerogatives were also trimmed back, which moved Alphonse XIII to withdraw the draft.

After a short phase of economic recovery, costly projects caused considerable financial problems, which could not be brought under control by tax increases. The plan for a higher taxation of the rich through income, luxury and profits taxes had to be dropped owing to the opposition of those concerned. Now the conservatives and the Catholic trade unions refused their support for the dictatorship. When the army and the king also withdrew their support, Primo de Rivera retreated in January 1930, and went into exile in France, where he died shortly afterwards. His successor, General Dámaso Berenguer, wanted to go back to the constitution of 1875. But Republicans, socialists and the Catalan Left united in the 'pact of San Sebastián' and demanded reforms such as the introduction of the republic. The municipal elections on 12 April 1931 brought an overwhelming victory for the allied Republicans and socialists in the towns; but in the country the monarchists stood their ground. Bloody contests followed, which Alphonse XIII prevented by following the ultimatum of the revolutionary committee and leaving Spain. On 14 April 1931 amid popular jubilation the Second Republic was called into existence. The system of restored monarchy was thus ended, the project of authoritarian modernization by a dictator defeated for the time being, and the way was open to break out of inherited socio-economic and political structures.

The new regime of republican modernization undertook a modification of the agrarian structures and a democratization of society. In this process three parties contended for political supremacy: the Catholic and conservative Right, the bourgeois and liberal Centre, and the anarchist and socialist Left. The bourgeois-liberal forces whose hand was on the tiller through this bloodless 'bourgeois revolution' had a reform programme; this embraced a liberal and *laïque* state with a democratic constitution and reforms in the educational and agricultural sector. They were moreover resolved to represent the interests of the labouring and unpropertied populace. In the view of employers and landlords these reforming ideas went too far. For the first time in Spanish history they were not the favoured groups. Within the republican-socialist coalition government considerable differences soon arose, party wings formed and there were controversies. In the elections to the Constitutional Assembly in June 1931, the Socialists and Republicans received an overwhelming majority and dominated the Cortes. If the Right in 1931 were still crippled, they succeeded two years later in forming a respectable election alliance, with the help of which they were able to win the election victory, while the Socialists and Republicans fragmented. The Right represented the interests of the old oligarchy, and hence called upon the social teaching of the Catholic Church. Their fight was against socialist and laicist legislation.

Between 1931 and 1933, in the first phase of the republic, the allied Socialists and Republicans had set about the necessary reforms. In the second phase the conservatives had undone many of these reforms especially in the agrarian sector, and in the third phase, between February 1936 and the beginning of the civil war in July, the development in the agrarian region began to look revolutionary. The first step in the reform phase was the working out of a constitution, which in its final shape revealed the powerful influence of the Weimar constitution in Germany. Although the Weimar constitution had for long periods during 1931 been set aside by emergency ordinances in Germany, its principles had been accepted in Spain. Among the complications in the constitutional text most in need of solution from the start were the relations between the provinces and the central State, the relations between Church and

State and, connected with them, social and political questions like divorce and educational policy. In the question of property and the possibility of expropriation, bourgeois-liberal and socialist ideas clashed and had to find a solution in constructive compromise. The constitution of 1931 guaranteed freedom of conscience and worship and treated all religions equally. Even the Roman Catholic Church was classified as an association; it therefore lost all its privileges. Activity in the commercial and educational sectors was forbidden to the religious orders. The Church lost its licence to teach, and the Jesuit order was forbidden. Church and State were separated with a clear *laïque* accent, and this led to the Church's adoption of a role as critic of the Republic, and becoming a melting pot for all the opposition forces. In the right wing of the conservative election alliance the Church had powerful backing. In his circular *Dilectissima nobis* of 3 June 1933[539] Pius XI objected to the legislation separating Church and State and all the other measures deemed hostile to the Church. The question of the position of the Church in Spain was of such high significance that the civil war which began in 1936 was often described as a war of religion, and quite certainly had the character of a clash of cultures.[540]

The entry into the government of the conservative Confederación Española de Derechas Autónomas in October 1934 was interpreted by the Socialists as a fascist seizure of power. A general strike was called and in some regions this broadened out into a social uprising. The central government called in the army to put down the revolt, and thus also prevented the secession of Catalonia. The events of October led to a polarizing of Right and Left. The Right viewed itself as a bulwark against separatism, atheistic liberalism and attempts at social revolution; the Left feared – with developments in Italy, Germany and Austria before their eyes – fascist counter-revolution in Spain too.

Corruption and mismanagement finally forced the conservative election alliance in January 1936 to dissolve the Cortes and to call new elections. The Left now again received an overwhelming majority. In face of world-wide depression the economic situation was tense. Strikes by farm labourers and wild expropriations put pressure on the government of the new Popular Front. Between March and July 1936 they drove through a high-speed partition of rural property in order to calm the agricultural proletariat. But their efforts were abruptly interrupted by the military uprising of 18 July 1936. The unwillingness of the old oligarchy to face reform, their desire to stick to the power relations and the archaic social structure of the nineteenth century, threw the country into a civil war. The Popular Front and the National Front faced each other irreconcilably as two great political blocks.

The insurgents could not win through in every part of the country. The whole of the east and north of the land as well as great parts of the south remained in republican hands. Above all the larger cities and economic centres stood on the side of the legal government. By and large the overwhelming part of the population rejected the coup and stood behind the government, which also had the industrial resources at its disposal. But from the beginning the insurgents possessed the numerically stronger army. Up to the spring of 1937 they were able – with the help of German aircraft which brought the Foreign Legion and Moroccan troops on to the mainland – to conquer about a third of the country. Between the spring of 1937 and the spring of 1938 they conquered the northern provinces. In this they were supported from the air by the German Condor legion requested by Franco. In mid-April 1938 Catalonia was cut off from the other republican territories. Barcelona fell at the end of January 1939, Madrid at the end of March 1939.

Fighting on the republican side were the so-called 'International Brigades' – from 40,000 to 60,000 men, of whom about 5000 were German. In November 1938 they were disbanded. Great Britain, France and the USA stuck officially to the principle of non-intervention (Non-intervention committee); the USA and financial circles from other western states of course supported Franco indirectly,[541] because they knew their economic interests would be better served by him than by a Popular Front government which was under increasing communist influence. The President of the French Popular Front government, Léon Blum, showed himself ready on 20 July 1936 to answer a request for help from the legal Spanish government; his cabinet, however, resolved on non-intervention. Only the Soviet Union openly supported the republicans. There are still no exact data as to the extent of their aid. The government paid for Russian military assistance with the gold reserves of the Bank of Spain.

Shortly after the beginning of the war the insurgents set up a provisional Junta in the Nationalist capital of Burgos, which in the occupied areas prohibited trade unions, dissolved parties, and brutally suppressed any resistance. Agrarian reforms were undone, the soil returned to its former owners. At the end of September 1936 the Junta de defensa nacional nominated General Franco to be Generalissimo and head of state. He saw to it that the heterogeneous state party with its falangist ideology did not dominate the state machine. Moreover, he sought to preserve for himself a certain independence from his civil war allies,

Italy and Germany. Mussolini had already from 1934 contributed to the destabilizing of the republic, when he supported fascists and other forces of the Right. Without the massive military intervention of Germany in the civil war the coup would have been quickly put down. On the motives for German intervention there is no agreement. Consideration of strategic alliances in the sense of anti-communist front-building certainly played an important role. Finally the common action in Spain formed the foundation of the 'Berlin–Rome axis'.

The fascist Falange was a party with which Franco was originally unconnected. Its founder was the son of the former dictator, Miguel Primo de Rivera, José Antonio Primo de Rivera, an intellectual inspired by the rise of Hitler, who in the first months of the war had been executed by a republican firing squad. His cult still lives.[542] Franco took over the party and blended it with the traditionalist Carlists, a party originally clerical and absolutist which originated in the 1930s. The programme of the new Falange was impressed by conservative and monarchist thought. The Caudillo used it to construct the 'New State'. Alongside the party the latter rested on two other pillars: the Church and the army. With two exceptions the Spanish bishops took the side of the insurgents in July 1937.[543] In every area relevant to public life the Church maintained a presence. In May 1938 the Jesuits were allowed to return to Spain.

On the republican side the governments changed constantly up to May 1937. Hence both bourgeois and socialist cabinets were turned out and driven against one another. Finally in May 1937 a communist and socialist government was formed under the socialist Prime Minister Juan Negrin which remained in office till the end of the war. From the internal power struggles of the republican block the communists dependent on Moscow (Partido Comunista de España, PCE) emerged victorious. This was due partly to the fact that they organized the International Brigades and – with the aid of Soviet arms deliveries from late autumn 1936 to March 1938 – built up the republican army. While the insurgents put a stop to almost all reforms, the republicans moved ever more decisively to the Left. Their object was to create a socialist economic system in a society free of domination and with soviet-like institutions. With great speed they pushed on the collectivization of the rural economy, of industry and other sectors. Pitted against the openly anarchist and libertarian revolutionary movements were the communists and the other parties of the Popular Front.

The civil war cost hundreds of thousands of lives. About 200,000 died at the fronts, and about as many again were killed without legal proceedings. Numerous republicans who fled before Franco to France were later given up to him by the Vichy government or by the German army of occupation.

From the beginning Franco followed a Spanish *Sonderweg* [special route] which condemned all the modern ideologies (demo-liberalism), secularization and Western democratization (constitution, separation of powers etc.) as alien to the 'essence of old Spain'. His 'New State' aimed to return to ancient Spanish values and traditions. By this he implied conservative, Catholic and military traditions together with the ideology of the Falange. He derived the supreme legitimation for his system from the doctrines of the Catholic Church. His concept of national Catholicism recalls the analogous Polish thought of the 1930s.[544] Instead of a constitution Franquism came out with 'basic laws' of an ideological and dogmatic character – the basic law of labour, for example, which included a proclamation of the right to work, of private property and family protection. These basic laws were typified by their paternalistic character, their view of the State as a family, their simple denial that there could be clashes of interest between specific groups in society.

At the same time the Falangists functioned as a modernizing elite, propagating a revolutionary 'Third Way' with socialist elements between 'liberal capitalism' and 'Marxist materialism'. In practice of course the traditional power elites – Church, large landowners and financial bourgeoisie – prevailed. Under Franco they could attain their objects – the pre-republican conditions they strove for – and had to accept no economic losses. There was, for example, no agrarian reform during the entire Franco dictatorship. 'In this sense the early phase of Franquism can be called a counter-revolutionary dictatorship with fascist elements.'[545]

Who it was in Spain that had the say became clear too in the Second World War. The great landlords, the financial oligarchy and the military were against entering the war, the Falangists for it. Franco tacked successfully between the warring parties, at first supporting the German side with deliveries of raw materials and the 'Blue Division' – then, when the outcome of the war was foreseeable, veering to the allies, who were to use Spanish airfields.

Between 1936 and 1939 the political opponents of Franco were locked up in concentration camps, 're-educated' in religion and ideology, and subjected to forced labour. There were at least 104 concentration camps on Spanish territory, in which some 367,000 men were interned.[546] These camps, often filled to overflowing, continued after the civil war – to about 1942. German Gestapo agents had access to them. The attitude of the Spanish episcopate in the conflict was perfectly clear: the civil war was conceived as a *cruzada*, as a crusade against the Reds, promising after Franco's victory the complete reestablishment of the earlier power-position of the Catholic Church.[547] Although Pius XI in June 1933 in his encyclical *Dilectissima nobis* had condemned the anticlerical legislation of the Second Republic and under the influence of the Spanish Primate, Cardinal Pedro Segura, put off recognition of the new regime, he did not at first strike this note. Impressed by the reports of abominations, which Segura's successor, Cardinal Isidro Gomá y Tomás, Archbishop of Toledo, sent to Rome, the *Osservatore Romano* then veered in the autumn of 1936 briefly to the thesis of a 'war of religion', and subsequently reported in ever more reserved terms. In reluctant understanding with the Holy See the Spanish episcopate issued a pastoral letter on 1 July 1937, in which they said:

> The white struggle of the February election of 1936 became as a consequence of civil and military conflict the bloody battle of a people who are split into two parties: into the spiritual party on the side of the insurgents, who set out to defend order, social peace, traditional civilisation and the fatherland and also [...] to defend religion; and, in the other party, the materialistic – be it now called Marxist, communist or anarchist – who wish to replace the old civilisation of Spain in all its aspects by the radical new 'civilisation' of the Russian soviets.[548]

A week after the common pastoral letter of the Spanish episcopate, Pacelli, during the Eucharistic Congress at Lisieux – in the country governed by the Popular Front administration of Leon Blum and which gave non-material support to the republican government in Spain – gave the assurance that the Church did not intend to favour or to oppose any particular political group, since it stood outside and above politics.[549] Yet there can be no doubt that the outcome of the Spanish Civil War was received in the Vatican with considerable relief and also with great approval. Spain, for centuries one of the states most loyal to the Pope, had joined the Catholic countries which favoured the model of the restorative corporative state. The danger of yet one more *laïque* state of the socialist stamp was thus ended. Franco's victory was thus also the victory of the Holy See.

3.13   The three papal encyclicals of March 1937

In the autumn and winter of 1936 the Pope faced a situation which had become very familiar to the Vatican since the 1920s from the complex of German-Polish relations: the national episcopate pressed the Holy See to enter some compromises in respect of the national interest with the socialist, the fascist or the Nazi government. Only in the case of the USA did Pacelli make a political engagement, for he, in common with the suffragan bishop of Boston, Francis Spellman, in the autumn of 1936, came out in support of the re-election of Franklin D. Roosevelt.[550] Among other things he hoped from his visit to the USA was the promotion of the acceptance of diplomatic relations.[551] Finally it was supposed in diplomatic circles that the situation of the Church in Mexico represented an important theme in the Pacelli visit.[552] While Pacelli promised himself no more from negotiations with the German Reich, and from the summer of 1936 was contributing to an encyclical condemning National Socialism, many German bishops after the conversation between Faulhaber and Hitler again raised the hope that an alliance could be forged on the basis of a common anti-communism, which might assist German Catholicism to recognition by the Nazi State. For the forces in the NSDAP which were decidedly and deeply hostile to the Church, this perspective was a nightmare. All manner of disruptive manoeuvres and actions at subordinate levels, but also from SD-circles and the Brown House, which apparently were not agreed with Hitler and Goebbels, only strengthened the bishops in their pet notion that the two wings of the party were fighting it out.[553]

On 30 December 1936 Faulhaber sent a new pastoral letter to Hitler,[554] dated for 24 December. In his accompanying letter he referred to the meeting at the beginning of November, and spoke of 'our agreement'.[555] The meaning of this emerged from his letter: 'The new pastoral letter in the New Year will sound like a trumpet, and even abroad they will be unable to ignore this unanimous confession of the German bishops to the Führer and his mission in world history, his defence against Bolshevism.'[556] But Faulhaber could not get away from the fact that with a background of fresh anti-Church incidents the bishops had had to mention also their anxieties, 'in order to remain truthful and not fall into the un-German role of Byzantine Yes-men'. The pastoral letter spoke in apocalyptic terms of Bolshevism; it was 'a gate of hell, an advance guard of Anti-Christ'. The weapons of the Church – faith, the Word and prayer – were directed against it. The Catholic emigrant press, most of all Friedrich Muckermann in his *Deutsche Weg* [*The German Path*] reacted in horror.[557] But even the Nazis were not satisfied with the pastoral letter and viewed the loyal criticism as a frontal attack on the part of the Catholic Church.

While the bishops in feverish haste sent their Pastoral Word on its way, a letter from Pacelli of 21 December reached them on the 26th, inviting the three German cardinals together with Bishops Preysing (Berlin) and Galen (Münster) 'as soon as possible in the New Year' to a conference in Rome.[558] Bertram promised a visit to the Vatican for the period after the bishops' conference at Fulda in mid-January 1937.[559]

On 15 January 1937, already two days after the conclusion of the bishops' conference, the Cardinal Secretary of State received Cardinal Bertram and Faulhaber to a preliminary meeting.[560] The conversation turned on the severe illness of the Pope, on Bolshevism and the Berlin nuncio, on whose weak role the bishops were unhappily outspoken.[561] On the following meeting on 16 January, in which all five members of the German episcopate took part, we now have, along with Faulhaber's notes,[562] also Pacelli's report.[563]

The Cardinal Secretary of State noted the assessment of the bishops that the Nazi party was completely ignoring the Reich Concordat and was behaving in open enmity to the Church. 'For the Church it is at the moment a matter of life and death: bluntly they want its annihilation.'[564] Even if Hitler had wished it otherwise, it was felt that he could scarcely contend against the party dictatorship any more. Neither the Rome official nor the Germans believed any longer that Catholicism in the Reich was capable of a 'counter-offensive'. Instead of this, the visitors appealed to the Vatican to intervene energetically in cases where the concordat was breached. While Bertram's proposal that the Holy Father should send a letter to Hitler met with refusal by Pacelli,[565] the Breslau Cardinal put the brakes on when Pacelli steered towards a public position in the form of a papal encyclical.[566] Galen and Preysing, in contrast, supported the project. They viewed the situation of the Church in Germany and the errors of National Socialism as the core of the doctrinal writing.[567] Pacelli thought that 'the foreign policy situation must suggest to the government not to take things too far', and hence held the moment exactly right for the issuing of a papal teaching document.[568] Moreover it was apparent to members of the group that the encyclical on the Church's situation in Germany was to complete the two encyclicals that had already been issued, the one against communism and the one on the position of the Church in Mexico.[569] Pacelli asked the Munich cardinal first for a written sketch, then for a formal draft, which Faulhaber handed in on 21 January.

On 17 January the Cardinal Secretary of State acquainted the German bishops with his notes of the previous day. Afterwards the clergy set out for the papal audience. At the start Pacelli handed over his report to the Pope. He prepared precise minutes of the conversation.[570] After this each bishop spoke in turn and represented – partly with a regional emphasis – the oppression of the Church by the Nazi State.

At first Pius XI answered the first speakers individually, then, doubtless from weakness, he waited for several votes before he spoke. Despite the infringements on the concordat he defended the treaty. 'Already when it was concluded on practical grounds we knew what sort of people we had to deal with. But such a measure of disloyalty towards a word pledged we neither believed nor expected. But even under present conditions the concordat is still of value, at least if one takes a stand upon the law.'[571]

In enumerating the misfortunes of the present, the Pope included not only events in Germany, Russia and Mexico but also those in Spain. At this moment the situation seemed to him so uncertain that he was still reckoning with a possible defeat of the Franquists. 'We suffer with: Germany, Russia, Spain, Mexico, all those parts of the mystical body of Christ which suffer more than the others.' The special praise which the Pope gave to Bishop von Galen alone is striking: 'We hear many glorious things about you.' After Galen had spoken, Pius XI continued in the same strain: 'Our especial blessing on all your bold warriors. Our cause will certainly triumph. [...] Our cause is in God's hands.'

Seen against the background of the drafts of the syllabus, the encyclical *Mit brennender Sorge* appears as a diplomatic compromise. 'This encyclical', thinks Godman, 'still hailed as the most courageous attack made by the papacy on Hitler and his followers, in fact marks a retreat.'[572] The unanimous opinion in the German episcopate and in the Vatican was that if a doctrinal statement should be issued it should on no account provoke a repudiation of the concordat by the Nazi State.[573] To avoid all acerbity, Faulhaber, in his draft of 21 January, chose a pastoral, occasionally a teaching tone, took up the Pope's motif of suffering, and abstained from all harsh judgements.[574] Rather he pleaded for moderation in viewing race, state and nationalism, and throughout avoided the sharp theological distinctions, which had appeared in the drafts produced by the Holy Office, drafts which were still unknown to him. All he rejected as an 'error' was faith in a 'national God'.

In the revision of the draft Pacelli was concerned to justify his concordat policy.[575] He was bound to fear, as transpires from a report of the Italian ambassador to the Holy See, Pignatti Morano di Custoza, that the development would be to his personal disadvantage. 'The fact is that today where there are conversations about a conclave, even in whispers,

Pacelli is reproached with having wanted the concordat and that he was fooled by Nazism to get it.'[576] If this interpretation established itself, Pacelli knew that his career would end with the death of Pius XI. Hence he made it clear right at the beginning of his revision that the negotiations were taken up on the initiative of the Reich government and that the Vatican had solely 'agreed' to the invitation. The Hitler government had wanted the concordat; were they now to breach it, that would be their responsibility.

In substance as well as in language, Pacelli took up the notes to the German government again and complained of striking breaches of the law. Even in the area of doctrine the encyclical was much more cautious than the drafts of the Holy Office. Only in connection with the idea of a 'national God' and a 'national religion' does the concept of 'error' appear. National Socialism is nowhere named by name, and the defence against a deification of race and state lacks the doctrinal backing to everything which was said on it theologically or anthropologically in the documents of the supreme tribunal. So the Secretary of State added the following:

> Whoever removes race, or the nation, or the state, or the form of state, the holder of the power of the state or other values basic to the formation of human community – all of which occupy an essential and honourable place within the earthly order – from this earthly scale of values, and makes it the highest norm of all, even religious values, and idolizes it with idolatrous worship, he perverts and falsifies the God-given and divinely sanctioned order of things. [...] From the totality of His creation flows essentially the totality of His claim to obedience upon individuals and communities of all kinds.

The encyclical rejects indeed the use of religious language in relation to blood, race and nation, but in respect of the analysis and of the scope of the claim of the Church – for example in respect of human rights – goes nothing like as far as the Holy Office. Through the General of the Jesuit order, Ledóchowski, the already cautious formulations were weakened further.[577] After the grave transgressions of the law of the past three years the Vatican could keep silent no longer, but it did not wish to speak so whole-heartedly as, in view of the careful preliminary work, it could have done. 'The Pope', noted Pacelli, 'does not wish to exclude the hope, small as it may be, that the situation may improve.'[578] Pius XI did not share such considerations where communism was concerned. On 17 March 1937 the cardinals of the Holy Office advised upon a draft for a condemnation of communism.[579] When it was learned that the Pope was himself planning an encyclical on this complex of issues, the Supreme Tribunal decided to postpone its decision – a resolution which the Pope approved. On 19 March 1937 *Divini redemptoris* appeared. The text of the encyclical, sharply critical of 'atheistic Soviet communism'[580] differed only in style from the draft of the Holy Office.[581] Unlike the encyclical *Mit brennender Sorge*, countries, for example, were named, in which persecutions took place – namely, Russia, Mexico and Spain.

Instead of following the clearly worded arguments used by the Holy Office, the text of the encyclical was disjointed and given clear levels of criticism. Without question National Socialism received milder censure than did communism: in 1937, the violence of the latter seemed far more cruel than the violence of the former.[582] This state of affairs the Vatican wished to explain to the outside world by pointing to the numerous previous condemnations of communism:[583] yet 'notwithstanding these repeated fatherly warnings [...] the danger grows daily from the tireless subversive activities of skilful and unscrupulous agitators'[584] and *Mit brennender Sorge* viewed them with 'mounting dismay'.[585] Even the *Catholic Times* realized this hierarchy of criticism and headed its article: 'The Holy Father publishes two Papal encyclicals within four days. He condemns communism and social injustices, and he warns the Nazis.'[586]

The perspective on Mexico was similar to that on Russia: persecution of the Church had gone on for many years[587] – which may be the reason why the third encyclical of this month – *Firmissimam constantiam* of 28 March 1937 – turned out as sharp as *Divini redemptoris*.

Knowledge of what was going on in the Vatican makes this explanation of course unacceptable. For in view of the insights of the Holy Office, there was from a theological perspective no reason to accept such gradation – it was due to political considerations respecting Hitler, Mussolini and Franco. In fact there are references to the circumstance that at least Franco thought *Mit brennender Sorge* applied to him and, holding the encyclical to be entirely inopportune, tried to suppress it.[588]

Despite the still comparatively restrained criticism, the excitement over the encyclical *Mit brennender Sorge* was very great, the more so as the Nazis were entirely surprised by it.[589] Orsenigo feared from now on a completely open persecution of the Church in the form of a 'real anti-religious policy' because the encyclical unmasked the true intentions of the regime which might now dispense with prudential considerations.[590] From Italian diplomatic circles, in contrast, came indications that the German government did not want a breach with the Holy See.[591] When the Vienna nuncio Gaetano Cicognani reported that not only the revolutionary wing of the NSDAP but also Hitler himself pursued the Church with hatred, Hitler 'exploded' on mention of the encyclical and described Kaas as 'traitor to Germany',[592] the Cardinal Secretary of State answered: 'To tell the truth: the powerful feelings of enmity towards the Church on the part of the Chancellor of the German Reich have been known here for a long time.'[593]

Ten days later Cicognani reported a conversation with the Austrian Federal Chancellor and the Secretary of State for Foreign Affairs, Guido Schmidt. In it the head of the Austrian government said that the encyclical had fanned Hitler's hatred against the Church into 'a kind of exaltation', on which Schmidt commented in Latin: 'whom God wishes to destroy he first drives mad'.[594] When shortly afterwards the Chicago Cardinal George Mundelein made Hitler ludicrous by describing him in a speech as a bad Austrian wallpaperman,[595] the Italian ambassador to the Reich, Attolico, reckoned on the worst. Significant for the good relations between the Italian government and the Holy See was that Pignatti, the Italian ambassador to the Holy See, passed on the summary of the report of his Berlin colleague to Pacelli. Attolico thought that a proclamation of the concordat among the people would be 'not only not unpopular, but be received almost with triumph'[596] – so severely did the Germans feel injured by the insult to their Führer. They were particularly outraged in Germany by the fact that Pacelli had made no kind of arrangements through diplomatic channels to express his regrets at the Cardinal's gaffe. Nevertheless there were repeatedly vague signals of readiness for conversations. Thus on 6 December 1937 Hitler received the suffragan Bishop of Augsburg, Franz Xaver Eberle, who reported on the meeting to Faulhaber at once that the Führer had announced his readiness for peace.[597] Yet when the Archbishop and Pacelli requested more precise information, it was quickly apparent that the conversation yielded no serious starting points for a peace initiative.

3.14   The Austrian *Anschluss*

While the German bishops were in the Vatican in mid-January 1937, Göring was in Rome negotiating with the Fascist government over the Spanish question and the future of Austria.[598] He did not bother much about the affairs of Spain; he had always been interested in the union of German Austria with the Reich.[599] Between 1934 and 1937 the political situation in Europe had changed in such a way that Göring now saw realistic chances of attaining his foreign policy goal. To Count Ciano he explained that it must not be forgotten that the Austrian government was neither Fascist nor Nazi in character, but clerical. The country looked on National Socialism as Enemy no. 1, and formed a dangerous source of friction in relations between Germany and Italy.[600]

The clerical corporative state had indeed been able to annihilate the Left,[601] but not the Nazis, who, with the support of the German Reich, were acting with increasing aggression.[602] On 25 July 1934 members of the illegal SS-Standard 89, clad in uniforms of the Austrian army, gained access to the Federal Chancellery in Vienna and arrested the members of the government who were there. The Federal Chancellor Dollfuss attempted to flee and was shot. The putsch was quickly put down; no help was to be expected from Germany for the Italian fascist troops gathered on the Brenner and thus made it clear that they intended to protect Austria's integrity as a state. But Engelbert Dollfuss went down in the history of conservative Austria as the first sacrifice to National Socialism. He became the centre of a virtual cult.

Four weeks previously the 'Röhm putsch' had taken place in Germany. Hitler felt himself subject to pressure from the Nazis who looked for continuing revolution and gathered round the SA Leader Röhm, on the one hand, and the Catholic monarchist imperial reactionaries who followed in the wake of his Vice-Chancellor Franz von Papen, on the other, and he rid himself of both opponents in an act of immense brutality. Supported by the army and the SS, on 30 June 1934 he had 50 senior storm trooper leaders arrested and shot, on the grounds that they had apparently planned a coup. At the same time he used the opportunity to liquidate 35 political opponents from the conservative camp, including Gustav Ritter von Kahr, Erich Klausener, Herbert von Bose and Edgar Jung.[603] Von Papen himself at first was subject to house arrest, then left the office of Vice-Chancellor and went as a special ambassador to Vienna in order to regain diplomatic ground for the Reich[604] – after the Nazi attempted coup of 25 July and the murder of the Federal Chancellor Dollfuss.[605]

At any rate, the Vienna nuncio Sibilia took von Papen for a 'wolf in sheep's clothing'; the Vienna Cardinal Innitzer refused for two whole years to receive him officially,[606] but was ready to meet him 'twice on neutral territory'.[607] With the help of Hudal,[608] of whom he made use, Papen long sought vainly to win the Austrian episcopate for his idea of a Catholicizing of National Socialism. But gradually he succeeded in forming a connection with those 'bridge-builders', who, like Martin Spahn at the celebrations of the founding of the Reich at Cologne University in 1934, pointed to the close ideological relationship between the Austrian Christian Social movement and National

Socialism. At the same time, the circle around the paper *Der christliche Ständestaat* published by Dietrich von Hildebrandt fought Nazism and anti-Semitism with all the means at their disposal.[609] Like the Holy Office, they saw in Nazism the German form of Bolshevism, and hence turned resolutely against the 'Reich mystics' and 'bridge-builders' who gathered round von Papen.

In the middle of March 1934 Austria had concluded the Protocol of Rome with Italy and with Hungary which was under equally authoritarian rule.[610] This agreement and the summit in Stresa in April 1935 with Great Britain, France and Italy guaranteed the independence of the Austrian State.[611] But with the Anglo-German naval treaty of June 1935[612] and especially with the Abyssinian war[613] the Stresa front loosened; there were, for example, deeply rooted conflicts of interest between the Western powers and Italy, and, as a consequence, after 1936, a gradual rapprochement of an Italy, now increasingly diplomatically isolated, with Germany.[614] The support of Italy with German weapons and finally the Spanish Civil War prepared the ground for the 'Rome–Berlin axis'. On 25 October 1936 Galeazzo Ciano, Italian Foreign Minister since 9 June 1936, and the German Foreign Minister von Neurath signed in Berlin the basic agreement.[615] The war with Ethiopia and the victory of Italy had led to a further ideologizing of Italian politics, and to a displacement of the zone of Italy's chief interests to the Mediterranean area.[616]

Austria very soon felt the effect of these alterations.[617] In the German-Austrian reconciliation agreement of 11 July 1936[618] Germany guaranteed the sovereignty of Austria and abolished the thousand-mark limit,[619] but Austria had to confess itself as a 'German State' and must operate no more against the National Socialists. The Duce at first took no fundamentally altered position towards Austria and Germany, but understood himself now rather as a mediator between Hitler and the Austrian Federal Chancellor Schuschnigg. He strengthened the collaboration with Austria by a cultural agreement at that time new in style,[620] and in March 1936 renewed the Protocol of Rome.[621] As the price for Italian protection Schuschnigg must keep silent on the question of the South Tirol and put a stop to the anti-Italian activities of emigrants from the South Tirol in Austria.

The mood abroad was favourable to an *Anschluss*; and the Austrians themselves observed the apparently prospering neighbouring land and had ever fewer reservations against an integration into the 'Reich'. In the weekly *Schönere Zukunft*[622] the Catholic-national forces published propaganda with some success for an understanding between the two countries. When the Duce visited Germany in September 1937 he had already realized that by strengthening the axis he would have to swallow the *Anschluss* with Austria.[623] A decisive break in Italy's policy towards Austria was brought about by the conversation between Mussolini and the new German Foreign Minister, Joachim von Ribbentrop, in November 1937. The Duce expressed reluctance to protect Austrian independence from the Reich, an independence which the Austrians themselves did not want. Italy in future would concentrate more powerfully on the Mediterranean and her colonies. According to Ciano's diaries Mussolini finally gave up Austria about the turn of the year 1937/38.[624]

In the middle of February 1938 during a meeting arranged by von Papen in Berchtesgaden Hitler threatened Schuschnigg with a military intervention. He thus forced the Austrian Federal Chancellor to take the leader of the Austrian Nazis and a practising Catholic, Arthur Seyss-Inquart,[625] into his cabinet, and to guarantee the NSDAP free activity within the 'Fatherland Front'. He must also issue an amnesty for National Socialists, and stick strictly to the July Agreement of 1936.[626] Twelve days later Schuschnigg made a speech in a phoney session of the Austrian Federal Parliament, which was repeatedly interrupted by shouts of 'Heil Schuschnigg'. He concluded with the pathetic proclamation: 'Red-White and Red till death. Austria!'[627]

Hitler was outraged by the speech. Berlin and Seyss-Inquart raised new demands. To get out of his difficult situation Schuschnigg resolved, against the express advice of Italy, to hold a referendum on 'a free and German, independent and social, Austria, at once Christian and united'.[628] In close cooperation with Berlin, the 'national' ministers in the Schuschnigg cabinet, Seyss-Inquart and Glaise von Horstenau, sought a postponement of the referendum. Since all attempts to obtain help in Rome, London and Paris proved fruitless, Schuschnigg finally gave way, declared on 11 March that he wanted to do without the referendum, and a few hours later resigned.

At first the Federal President Miklas refused to nominate Seyss-Inquart to be Federal Chancellor, but finally gave way to pressure from the streets. In this way a legal seizure of power was stage-managed in the night of 11–12 March 1938, which of course was accompanied by the invasion by German troops.[629] Already on 13 March the German dictator was able to sign in Linz the law for the reunification of Austria with the German Reich. When on 15 March Hitler went from Schönbrunn to the Hotel Imperial, the bells rang in all the churches of Vienna. In agreement with Berlin, Seyss-Inquart immediately liquidated his State and held office henceforth as Reichsstatthalter [Governor] until the

Reichskommissar for the reunion, Gauleiter Joseph Bürckel, dismissed him. Hudal, the enthusiast for a 'great Germany' wanted to celebrate the union of Germany and Austria by a Te Deum in the Anima, but on the instructions of the Pope had to call it off.[630]

There can be no doubt that great sections of the Austrian people who received the German troops with shouts of *Heil*, genuinely welcomed the *Anschluss*. The protest notes of the Western powers fell totally flat.[631] But the governments of the Soviet Union and Mexico, condemned a year previously by the Holy See in encyclicals, protested with all their power against Germany's breach of treaties binding under international law.[632]

Shortly after the annexation of Austria, Magistrati, the chargé d'affaires of the Italian embassy in Berlin, discussed with Göring the future relations between Church and State in the Reich. Via the Italian ambassador to the Holy See, Pignatti, the minutes of the conversation reached the hands of Pacelli. The Reichsmarschall, according to Pignatti, made clear that they were well aware that there were now five and a half million more Catholics in the Reich. 'Chancellor Hitler sees all this precisely and is truly inclined to follow a path leading to a religious peace – always, of course, presupposing clearly and exactly that religion and politics are two quite distinct things.'[633]

Göring spoke of the 'great chance for the Vatican' now to clear up relations with the Reich. Instead of weeping over the fate of Austria, the Vatican should take care that the Austrian clergy behaved loyally. Hitler had given orders that no further actions be undertaken against the Catholic Church. Then the conversation turned to Pius XI about whom Göring spoke 'with a certain sympathy and deep respect'. But (according to Pignatti) Göring 'had had the vague impression that the Pope seemed to make no distinction between communism and National Socialism!' Obviously Pius XI had made his estimate of the two dictatorships so clear that even Göring must have understood it.

The popular vote throughout the Reich of 10 April 1938 on the *Anschluss* with Austria ended with overwhelming agreement.[634] Even the Social Democrat Renner and the Austrian bishops, above all Cardinal Innitzer, supported the 'Yes' to the *Anschluss*.[635] The Roman Catholic Church had lost one of its model states of corporative organization, and looked anxiously at the forced ideological rapprochement of Italy with the Reich: at the beginning of 1938 the propagation of anti-Semitism began in Italy.[636]

Papen indeed succeeded in building up a certain relationship with the nuncio accredited in Vienna since 1936. But even this contact could not stop the Austrian bishops' conference reacting to the encyclical *Mit brennender Sorge* by making a public declaration of sympathy for the German cardinals and bishops; nor did they leave any doubt as to their rejection of Nazism: we know 'that many are troubled that conditions which have developed with you may arise also in our state and help Godlessness to triumph'.[637] Papen telegraphed to the German Foreign Office on this: 'Have left no doubt that given the close relations between episcopate and government well known among us such publications could not be without consequences for German-Austrian relations.'[638]

Despite their declaration of November 1937, and despite the close connection of the Christian corporative State with the Catholic Church that had left its mark in numerous official gatherings of leading politicians with the upper clergy,[639] the bishops capitulated two days after the *Anschluss*.[640] Through the mediation of Seyss-Inquart and Papen the Vienna Cardinal Archbishop Theodor Innitzer paid Hitler a visit at the Hotel Imperial on 15 March 1938. He made a declaration of loyalty coupled with the request for the preservation of the liberties of the Church guaranteed in the Austrian concordat; in reply the Führer assured him of good cooperation, and even thought 'this religious spring [might] have its effect on the old Reich'.[641]

The first disappointment was not long in coming. When the cardinal wished to publish the substance of the conversation in a short pastoral letter, he had to ascertain that the Austrian papers and the radio would not carry it. On 18 March the Austrian bishops gathered at an extraordinary conference in Vienna. Bürckel, who had announced his visit to those assembled for the purpose of making a statement, sent instead three 'special commissioners', among them Josef Himmelreich. They met the complaints of the clergy with understanding and then presented the draft of a declaration, which Innitzer had seen two days before, and which they were to sign.

The Prince Archbishop of Salzburg, Sigismund Waitz,[642] whom Innitzer had previously informed, made a series of objections to the official draft, and informed the nuncio Cicognani. The latter required that in the introduction to the piece a sentence be accepted, by which the Church would be assured of the preservation of its rights. Instead of this Bürckel asked for 'trust', and after some 'to-ing and fro-ing' carried his version. The declarations signed by Innitzer and Waitz from 18 to 21 March 1938 finally read:

> Preface to the solemn declaration of the Austrian bishops in the matter of the referendum. After detailed consultations the bishops of Austria, recognizing the great historical moment which the people of

Austria is experiencing, and conscious that in our days the millennial yearning of our people for union in one great empire of the Germans is finding its fulfilment, have resolved to send the following call to all faithful people. We can do this with the less hesitation as the Führer's commissioner for the referendum in Austria, Gauleiter Bürckel, has made known to us the honest line of his policy, which is to be headed by the motto: 'Give to God what is God's and to the Emperor what is the Emperor's'.

Solemn declaration! From deepest inward conviction and of free will we the undersigned bishops of the Austrian church province declare on the occasion of the great historical events in Germany-Austria: We acknowledge with joy that the National Socialist movement has done and is doing great things in the area of national and economic construction, and also in social policy for the German Reich and people, and specifically for the poorest strata of the people. We are also of the conviction that through the working of the National Socialist movement the danger of godless Bolshevism destroying all before it is averted. The bishops support the work for the future with their blessings and will urge the faithful to do the same. On the day of the referendum it is a self-evident national duty to confess ourselves as Germans to the German Reich, and we expect of all faithful Christians that they know what is due to their people.[643]

In the accompanying letter to Bürckel Innitzer reaffirmed that 'we bishops voluntarily and without compulsion have fulfilled our national duty', and affixed (after the kingdom of heaven had first taught him that in the old Reich it was the general custom) under the civil formula of greeting, above the signature, in his own handwriting, 'Heil Hitler'. Without the agreement of the bishops the documents were duplicated by the million before the referendum and fixed to the advertisement pillars.

Waitz, however, had such great reservations about the documents for which he had joint responsibility that he sent the Curia a memorandum on the proceedings. According to the will of the Holy See, the President of the Austrian bishops' conference, Innitzer, ought to speak and answer for it in Rome. Bürckel and the Führer's adjutant, Fritz Wiedemann, tried almost everything to keep the Cardinal in Vienna, even promising him a conversation with Hitler. But the nuncios Cicognani and Orsenigo, who were also staying in the city, made it clear to him that he could not postpone his journey. On 5 April he was received by Pacelli and worked out with him an explanation which was to 'correct and complete' the explanation of the Austrian bishops.[644] Despite Innitzer's 'greatest reservations' the text was published in the *Osservatore Romano* on 6 April and also broadcast over Radio Vatican. The official paper had already reported that the Austrian bishops had acted without the knowledge and agreement of the Vatican. The audience with Pius XI, also on 6 April, turned out correspondingly frosty.

It was best known in the Berlin diplomatic corps how much was riding upon Innitzer's journey to Rome. On 6 April Weizsäcker told his American colleague Wilson 'that the actual object of Innitzer's visit was to clear up the situation which had arisen through the commentary in the *Osservatore Romano* and the latest radio broadcast from the Vatican, and to stop an open breach being conjured up from these happenings'.[645]

Back in Vienna, Innitzer was confronted by the severe disappointment of Bürckel. In the evening before the referendum, Hitler himself said to him: 'I wanted a binding declaration given in respect of the Catholic Church in Austria. After this explanation in Rome I must keep my distance from it.'[646] Yet he promised the Cardinal after the elections a model agreement between the Church and the National Socialist State. From May 1938 therefore it was clear that Hitler would not acknowledge the Austrian concordat, and that the Reich concordat would not be extended to the 'Ostmark'. In the meantime the 'bridge-builders' (with whom Hudal was also working in the background)[647] under the leadership of Karl Rudolf Pischtiak had united into a 'Working Group for Religious Peace' and together with Bürckel and his people had sketched out a non-intervention agreement. Their piece, put out in July 1938, bore the title 'Solemn Common Declaration of the Party and Catholic Church in Austria for Cultural Peace'. The episcopate showed itself as in agreement in principle, but were willing to sign the declaration only after it had been approved by the Vatican.

Archbishop Waitz and the Foreign Minister of the short-lived Seyss-Inquart cabinet, Wilhelm Wolf, were received by Pacelli, who pointed out that his note on the question of the Austrian concordat had still not been answered. In view of the declaration they had brought with them, the Cardinal Secretary of State formulated an alternative draft which worked out the rights of the Church with greater precision and detail, and was thought of as a kind of new pre-concordat for Austria. Yet Bürckel was not ready to negotiate further on the basis of the Rome draft. Through a series of anti-church measures pressure was to be exercised on the Austrian episcopate to bow to Bürckel's wishes. After various modifications of the text of the treaty, which appeared unacceptable to the Vatican, the bishops' conference finally broke off the negotiations on the instructions of the Holy See at the end of August 1938. Three months later Hudal wrote further memorials advocating personal reshuffles in the Austrian episcopate and recommended adaptation to the 'historic phenomenon' of National Socialism.[648] He advocated a reduction in the Church's claims as the basis for a modus vivendi and for the Church itself to discipline clergy with political ambitions. Cardinal Schulte of Cologne and the Bishop of Trier, Franz Rudolph Bornewasser, who were questioned about Hudal's explanations, rejected his views as completely mistaken.[649]

In a 1938 report of the Berlin SD-Zentrale (the headquarters of the intelligence service of the SS) it says triumphantly that the Roman Catholic Church is facing 'breakup'. It has lost one of its most important territories. 'Through the foundation of the Dollfuss-Schuschnigg-regime the Church acquired after 1933 a legally anchored power of such a kind that Austria could be described as a Church-state. When Dollfuss and Federal President Miklas visited the Vatican in 1933 they venerated the Pope as feudal lord.'[650] All this was now finished.

Against the background of the *Anschluss*, the American embassy in Berlin thought in the spring of 1938 that Hitler would take pains for an arrangement with the Catholic Church in order not to imperil the integration of Catholic Austria into the Reich. At any rate ambassador Hugh R. Wilson doubted that this would ever be possible. 'Looked at theoretically, the question finally boils down to whether an ultimate reconciliation between two such competitive, totalitarian outlooks is in fact possible.'[651] Orsenigo too saw little possibility of a change in the situation. 'He said that the relations of Church and State remained more or less the same in the last year or so, and that he saw little ground to hope for an immediate improvement.'[652]

While the nuncio had few worries about the steadfastness of grown Catholics in the faith, the influence of the Nazis upon young people worried him a great deal. Orsenigo said that he never discussed Church questions with Hitler personally, but only with the Foreign Office and the Reich Church Ministry. 'Although Hitler is nominally still a confessing Catholic, he is not an active church-member and seems (in the papal nuncio's view) to have very little interest in the affairs of the German Church, for he leaves it to his governors [Statthalter] to run them.'[653]

The fatal consequences of Innitzer's unauthorized proceedings come out in the report of the American embassy in Warsaw of 14 April 1938 on the attitude of the Church of England. In the report destined for Washington DC it says 'that the Archbishop of Canterbury and Lord

Halifax, a leading figure among the "Anglo-Catholics", were very angry at the papal attitude. Both had been thought very keen to stay on the Vatican line, and had believed Innizter's declaration had been approved by the Pope. In this belief they had been encouraged to tolerate the *Anschluss* in silence.'[654] Everywhere the Catholic world was dominated by great excitement.

Not least because of this Pacelli wrote a memorandum to explain the Catholic attitude towards the *Anschluss* with Austria which he handed to the Catholic diplomat Joseph P. Kennedy, who from 1938 to 1940 was American ambassador in Great Britain,[655] when he visited Rome in April 1938.[656] Although the Cardinal Secretary of State described the statements in the text as his 'personal, private views' 'given for your confidential use', he empowered Kennedy expressly to bring them to the notice of the American President. Since their meeting in Washington at the beginning of November 1936, which Kennedy had arranged, Pacelli had enjoyed warm relations with Franklin D. Roosevelt.[657]

Kennedy sent the memorandum to the White House on 19 April 1938. In the paper Pacelli explained that the 'unexpected declaration [of the Austrian episcopate] immediately after the invasion of the country had been agreed by the Holy See neither previously nor subsequently'.[658] The bishops had obviously been under immense political pressure and hence omitted 'in the text of the declaration to refer to the basic principles of Church liberty and getting rid of anti-Christian propaganda'.[659] The Holy See had not hesitated to distance itself from the declaration with great tact, but with equal firmness. From this proceeding it is apparent 'that the Holy See will never be prepared to sanction any agreement of any bishop or any undertaking of any government which may be opposed to the law of God or to the liberty and rights of the Church'.[660] On relations between Germany and the Vatican Pacelli affirmed that there were indeed diplomatic relations. Nevertheless in their attitude to the Reich concordat there were severe differences.

The fact is that shortly after the concordat was signed the German government took up a more or less open attitude of defiance to all the clauses which had been acknowledged in the concordat. The Holy See has used all the means at its disposal to safeguard the freedom of the Church and of Catholics, and was always ready to bring about the best possible settlement so that any further bitter conflict may be avoided; it was always driven by the wish to prevent any further aggravation of the situation.[661]

After this clarification of the clearly bad relations between the Vatican and the Third Reich, Pacelli reminded the American diplomat of the considerations they had proposed two years before in the United States. These plans 'to ensure peace for all peoples' must now be pushed forward. Here he left no doubt that he saw the USA in a leadership role – a position which in his mind they had had since the First World War.[662]

> It would assist the world to this end, in the face of the present difficulties to consider the ever growing necessity to remain allied with the highest moral powers of the world, who come forward, for the time powerless and isolated, in their daily struggle against all kinds of political excess on the side of the Bolsheviks and the new heathen descended from the circle of the young 'arian' [sic] generations.[663]

Charles R. Gallagher, the historian of Boston, who found this document, links with his interpretation considerations of the gradual alteration of diplomatic style during the Pacelli era. Educated in the diplomatic customs of the late nineteenth century, the Cardinal Secretary of State vacillated between the maxims of a diplomacy at once discreet and secret and the beginnings of modern diplomacy, distinguished by open conferences, detailed debates and personal connexions between the leading diplomats. Hence Pacelli preferred to utter harsh criticism of the Nazi regime in personal conversations with high-ranking diplomats and Church people, and not to proclaim such views in public. 'Like many diplomats of his time he was not capable of breaking altogether with the old rules of diplomatic behaviour.'[664]

The Munich contemporary historian, Thomas Brechenmacher, has drawn attention to the fact that this document with its clear rejection of both Bolshevism and neo-pagan Nazism is not a solitaire.[665] In May 1938, just a few weeks after Joseph Kennedy, Mosche Waldmann, a delegate of the pre-state Jewish community in Palestine, visited the Holy City, to win it for his cause. Pacelli did not receive him, but through the Roman Chief Rabbi Prato, who was on constant conversational terms with the Cardinal Secretary of State, he got to know the attitude of the Holy See towards Nazism.

It was Prato's impression that the 'opposition of the Vatican to the neo-paganism of National Socialism [is] fundamental. Through this fact [thus David Prato] a peculiar psychological condition has developed, viz. a greater openness towards Jewish demands.'[666] Pacelli and Pius XI were now more ready to back Jewish interests, and had intervened to exercise restraint upon anti-Semitism in Polish Catholicism and upon anti-Semitic legislation in Hungary. The Curia was not ready to give strong backing to Waldmann's project, the foundation of a Jewish state in Palestine, but he could at any rate report to Jerusalem that the Holy See no longer gave support only to Catholics of Jewish descent, but also for Jews themselves.

In a third document from the year 1939 the former Berlin General Consul of the USA, Alfred Will Klieforth, reports his impression of a three-hour conversation with Pacelli. 'He [i.e. Pacelli] opposed from his side every compromise with National Socialism. He regarded Hitler as more than an unreliable scoundrel, he was a basically evil person. Despite the outward appearance he believed him incapable of moderation and he totally supported the German bishops in their anti-Nazi attitude.'[667]

3.15 The draft encyclical on racism

After the annexation of the Catholic corporative state by the Third Reich, Pius XI took up the question of the condemnation of racism once more.[668] On 22 June 1938 he commissioned the American Jesuit, John LaFarge, to compose an encyclical on the questions of nationalism and racism.[669] LaFarge requested the General of the Order, Count Wlodimierz Ledóchowski, for support from two scholars who should prepare the actual draft of the text. The choice fell on his brethren in the order, Gustav Gundlach and Gustave Desbuquois. They planned not a syllabus but a magisterial disputation in the style of the encyclical *Divini redemptoris*. Why the Pope did not commission the Holy Office and why there was no return to the corresponding pattern of the years 1935/36 is totally obscure.

The drafts of Gundlach and Desbuquois differed significantly from each other. For this reason all the versions – French, German and English – were handed over by LaFarge at the end of September 1938 to the Jesuit General. Whether Pius XI ever handled them is uncertain. Why Pacelli did not take them up when he became Pope cannot be answered from the sources at present available. Given the usual lengthy procedures and assessments in the Vatican many variants are conceivable. Gundlach, the actual author of the text, proposed to let the encyclical begin *Societatis unio* (The Unity of Mankind). Despite the somewhat 'heavy, academic style'[670] of Grundlach, his draft included principles which outdid all the previous work since the mid-1930s:

[T]he so-called Jewish question is in its essence a question neither of race, nor nation, nor affiliation to the state, but it is a question of religion, and, since Christ, a question of Christianity. [...] Today the Church sees only with indignation and pain how the Jews are treated on the basis of legislation which is contrary to the law of nature and does not deserve the honourable name of law. The very basic clams of justice and love are violated without shame and inhibition.[671]

In conclusion Gundlach referred back to the condemnation by the Holy Office on 25 March 1928 in which 'that quite special hatred which today is accustomed to go by the name of anti-Semitism'[672] is denounced. The meaning of this was that the Roman Catholic Church had not changed its opinion in the last ten years.

At the beginning of October 1938, a month after the submission of the draft, in the resolutions of the Gran Consiglio del Fascismo of Italy anti-Semitism was endorsed, and in mid-November a legal decree was issued – based, indeed, not on racial but on a national-cultural foundation.[673] By these measures Jews were excluded from the national community, and sent back into the ghetto. They could no longer attend public schools, visit public places, and marry non-Jews.[674] Whatever ideological land-slip underlay this reorientation becomes clear when it is observed that Mussolini, only four years before, had despised Hitler's racial theories as utter nonsense.[675] At the end of May 1934 he wrote again: 'Cult of Race at 100 per cent. Against each and all: yesterday against Christian civilisation, today against Latin civilisation, tomorrow perhaps the civilisation of the whole world!'[676]

Pope Pius XI, who already on 28 July 1938, on the occasion of a public audience, vigorously rejected the new Italian racism, complained that the concordat would be damaged by the proposed regulations about marriage. In secret conversations it was in fact secured that the article concerned was modified in the planned decree.[677] But this alteration did not include that marriages of converted Jews blessed in church would be recognized by the State. This conflict escalated up to the death of Pius XI on 11 February 1939 and was then set aside because Pacelli wanted every direct confrontation with Italy out of the way in order to be able to use Mussolini as a mediator with Germany and the Western powers.

Despite the growing rapprochement of fascist Italy with the ideology of National Socialism, striking differences remained. This became clear from a speech given by Roberto Farinacci, the leading figure of anti-Semitism within the fascist movement, on 7 November 1938, on the occasion of the opening celebrations of the Fascist Institute of Culture in Milan. In his lecture, entitled 'The Jewish Problem in the History of the Church', Farinacci sought to proclaim a peculiar Jewish policy, independent of Germany, which in his view was based upon an anti-Semitic Christian tradition. 'We establish quietly to the comfort of our own souls that when we as Catholics became anti-Semites, we owed this exclusively to the doctrines which the Church has mediated to us for 2000 years. [...] Rome is and will always be anti-Jerusalem.'[678]

Farinacci quoted for pages from the anti-Jewish writings of the Church Fathers and came to the conclusion that the 'aryan race principle' was 'considerably more strictly applied by the Jesuits [...] than in Germany'.[679] Under the influence of the ideals of the French Revolution, the Roman Catholic Church ceased to grow, so that many baptized Jews had been able to infiltrate deep into the clergy. But now the Fascist State had undertaken to solve the 'Jewish question'.

> We know that the spirit of Christianity is the greatest source of energy which sustains men and the European nations, and leads them in the struggle for the service of God. We are not willing that the Church should lose sight of its chief educational mission, and concern itself with political things which belong exclusively to Fascism. For Fascism obeys history and preserves and increases the heritage of Rome for those who come after us.[680]

The Nazi ideologists commented in the SD [Security Service] quite justly that the pro-German Farinacci had 'opened up [the problem] completely wrongly'. For to the Church it was always only a question of 'forcing Jews into baptism' by their measures.[681] The Catholic Church did not understand that the 'core problem' lay in race, but only wished to establish an 'international claim to Catholic culture'.

On the other side there was within Italian fascism always a hard-line anti-Semitic pro-Nazi movement which gathered round the semi-official daily paper *Il Tevere* and its editor Telesio Interlandi.[682] He had Mussolini's ear, and in his organ defended with the silent agreement of the Duce – even before 1933 – the anti-Semitic policy of Hitler. Count Ciano noted in the middle of September 1939 that the ultra-German sheet *Il Tevere* would be known in Rome only as 'Rheingold'.[683] Since a general anti-Semitism was not accepted in Italy, Interlandi accused all Italian Jews of Zionism.

Mussolini's position on racism altered after the Abyssinian war. If he had been previously reckoned as 'pro-Semitic', he thought in mid-May 1936 he must fight against the 'terrible danger' of racial mixture between Italians and Africans. This attitude did not of course concern the Jews, but it was something like an 'entry' into racist thought.[684] The book published in the autumn of 1936, *Il Razzismo*, by Giulio Cogni, a friend of Interlandi, denied indeed that there was a 'Jewish problem' in Italy. But because of its pagan content the Church put the book upon the Index in June 1937.[685] At the end of May 1937, Mussolini moved in several announcements into Interlandi's anti-Semitic course.[686] Finally, in agreement with Mussolini's directives, the anthropologist Guido Landra, likewise a supporter of Interlandi, formulated the *Manifesto della razza*. After Hitler's visit to Rome Mussolini dropped all the ambiguities which he had hitherto cultivated with a view to the 'race question'. On 14 July 1938 the *Manifesto della razza* was published in *Il Giornale d'Italia*.

3.16   Hitler in Rome, the Instruction against Racism and the Reich Pogrom Night 1938

Between 3 and 9 May 1938 Hitler paid his first visit to Rome.[687] The first meeting of the two dictators had taken place four years before in Venice, and at the end of September 1937 the Duce had visited Hitler in Berlin.[688] It was usual that heads of state who currently maintained diplomatic relations with the Holy See made use of their stay for an audience with the Pope. Even Reich Chancellor Brüning had had to submit to this unwelcome duty in 1931.[689] Pius XI wanted a visit of this kind,[690] hoping to clear up Church affairs in Germany face-to-face.[691] Yet the German diplomats strenuously advised against such a visit,[692] and declared that the meeting between the Führer and the Duce, given the background of the ideological alliance, was a visit to which the 'special character'[693] was attached and was not comparable with the usual state visits. Yet the papal secretariat of state made a last attempt through ambassador von Bergen even during Hitler's stay in Rome to hinder the 'very painful case of precedence' and move the Reich Chancellor to a visit in the Vatican.[694]

Even Hitler's host was apparently pained by the affront. The Italian chargé d'affaires in Berlin, Massimo Magistrati, spoke up for an audience, in order to avoid the impression that the German Chancellor was coming to Rome 'in an anti-Catholic attitude'.[695] A note of the Vatican of 3 May 1938 says that neither from the side of the Apostolic Nunciature in Berlin nor from the German embassy to the Vatican in Rome had any communication arrived on the possibility of a visit from the Chancellor to the Holy Father.[696]

In the run-up to the Hitler visit, which Mussolini had prepared with all pomp, the Vatican protested against plans festively to decorate even

church buildings to the honour of the German guest.[697] The Italian
government was anxious to avoid as far as possible the more sparsely
illuminated Vatican City on Hitler's and Mussolini's journey through
Rome; this of course could not be avoided in one case on technical and
traffic grounds.[698]

On the evening of 4 May a great rally of all Germans living in Rome
took place in the Basilica of Maxentius on the Forum to the honour
of their Führer, which Hudal also did not wish to miss. Without the
permission of the Secretariat of State he not only took part but also
forced himself close to Hitler, so that on the published photographs he
was clearly to be seen at his side.[699]

Given the just completed *Anschluss* Hitler's visit to Rome attracted all
eyes in diplomatic circles. Already in the run-up, the American embassy
in Warsaw speculated upon the repercussions of the conflict upon the
Axis powers:

> Mussolini was touched scarcely less painfully by the Berlin–Vatican
> dispute. It would become very difficult for him, to welcome the Führer
> to the Eternal City, unless his diplomacy (on which in this respect no
> pains were spared) succeeded from now on [14 April] to the beginning
> of May, in smoothing over some of the essential differences between
> the Nazi Reich and the Holy See. Thus Ciano had a report published
> in the press which suggested that the Pope would receive Herr Hitler
> on his visit to Rome. However, Pacelli immediately had a denial
> published, according to which the Pope intended nothing of the
> kind.[700]

The version propagated at the time was that the Pope would discretely
withdraw to his summer palace and simply ignore Hitler's visit to Rome.
It survives in many accounts to this day.[701]

In reality Pius XI waited until the penultimate day of Hitler's stay for a
sign from the Reich Chancellor. Then Ratti travelled to Castel Gandolfo,
leaving a message that he would return at any time to receive the Führer.
But it never came to this. For Hitler was not ready to give an explanation
which would have raised the prospect of a change of course in religious
policy.[702]

The American embassy in Rome reported on 18 May 1938 to Washington DC that it was not even known in the Vatican whether and
what efforts Mussolini had undertaken to improve relations between the
German government and the Vatican.[703] At any rate diplomatic circles
were counting on an intervention of this kind!

Despite all the differences, relations between the fascist state of Italy and the Curia were based on singular presuppositions. Only against this background is it comprehensible that, shortly before Hitler's visit to Rome, the Duce addressed the Jesuits and the Vatican middleman, Tacchi Venturi, even on the idea of an excommunication of the Führer, in order to break Hitler's firm anti-religious stance and to force him in the interests of the common struggle against communism to peace with the Vatican.[704] In crisis situations the 'collaborators' were accustomed to remind each other of what one had done for the other. Thus in September 1936 for example Ratti reminded the Duce of the support which he had received from Catholics in the Abyssinian campaign.[705] Mussolini was incensed that he had not succeeded in making the Church a tool, and the Pope was worried that a Catholicizing of Fascism had come to nothing. At a meeting of the Grand Council on 6 October 1938 Mussolini gave vent to his annoyance: 'I declare that this Pope has had a bad influence on the fate of the Catholic Church.'[706] Shortly afterwards he described the Vatican as a 'ghetto'.[707] In mid-December when with Ciano he got carried away in an 'outburst of wrath against the Pope' even to the point of remarking that he hoped the Pope 'would die at the earliest possible date'.[708] Yet both sides had an interest in finding a modus vivendi and this included the possibility that Mussolini would approach the German government as a mediator in religious affairs.[709] Hence the relations between the Holy See and fascist Italy bear no comparison with those between Hitler's Germany and the Vatican.[710] Of course it was hard for Pius XI to bear that Mussolini received the hateful blasphemer Hitler in the Holy City with all pomp. Did not the Duce here offend against the spirit of the Lateran treaties?[711] To Mussolini in contrast it seemed in foreign-policy terms unthinkable to put good relations with Berlin at risk for the sake of the Vatican. Hence Ciano and other Italian diplomats repeatedly advised the Curia to patience and moderation. The Pope should not contemplate 'extreme sanctions' like excommunication,[712] but on the contrary give more evidence of elasticity and readiness for compromise.[713]

When Hitler's visit was absolutely imminent, Pius XI resolved to give an instruction to the Congregation for Universities and Faculties, whose direction he had taken over, since the post of Prefect was vacant. From 13 April 1938 this instruction, which embodied a simple condemnation of the Nazi ideology of blood and race, was ready.[714] On 1 May 1938 the text appeared in *La Croix* and on 3 May 1938, on the day of Hitler's arrival in Rome, in the *Osservatore Romano*.[715] Pius XI had fallen back on the material of the Holy Office of 1935/36;[716] he had nevertheless produced a more cautious formula, presented only a small selection from the documents, and avoided express reference to Germany. According to the instruction, the directors of Catholic Universities and faculties were to reject the 'ludicrous' doctrines according to which 'race and purity of blood [...] must be preserved and cultivated'.

On 5 May 1938, Pius XI complained of the fact that on the day of the Holy Cross in Rome a cross will be put on show in Rome, which was 'not the cross of Christ' – but the crooked cross [swastika]. There is a series of references to the fact that in the last months of his life Pius took a different attitude to the Jews.[717] Thus he spoke on 6 September 1938 to Belgian pilgrims: 'Antisemitism cannot be tolerated. In the spiritual sense we are semites.'[718]

Peter Godman has described the departmental wrangling between the Dikasterien, the central administrative organs of the Roman Curia in the Vatican,[719] and against this background makes clear that the Congregation for Extraordinary Church Affairs, somewhat piqued at the Instruction to the Congregation for Universities and Faculties, reacted, because it fell primarily into their area of responsibility.[720] It was not only the European dictatorships which harboured polycratic structures but also those in the Vatican.

The Vatican was informed in detail about the pogrom night in the Reich on 9/10 November 1938 by a report from Orsenigo.[721] The Reich nuncio spoke of 'antisemitic vandalism'. The 'suspicion was that the order or the permission to act came from the top'; Orsenigo was right in his assessment of the origin of the pogrom. The diplomats had greatly concerned themselves with 'these vandalisms', and the representatives of Great Britain and the Netherlands 'energetically intervened to defend Jewish property' so far as it concerned their own citizens. Soon afterwards Orsenigo reported upon the possible consequences of anti-Jewish marriage legislation for converted Jews.[722] Despite these alarming reports the Vatican was silent and did not break off diplomatic relations with the Third Reich. They preferred rather to leave the initiative for this step to the Nazis, in order then to be able to use the situation morally for the Holy See: 'The world will then see that we have tried everything to live in peace with Germany';[723] this was Pacelli's thought at a meeting with German cardinals on 9 March 1939.

At the same time, a cautious political development is to be observed in which the course of the Vatican gradually distanced itself from political dependence on the authoritarian and totalitarian dictatorships and sought a cautious union with the Western democracies. There is no doubt that in this connection that Pacelli's contacts in the USA played a key role. Of course it must not be overlooked that the USA despite a large number of Catholic citizens – about 21,403,000 – at the end of the 1930s was reckoned a 'Protestant' nation, and Protestant circles reacted excitedly to the incipient diplomatic contacts with the Vatican.[724]

At the end of 1938 this reorientation of the Vatican left its mark on the diplomatic correspondence of the United States. Thus the Polish Foreign Minister Józef Beck reported to the American diplomat accredited in Warsaw, A. J. Drexel Biddle: 'The Minister [i.e. Beck] informs me that he has learned from a reliable source that an influential team in the highest Catholic circles of Rome is now pressing the Vatican to orient itself in its proceedings more strongly to the political attitudes of the democracies; the practical result of the concerns of this team remains to be seen. Yet there are signs that the campaign is gaining ground.'[725]

3.17 The death of Pius XI, the election of Pacelli as Pope and the threat of war

From the beginning of his eightieth year in the summer of 1936 Pius XI began to suffer the complaints and illnesses of old age. Events in Austria, Hitler's state visit to Rome and the growth of racism were further burdens on the weak health of the old man. At the end of November 1938 speculation in diplomatic circles increased over a possible successor to Pius XI, now seriously ill. At this time he suffered two severe heart attacks, from which he did not recover. Because of the Pope's poor condition of health the ability of the Vatican to do business was very greatly impaired.

When, on 10 February 1939, the Pope finally died, an atmosphere of the tensest attention reigned in the diplomatic world, and in the Catholic world as well. The wildest rumours of Ratti's last wishes went the rounds;[726] there was the greatest excitement about the election of the new Pope.

On 18 February the American embassy in Berlin reported to Washington:

> The election of the new pope will be awaited in Germany with burning interest both on the official side and in Catholic circles. It is imagined that this will be an affair of possibly powerful consequences for the future situation of the Church in Germany – whether indeed the choice falls on a pope who like his predecessor will stand up to Nazism or upon a so-called unpolitical pope. Moreover the belief here

is that the question of the future relations of the Vatican to authoritarian governments could themselves play a role in the choice.[727]

On the mood in Catholic circles it reports:

It is interesting to discover that in Catholic circles here the idea is going the rounds that in the event that an unpolitical pope is elected and it should be possible to bring all the groups in the German Church together, the opportunity could finally be seized to make peace with the state. However great the fundamental differences between Catholicism and National Socialism may be, the sense is that it may still not be too late to negotiate an agreement over something less than the conditions of the present concordat which could also be acceptable to the Church. It is noted that some Catholics here are convinced of the necessity of this undertaking because they are afraid that – should the present conflict drag on – the state could go so far as to confiscate church property.[728]

Under the impression of the imminent election of a pope, the Italian ambassador to the Holy See, Pignatti, and his German colleague von Bergen met on 18 February to exchange views. They were agreed that the attitude of the German cardinals would play a 'prime, indeed a decisive' role.[729] Pignatti once again made clear the desire of his government for improved relations between the Vatican and the Reich and asked his German colleague to use his influence to save the deceased Pope and members of the Curia from personal attacks in the German press.

In view of the succession the Roman Catholic Church abandoned a tradition centuries old: in a conclave of only a single day Pacelli was elected, although he had exercised power for years as Cardinal Secretary of State, had held the functions of Chamberlain of the Holy Roman Church since 1935,[730] and hence was not actually eligible.[731] Already Pius XI was of course said to have looked on him as his favourite candidate,[732] and had repeatedly sent his Cardinal Secretary of State abroad as a legate.[733] Alongside Pacelli's towering abilities, the elections of course also showed that in the Curia the political situation was regarded as so threatening that they should elect to the head of the Church a man with diplomatic experience and with a world-wide reputation already.

On 2 March, by chance his sixty-third birthday, the conclave decided for Pacelli on the third ballot. After more than two centuries a native Roman again represented the Church, and more than that: the nomination of the little-known diplomat Luigi Maglione[734] from Naples to be the new Secretary of State sent a signal to all the world that this Roman was determined 'to take all essential decisions in this perilous time in person'.[735] The handling of the 'German question' he had already 'expressly reserved' to himself.[736]

Through the Polish Catholic Press Agency KAP the election of Pacelli was received in Poland with great joy.[737] In an article 'From Pius XI to Pius XII' the German monthly *Das XX. Jahrhundert* [*The Twentieth Century*] commented on the papal election thus:

> A political pontificate! The continuation of that bold policy of concordats, of approaches in friendship to willing governments in great alliances. The most fought over and the strongest man of the Curia has taken over its leadership. This is one of the most remarkable adaptations to the spirit and forms of the twentieth century. Will Pius XII beat this epoch with its own methods?[738]

Nazi Germany observed the reactions of the democratic states to the death of Pius XI and the election of his successor with the greatest suspicion.[739] Especially the American, British and French press represented Pope Ratti as a 'friend of the democratic world' or a 'Roosevelt in a tiara' as *Il Giornale d'Italia* wrote in scorn,[740] and an outright opponent of National Socialism. In the eyes of the democratic states the autocratic Pope had been transformed on his deathbed into a liberal.[741]

While this view of things was scarcely comprehensible,[742] emphasis on the anti-racist attitude of the pope, documented by telegrams of condolence from leading Jewish personalities throughout the world,[743] appears very interesting. This perspective underlines that Ratti's initiatives against racism had obtained a wide publicity. His testimony of 6 September 1938, 'In the spiritual sense we are all Semites' and other aphorisms[744] and the Instruction against the Nazi blood-and-race ideology of Spring 1938 had obviously remained firmly rooted in the collective memory.

In the commentaries of Western statesmen and in the media there were clear expressions of a desire for continuity in the views of Ratti's successor. Logically the election of Pacelli was greeted in the democratic states with great jubilation. The *New York Times* of 3 March 1939 wrote: 'Today once more the Catholic Church, on the broad issue, stands side by side with the democratic peoples in defending the integrity of the human spirit and the brotherhood of mankind against the spiritual servitudes of the new barbarians.'[745] And the French communist

L'Humanité wrote a day later: 'It is Pius XII. Will he not along with the name also take up the work of that man whose colleague he was as a Secretary of State during the last years? For when it was a question of the nonsense of racial doctrine, Nazi persecution and the attacks of Fascism and freedom of conscience and human dignity, Cardinal Pacelli and the Pope were not to be separated'.[746]

In the Catholic part of the German people the election of Pacelli released unanimous and great rejoicing. According to the analyses of the SS-security service, it was particularly the French, American, Italian and Latin American cardinals who promoted the election of Pacelli. The German cardinals had at the beginning shown little inclination to opt for the former Reich nuncio. But since they could not produce an attractive candidate in opposition, they finally also changed front. Pacelli came from the school of Cardinals Rampolla and della Chiesa.

> We in Germany have nothing to expect from this Pope! He will try [...] to come to agreements; he will outwardly also be conciliatory – but beware! [...] When Austria came home to the Reich, he suffered his first great set-back. How he had depended on this 'Christian state', [...] how he relied on Prague, [on the fact] that the nomination of the Prague Archbishop Kaspar to be a cardinal was traced back to him alone! [...] And now everything is in his game of chess. [...] The Church under Pius XII will play at politics more than ever, but less raw and noisily than under Pius XI, finer, more discreet, more upright. Perhaps also more verbose.[747]

Almost the whole world sent special deputations to the enthronement of Pius XII on 12 March 1939. At the head of the Italian group stood the representatives of the Italian royal house, and for fascist Italy the Foreign Minister, Count Ciano. The National Socialist government was among the very few which did not send a delegation.[748] Yet after the election of Pacelli a new phase of détente in the relations between the Nazi State and the Catholic Church set in, which was immediately noted in diplomatic circles.[749] On 8 May 1939 Hitler had a long conversation with Orsenigo on the situation of the Catholic Church in Germany. On this the nuncio reported not only to the Vatican but also to his American colleague, Geist:

> According to that source Hitler took the opportunity to show a friendly and understanding attitude and gave grounds to hope that he would give attention to the problem of the Church. While there is

so far no positive sign of decisive steps being taken in this direction, and while resistance to an agreement friendly to the Church is to be expected from extremist circles in the party, the conversation will be looked on as significant for the improvement of the atmosphere in relations between the party and the Church, which began with the enthronement of the new Pope, and showed itself moreover in the armistice which has characterized the Church–State conflict during the last weeks.[750]

A few days later there was news from the American embassy in Berlin:

By virtue of information which the American consuls have received from Munich and Cologne where cardinals hold office, it has become clear that Nazi officialdom is exercising less political pressure on the Catholic Church, and the impression prevails that in the rest of the country – as is confirmed at least by observers in Berlin – interference has come to a stop. It is quite clear that the friendly style with which the Vatican has approached Hitler on the international situation has contributed in part to the improvement of the situation of the Church in Germany; it must, however, be admitted that at the moment there is no indication that the government of the Reich intends to react favourably to the diplomatic initiative of the Pope. In this connexion the Papal nuncio here told me in the course of a short conversation how Hitler had received the news of the Pope with great courtesy, news which had been brought over to Berchtesgaden by him [i.e. Orsenigo] and he has not rejected the representations which were made to him at that time. The nuncio at any rate added that the effect of the papal démarches will only be able to be inferred from the future course Hitler takes. Again it is not possible to determine whether the authorities of the Reich have partially altered their policy from respect for the Church, as, so to speak, a prelude for concern for a new agreement by revision of the concordat, or whether on the other hand they want to push through an armistice not merely on this account, because they want to get Catholic dissatisfaction out of the way during this critical moment in international affairs. According to reports of journalistic circles in Berlin the Pope is keen on an improvement of relations with Germany.[751]

In fact Pacelli used every opportunity which offered for de-escalation. After von Bergen had delivered the 'congratulations of the Führer and Reich Chancellor and the Reich government',[752] the Pope invited the

Ambassador to a private audience, in order to declare 'his warmest wish for peace between Church and State'.[753] In this connexion Pacelli made it clear once again that the form of government of dictatorship would not upset the relationship between the Vatican and the Reich. 'The church is not called to be a party in purely earthly things and purposes not to choose between various systems and methods which may come into question in overcoming the emergencies of the present day.'[754] To calm the situation both sides instructed the press to be cautious and objective.[755] Clearly encouraged by this development, Alois Hudal proposed an initiative for 'peace between Church and State in Germany' at the end of March 1939.[756] As a symbolic date for this step, he had in mind the jubilee of the Anima or Hitler's fiftieth birthday.[757] He gave vent to his anxieties over the threatened formation of a German national Church, and proposed the resumption of negotiations on the part of the German episcopate. The presupposition for the success of such concerns was of course the retirement of Faulhaber, a course for which he was ready. 'Any sacrifice will be good for the party. I am ready to be the Jonah, if the storm is then truly stilled.'[758] Again he found no positive echo for his proposal.

The Pope began his pontificate as 22 years previously he had begun his Munich nunciature – with a peace initiative. After the dissolution of the agreement between Germany and Poland[759] and of the German-British naval agreement in April 1939, he seized the initiative and proposed to the governments of France, Germany, Great Britain, Italy and Poland a five-power conference to settle European tensions.[760] The whole experience turned out to be one of déjà vu. For in the middle of May 1939 it became clear that none of the governments he approached had a real interest in a conference of this kind. Nevertheless the Pope required the papal nuncios to conduct uninterrupted conversations and report on them.[761] Thus Berlin received through the Italian government also the simple message that Great Britain would stand by its treaty obligations on the Danzig question.

Along with the intensive diplomatic activities, the Pope turned to his opponents in several addresses and counselled them to peace. In a radio address of 24 August 1939 he reminded governments that with 'peace [...] nothing was lost'. 'But with war everything can be lost.'[762] Again on 31 August Pius XII considered going to Berlin and Warsaw but gave up the idea and pleaded in a letter to the governments of Poland and Germany 'to avoid everything which could lead to any accidents and to take no measures which could aggravate the present serious tensions'.[763] He begged the governments of Great Britain, France and

Italy to support his efforts. Yet both sides had already ordered mobilization. On 1 September 1939 Hitler's armies invaded Poland.

The peace activities of Pius XII suffered – in the eyes of the democratic
states and their churches – from their diplomatic impartiality. After
Hitler's invasion of 'remaining Czechoslovakia' on 15 March 1939, the
Archbishop of Canterbury, Cosmo Gordon Lang, on the occasion of a
speech in the House of Lords, invited the Pope in the name of all the
Christian churches to lead an international protest movement against
the European dictatorships.[764] Since the end of June Paris had waited
in vain for a condemnation of the aggressors by the new Pope.[765] In
the end there were reactions in France to the Pope's broadly exercised
neutrality, with open polemic against the Church.[766]

On 24 August the French Ambassador in Rome, François-Poncet,
lodged a complaint in the office of the Cardinal Secretary of State,
and required a condemnation by the Vatican of the imminent German
aggression against a Catholic land.[767] Shortly afterwards the Polish
ambassador Papée demanded a similar statement. Two days later Papée
again asked that in the event of a German attack the Holy See might
declare on whose side justice and ethics stood.[768] On 28 August the
French ambassador proposed to the Pope to make a public declaration
in favour of Poland.[769] Yet the Vatican again refused, because it did not
want to appear partisan. Through the Holy See's constant pressure on
the Italian government to exercise influence on Berlin, their relations
to the government of Mussolini finally deteriorated also.

On 11 June 1940 shortly after Hitler's armies also marched into France,
the French curial cardinal Tisserant wrote to Cardinal Suhard: 'I fear
history will have to reproach the Holy See with having followed a policy
of convenience for itself and not much more. This is extremely sad,
especially for anyone who has lived under Pius XI.'[770]

If the beginning of the war is included, papal aspirations to societies with a Catholic structure in the heart of Europe had suffered a
cruel defeat. Almost all the political endeavours of the last twenty years
seemed to have failed. Arrangements with the atheistic Soviet Union
were not possible, Nazi Germany had revealed itself as Bolshevism
in another form, Italy, from an ideological viewpoint, increasingly
resembled its northern partner, and Hitler's Wehrmacht had totally
routed Catholic Poland; the land was crushed and incorporated in the
German and Soviet power blocs. How hopeless the situation was could
be seen from the fact that the Primate of Poland, Cardinal Hlond, emig-
rated in haste to Rome against the will of the Vatican. There remained
only Portugal and Spain – both of them weak states on the fringe of

Europe, and one of them economically and militarily dependent on Italy and Germany.

3.18 The 'Totality of the Divine Claim to Obedience', the authoritarian Catholic ideal of the State and the totalitarian states

When Peter Godman writes: 'Authoritarian or democratic, the form of the state was indifferent to the Church',[771] his thesis is only partly correct. Even apart from the fact that the Vatican State itself is a political structure under absolutist leadership, Ratti, an authoritarian personality par excellence, made no bones about his sympathy for 'Catholic states under strict leadership'. Democratic ideals like freedom, independence and individual initiative on the contrary he regarded as 'illnesses [on] the ailing body of Christendom'.[772] As a cure for such things he recommended Catholic institutions – schools, hospitals, banks and newspapers – and the union of Catholics in Catholic Action. His object was a Catholicizing of societies and the pressing of the respective states into the service of establishing Catholic ideals. He wanted to set up the power of Christ – a power which was to be acknowledged unconditionally by individuals and by society.[773]

In all this he knew that he was at one with his Cardinal Secretary of State. In the middle of July 1937 Pacelli said in an interview with the *Osservatore Romano*:

> The sooner and the more completely everyone acknowledges that between the mission of salvation peculiar to the Church of Christ and the progress and the greatness – even the earthly greatness, of nations there exists a sacrosanct, unalterable correlation, the more will the way be open to that divinely appointed harmony in the peaceable unity of each individual people and of peoples one with another, for which the contemporary world strives tirelessly but in vain, and which yet, the more difficult it seems to be to attain, the more it represents the most inward yearning and most glowing striving of all men of good will.[774]

Of course Pius XI exercised his spiritual rule not from his own perfection of power but at the behest of God. The dictators also laid claim to this boast for themselves. The dictators as well as the Church called upon the will of 'providence'.[775] But who represented the will of God better than the Church? She and she alone represented the power of Christ upon earth.[776] In so far as lordship remained firmly tied to salvation, the Pope sat with the others in temporal government.

A controversy between the nationalist Catholic Flemish People's Party and the Belgian episcopate at the beginning of 1930 illustrates the understanding of the Church prevalent among the Catholic clergy. To the objection of the bishops against their political course, the Volkspartei turned against the bishops and questioned their ecclesiastical authority in political matters. The episcopate thereupon issued a declaration in which it referred 'to the respect due to the Church [...] from the leaders of a party calling itself Catholic'.[777]

> Not to respect Church authority means to take up a position against Christ and his Church. You know the word of the Redeemer: 'who listens to you, hears me; who despises you, despises me; but who despises me despises him who sent me' (Luke X, 16). [...] If you venture to maintain that, when the bishops are against you, the highest Church authority approves Flemish nationalism and the common father of Christendom is with them, we reply without hesitation – and we know what we say – that you have lied. [...] This is how the sad story of all apostates generally begins. When the Pope had to condemn you publicly you still maintain that God is with you! [...] Much beloved brethren, fulfil your Christian duty: Turn from those who wish to lead you astray, and imperil your adherence to the Church! Avoid reading and supporting nationalistic daily and weekly papers [...].

At the level of practical lordship there was at any rate one distinction between the Vatican and the totalitarian states to which Godman refers: 'The Pope might be an autocratic ruler, but he was not absolute. More than a totalitarian dictator, he relied on his experts.'[778] And this situation, be it noted, had been reached gradually. In his first years of office Pius XI ruled high handedly as an absolute monarch; then he showed himself more open to the advice of his colleagues; and finally in his last years on grounds of health had in practice to leave many decisions to Pacelli. The period between 1937 and 1939 formed a kind of vacancy in the see.

The student of Fascism, Roger Eatwell, points out that the corporatism of the corporative state with its cooperative social institutions, as it developed in the encyclical *Rerum novarum* of Leo XIII in 1891 and was reinforced by Pius XI in the encyclical *Quadragesimo anno*,[779] exercised a great fascination on parts of Italian Fascism from 1922. 'Albeit the motives were very different, there was created here a direct point of contact with the important group of early Fascists who were converts from syndicalism.'[780] More than this, they forged the common critics of Catholicism and Fascism together: the weak liberal state and the anti-nationalist Left with its pre-bolshevist tradition of force.[781] Many Catholics saw in the Fascists those who had successfully defied the Left and established a stable conservative government in Rome. By this means, Mussolini achieved integration, absorbing rebellious groupings and Right-oriented parties into the governing coalition.

Only Fascism seemed to make it possible, to prevail against all the contemporary processes of decay at home and abroad, and restore a unitary, that is, pre-Reformation, medieval Christendom. The principles of the French Revolution, Liberalism, popular sovereignty, socialism, Enlightenment rationalism, parliamentarism, with its parties, materialism and egalitarianism – all this seemed to have triumphed but was now swept away at once by Fascism. After a catastrophic period of decline the law of God seemed to have triumphed over the rights of man.[782] Authority, hierarchy and order were back in vogue, and had created for the Church, the sole proprietor of Christian truth, once again the place in society appointed for it, indeed determined the social body as Christian once more.[783]

The Vatican made nothing at all of the concept of a plural society – on the contrary. The anti-liberal and monopolistic authoritarianism of Mussolini was no offence to the Pope so long as the regime permitted every freedom to Catholic Action, and guaranteed the Church its rights over family and education. The Holy See was buoyed up with the hope that in the authoritarian, hierarchical Fascist state it would achieve its own social and political ideals, that it would be able to Catholicize Fascism. The Catholic penetration of the body of the people was also the object of the religious hijacking of Fascist festivals such as the anniversary of the march on Rome.[784] The yearly commemoration of this event was ceremonially begun in the churches. In opposition to those Catholics – among them the conservative Bishop of Milan, Achille Ratti – who had openly supported the young Fascist movement, others condemned Fascism because in their view it was based on a dangerous radical ideology. Their most prominent exponent was Don Luigi Sturzo, the founder of the *Partito Popolare Italiano* of 1919. He it was also who coined the term *clerico-fascismo*. Sturzo contrasted the scenes of Fascist violence with the central values of the Christian faith and feared that Fascism intended to extinguish every kind of opposition. Calling upon Leo XIII's encyclical *Immortali Dei* (1885),[785] he spoke out in 1932 for a 'diarchy', a mutual cooperation of State and Church. Since Catholic political parties had become involved in democracy, they had contributed 'to the moral and political reform of various lands' and given birth to the system of 'Christian Democracy'.[786] In a 'hypercentralistic' state, by contrast, every freedom was lost because this regime claimed 'all social activities' for itself, and set up a 'dangerous monopoly of morality'.[787] It was these ideals of democracy and freedom on the one side and the readiness for joint action with the socialists on the other which produced the opposition between Sturzo and Pius XI.

Ratti, by contrast, after becoming Pope in February 1922, 'actively supported a politically united front against the Left, sharply reprimanding the Popolari; the latter were willing to ally themselves with the socialists and others against the meteoric rise of the Fascist party'.[788] In the destruction of the Partito Popolare the Fascist state and the Vatican worked 'hand in hand'.[789] Pacelli and Orsenigo pursued – though with much less success – a similar policy in Germany.[790] They also tried repeatedly to get the Centre Party to give up coalitions with the Social Democrats and replace them with the 'national' parties under the influence of the NSDAP. In Italy there were in the sphere of La Civiltá Cattolica groups of clergy who thought the Fascists had successfully absorbed the value of the Partito Popolare Italiano and thus made the Christian party superfluous.[791]

When the Fascists established a dictatorship in 1926, the Catholic hierarchy (according to Eatwell) gave them their consent. Already they had been thankful for previous concessions from the Fascist state – for example, for the introduction of religious instruction and the hanging of crucifixes in class rooms. Miccoli mentions further help from the fascist state: the making available of three million lire for the restoration of war-damaged churches, the building-up of priest's stipends, gifts to the Vatican and the rescuing of the Bank of Rome in January 1923.[792] The atmospheric disturbances two years after the conclusion of the Lateran treaties were occasioned by the subversive, squadristic[793] and anti-clerical wing of the Fascist Party.

Against this background it is not surprising that the Curia in dealing with the NSDAP stuck tenaciously to the hypothesis of a radical wing; on this view, the anti-Church features of the party's policies could be ascribed to radical forces which Hitler, Göring and other 'moderates' were not able to restrain. Despite the uncontestable detailed knowledge of Germany and Nazism which a man like Pacelli doubtless possessed, the Italian style of the Vatican remained unmistakeable.

Roman conditions, especially experiences with Italian Fascism, moulded the political guidelines of the Holy See – even in relation to Germany.

During the Abysinnian War as during the Spanish Civil War the Church continued to give the Fascist regime significant ideological support. 'However, historians are not agreed how large or how useful that "consensus" was; in general it seemed to rest more on passive acceptance than upon fanatical and active support of the Duce, not to mention the increasingly corrupt PNF.'[794] After 1936, Italian Fascism got closer ideologically to the Nazi State, but this produced no breach with the Vatican – a development for which the radicals in the Fascist Party may perhaps have hoped.[795] Pius XI at any rate fought the 'Rome–Berlin axis' between 1936 and 1939, because he saw that the alliance between Fascism and Nazism endangered the religious peace in Italy and with it an important part of his life's work – the Lateran treaties.[796]

Eatwell has no doubt 'that Pacelli encouraged the Centre Party to dissolve itself and to accept the Nazi Dictatorship'.[797] He sees the future Pope as representative of the chief line of German Catholicism: he supported neither the Catholic opposition nor those forces in the Catholic Church which wanted a synthesis with National Socialism.

While the Western constitutional states barred the State from putting or answering the religious question, in the ideological dictatorships the states themselves developed the responsibility for the religious question, since they – or the appropriate department of the ideological party – developed a 'political religion'.[798] The corporative type of state claimed the right to answer the religious question and laid claim also to a Catholic ethic of the political based on natural law. The Vatican itself supported it in this attitude, for it had thus a guarantee that these states were based on a 'Catholic ideology' and in practice left the whole system of values and education to the Church. This was the precise distinction between the authoritarian 'Catholic' states and the Fascist states proper. Even where, as in Italy, the Church was accepted as an important cultural entity, the State wanted to pursue its own cultural policy, based upon ideals other than those of the Church.

Antonio Canepa, one of the leading philosophers of Fascism,[799] emphasized in 1937 the universal claims of his movement.[800] Citing the Duce, he distinguished between Fascism as a universal idea and its national realization. Not all the principles of Fascism possessed a universal character but only the 'spiritual, intellectual values, such as patriotic feeling, feeling of duty, the feeling for the heroic life [...], because they represent a moment in the history of the human spirit'.[801]

Canepa distinguished between universality and totality:

> If it is said that the fascist doctrine is totalitarian or integral, this
> means that its principles relate to all the activities of men. [...] Fascist
> principles are totalitarian in so far as they embrace all areas in their
> totality, all the problems which beset the human spirit. [...] What
> Fascism understands by values is altogether totalitarian, yet in a signi-
> ficance which does not coincide with that on behalf of which it is
> universal. It is observable [...] that the totalitarian character is not
> peculiar to the value-principles alone, but to all doctrinal principles:
> it is a question of a peculiar attribute of doctrine instead of the indi-
> vidual principles of which it is composed.[802]

The dogmaticians of the Vatican could not have spoken more
precisely. Giulio Ulderigo Bruni sought in 1939 to work out the positive
'essence of the totalitarian state', setting up an all-embracing concept
of politics. 'The totalitarian state is the empire of integral politics'; it
'includes in itself the totality of the manifestations of social life, which
is orientated, guided and dominated entirely to political ends. [...] The
community of blood, the community of labour, the community of ideals
represent the natural and organic foundations on which alone the total
state can rise'.[803] It was thus a reciprocal misunderstanding if the Vatican
and the Fascist State in practice thought that there was a possibility of
delimiting one sphere of influence from the other. The historian Lutz
Klinkhammer (German Historical Institute in Rome) shows in detail
that 'in the course of the 1930s there was doubtless a Christianising of
Fascism, [...] but Italian Catholicism became tarred in the same degree
with the Fascist brush'.[804] The political claim to totality of the Fascist
State extended deep into the sphere of the religious, as the Fascist
'liturgy', the cult of the dead, the special rituals, the religious veneration
of Mussolini and the 'martyrs' of the movement, the elevation of Fascist
ideology to the status of dogma, sufficiently verify.[805] And in all this
National Socialism emulated it.[806]

Conversely the religious claim to totality of the Holy See forced its
way deep into the area of the social and political, for by calling on
the law of God and the law of Nature, it legitimated comprehensive
claims to shape the common life. In the framework of this tense coexistence it came – for example, in connection with the Ethiopian war –
some times to alliances; but, because of practical competitiveness, it
also came to conflicts – as in 1931 because of Catholic Action. The
one-sided emphasis on conflicts 'arose already in 1944, in order to free

Catholic Italy from the reproach of collaboration with Fascism'.[807] The reasons that the Vatican became so intimately involved with Fascism, Klinkhammer thinks, were the advantages to the Roman Catholic Church in the middle and longer term. '*À la longue* the *ventennio fascista* signified protection against laicism and implied a recatholicisation of the country, which found its high point only in the excommunication of the communists in 1949 and Pius XII's moralisation campaigns in the early post-war years.'[808]

Although the Vatican was concerned for political reasons for a rapprochement with the democratic constitutional states, its isolation from the modern state and modern society remained. At the level of theology and ideology it continued to support the authoritarian overthrow of modern individualism and the democratic parliamentary systems. Both before and after the evolution of the Christian corporative state with a single state religion guaranteed by concordat – as was the case in Austria and Spain – the political ideal of the Holy See remained the same, even when it repeatedly proclaimed its ability to fit in with every form of government. Hudal's 'golden mean' between democracies and dictatorships did not apply, for the Christian corporative states were authoritarian regimes. Their practical support by the Church permits the conclusion that Catholicism had a simple preference for this form of government.

This continued close identification of Church and State was not an arbitrary decision of the pope but was inherent in the Catholic concept of the Church.[809] A church which concentrated on the sacramental mediation of salvation must be concerned to keep this function going under all circumstances. In order to lead men to salvation, social institutions guaranteed by the State and grounded in dogma (the Christian school, the Christian family, the Christian ethic of individual and society) – not to mention the Christian understanding of the State – were necessary. At the same time, everything must be kept away from believers which might imperil their way to salvation – even if it could only be done by force. By the standard of eternal salvation and its visible endangering, all earthly freedoms shrank to the proportions of marginal entities or swelled to extremely problematic potentials for danger which must hence be excluded.

A plural social model which itself exercised a philosophical abstinence and could allow several understandings of the meaning of man, the world and life to subsist beside each other could not satisfy the Church's claim to the truth. Pius XI stood in a clear line of anti-modernist tradition, which could scarcely allow doubt in this view of things to arise. But a totalitarian regime like Soviet Russia, which had shown itself as simply anti-Church and hence made the saving function of the Church practically impossible, must encounter the decided rejection of the Vatican. However different the motives might be, there were in these political and ethical fields great agreements and common fronts with the 'national movements'. The realized common ground created the impression in the crisis-ridden conditions of the 1920s and 1930s that the obvious differences between Italian Fascism, German National Socialism and the Church were rather small.

This background explains why the Vatican agreed to Italian Fascism and to Hitler's takeover of power in 1933. Against every probability the wheel of history seemed culturally to turn back again and to offer against all hope the opportunity of correcting all the mistakes from the Reformation via the Enlightenment to the philosophically neutral liberal state. In this the Vatican did not take up an 'extreme' position; it saw itself within the Catholic world between the forces 'made sick' by the democratic spirit of the age of political and parts of social Catholicism on the one side and the energetic 'bridge-builders' to dictatorship on the other. Both must be domesticated by 'rechurching' or 'depoliticizing', and, if this did not succeed, then if necessary they must also be made harmless. From this perspective the end of the Catholic parties weighed none too heavily.

In contrast, the Right Catholic ideology of the Reich threatened to undermine the last reservations of the Vatican towards dictatorship, and to lead to an identification with the 'new Reich' which was bound to colour Catholicism brown. Anti-democratic and anti-pluralistic sentiments were here at home, Christianity was seen as the antithesis to democracy and as a guarantor for the authoritarian state. As Klaus Breuning summed it up already in 1969, the idea of a *sacrum imperium* [holy empire] 'performed as a political theology an unintended delivery service for the Third Reich'.[810]

On the side of the Vatican, unlike that of the national Catholicisms, it is mostly not possible to establish excess religious legitimation in the sense of a 'political theology'.[811] On the contrary: rational analyses and in principle an emotional distance towards the dictators determine the picture. Unlike in German Protestantism, for example, there is scarcely a trace of nationalistic 'intoxication', of partial conversion to National Socialism or Fascism.[812] Rather when political decisions had to be made cool considerations of utility were in the foreground.

In view of the potential for analysis released through studies of the Holy Office, the discrepancy between this fund of knowledge on racism, totalitarianism and nationalism on the one side and on the other the political decisions of the Secretaryship of State apparently largely untouched by them is conspicuous. One cannot avoid the impression that the rich background knowledge at the disposal of the Holy See for political action remained practically unused. At any rate no inner connection between theological reflection and political action can be established. These findings strengthen the impression of double vision in the Roman Catholic Church: faith and power, bound together in an institution, fall apart when it comes to practical application.

One cause for this remarkably unconnected coexistence could lie in the self-imposed limitation of theoretical considerations to the field of the relations of State and Church. The 'divine or natural law' seems not to develop anything else even in relation to the 'common good'.[813] There was no consideration given to various forms of government and their social and political implications, although the rapprochement with the democratic constitutional states of the West, mentioned above, might have suggested such a train of thought.

'The Catholic Church has bound its fate with that of Fascist politics',[814] wrote the Protestant theologian Reinhold Niebuhr, in 1938 in the *Christian Century*, thus expressing the discomfort of a majority of American citizens over the policy of the Vatican and the swing to the right of American Catholics.[815] Many liberals in the USA sympathized with the Mexican President Plutarcho Calles, and regarded his *laïque* policy as a just reward for the fanatical bigotry of the Mexican Catholic Church. By contrast the Holy See was at odds with the passivity of the USA. Already at the beginning of January 1927 Cardinal Secretary of State Gasparri said it was to him 'inconceivable that they [i.e. the government of the USA] should tolerate in their immediate neighbourhood such excesses of fanatical hate against the Church [...], when it would only require a nod on their side, to put a stop to the trouble'.[816] The anti-Church policy of Mexico was preparing 'the ground for Bolshevism'.

A request of Pacelli, occasioned by Gasparri, to the German government, to intervene with the Mexican government, was rejected in Berlin.[817] The protest meetings against Mexican religious policy organized by German lay Catholics and by the episcopate in various large cities[818] had already led to diplomatic reactions by the Mexican government.[819] The Catholic clergy in the United States also delivered declarations on persecution of the Church in Mexico.[820] One of the things which told against the Catholic presidential candidate Al Smith[821] was the fear of many electors that he would influence American policy towards Mexico in the direction desired by the Vatican. The Catholic minority in the USA had a hard job to defend the Vatican because Pius XI and his Cardinal Secretary of State viewed 'the processes of compromise and negotiation which were native to the democratic form of polity with suspicion, and preferred concordats which were dedicated to the protection of Catholic interests to the support of independent Catholic groups'.[822]

Similar reservations were made by liberal Democrats in the USA against Vatican policy in Germany and Italy, and against the attitude of the Catholic Church in the Spanish Civil War. The journalist Herbert Matthews judged that this conflict divided the USA along religious and political breachlines as had no other.[823] In a manifesto published in New York in 1937 entitled *American Democracy vs. the Spanish Hierarchy* it says: 'We cannot avoid being disturbed by the fact that no leaders of the Catholic Church in America have raised their voices to reject the attitude of the Spanish hierarchy.'[824]

Taken together all these observations had the cumulative effect that in the perception of democratic America there were obvious 'connections between Catholicism and Fascism'.[825] The 'Church has chosen to ally itself with democracy's chief enemy, fascism',[826] wrote Lewis Mumford in mid-May 1938, expressing the view of a broad majority in the United States. The stubbornness of Catholics towards civic liberties seemed to Americans to confirm their thesis that they had a certain affinity with Fascism. The sociologist John Mecklin explained in 1938 that the Catholic Church harboured only little sympathy for the democratic ideas of free speech and favoured a 'medieval concept of freedom'.[827] Various scholars, among them the sociologist Talcott Parsons, reproached the Catholic Church with wanting to limit academic freedom.[828] From 1937/38 the situation was aggravated by fears in the USA of a Nazi or Fascist coup in the Catholic states of Latin America.[829] Fascism moved ever closer to democratic America; it was no longer a distant European problem. That there was indeed the intention on the side of the European dictators to make use of the Vatican and the Catholic population of America against liberal America emerges from an exchange of information between Ciano and Franco. According to this, the Caudillo proposed to the son-in-law of the Duce in the summer of 1939 that they should mobilize the Catholics of America against a re-election of Roosevelt.[830] The German Foreign Office took up these suggestions[831] and asked von Bergen 'whether we should not through our ambassadors in Madrid and at the Quirinal go to the Spanish and Italian governments with the request that they through their representatives at the Vatican should give an invitation to appropriate action to influence American Catholics'.[832]

There were similar reservations towards the Vatican in Great Britain as in the USA, and especially in the Church of England.[833] Thus, for example, Sir Charles Grant Robertson, Vice-Chancellor of Birmingham University, wrote to the Bishop of Chichester, George Bell: 'For the politics of the Vatican are ultimately determined by high political considerations and, to speak plainly, the Vatican will not separate the purely religious problem from its politics either in Italy, where it has in fact capitulated to Mussolini, or in Spain or elsewhere.'[834]

To many in Britain the relation of politics and religion in Roman Catholicism seemed unclear. The politics of the Vatican were taken as 'exceedingly opportunistic and resting on general temporal considerations in which the Vatican is continually immersed'.[835] The Pope was driven by a deep fear of communism, 'so far as the purely political side is concerned, his personal sympathies lie with the Fascist states'.[836] On these grounds it could be accepted with assurance that he would take an extremely cautious position when it was a question of judging a dictatorship which understood itself as a bulwark against Bolshevism. In the Anglo-American countries Pius XI was reckoned more or less as a fellow-traveller of the authoritarian or totalitarian states, and as no friend of the democratic constitutional states. Such an assessment was bound to put sharp limits to the trust of these states in the Holy See and its policy.

In fact the relation of the Catholic Church and liberal democracy formed the central problem in view of the relationship of the Church and the corporative state, Fascism and National Socialism. Even the forming of a Christian democracy with a corresponding party structure encountered resistance from the Holy See and repeatedly issued in defensive movements.[837] Even after the arduous recognition of democracy in 1944 by Pius XII,[838] he sought to construct another exclusive connection of this form of state to Christianity. Such bracketing strategies concealed the danger of 'debasing the really existing pluralistic democracies by confrontation with normative-natural-law or special Church-Catholic postulates, and by this means to lead again to expecting from these special viewpoints better relations from authoritarian regimes'.[839] Ernst-Wolfgang Böckenförde, who studied the problem of this Catholic political thought already at the beginning of the 1960s came to this judgement on its denial in principle of historically developed realities: 'This is the inner process of thought of every ideology.'[840]

It is – despite all the Christian-democratic and liberal-Catholic roots in the nineteenth and early twentieth centuries – impossible to mistake that, when the rapprochement of the Catholic Church with democracy took place after 1945, it was a question of a movement indebted to altered conditions of power, and catching up with them, and not of a new orientation springing from its own strength and insight.[841] Again in 1845 Adolfo Omodeo in an essay on *Totalitarismo cattolico* could write: 'Noone [...] should ignore the circumstance that the first and oldest totalitarianism is that of the Catholic Church. [...] The Church as part of the universality of things demands for itself the right and the boast of totality. Of course this violent and material demand for totality had the consequence of the persecution of unbelievers, heretics, schismatics [...]'.[842]

Abbreviations

AA	Auswärtiges Amt
AA.EE.SS.	Affari Ecclesiastici Straordinari
AAS	Acta Apostolicae Sedis
Abt.	Abteilung
ACDF	Archivio della Congregazione della Fede
ADAP	Akten zur deutschen Auswärtigen Politik
ADSS	Actes et documents du Saint Siège relatifs à la seconde guerre mondiale
AHP	*Archivum Historiae Pontificiae*
ANM	Archivio della Nunziatura Apostolica in Monaco
APuZ	*Aus Politik und Zeitgeschichte* (Beilage zu *Das Parlament*)
ASI	*Archivio Storico Italiano*
ASMAE	Archivio Storico-Diplomatico del Ministero degli Affari Esteri italiano
ASS	Acta Sanctae Sedis
ASV	Archivio Segreto Vaticano
BA	Bundesarchiv
BayHStA	Bayerisches Hauptstaatsarchiv München
Bearb.	Bearbeiter (editor)
Best.	Bestand
BVP	Bayerische Volkspartei
CC	*La Civiltà Cattolica*
Cf.	Confer
ChC	*Christian Century*
CIC	Codex Iuris Canonici
cit.	Cited, citation
CRST	*Cristianesimo nella Storia*
CŠR	Republic of Czechoslovakia
DDI	I Documenti diplomatici italiani
DDP	Deutsche Demokratische Partei
DHI	Deutsches Historisches Institut
Dipl.	Diploma
Diss. phil.	Dissertatio philosophiae
DNVP	Deutschnationale Volkspartei
Doc.	Document
DÖV	*Die öffentliche Verwaltung. Zeitschrift für öffentliches Recht und Verwaltungswissenschaft*
DVP	Deutsche Volkspartei
EAM	Erzbischöfliches Archiv München
EDG	Enzyklopädie deutscher Geschichte
Emo.	Eminentissimo (Highest Eminence)
Ew. H. E.	Eure Hochwürdigste Eminenz (Your Highest Eminence)

f./ff.	following page/following pages (or years)
fasc.	fascicolo (file, dossier)
FAZ	*Frankfurter Allgemeine Zeitung*
fol./fos	folio/folios
GuG	*Geschichte und Gesellschaft*
HJ	*Historisches Jahrbuch der Görresgesellschaft*
HKG	*Handbuch der Kirchengeschichte*
Hl.	Heilig (Sacred, Saint)
HPM	*Historisch-Politische Mitteilungen*
HZ	*Historische Zeitschrift*
JCH	*Journal of Contemporary History*
JHK	*Jahrbuch des Historischen Kollegs München*
JMIS	*Journal of Modern Italian Studies*
KAP	Katolickie Archiwum Państwowe (Catholic Press Agency in Poland; existed until 1948)
KPD	Kommunistische Partei Deutschlands
KZ	Konzentrationslager (concentration camp)
KZG	*Kirchliche Zeitgeschichte*
Lfd. Nr.	Laufende Nummer (shelf number)
LPL	Lambeth Palace Library London
LThK	*Lexikon für Theologie und Kirche*
MS	Manuscript
Msgr	Monsignor (Title of high Catholic clergymen)
MSPD	Mehrheits-SPD
NA	National Archives at College Park, MD (Archives II) Washington DC
NDH	*Neue deutsche Hefte*
NL	Nachlass (literary remains)
NS	National Socialism, National Socialist (Nazi)
NSDAP	Nationalsozialistische Deutsche Arbeiterpartei (National Socialist Party)
NZZ	*Neue Züricher Zeitung*
OP	Ordo Predicatorum (Dominikanerorden)
OSB	Ordo Sancti Benedicti
PA/AA	Politisches Archiv des Auswärtigen Amtes
PCE	Partido Comunista de España
PNF	Partito Nazionale Fascista
Pos.	Position
PPI	Partito Popolare Italiano
r	recto (front of a folio page)
Rev.	Reverend
RGBl.	Reichsgesetzblatt
RQ	*Römische Quartalsschrift*
R.V.	Rerum Variarum
SA	Sturmabteilung (armed and uniformed branch of the NSDAP)
SCont	*Storia contemporanea*
SD	Sicherheitsdienst des Reichsführers SS
SdZ	*Stimmen der Zeit*
SJ	Society of Jesus (Jesuits)

S.O.	Sant'Offizio (Holy Office)
SPD	Sozialdemokratische Partei Deutschlands
St	Saint
StSt	*Studi Storici*
TMPR	*Totalitarian Movements and Political Religions*
TRE	*Theologische Realenzyklopädie*
USA	United States of America
USPD	Unabhängige SPD
USSR	Union of Socialist Soviet Republics
UTB	Uni-Taschenbücher
v	verso (back of a folio page)
VB	*Völkischer Beobachter*
VfZ	*Vierteljahrshefte für Zeitgeschichte*
VKZG.F	Veröffentlichungen der Kommission für Zeitgeschichte, Reihe B: Forschungen
VKZG.Q	Veröffentlichungen der Kommission für Zeitgeschichte. Reihe A: Quellen
Vol.	Volume
WRV	Weimarer Reichsverfassung (Constitution of the Weimar Republic)
WuW	*Wissenschaft und Weisheit*
ZaÖRV	*Zeitschrift für ausländisches öffentliches Recht und Völkerrecht*
ZevKR	*Zeitschrift für evangelisches Kirchenrecht*
ZfO	*Zeitschrift für Ostmitteleuropa-Forschung*
ZfP	*Zeitschrift für Politik*
ZKG	*Zeitschrift für Kirchengeschichte*
ZRG KA	*Zeitschrift der Savigny-Stiftung für Rechtsgeschichte. Kanonistische Abteilung*

Notes

Preface

1. German title: *Der Stellvertreter*. Published as *The Deputy* in the United States.
2. Cf. J. Cornwell, *Hitler's Pope*; G. Miccoli, *Dilemmi*; M. Phayer, *Pius XII*; S. Zuccotti, *Vaticano*.
3. Cf. S. Friedländer, *Pius XII*; G. Lewy, *Katholische Kirche*.
4. Cf. D. J. Goldhagen, *Moral Reckoning*; see also G. Besier, *Pacelli*.
5. See e.g. D. I. Kertzer, *Popes*; J. Carroll, *Constantine's Sword*.
6. Cf. G. Grössl, *Papst Pius XII*; R. Rychlak, *Hitler*; J. Sánchez, *Pius XII*; P. J. Gallo, *Pius XII*.
7. Cf. R. Morsey, *Ende*.
8. Karl Jaspers to Hannah Arendt, 29 October 1963, in L. Kohler/H. Saner (eds), *Hannah Arendt/Karl Jaspers, Correspondence*, 526–8.
9. H. Arendt, *Stellvertreter*, 114 (own re-translation).
10. K. Jaspers, *Stellvertreter*, 472.
11. Cf. W. Brandmüller, *Streit*, 371–81.
12. In a letter of 25 June 2004 Walter Brandmüller, President of the Papal Committee for Historical Science in Rome, informed the authors that the 'Commission which has to report on access to the archive of the Anima College [...] does not see itself in a position' to answer the proposal, 'since the presuppositions for access to the documents were not given'. Cf. also Chenaux, *Pacelli, Hudal*.
13. In German P. Blet, *Papst Pius XII*.
14. H. Tittmann Jr, *Inside*.
15. Cf. J. Bottum/D. G. Dalin (eds), *Pius War*; M. L. Napolitano/A. Tornielli, *Papa*; A. Tornielli, *Ebrei*; M. L. Napolitano, *Pio XII*; J. G. Lawler, *Popes*.
16. J. Bottum, *End*.

1. The German and European policy of the Vatican 1904–20

1. Cf. here and for the following Ph. Chenaux, *Pie XII*, 21–34; M. Feldkamp, *Pius XII*, 8–10; H. Hoberg, *Papst Pius XII*, 9–28; M. Marchione, *Consensus and Controversy*, 18ff.
2. Cf. St. Samerski, *Primat*, 6.
3. Cf. W. Sandfuchs, *Aussenminister*, 94ff.
4. Cf. H. Tüchle, *Pietro Kardinal Gasparri*.
5. After the death of Pius X, the 'progressive' cardinals hoped that Gasparri would succeed him. Cf. G. Schwaiger, *Papsttum und Päpste*, 162.
6. Cf. E. Pacelli, *Personalità*.
7. Cf. G. Schwaiger, *Papsttum und Päpste*, 187–8.
8. Ibid., 161–92 et passim; A. Melloni, *Konklave*, 82ff.

9. Cf. *Livre blanc du S. Siège.* See also K. Rothenbücher, *Trennung.*
10. Cf. R. Astorri, *Diritto comune.*
11. The example of Portugal shows what changes – in this case, from a laicist state to a Catholic state of order – were possible. See more on this below, Chapter 3.3.
12. Cf. on this E. Nolte, *Faschismus,* 102–6; J. Prévotat, *Catholiques,* 280ff.
13. Cf. below, Chapter 2.2.
14. Cf. A. Melloni, *Konklave,* 73ff. See also L. Wahrmund, *Exklusive.*
15. On the tense relations between Italy on the one side and the German Reich and Austria-Hungary on the other on account of the latter's continued possession of areas in northern Italy, cf. DDI 4, Vf.
16. Cf. on the *Osservatore Romano,* F. Rossi, *Vatikan,* 85–6; F. Sandmann, *Haltung.*
17. Cf. A. Melloni, *Konklave,* 79ff.
18. Cf. Ph. Chenaux, *Pie XII,* 56–7.
19. Ibid., 49–50.
20. Cf. also ibid., 52–3.
21. Thus G. Schwaiger, *Papsttum und Päpste,* 155.
22. Ibid.
23. Cf. J. Cornwell, *Hitler's Pope,* 48ff.
24. H. Batowski, *Bestimmungen.*
25. On this and the following, see Ph. Chenaux, *Pie XII,* 76–84; H.-J. Härtel/R. Schönfeld, *Bulgarien,* 170ff.
26. Cf. on this and the following A. Rigoni, *Concordato.*
27. Cf. R. Astorri, *Diritto comune,* 687 n. 9.
28. Cf. M. Feldkamp, *Pius XII,* 19.
29. Cf. Th. Grentrup, *Rechtslage,* 144–7.
30. Cf. J. Schmidlin, *Papstgeschichte,* vol. 3/1, 19–195.
31. Cf. AAS 6 (1914), 565–81.
32. Cf. M. Jürgs, *Frieden,* 68, 294–6.
33. See also the pamphlet published by Ludendorff's wife (M. Ludendorff [ed.], *General und Kardinal*). On the burial of Ludendorff on 22 December 1937 the Ministry of the Interior required that all public corporations should fly flags at halfmast. The Roman Catholic Church refused. Cf. Orsenigo to Pacelli (24 December 1937), AA.EE.SS., Germania, Pos. 604 P.O. fasc. 115 fos 47r–48r. Printed in G. Sale, *Hitler,* 505–6. (The author was by and large careless in his copying: there is a series of errors in his published versions, the more important of which will be pointed out.)
34. Cf. G. Ritter, *Staatskunst und Kriegshandwerk,* vol. 4, 27; W. Steglich, *Friedenspolitik,* 117.
35. Cf. O. Chadwick, *Britain,* 2; St. Stehlin, *Weimar,* 21.
36. Report of M. Buccarini to Pacelli (26 March 1918), ANM Pos. 307 fasc. 4 fo. 277r.
37. Cf. Fr. Engel-Janosi, *Österreich,* vol. 2, 190ff.
38. Benedict XV first tried to keep Italy out of the war, and then to press a separate peace with Austria. On this see also R. Lill, *Papato,* 385ff.
39. Frühwirth was nuncio in Munich from 1908 to 1915. Cf. A. Walz, *Andreas Kardinal Frühwirth.*
40. Cf. M. Feldkamp, *Aufhebung,* 221.
41. Cf. L. von Pastor, *Tagebücher,* 689 (6 July 1920).

42. Cf. Ritter zu Groenensteyn to the President of the Bavarian Council of Ministers, Minister of State von Hertling, on 16 April 1916 and 18 March 1917, BayHStA, Bayerische Gesandtschaft, Päpstlicher Stuhl, 949, fo. 3; 20–1.
43. G. Ritter, *Staatskunst und Kriegshandwerk*, vol. 4, 24.
44. Groenesteyn to Hertling (23 April 1917), BayHStA, Bayerische Gesandtschaft, Päpstlicher Stuhl, 949, fo. 55–6. Cf. also K. Scholder, *Kirchen*, vol. 1, 54–5.
45. Cf. H. Hürten, *Faulhaber*; P. Pfister (ed.), *Faulhaber*.
46. Cf. *CIC*, can. 329, 1 resp. 179–82.
47. Cf. Hertling to Groenesteyn (29 May 1917), BayHStA, Bayerische Gesandtschaft, Päpstlicher Stuhl, 949, fo. 85. On the relations between Faulhaber and Pacelli cf. P. Pfister, *Spanngsfeld*, esp. 204ff.
48. St. Samerski, *Primat*, 22.
49. F. Rossi, *Vatikan*, 69.
50. St. Samerski, *Primat*, 22.
51. Cf. J. Höcht, *Fatima und Pius XII*, esp. 105ff.
52. Groenesteyn was so taken with Pacelli that he wrote to Hertling on the 15 May 1917: 'He is a character of whom one could well believe that one day if the circumstances are right he could even be elected Pope.' BayHStA, Bayerische Gesandtschaft, Päpstlicher Stuhl, 949, fo. 70.
53. Cf. J. Dülffer (ed.), *Bethmann Hollweg*, 382. Cf. also Wilhelm II, *Ereignisse und Gestalten*, 223ff.
54. Cf. W. Steglich, *Friedensappell*, 120.
55. Cf. on this and the following W. Mommsen, *Bürgerstolz*, 761–4.
56. J. Dülffer (ed.), *Bethmann Hollweg*, 382. Cf. also Wilhelm II, *Ereignisse und Gestalten*, 223ff.
57. Cf. J. Cornwell, *Hitler's Pope*, 65; E. Fattorini, *Germania*, 48; M. Feldkamp, *Pius XII*, 26; [Pius XII], *Papst*, 17; H. Rall, *Wilhelm II*, 322ff.; W. Steglich, *Friedensappell*, 655ff.
58. Cf. Fr. Engel-Janosi, *Österreich*, 209ff.; W. Steglich, *Friedenspolitik*, 123.
59. *Verhandlungen des Reichstags*, 3573–5, esp. 3573.
60. Cf. W. Steglich, *Friedensappell*, 122ff.; the same, *Friedenspolitik*, 131.
61. Text: AAS 9 (1917), 417–20.
62. Cf. R. Leiber, *Friedenstätigkeit*, 273.
63. Cf. M. Hildermeier, *Geschichte*, 83.
64. Cf. B. Schneider, *Friedensbemühungen*, 39.
65. Cf. G. Ritter, *Staatskunst und Kriegshandwerk*, vol. 4, 65–6, 73.
66. Cf. W. Steglich, *Friedenspolitik*, 146–231. Di Bonzo was reckoned an Italian patriot, and in these years played a dubious part. Cf. on this E. Kovács, *Österreich-Ungarn*.
67. Here the active diplomatic contacts between Rome, the Munich nunciature and the envoys of the Central Powers in Switzerland as well as the peace efforts of Erzberger were followed with extreme mistrust. Cf. G. Ritter, *Staatskunst und Kriegshandwerk*, vol. 4, 28ff. J. Schmidlin, *Papstgeschichte*, vol. 3/IV, 12.
68. Cf. W. Steglich, *Friedenspolitik*, 216.
69. B. Schneider, *Friedensbemühungen*, 41.
70. Cf. J. Cornwell, *Hitler's Pope*, 69.
71. Cf. G. Schwaiger, *Papsttum und Päpste*, 181.
72. Cf. St. Stehlin, *Weimar*, 21.

73. Cf. W. Michalka, *Erzberger*, esp. 43ff.
74. Cf. K. Epstein, *Erzberger*, 170ff., 210–11, 240–1, 244–5; E. Fattorini, *Germania*, 78–80; R. Morsey, *Erzberger*, esp. 108; St. Stehlin, *Weimar*, 46.
75. M. Feldkamp, *Pius XII*, 32.
76. Cf. on this also Burkard, *Häresie*, 239–52, 252–8.
77. ANM Pos. 328 fasc. 1 fo. 41r.
78. Ibid.
79. See e.g. fo. 41r.
80. Ibid.
81. Ibid.
82. M. Erzberger, *Erlebnisse*, 277–8.
83. Gasparri to Pacelli (26 June 1920), ANM Pos. 328 fasc. 1 fo. 74r–v.
84. Cf. on the following M. Feldkamp, *Pius XII*, 45–9.
85. Cf. Groenesteyn's report of 18 January 1927, BayHStA, Bayerische Gesandtschaft, Päpstlicher Stuhl, 967, fo. 189.
86. Cf. G. May, *Ludwig Kaas*. Kaas destroyed his own papers at the behest of Pius XII in Rome. Certain of his papers are to be found in the Bundesarchiv Koblenz.
87. *Tägliche Rundschau* 3 September 1922; cf. W. Steglich, *Verhandlungen*, 338.
88. Cf. J. Dülffer (ed.), *Bethmann Hollweg*, 254, 381ff.
89. Cf. Wilhelm II, *Ereignisse und Gestalten*, esp. 225–7.
90. Cf. E. Severus, *Herwegen*; M. Albert, *Benediktinerabtei Matia Laach* which does not mention this episode.
91. Cf. *Germania* of 17 October 1922 and *Osservatore Romano* of 19 October 1922; see also [Pius XII], *Papst*, 17ff.; W. Steglich, *Friedensappell*, 659ff. See also Groenesteyn's reports of 6 October 1922 and 13 October 1922. BayHStA, Bayerische Gesandtschaft, Päpstlicher Stuhl, 967, fos 166, 168.
92. Cf. B. Grau, *Eisner*.
93. Pacelli to Gasparri (8 November 1918), ANM Pos. 397 fasc. 1 fo. 2r.
94. Pacelli to Gasparri (10 November 1918), ANM Pos. 397 fasc. fo. 3r.
95. Pacelli to Gasparri (11 November 1918), ANM Pos. 397 fasc. fo. 11r. Cf. also Pacelli to Gasparri (11 November 1918), ANM Pos. 397 fasc. fo. 5r.
96. Gasparri to Pacelli (13 November 1918), ANM Pos. 397 fasc. fo. 6r (emphasis in the original).
97. Gasparri to Faulhaber (9 December 1918) EAM NL Faulhaber no. 1200/1.
98. On this see the report of Groenesteyn of 21 February 1919, BayHStA, Bayerischer Gesandtschaft, Päptslicher Stuhl 967, fo. 195.
99. On this and the following, cf. H. Hürten, *Legenden*.
100. Faulhaber's *Autobiographie* (Part 2) relates: 'It was a frightful sight for me to see on 8 November at 3 in the morning the first soldiers marching in column [...] behind the red flag. [...] How could a people whose loyalty to the king was proverbial be roused by a foreign Galician scribbler and overnight without a shot or shedding a drop of the blood of heroes, swing over to the republican camp and have its king taken off to exile' (466). 'With the progressive radicalisation of the revolution the attitude to the Church became steadily more hostile. Kurt Eisner wanted on the very first night "to take revenge on the parsons", but was restrained by the quieter elements, like Erhard Auer [...] At the bottom the revolution was directed

as much against the altars of the Church as against the throne' (476). EAM
NL Faulhaber, no. 9272–3.

101. Cf. On this B. Grau/G. Treffler, *Unter Republikanern*.
102. L. Volk, *Akten Kardinal Michael von Faulhabers*, vol. 1, no. 94.
103. B. Grau/G. Treffler, *Unter Republikanern*. The diplomatic representative of
the German federal states also all sought to avoid any appearance of a diplomatic recognition of the Eisner government. Cf. E. Fattorini, *Germania*,
313–14.
104. In an explanation for the documents of 7 July 1921 Faulhaber repeats this
openly. EAM NL Faulhaber no. 1320.
105. Pacelli to Gasparri (20 November 1918), ANM Pos. 397 fasc. 1 fos 22r–24r.
106. Cf. J. Cornwell, *Hitler's Pope*, 73.
107. Cf. E. Fattorini, *Germania*, 328–30; P. Lehnert, *Erinnerungen*, 21; N. Padellaro, *Pius XII*, 143.
108. According to Groenesteyn's report of 11 June 1919 Pacelli returned to
Munich only 'in February'. BayHStA, Bayerische Gesandtschaft, Päpstlicher
Stuhl, 967, fo. 167.
109. Cf. H. Möller, *Weimarer Republik*, 127; H. Winkler, *Weg*, 396ff.; Winkler,
Weimar, 76ff.
110. ANM Pos. 397 fasc. 2 fos 72r–73r. Cf. also Pacelli to Gasparri (22 February
1919), ANM Pos. 397 fasc. 2 fo. 79r.
111. Pacelli to Gasparri (23 February 1919), ANM Pos. 397 fasc. 2 fos 86r–88v.
Printed (in Italian) in E. Fattorini, *Germania*, 314–18.
112. Pacelli to Gasparri (4 March 1919) ANM Pos. 397 fasc. 2. Faulhaber wrote in
his biography (Part 2): 'On the burial of Kurt Eisner on 26 Feb. the Church
took no part, although general public mourning was required, and public
buildings had to be flagged. The ringing of bells and the hanging out of
mourning flags were forcibly required by the soldiers' soviets' (483). EAM
NL Faulhaber no. 9272–3.
113. Cf. H. Fischer, *Geschichte*, 168ff.; Z. Nagy, *Geschichte*, 8–9.
114. Report of Pacelli to Gasparri of 3 May 1919, ANM Pos. 397 fasc. 2 fos
105r–111v.
115. Cf. *Bayerische Staatszeitung* of 9 April 1919, Bay HStA, Bayerische
Gesandtschaft, Päpstlicher Stuhl, 967, fo. 192. Cf. also the *Bayerischen Kurier*
12/13 April 1919, Bay HStA, Bayerische Gesandtschaft, Päpstlicher Stuhl,
967, fo. 191.
116. Pacelli to Gasparri (18 April 1919), ANM Pos. 397 fasc. 2 fos 154r–155v.
Emphases in the original. Printed (in Italian) in E. Fattorini, *Germania*, 322–3.
117. See also the account, based on the documents of the BayHStA (Bayerische
Gesandtschaft, Päpstlicher Stuhl, 967, fo. 190), by H. Stehle, *Geheimdiplomatie*, 22–3.
118. Cf. E. Fattorini, *Germania*, 322–5.
119. Cf. Fattorini, *Germania*, 116 (Pacelli's report); Bay HStA, MA 99878
(Schioppa's report according to the *Corriere d'Italia*).
120. After the victory of the government troops, the doorman of the nunciature,
Alois Haindlmaier, testified in favour of Mehrer who had to appear in court.
Cf. ANM Pos. 397 fasc. 3 fos 15r, 17r–v.
121. Cf. Pacelli's report to Gasparri of 30 April 1919, ANM Pos. 397 fasc. 3 fos
4r–8r.

122. ANM Pos. 397 fasc. 3 fo. 8r.
123. Cf. report of Pacelli to Gasparri (5 May 1919), ANM Pos. 379 fasc. 3 fo. 10r–v. The report is headed 'The Nunciature palace under Machine-gunfire'. Printed by E. Fattorini, *Germania*, 325–7.
124. Cf. B. Zittel, *Vertretung*, 485.
125. Thus also Schioppa's report according to the *Corriere d'Italia*, Bay HStA, MA 99878. See also Groenesteyn's report of 18 July 1919, BayHStA, Bayerische Gesandtschaft, Päpstlicher Stuhl, 967, fo. 157–8.
126. Gasparri to Pacelli (8 May 1919), ANM Pos. 397 fasc. 3 fo. 11r.
127. Cf. Pacelli to Gasparri (9 May 1919), ANM Pos. 397 fasc. 3 fo. 12r.
128. Cf. Gasparri to Pacelli (10 May 1919), ANM Pos. 397 fasc. 3 fo. 13r.
129. Pacelli to the Foreign Ministry of the Bavarian People's State in Munich (11 May 1919), ANM Pos. 397 fasc. 3 fo. 14r.
130. Cf. H. Hillmayr, *Terror*, 143–9.
131. Erzberger to Pacelli (8 April 1919), ANM Pos. 395 fasc. 1 fo. 112r.
132. Cf. Pacelli to Gasparri (10 April 1919), ANM Pos. 395 fasc. 1 fo. 113r–v.
133. Cathedral canon to Fritz Albert, council member in the Ministry of State for Education and Public Worship, Munich (14 November 1928), EAM NL Faulhaber no. 5922.
134. Pacelli to Gasparri (19 June 1919), ANM Pos. 397 fasc. 2 fos 178r–183r.
135. St. Samerski, *Primat*, 8.
136. Cf. E. Fattorini, *Germania*, 324.
137. Quoted in H. Stehle, *Geheimdiplomatie*, 23.
138. Cf. P. Lehnert, *Erinnerungen*, 15–16.
139. Cf. H. Hürten, *Legenden*.
140. Cf. K. Epstein, *Erzberger*, 328.
141. Cf. H. Stehle, *Geheimdiplomatie*, 63–72.
142. Pacelli to Gasparri (2 November 1918), E. Fattorini, *Germania*, 164.
143. J. Cornwell, *Hitler's Pope*, 72ff.
144. Cf. M. Feldkamp, *Pius XII*, 36.
145. Quoted in J. Cornwell, *Hitler's Pope*, 70.
146. E. Kovács, *Papst Benedikt XV*. Also every concern for the consolidation of the Habsburg monarchy ('Danube confederation') came to nothing. The division of Austria-Hungary and the partition of the Tyrol were logically carried through by the Entente Powers. Cf. R. Lill, *Südtirol*, 34ff.
147. G. Adriányi, *Geschichte*.
148. On this and the following cf. St. Samerski, *Heilige Stuhl*, 357.
149. On the 2 January 1919, Engelbert Baron von Kerckerinck zur Borg wrote to Pacelli: 'Your Excellency represented to me in that audience [on the 30 October 1917] that we overestimated the effect of the U–boat war, and that the strength of America was by contrast underestimated. The political vision of Your Excellency had been justified by events.' ANM Pos. 395 fasc. 1 fos 47r–48v.
150. Cf. St. Samerski, *Heilige Stuhl*, 372.
151. Cf. M. Keipert/P. Grupp (eds), *Biographisches Handbuch*, 116–17.
152. Cf. Pacelli to Gasparri (15 September 1918) (report no. 9263) AA.EE.SS., Germania, Pos. 1317 fasc. 470 vol. XII (no foliation).
153. Cf. Pacelli to Gasparri (6 October 1918) (report no. 9776), AA.EE.SS., Germania, Pos. 1317 fasc. 470 vol. XII (no foliation).

154. Cf. Benedict XV to Wilson (11 October 1918). MS draft (telegram no. 31) of 7 October 1918, sent by Gasparri to Giovanni Bonzano (Apostolic Delegate in the USA); Bonzano wrote under the date 28 October 1918 to Gasparri that he had received the telegram on 11 October and immediately had it brought to President Wilson in translation. With it he circulated Wilson's answer of 17 October 1918 to the Vatican. All these documents AA.EE.SS., Germania, Pos. 1317 fasc. 470 vol. XII (unfoliated).
155. Cf. Pacelli to Gasparri (2 November 1918) (report no. 10502), AA.EE.SS., Germania, Pos. 1317 fasc. 470 vol. XII (unfoliated).
156. Cf. von Hartmann to Benedict XV (12 December 1918), AA.EE.SS., Germania, Pos. 1317 fasc. 470 vol. XII (unfoliated); von dem Bussche to Pacelli (15 November 1918), AA.EE.SS., Germania, Pos. 1317 fasc. 470 vol. XII (unfoliated).
157. Cf. also Erzberger to Pacelli (21 January 1919), AA.EE.SS., Germania, Pos. 1317 fasc. 470 vol. XII.
158. Pacelli to Gasparri (4 April 1919) (report no. 12487), AA.EE.SS., Germania, Pos. 1317 fasc. 470 vol. XVII (unfoliated).
159. Cf. Erzberger to Benedict XV (9 May 1919), AA.EE.SS., Germania, Pos. 1317 fasc. 470 vol. XVII (unfoliated).
160. Telegram Pacelli to Gasparri (11 May 1919), AA.EE.SS., Germania, Pos. 1317 fasc. 470 vol. XVII (unfoliated).
161. Cf. Nicotra to Gasparri (12 May 1919) (letter no. 41), AA.EE.SS., Germania, Pos. 1317 fasc. 470 vol. XVII (unfoliated).
162. Cf. Gasparri to House (13 May 1919) (kept as a copy, letter no. 90172), AA.EE.SS., Germania, Pos. 1317 fasc. 470 vol. XVII (unfoliated).
163. Cf. Gasparri to Pacelli (14 May 1919), AA.EE.SS., Germania, Pos. 1317 fasc. 470 vol. XVII (unfoliated).
164. Cf. Pacelli to Gasparri (19 May 1919), AA.EE.SS., Germania, Pos. 1317 fasc. 470 vol. XVII (unfoliated).
165. Cf. E. Fattorini, *Germania*, 167–8; G. die Hankel, *Leipziger Prozesse*, 74–87; L. von Pastor, *Tagebücher*, 730; St. Samerski, *Wilhelm II*, esp. 230ff.; W. Schwengler, *Völkerrecht*, 74–82; St. Stehlin, *Weimar*, 44, 106–16.
166. Cf. Fr. Engel-Janosi, *Chaos*, 35–8; E. Fattorini, *Germania*, 163–6; St. Stehlin, *Weimar*, 41.
167. E. Fattorini, *Germania*, 88.
168. Cf. Autobiographie Faulhaber Part 2, 499 (EAM NL Faulhaber no. 9272–3).
169. AAS 12 (1920), 209–18.
170. E. Fattorini, *Germania*, 187–99; St. Stehlin, *Weimar*, 23–35.
171. Cf. St. Samerski, *Heilige Stuhl*, 373ff.
172. Cf. G. Besier, *Kirche im 19. Jahrhundert*, 20ff., 107ff.
173. On this and the following, cf. St. Samerski, *Aufnahme*, 325–68.
174. Cf. L. von Pastor, *Tagebücher*, 686–7.
175. Cf. St. Samerski, *Aufnahme*, 327.
176. Cf. L. Bruti Liberati, *Santa Sede*, 129–30, 146.
177. Cf. St. Stehlin, *Weimar*, 13.
178. Cf. *Germania*, no. 68 of 10 February 1917 and no. 96 of 27 February 1917.
179. Cf. Aversa to Gasparri (11 February 1917), AA.EE.SS., Germania, Pos. 1716 P.O. fasc. 896 fos 25r–27v. Printed in St. Samerski, *Aufnahme*, 362ff.

180. Cf. H. Wolf, *München*, 233ff.
181. Cf. Erzberger to Aversa (27 February 1917), AA.EE.SS., Germania, Pos. 1716 P.O. fasc. 896 fo. 37r.
182. Cf. Gasparri to Aversa (21 February 1917), AA.EE.SS., Germania, Pos. 1716 P.O. fasc. 896 fo. 30r.
183. Aversa to Erzberger (28 February 1917), AA.EE.SS., Germania, Pos. 1716 P.O. fasc. 896 fo. 38r.
184. Erzberger to Aversa (2 March 1917), AA.EE.SS., Germania, Pos. 1716 P.O. fasc. 896 fos 39r–41r.
185. Cf. von Gerlach to Pacelli (22 March 1917), AA.EE.SS., Germania, Pos. 1716 P.O. fasc. 896 fo. 35r.
186. Cf. Pacelli to von Gerlach (31 March 1917), AA.EE.SS., Germania, Pos. 1716 P.O. fasc. 896 fo. 45r.
187. Cf. Pacelli to Aversa (31 March 1917), AA.EE.SS., Germania, Pos. 1716 P.O. fasc. 896 fo. 46r–v.
188. Cf. Pacelli to Gasparri (27 May 1917), AA.EE.SS., Germania, Pos. 1716 P.O. fasc. 896 fos 50r–51r.
189. Cf. Report from Mühlberg (27 July 1918), PA/AA, R9353.
190. Cf., with respect to Prussia, Pacelli to Gasparri (6 April 1919), AA.EE.SS., Germania, Pos. 1718 P.O. fasc. 897 fos 44r–48r.
191. Cf. G. Mai, *Europa*, 147–8.
192. Cf. AAS 13 (1921), 521–4.
193. Cf. E. Fattorini, *Germania*, 187; St. Samerski, *Delbrueck*, 338.
194. Report from von Bergen (5 December 1919) (telegram no. 53), PA/AA, R 9349.
195. Cf. A. Kotowski, *Polnischer Staat*.
196. Cf. St. Wilk, *Staaten*, 254.
197. Cf. St. Stehlin, *Weimar*, 25.
198. Cf. Pacelli to Gasparri (1 March 1919), AA.EE.SS., Germania, Pos. 1716 P.O. fasc. 896 fos 53r–54r.
199. Cf. E. Fattorini, *Germania*, 164.
200. Cf. G. Anschütz, *Verfassung*, 415–23.
201. Cf. Pacelli to Gasparri (1 March 1919), AA.EE.SS., Germania, Pos. 1716 P.O. fasc. 896 fos 53r–54v; G. Franz-Willing, *Bayerische Vatikangesandtschaft*, 168–9.
202. Cf. Report of Pacelli of 28 August 1919, AA.EE.SS., Baviera, Pos. 62 fasc. 40 fo. 77r.
203. Cf. E. Fattorini, *Germania*, 207; K. Scholder, *Kirchen*, vol. 1, 63–4.
204. Cf. Pacelli to Gasparri (6 October 1919) AA.EE.SS., Baviera, Pos. 62 fasc. 40 fos 78r–92v.
205. President of the Prussian Ministry of State to AA (18 July 1919) and AA to the Prussian Ministry of State (29 July 1919), PA/AA R 130193.
206. Cf. R. Morsey, *Deutsche Zentrumspartei*, 109 n. 27; Report of von Bergen (26 August 1919) and von Bergen to Mathieu (15 August 1919), PA/AA R 130193.
207. Cf. Erzberger to von Bergen (7 June 1919), PA/AA R130193.
208. E. Deuerlein, *Reichskonkordat*, 8–9; St. Stehlin, *Weimar*, 26.
209. Cf. Pacelli to Gasparri (6 October 1919), AA.EE.SS., Baviera, Pos. 62 fasc. 40 fos 78r–92v.

210. Cf. Pacelli to Gasparri (25 October 1919), AA.EE.SS., Baviera, Pos. 62 fasc. 40 fos 78r–92v.
211. Minutes of the sitting of the AA (22 October 1919), report of Zech (29 October 1919), and Adolf Müller to Hoffmann (1 November 1919), PA/AA, R 9349.
212. Cf. AA to von Grunau (17 November 1919), PA/AA, R 9349.
213. Cf. Report of Zech (26 December 1919), PA/AA, R 9349; E. Fattorini, *Germania*, 164–5.
214. Cf. Akten der Reichskanzlei, *Kabinett Bauer*, 321.
215. Cf. Report of the Bavarian embassy to the Holy See (11 November 1919), PA/AA, R 9349. In the farewell audience for the Bavarian ambassador Benedict XV said 'that the Papal See suffered under the pressure which the Entente and especially France sought [*sic*] to exercise upon it even after the war and it would suit him to find a backing in Germany'.
216. Cf. Report of von Bergen (5 December 1919) (telegram no. 53), PA/AA, R 9349.
217. Cf. Report of Zech (19 December 1919), PA/AA, R 9349.
218. Cf. Report of Zech (16 January 1920), PA/AA, R 9349.
219. Gasparri to Pacelli (12 January 1920), AA.EE.SS., Baviera, Pos. 62 fasc. 40 fo. 110r.
220. Cf. Pacelli to Gasparri (9 January 1920), AA.EE.SS., Baviera, Pos. 62 fasc. 40 fo. 110r.
221. Cf. Gasparri to Pacelli (27 January 1920), AA.EE.SS., Baviera, Pos. 62 fasc. 40 fos 114r–115v.
222. H. Müller to von Bergen (1 February 1920), PA/AA, R 9439.
223. Cf. Hirsch to AA (22 February 1920), PA/AA, R 130195.
224. The resumption of diplomatic relations with France – preceded by the canonization of the Maid of Orleans in the previous year (9 May 1920) – was part of the comprehensive curial diplomatic conception of peace.
225. Cf. M. Feldkamp, *Pius XII*, 41.
226. Cf. Report of von Bergen (10 March 1920), PA/AA, R 9349.
227. Cf. Hermann Müller to Zech (23 March 1920), PA/AA, R 9439; Report of von Bergen (30 April 1920), PA/AA, R 72079.
228. Cf. Gasparri to Schioppa (31 March 1920), AA.EE.SS., Germania, Pos. 1716 P.O. fasc. 896 fo. 67r.
229. Cf. E. Deuerlein, *Reichskonkordat*, 11–12; Report of von Bergen (30 April 1920) (telegram no. 144), PA/AA, R 72079.
230. Cf. St. Samerski, *Aufnahme*, 353ff.
231. Cf. telegram from Faulhaber to Gasparri (21 May 1920), AA.EE.SS. Germania, Pos. 1716 P.O. fasc. 897 fo. 3r.
232. Report of von Bergen (11 May 1920) (telegram no. 161), PA/AA, R 72229.
233. Cf. Pacelli to Gasparri (3 June and 25 June 1920), AA.EE.SS., Germania, Pos. 1716 P.O. fasc. 897 fo. 9r–v.
234. Cf. Gasparri to Pacelli (26 May 1920), AA.EE.SS. Germania, Pos. 1716 P.O. fasc. 897 fo. 4r. Printed in E. Fattorini, *Germania*, 356.
235. Cf. AA (Haniel) to Rome (24 June 1920) (no. 123; A 424), PA/AA Embassy to the Holy See, Best. 9 Umwandl./Lfd. No. 283 (unfoliated).
236. Cf. Pacelli to Gasparri (30 June 1920), AA.EE.SS. Germania, Pos. 1716 P.O. fasc. 897 fo. 15r.
237. [Pius XII], *Papst*, 22.

238. Cf. R. Morsey, *Pacelli*, 115.
239. [Pius XII], *Papst*, 22–3.
240. Cf. Report of von Bergen of 3 July 1920 (telegram 130), PA/AA, R 72229;
     Report of von Bergen to AA (8 July 1920) (no. 232; A 431); PA/AA, Embassy
     to the Holy See, Best. 9 Umwandl./Lfd. no. 283 (unfoliated).
241. Cf. Ritter zu Groenesteyn to the Bavarian Ministry of Foreign Affairs of 3
     October and 12 October 1923, BayHStA MK 49127; Gasparri to Pacelli of 5
     October 1923, AA.EE.SS., Germania, Pos. 1716 P.O. fasc. 897 fo. 29r; tele-
     gram Wirth to the Vatican (7 December 1921) (no.134), PA/AA, Embassy
     to the Holy See, Best. 9 Umwandl./Lfd. no. 283 (unfoliated); von Bergen
     to AA (28 June 1924), PA/AA R 72229.
242. Draft letter of Gasparri to Pacelli (30 May 1923), AA.EE.SS., Germania, Pos.
     597 P.O., fasc. 17 fo. 74r–v.
243. Ibid.
244. Cf. St. Samerski, *Katholizismus*, 67–8.
245. The dissolution of the Landtag occasioned further delay. Pacelli wrote
     bitterly to Groenesteyn on 6 February 1924: 'Speaking strictly confiden-
     tially, it is incomprehensible that the Bavarian Volkspartei should itself have
     prompted the dissolution of the Landtag! In any other case we would have
     had enough time to get the concordat all wrapped up with this Landtag',
     BayHStA, Bayerische Gesandtschaft. Päpstlicher Stuhl, 973, fo. 366.
246. Pacelli to Bertram (14 March 1924), ANM Pos. 396 fasc. 7 fo. 31r.
247. Cf. E. Huber/W. Huber (eds), *Staat und Kirche*, vol. 4, 294–315; H. Hürten,
     Deutsche Katholiken, 101; J. Listl, *Konkordatäre Entwicklung*, 447ff.
248. Paul Stengel to Groenesteyn (28 November 1924), BayHStA, Bayerische
     Gesandtschaft, Päpstlicher Stuhl, 973, fo. 443.
249. AAS 17 (1925), 41–54.
250. AAS 14 (1922), 577–81.
251. AAS 17 (1925), 273–87.
252. AAS 21 (1929), 441–54.
253. AAS 19 (1927), 425–33.
254. AAS 21 (1929), 319–20.
255. AAS 21 (1929), 275–94.
256. AAS 21 (1929), 521–41.
257. AAS 25 (1933), 177–94.
258. AAS 25 (1933), 385–431.
259. Cf. on the whole group R. Minnerath, *L'Église*, 43ff., 57ff., 441ff; Au.
     Scheuermann, *Konkordatspolitik*.
260. AAS 19 (1927), 9–12.
261. AAS 20 (1928), 65–6. See also Hrabovec, *Slowakei*.
262. AAS 20 (1928), 129–33.
263. L. Schöppe, *Konkordate*, 87–91.
264. Cf. O. Gritschneder, *Bewährungsfrist*; H. Möller, *Die Weimarer Republik*,
     167ff.; H. Winkler, *Weg*, 443–4; Winkler, *Weimar*, 234–5.
265. Report of Groenesteyn (9 November 1923), BayHStA, Bayerische
     Gesandtschaft, Päpstlicher Stuhl, 996, fo. 71. It says further: 'In the Vatican
     there seems to be doubt whether it would be possible to conclude a
     concordat with a dictator, because it is to be feared that its legal validity
     might subsequently be contested by the representative of the people.'

266. Pacelli to Gasparri (9 November 1923), ANM Pos. 396 fasc. 7 fo. 3r.
267. Pacelli to Pizzardo (10 November 1923), AA.EE.SS., Germania, Pos. 511 P.O. fasc. 24 fo. 87.
268. Pacelli to Gasparri (12 November 1923), ANM Pos. 396 fasc. 7 fo. 4r. Cf. also EAM NL Faulhaber 7150–5.
269. ANM Pos. 396 fasc. 7 fo. 5r.
270. Cited after Th. Brechenmacher, *Held*. The author quotes from the documents of the Vatican Archive (AA.EE.SS., Baviera, ANM Pos. 396 fasc. 7 fo. 6f.).
271. Pacelli to Gasparri (24 April 1924), ANM Pos. 396 fasc. 7 fos 6f. Quoted from P. Godman, *Hitler and the Vatican*, 5. On the other side, Groenesteyn reported on 27 July 1924, in relation to an article in the *Osservatore Romano*, also in the following terms: 'All the concerns of the Jews to attain a position of power had from the beginning reinforced the struggles with Catholicism and hence in the provinces which turned from the Catholic Church, had had the easier game. Hence the Jews sympathized even now with everything which is anti-Catholic.' BayHStA, Bayerische Gesandtschaft. Päpstlicher Stuhl, 996 (unfoliated).
272. Cf. L. Volk (ed.), *Akten Kardinal Michael von Faulhaber*, vol. 1, 320–4.
273. Report of Groenesteyn (12 January 1924), BayHStA, Bayerische Gesandtschaft, Päpstlicher Stuhl, 996, fo. 71. Cf. also report of Groenesteyn (2 March 1924), ibid. fo. 42.
274. Cited from Th. Brechenmacher, *Held* (ANM Pos. 396 fasc. 7 fos 75r–76v).
275. ANM Pos. 396 fasc. 7 fos 9r–10v. Cf. also EAM NL Faulhaber 8028, 8029 (Ludendorff movement).
276. ANM Pos. 396 fasc. 7 fo. 9v.
277. ANM Pos. 396 fasc. 7 fos 39r, 40r.
278. Telegram Pacelli to Gasparri (5 April 1924), ANM Pos. 396 fasc. 7 fo. 66r; cf. telegram Gasparri to Pacelli (9 April 1924), ANM Pos. 396 fasc. 7 fo. 68r.
279. Draft report of Pacelli (10 April 1924), ANM Pos. 396 fasc. 7 fos 69r–72v; here 69r.
280. ANM Pos. 396 fasc. 7 fo. 72v.
281. Pacelli to Gasparri (26 April 1924), ANM Pos. 396 fasc. 7 fos 75r–76v.
282. ANM Pos. 396 fasc. 7 fo. 76v.
283. Draft letter of Pacelli to Gasparri (1 May 1924), ANM Pos. 396 fasc. 7 fo. 79v.
284. St. Samerski, *Aufnahme*, 361. Cf. Paul Stengel to Groenesteyn (18 August 1925), BayHStA, Bayerische Gesandtschaft, Päpstlicher Stuhl, 949, fo. 219.
285. Pacelli to Pizzardo (8 December 1925), AA.EE.SS., Germania, Pos. 511 P.O. fasc. 24 fos 95r–96r; here: 95r.
286. Pacelli to Pizzardo (17 December 1925), AA.EE.SS., Germania, Pos. 511 P.O. fasc. 24 fo. 99v.
287. Cf. Leopold von Hoesch to AA (17 November 1925), ADAP, A, vol.14, 616.
288. Cf. R. Morsey, *Pacelli*, 135.
289. Pacelli to Pizzardo (21 November 1925), AA.EE.SS., Germania, Pos. 511 fasc. 24 fo. 91r.
290. AA.EE.SS., Germania, Pos. 511 P.O. fasc. 24 91v.
291. Ibid.
292. Pacelli to Pizzardo (24 November 1925), AA.EE.SS., Germania, Pos. 511 P.O. fasc. 24 fo. 92r.

293. Ibid.

294. Cf. St. Samerski, *Delbrueck*.

295. Report of Groenesteyn no. 105 (3 October 1923), BayHStA, Bayerische Gesandtschaft. Päpstlicher Stuhl, 949, fo. 194.

296. Report of Groenesteyn no. 107 (12 October 1923), BayHStA, Bayerische Gesandtschaft. Päpstlicher Stuhl, 949, fo. 195. On 23 March 1925, Groenesteyn reported: 'As was to be expected, the German ambassador has been recently directed, as of now, after the concordat has come into force, to request very energetically the detailing of Monsignor Pacelli to Berlin, and to intimate that the Reich government is beginning to become sensitive to the undue length to which this question has been drawn out, and that the long-term presence of the nuncio in the Reich capital is urgently desired not only by the Reich government, but also by the Prussian government, the north-German bishops and the diplomatic *corps*.' BayHStA, Bayerische Gesandtschaft. Päpstlicher Stuhl, 949, fo. 211.

297. Cf. Pacelli to Gasparri (19 July 1923), AA.EE.SS., Germania, Pos. 535 P.O. fasc. 64 fos 71r–72v.

298. Cf. St. Samerski, *Bistum Danzig*, 95–6.

299. F. J. Köhler, *Bertram*.

300. Telegram from von Bergen to AA (no. 69; A 967), PA/AA, Embassy at the Holy See, 8 Nuntius/Lfd. no. 284 (unfoliated).

301. St. Samerski, *Bistum Danzig*, 95–6.

302. Cf. Decree of Schubert (27 June 1924) and the report of von Bergen (28 June 1924), PA/AA, Embassy at the Holy See, 8 Nuntius/Lfd. no. 284 (unfoliated).

303. Cf. Report of von Bergen (9 January 1925), PA/AA, Embassy at the Holy See, 8 Nuntius/Lfd. no. 284 (unfoliated).

304. Cf. St. Samerski, *Aufnahme*, 360.

305. Cf. M. Feldkamp, *Pius XII*, 45.

306. Cf. E. Deuerlein, *Reichskonkordat*, 2; G. Franz-Willing, *Bayerische Vatikangesandtschaft*, 248; Fr. Hanus, *Preussische Vatikangesandtschaft*, 409.

2. Vatican Foreign Policy 1920–29

1. Cf. St. Payne, *History of Fascism*, 106; Z. Sternhell/M. Asheri, *Entstehung*, esp. 285ff.

2. Cf. G. Schwaiger, *Papsttum und Päpste*, 187, 199–200.

3. Cf. also F. de Giorgi, *Linguaggi militari*.

4. Cf. H. Roos, *Geschichte*, 41ff.; cf. also N. Davies, *Herzen Europas*; A. Koryna, *Wojna*.

5. Cf. H. Winkler, *Weg*, 443–4; J. Schmidlin, *Papstgeschichte*, vol. 3/IV, 11. On Ratti's attitude to east-european Jewry, cf. Brechenmacher, *Vatikan*, 146ff. Unlike his closest colleague Ermenegildo Pellegrinetti, Ratti revealed no antisemitic stereotypes, but opted against 'a kind of Toleration Act for Protestants and Jews' (ibid., 148) in Catholic Poland.

6. On the relations between the Vatican and the Ukraine – and here too Ratti was involved – see M. Mróz, *Watykan y Ukraina*.

7. H. Stehle, *Geheimdiplomatie*, 24.

8. Cf. K. Kowalec, *Dmowski*; A. Micewski, *Dmowski*, 227–8.

9. Cf. St. Samerski, *Katholizismus*, 29–30.
10. Cited from B. Grott, *Polnische Parteien*, 75.
11. Cf. B. Grott, *Polnische Parteien*, 76–7.
12. Cf. on this K. Sadowski, *Catholic Power*.
13. Cf. H. Hein, *Piłsudski-Kult*, 19ff., 34ff.
14. Cf. St. Wilk, *Staaten*, 254.
15. Ratti to Sapieha, 6 June 1919 (AKMK, TS XII), 11 and 19 August 1919 (AKMK, TS XII, 14).
16. Cf. W. Meysztowicz, *Nunziatura*, 180ff.
17. Cf. Meysztowicz, *Nunziatura*, 188.
18. Cf. Fr. Steffen, *Diözese Danzig*, 78–9.
19. Cf. H. Roos, *Geschichte*, 83.
20. Cf. Fr. von Lama, *Papst und Kurie*, 247.
21. Cf. E. Fattorini, *Germania*, 236; St. Stehlin, *Weimar*, 108ff.
22. Cf. J. Schmidlin, *Papstgeschichte*, vol. 3/IV, 15.
23. Cf. E. Fattorini, *Germania*, 236; St. Stehlin, *Weimar*, 110–11.
24. Cf. St. Stehlin, *Weimar*, 117.
25. Cf. on this T. Falecki, *Stolica Apostolska*.
26. Cf. St. Stehlin, *Weimar*, 117.
27. Cf. ibid., 118–19.
28. Cf. J. Myszor, *Beziehungen*.
29. Cf. E. Fattorini, *Germania*, 240.
30. Cf. W. Marschall, *Geschichte*, 157; Fr. von Lama, *Papst und Kurie*, 253; E. Fattorini, *Germania*, 232–4; St. Stehlin, *Weimar*, 114ff.
31. Ratti to Sapieha (30 May 1919), AKMK, TS XII, 9.
32. Cf. E. Fattorini, *Germania*, 246–7.
33. Thus G. Schwaiger, *Papsttum und Päpste*, 204.
34. Cf. E. Fattorini, *Germania*, 249; Fr. von Lama, *Papst und Kurie*, 254.
35. Cf. J. Topolski, *Polska*, 73.
36. B. Grott, *Polnische Parteien*, 81–2.
37. Cf. E. Kneifel, *Geschichte*, esp. 203ff.
38. Cf. J. Kochanowski, *Horthy und Piłsudski*, 90–1; Warszawski, *Piłsudski a religia*.
39. Cf. *Gazeta Wyborcza* (27 August 2004), 16.
40. Cf. H. Hein, *Piłsudski-Kult*, 319.
41. Cf. A. Kotowski, *Hitlers Bewegung*, 126ff.
42. W. Lipiński, *Piłsudski*.
43. Cf. J. Rogall, *Posener Land*, 137, 140; M. Scheuermann, *Minderheitenschutz*, 22ff., 88ff.
44. Cf. O. Wagner, *Geschichte*, 134. Cf. on the status of Catholics of German descent in Poland LON Archives, Geneva, R 3906, 41/5154/560 and R3906, 41/6274/560.
45. Cf. St. Wilk, *Staaten*, 258. For the further development, see also Hoover Institution Archives, Poland. Ambasada (Catholic Church) Records, 1924–45.
46. Cf. St. Zimniak, *Cardinale August J. Hlond*.
47. Thus H. Stehle, *Geheimdiplomatie*, 22. See also W. Rood, *Rom und Moskau*, 30.
48. Cf. on the following also K. Repgen, *Pius XI*, 6ff.
49. On this and the following, see J. Karlov, *Vatikan*, 158; W. Rood, *Rom und Moskau*, 29ff.

50. Cf. W. Rood, *Rom und Moskau*, 30.
51. Cf. ibid., 44ff.
52. O. Barkowez/F. Fjodor/A. Krylow, *Zar Nikolaus II*, 345–60.
53. Cf. on this and the following see J. Karlov, *Vatikan*, 158ff.; H. Stehle, *Geheimdiplomatie*, 25ff.; A. Wenger, *Rome et Moscou*, 132ff.
54. Cf. W. Rood, *Rom und Moskau*, 52ff.
55. Text: ibid., 57–9.
56. Cf. H. Stehle, *Lenins Mann*.
57. Cf. St. Samerski, *Konsultor*, esp. 270ff. On W. von Braun see also H. Stehle, *Lenins Mann*, 35–9.
58. The American Jesuit Edmund A. Walsh was the first to be put in charge of the charitable aid, then the Steyler Missionary father Eduard Gehrmann. M. Feldkamp, *Pius XII*, 50; St. Samerski, *Konsultor*, 272; H. Stehle, *Geheimdiplomatie*, 37.
59. Cf. W. Rood, *Rom und Moskau*, 47ff.
60. Cf. H. Winkler, *Weimar*, 167ff.
61. Cf. C. Fink, *Genoa Conference*, 147–8, 201.
62. Cf. M. Hildermeier, *Geschichte*, 355ff., 360ff.
63. Cf. in detail H. Stehle, *Geheimdiplomatie*, 39ff.
64. Cf. J. Karlov, *Vatikan*, 177.
65. Cf. G. Rosenfeld, *Sowjetunion und Deutschland*, 126ff.
66. Cf. St. Samerski, *Katholizismus*, 64. Samerski rightly notes that the German Centre Party abandoned the 'Eastern course' again from spring 1923 and under Foreign Minister Stresemann (August 1923 to October 1929) swung logically to an understanding with the West (ibid., 65–6).
67. Cf. H. Winkler, *Weimar*, 169–70.
68. Cf. H. Stehle, *Geheimdiplomatie*, 61.
69. Cf. St. Payne, *History of Fascism*, 83–4, 126.
70. On the concept of Fascism cf. W. Schieder, *Faschismus*.
71. S. Nosov (ed.), *Papstvo*, 61, links the recognition with the expulsion of Herbigny. The support of the Vatican was no longer needed.
72. J. Karlov, *Vatikan*, 184.
73. Cf. ibid., 182.
74. Ibid.
75. Cf. ibid., 183.
76. Worowski had been murdered in Lausanne in May 1923. Ibid.
77. Cf. H. Stehle, *Geheimdiplomatie*, 62–3.
78. Cf. D. Colas, *Einheitspartei*, 155; Colas, *Léninisme*, 296–70.
79. Cf. H. Stehle, *Geheimdiplomatie*, 71, 78.
80. J. Karlov, *Vatikan*, 183.
81. Cf. M. Feldkamp, *Pius XII*, 50; H. Stehle, *Geheimdiplomatie*, 80ff.
82. AAS 16 (1924), 294–5.
83. Cf. Pacelli to Pizzardo (24 November 1925), AA.EE.SS., Germania, Pos. 511 P.O. fasc. 24 fo. 92r.
84. Cf. U. von Hehl, *Wilhelm Marx*, esp. 288ff.
85. Cf. St. Payne, *History of Fascism*, 114–15; G. Sale, *Matteotti*.
86. Cf. M. Schäfer, *Luigi Sturzo*.
87. Cf. J.-L. Pouthier, *Émigrés*.

88. In order not to strengthen the anti-fascist centre in Paris any further, the Holy See required that Sturzo remain in London exile. He came back to Italy only at the beginning of September 1946. Cf. J.-L. Pouthier, *Émigrés*, 482.
89. Cf. J. Molony, *Emergence*, 167, 192. The emigration was, of course, represented as a measure of protection for the Christian Democrats. Cf. ibid., 191.
90. Cf. Fr. Engel-Janosi, *Chaos*, 65.
91. Cf. Corrin, *Catholic Intellectuals*, 223–4.
92. Thus Corrin, *Catholic Intellectuals*, 231. The Catholic priest James M. Gillis was one of the very few who raised their voice against Italian Fascism. Cf. Gribble, *Guardian*.
93. For this and the following cf. H. Stehle, *Geheimdiplomatie*, 83–4.
94. On the further proposals and on Soviet strategy in detail, see T. Tokareva, *Hierarchy*, 144–5.
95. Cf. N. Cimbaev, *Russische Kirche*, 186; G. Stricker, *Religion*, 86–7.
96. Cf. H. Stehle, *Geheimdiplomatie*, 114.
97. Cf. Stehle, *Geheimdiplomatie*, 114ff. After a few days the Jesuits were expelled from the country.
98. Cf. on the relation between Pacelli and Brockdorff-Rantzau ADAP, B, vol. 5, 254–8; H. Stehle, *Geheimdiplomatie* 117–18. See also W. Rood, *Rom und Moskau*, 106ff.
99. Cf. von Bergen to AA (24 October 1927), ADAP, B, vol. 7, 113.
100. Cf. S. Nosov (ed.), *Papstvo*, 76.
101. Cf. M. Hildermeier, *Geschichte*, 362.
102. Cf. W. Rood, *Rom und Moskau*, 74ff.; D. Alvarez, *Spies*, 130ff.
103. G. Schwaiger, *Papsttum und Päpste*, 260–2; L. Tretjakewitsch, *Bishop Michel d'Herbigny*.
104. AAS 16 (1924), 5–11.
105. Cf. H.-G. Franzke, *Laizität*; Z. Giacometti, *Quellen*, 383–6; G. May, *Konkordatspolitik*; J. Schmidlin, *Papstgeschichte*, vol. 3/IV, 115–22.
106. AAS 16 (1924), 5–11; cf. Z. Giacometti, *Quellen*, 383–6; J. Schmidlin, *Papstgeschichte*, vol. 3/IV, 115–22.
107. Cf. B. Bruneteau, *Antiliberalismus*; J. Prévotat, *Catholiques*, 280ff.
108. Pius XI to Andrieu (5 September 1926); cf. J. Schmidlin, *Papstgeschichte*, vol. 3/IV, 118–19. Pacelli too was exposed to the attacks of the *Action Française*. Cf. on this the report of von Bergen to AA (24 January 1930) (No. 7; A54), PA/AA, Best. 29, vol. 1/Lfd. No. 441 (no pagination). Hoesch reported from the German embassy in Paris on 11 February 1930 to the AA (A583): 'That the *Action Française* would take the final nomination of Pacelli [namely, to be Cardinal Secretary of State] coolly, if not be absolutely hostile, was to be expected. Yet it is noticeable that Charles Maurras at least exercises a certain reserve in what he says. After some thrusts against the earlier Nuncio in Paris, Cardinal Cerretti, Maurras points to the popularity and skill with which Pacelli has worked in Berlin, and concedes the possibility that he will administer his new high office in Rome with the same skill.' PA/AA, Best. 29, vol. 1/Lfd. No. 441 (no pagination).
109. Cf. H. Stehle, *Geheimes*.
110. Cf. G. Schwaiger, *Papsttum und Päpste*, 262.

111. S. Nosov (ed.), *Papstvo*, 76.
112. Archepiscopal Secretary to Prälat Münch (15 November 1929), EAM NL Faulhaber, no. 7222.
113. EAM NL Faulhaber, no. 7222.
114. G. Schwaiger, *Papsttum und Päpste*, 207.
115. Cf. H. Stehle, *Geheimdiplomatie*, 73.
116. Thus EAM NL Faulhaber, no. 7222, 82 (emphasis in the original).
117. Cf. on this and the following, St. Samerski, *Katholizismus*, 50–1; Samerski, *Kirche*, 66ff.
118. Cf. St. Samerski, *Kirche*, 68.
119. Cf. H. Böttcher, *Freie Stadt Danzig.*
120. Cf. St. Samerski, *Bistum Danzig*, 39–52.
121. Cf. AAS 14 (1922), 577–81.
122. Cf. St. Samerski, *Kirche*, 77.
123. Cf. ibid., 46.
124. Pacelli to Gasparri (27 February 1922), AA.EE.SS., Germania, Pos. 507 P.O. fasc. 16 fos 10r–11v; here: 10v. Printed in E. Fattorini, *Germania*, 376–8.
125. AA.EE.SS., Germania, Pos. 507 P.O. fasc. 16 fos 10r–11v.
126. AA.EE.SS., Germania, Pos. 507 P.O. fasc. 16 fos 10r–11v
127. AA.EE.SS., Germania, Pos. 507 P.O. fasc. 16 fos 10r–11v. See also the draft reply of Gasparri to Pacelli (March 1922), AA.EE.SS., Germania, Pos. 507 P.O. fasc. 16 fos 10r–11v.
128. On the negotiations for the Polish concordat and the preliminary drafts, see in detail AKMK, TS XII, 7; TS XII, 9.
129. Cf. St. Samerski, *Kirche*, 78–9.
130. On 4 January 1928, the so-called 'Observation' [*Feststellung*] was signed, but this was ratified neither by the Roman Curia nor by the Volkstag. Cf. St. Samerski, *Bistum Danzig*, 49.
131. Cf. St. Samerski, *Kirche*, 136ff. See also the same, *Bistum Danzig*, 9ff.
132. Cf. St. Samerski, *Kirche*, 149.
133. Cf. on this and the following St. Stehlin, *Weimar*, 130ff.
134. Soon Hlond fell into conflict with the League of German Catholics in Poland, which opposed his diocesan administration. In 1926 the League presented Hlond with a written accusation, which he answered in the following year. Cf. J. Myszor/J. Konieczny (eds), *Korespondencja*; J. Myszor, *Beziehungen.*
135. Thus J. Myszor, *Beziehungen.*
136. Cf. St. Stehlin, *Weimar*, 134–5.
137. Cf. ibid., 137. In 1931, ten years after the plebiscite in Upper Silesia, Pacelli feared demonstrations for the return of those areas to Germany – and indeed that the Catholic Church might be involved (cf. Pacelli to Orsenigo [26 February 1931], AA.EE.SS., Germania, Pos. 604 P.O. fasc. 112 fo. 55r). Yet Orsenigo was able to calm him down: 'At the great demonstration in Beuthen, which is scheduled for the 22 March 1931 the Church will take no part. All that will happen is that the bells will be rung and Bertram will make a short speech' (AA.EE.SS., Germania, Pos. 604 P.O. fasc. 112 fo. 56r–v).
138. On the negotiations in connection with the Polish concordat cf. St. Samerski, *Katholizismus*, 93ff.

139. Cf. St. Stehlin, *Weimar*, 136.
140. Cf. ibid., 138.
141. Pacelli to Gasparri (7 December 1923), AA.EE.SS., Germania, Pos. 511 P.O. fasc. 21 fos 33r–34r.
142. Ibid.
143. Cf. H. Winkler, *Weg*, vol.1, 452–3.
144. Pacelli to Gasparri (7 December 1923), AA.EE.SS., Germania, Pos. 511 P.O. fasc. 16 fos 33–4.
145. Ibid.
146. Cf. Pacelli to Gasparri (23 July 1922), AA.EE.SS., Germania, Pos. 507 P.O. fasc. 16 fo. 84r–v.
147. Cf. L. Volk, *Reichskonkordat*, 5.
148. It was a question of Art. 10 (1), 137, 138, and 143–9. Cf. on this G. Anschütz, *Verfassung*, 87, 629ff., 666ff.
149. Cf. R. Morsey, *Deutsche Zentrumspartei*, 235.
150. *Reden*, 4.
151. Ibid., 204–5.
152. Cf. Wirth to Faulhaber (21 August 1922) and Faulhaber's answer (14 September 1922): L. Volk (ed.), *Akten Kardinal Michael von Faulhabers*, vol. 1, 26–7, 275–6. See also Wirth to Pacelli (30 October 1922); Stegerwald to Wirth (3 October 1922): 'The assumption concerning the attached letter of Cardinal Faulhaber, that you had in Franfurt before the beginning of the Catholic assembly in the Augustinerverein attempted to influence the mood against Bavaria, is certainly a mistake [...] Cheap propaganda against Bavaria, as I recollect very clearly was not made by you on the occasion of the General Assembly of the Augustinerverein in Frankfurt' (EAM NL Faulhaber, no. 3503).
153. Cf. Faulhaber to Pacelli (19 October 1922), EAM NL Faulhaber, no. 3503, 289–90. See on the whole question H. Hürten, *Deutsche Katholiken*, 59–62.
154. Faulhaber to Pizzardo (19 September 1922), EAM NL Faulhaber, no. 1200/1.
155. Reichstag election statement of the BVP-provincial presidency of 26 April 1924. Wirth defended himself against the reproaches and asked Faulhaber to mediate. EAM NL Faulhaber, no. 7228. See also Stresemann's appeal to Faulhaber of 13 October 1923 in which he expresses his anxiety about the disintegration of the Reich, and requests the Cardinal to support his policy. EAM NL Faulhaber, no. 7229.
156. Thus R. Morsey, Discussion, 187. On 9 August 1962, Adenauer wrote to Msgr Dr Josef Weissthanner: 'After this speech Cardinal Faulhaber accused me of having attacked the Bavarian royal house. I had no success in overcoming this disagreement. Indeed I had to refuse an invitation to a banquet. Much as I regret this controversy, I must claim even today to have been justified in what I said.' EAM NL Faulhaber, no. 3503.
157. Cf. J.-L. Pouthier, *Émigrés*, 487.
158. Cf. St. Samerski, *Delbrueck*.
159. O. Braun, *Weimar*, 155.
160. On the Münster Church historian and Centre deputy Georg Schreiber, see R. Morsey, *Machtkampf*.
161. Cf. Delbrueck's report in R. Morsey, *Vorgeschichte*, 244–6; see also G. May, *Ludwig Kaas*, vol. 2, 361; G. Schreiber, *Kirchenpolitik*, 38. In January 1920,

the Fulda Bishops' Conference called the Trier canon lawyer Kaas to be the
go-between between the Bishops' Conference and the nuncio – a mediating
function which he was to fulfil till the conclusion of the Reich concordat
in 1933. Cf. M. Höhle, *Gründung*, 72–3.

162. Reprint of the text in A. Kupper (ed.), *Staatliche Akten*, 437–9; cf. L. Volk,
Reichskonkordat, 8.
163. Thus D. Golombek, *Vorgeschichte*, 13.
164. Cf. L. Volk, *Reichskonkordat*, 7ff.
165. Cf. St. Samerski, *Delbrueck*, 341.
166. Cf. L. Volk, *Reichskonkordat*, 21.
167. Reprint of the results of the conversation in Morsey, *Vorgeschichte*, 247–50.
168. Reprint of the guidelines of the Ministry of the Interior (Koch-Weser
directive) of 6 January 1921, in A. Kupper (ed.), *Staatliche Akten*, 441–7.
169. Cf. Debrueck to the Bavarian embassy (12 March 1921), PA/AA, R72088.
170. Text in A. Kupper (ed.), *Staatliche Akten*, 441–7.
171. Cf. E. Deuerlein, *Reichskonkordat*, 30.
172. L. Volk, *Reichskonkordat*, 13.
173. Volk, *Reichskonkordat*, 18–19. Cf. K. Scholder, *Kirchen*, vol. 1, 66ff.
174. A. Kupper (ed.), *Staatliche Akten*, 441–7.
175. St. Samerski, *Katholizismus*, 78.
176. Cf. Pacelli to Gasparri (26 May 1922), AA.EE.SS., Germania, Pos. 507 P.O.
fasc. 16 fos 53r–60v.
177. Pacelli to Gasparri (18 April 1922), AA.EE.SS., Germania, Pos. 507 P.O. fasc.
16 fos 75r–76r.
178. AA.EE.SS., Germania, Pos. 507 P.O. fasc. 16 fo. 75r.
179. Pacelli to Gasparri (27 March 1923), AA.EE.SS., Germania, Pos. 507 P.O.
fasc. 17 fo. 12r.
180. Pacelli to Gasparri (24 February 1923), AA.EE.SS., Germania, Pos. 507 P.O.
fasc. 17 fo. 7r.
181. AA.EE.SS., Germania, Pos. 507 P.O. fasc. 17 fo. 28r.
182. Cf. in the overview of K. Keller, *Landesgeschichte*, 268ff., 361–2.
183. Pacelli to Gasparri (23 December 1928), AA.EE.SS., Germania, Pos. 515 P.O.
fasc. 25 fos 14–15.
184. Pacelli to Gasparri (24 August 1929), AA.EE.SS., Germania, Pos. 515 P.O.
fasc. 17 fos 24–5.
185. Text in E. Huber/W. Huber (eds), *Staat und Kirche*, vol. 4, 346–8.
186. Text in ibid., 689–92.
187. Cf. *Verhandlungen des Sächsischen Landtags, 3. Wahlperiode, 1928/9*, Draft
no. 74.
188. Cf. *Verhandlungen des Sächsischen Landtags, Wahlperiode, 1929/30*, 707ff.
189. Cf. Centoz to Pacelli (18 March 1930), AA.EE.SS., Germania, Pos. 515 P.O.
fasc. 25 fo. 26.
190. See the report of Orsenigo to Pacelli of 22 July 1937, AA.EE.SS., Germania,
Pos. 515 P.O. fasc. 25 fos 51–2.
191. Cf. K. Scholder, *Kirchen*, vol. 1, 69.
192. Cf. F. von Papen, *Wahrheit*, 313–18; J. Petzold, *Papen*.
193. E. Huber/W. Huber (eds), *Staat und Kirche*, vol. 1, 204–21.
194. Cf. R. Morsey, *Vorgeschichte*, 262ff.
195. Cf. on this E. Wende, *C. H. Becker*, 272.

196. Cf. D. Golombek, *Vorgeschichte*, 48.
197. Cf. H. Hömig, *Zentrum*, 189–90; E. Gräfin Rittberg, *Kirchenvertrag*, 94–5, 98–9.
198. Cf. already Pacelli's report to Gasparri of 18 December 1922 (AA.EE.SS., Germania, Pos. 507 P.O. fasc. 16 fos 97r–98r), in which he reports upon the activities of the Evangelische Bund against the concordat.
199. Resolution of the Prussian general synod on the concordat question of 12 May 1927, in: E. Huber/W. Huber (eds), *Staat und Kirche*, vol. 4, 319–20.
200. Thus Pacelli to Gasparri (2 February 1923), AA.EE.SS., Germania, Pos. 507 P.O. fasc. 17 fo. 39v.
201. Cf. in detail M. Höhle, *Gründung*.
202. Texts: E. Huber/W. Huber (eds), *Staat und Kirche*, vol. 4, 337–9.
203. Cf. ibid., 337.
204. On these see below, Chapter 2.6.
205. Cf. on this now especially A. Hamers, *Konkordatspolitik*.
206. Cf. Pacelli to Gasparri (30 June 1928), AA.EE.SS., Germania, Pos. 511 P.O. fasc. 23 fos 6–7.
207. Already with the Trunk cabinet, which was in office from November 1925 Pacelli had had confidential conversations. On 20 May 1927 he wrote to Gasparri: 'Despite the great difficulties and the opposition of the Liberals and Democrats, President Dr. Trunk, various ministers and the Centre leader Schofer, promised to do everything to attain that end [i.e. the conclusion of a concordat]' (AA.EE.SS., Germania, Pos. 565 P.O. fasc. 81 fo. 25). Cf. also Pacelli to Gasparri (1 December 1925), AA.EE.SS., Germania, Pos. 565 P.O. fasc. 81 fo. 9.
208. Cf. E. Föhr, *Geschichte*, 14–15. On the further negotiations over the Baden concordat, see below, Chapter 3.6.
209. Pacelli to Gasparri (4 December 1928), AA.EE.SS., Germania, Pos. 511 P.O. fasc. 23 fos 41r–42r.
210. Cf. The draft answer of Gasparri to Pacelli, AA.EE.SS., Germania, Pos. 511 P.O. fasc. 23 fo. 45r. Ibid. for the following quotation (emphasis in the original).
211. Pacelli to Gasparri (20 July 1929), AA.EE.SS., Germania, Pos. 511 P.O. fasc. 23 fo. 64r–v.
212. Draft answer of Gasparri to Pacelli of 31 July 1929, AA.EE.SS., Germania, Pos. 511 P.O. fasc. 23 fos 67r–68r.
213. Cf. M. Feldkamp, *Pius XI*, 62–4.
214. Feldkamp, *Pius XI*, 63.
215. J. Mayer, *Unfruchtbarmachung*.
216. Cf. on this and what follows Pacelli to Gasparri (7 November 1928), AA.EE.SS., Germania, Pos. 565 P.O. fasc. 81 fos 33–4.
217. *Collectanea*, no. 1897, 321.
218. P. Godman, *Hitler and the Vatican*, 59–60; citation: 60.
219. Cf. G. Besier, *Kirchen*, 869–70; D. Dietrich, *Josef Mayer*; I. Richter, *Nationalsozialismus*; W. Stüken, *Hirten* 63–6; H.-J. Wollasch, *Priester*.
220. AA.EE.SS., Germania, Pos. 632 P.O. fasc. 150 fo. 51, cited from P. Godman, *Hitler and the Vatican*, 37.
221. Pacelli to Orsenigo (10 August 1933), AA.EE.SS, Germania, Pos. 632 P.O. fasc. 150 fo. 56; cf. G. Besier, *Kirchen*, 869ff.

222. Cf. P. Godman, *Hitler and the Vatican*, 40ff.
223. Godman, *Hitler and the Vatican*, 40ff. (ACDF, Best. S.O. 535/30; R.V. 1934, 12).
224. Godman, *Hitler and the Vatican*, 46–7 (ACDF, Best. S.O. 1413/30 i).
225. Cf. B. K. Vocelka, *Geschichte Österreichs*, 281; B. Wedemeyer-Kolwe, *Körperkultur*. See also EAM NL Faulhaber, no. 3703 (Struggle against Immorality); 5919 (Church objections against the establishment of family bathing); 6015 (organized dancing during seasons of fasting); 6016 (ladies' fashions); 6017 (inadequate dress of female gymnasts); 6020 (sexual enlightenment); 7033 (Catholic Church, body culture and fashion).
226. Cf. R. Heinemann, *Familie*.
227. Pacelli to Gasparri (26 May 1926), AA.EE.SS., Germania, Pos. 565 P.O. fasc. 81 fo. 104.
228. Cf., for example, the attitude of Cardinal Donato Sbarretti, reported in P. Godman, *Hitler and the Vatican*, 26–7.
229. Cf. EAM NL Faulhaber, no. 9899 (Evangelischer Bund against the Pope and Cardinal Faulhaber).
230. On this and what follows, see K. Repgen, *Pius XI*, 7ff.; Repgen, *Pius XI und das faschistische Italien*.
231. Cf. M. Berezin, *Fascist Self*, esp. 70ff.; E. Gentile, *Via Italiana*, esp. 129ff.
232. R. Lill, *Katholische Kirche*, 210.
233. Already in 1931 there were the first conflicts on account of Catholic Action, which it proved possible to remedy quickly. Cf. R. Lill, *Katholische Kirche*, 212–13; St. Payne, *History of Fascism*, 216–17.
234. Cf. St. Payne, *History of Fascism*, 107–8.
235. Cf. ibid., 119.
236. Cf. ibid., 121ff. Volker Reinhardt (*Geschichte*, 265) thinks 'that totalitarianism in Mussolini's understanding was to signify primarily a distinctive predominance in patronage and prestige in a society structured on a basis of clientage'. See, in contrast, on 'authoritarian fascism and totalitarian fascism', E. Gentile, *Via Italiana*, 136ff. On the totalitarian character of Italian fascism, see also Schlemmer/Woller, *Faschismus*.
237. Thus F. Rossi, *Vatikan*, 19.
238. Cf. H. Köck, *Pius XII*; A. Steinmaus-Pollak, *Katholische Aktion*. See also EAM NL Faulhaber, nos 6580–6.
239. Cf. H. Maier, *Politische Religionen*, 27.
240. R. Lill, *Katholische Kirche*, 210.
241. Cf. J.-L. Pouthier, *Émigrés*, 488–9.
242. Pouthier, *Émigrés*, 484.
243. *Lateranverträge*.
244. Cf. also the evaluation of the Lateran treaties by Alois Hudal (A. Hudal, *Schaffen*, 206–11).
245. Cf. F. Rossi, *Vatikan*, 88; *Kölnische Zeitung*, no. 78 of 13 February 1931.
246. Cf. Pacelli, *Diario*.
247. 'Gasparri, who had successfully brought to conclusion the complex and prolonged negotiations for the Lateran Treaty with Italy in February, 1929, was forced to resign at the beginning of 1930. The strong-willed Pope had been carrying on violent polemics with Mussolini over the interpretation of that treaty and had felt for some months that his Secretary of State, a

man of great intelligence and with a personality as strong as his, did not approve of his views and methods in dealing with that particular phase of Italo-Vatican relations. Pacelli, who had been for years Gasparri's right hand before his diplomatic missions, was chosen to replace the man who, twenty-nine years before, had invited him to enter the Vatican diplomatic service' (C. Cianfarra, *War and the Vatican*, 78).

248. Cf. C. Casula, *Segreterie di stato*, 424–5. A Cardinal Secretary of State remains until the death of 'his' Pope in office (cf. article 'Secrétairerie d'état' in Ph. Levillain [ed.], *Dictionnaire*, 1555ff.), e.g. Mariano Rampolla del Tindaro up to the death of Leo XIII in 1903, or Rafael Merry del Val under Pius X up to 1914. After Domenico Ferrata died unexpectedly after only a month in office, Pietro Gasparri was nominated Secretary of State by Benedict XV, and, after his merely seven years in office, was taken over by Pius XI; he surely reckoned on occupying this office till his death or that of the Pope. In his short, unwanted retirement he managed nothing more towards writing his memoirs, some of which were published by the historical journalist and politician Giovanni Spadolini in the volume *Il Cardinale Gasparri e la questione romana*; cf. C. Casula, *Segreterie di stato*, 425 n. 29. Cardinal Gasparri died on 18 November 1933.

249. Cf. P. Godman, *Hitler and the Vatican*, 28–9.

250. When the cardinals were created nuncios and put on the biretta, they usually worked in Catholic states with the heads of state. The Reich government showed great interest in an act of this kind. Yet Kaas the president of the Centre Party made it clear that such a favour could only be guaranteed in purely Catholic states. Cf. von Bergen to AA, 27 November 1929 (no. 93; A 680). PA/AA, Embassy to the Holy See, Best. 9 Umwandl./Lfd. No. 283 (no foliation).

251. On 24 January 1930, von Bergen telegraphed to AA (no. 8; A55): 'Cardinal Secretary of State [i.e. Gasparri] disclosed to me today that his Holiness has read the answer of the Reich President to the letter of recall of former Nuncio Pacelli with lively satisfaction; the letter [he said] was very friendly, and moreover, as he added with a smile when alluding to the impending change of personnel, extremely complimentary for his Secretary of state.' PA/AA Embassy to the Holy See, Bestand 29, vol. 1/Lfd. No. 441 (unfoliated).

252. Cf. P. Lehnert, *Erinnerungen*.

253. Cf. W. Steglich, *Friedenspolitik*, 120. D. Alvarez/R. Graham, *Nothing Sacred*, 3, speak of a 'friendship' which is said to have bound the two men.

254. Cf. von Bergen to AA (8 March 1930) (no. 68; A 206), PA/AA, Best. 29 vol. 1/Lfd. No. 441 (unfoliated).

255. Cf. esp. EAM NL Faulhaber, no. 7480.

256. On the role of Faulhaber in the negotiations for the Reich concordat cf. EAM NL Faulhaber, nos 7302–8.

257. Report no. 93 (A284) of the German embassy to the Holy See to the AA, 24 April 1931; cf. report of 17 April 1931 (AA II. Vat. 29; A 265); Report of 27 May 1931 (no. 21; A350); Report of Klee to the AA of 24 March 1934 (no. 143; A 218); Report of Klee (6 December 1934) (no. 78; A 724). PA/AA, Embassy to the Holy See, Best. 29, vol. 1/Lfd. No. 441 (unfoliated).

258. Report of von Bergen (26 June 1934) (no. 267; A400), PA/AA, Embassy to the Holy See. Best. 29, vol. 1/Lfd. No. 441 (unfoliated).

259. Cf. Wolf/Unterburger, *Eugenio Pacelli*.
260. Pacelli to Perosi (18 November 1929), AA.EE.SS., Germania, Pos. 511 P.O. fasc. 24 fo. 4r.
261. AA.EE.SS., Germania, Pos. 511 P.O. fasc. 24 fo. 6r.
262. AA.EE.SS., Germania, Pos. 511 P.O. fasc. 24 fo. 10v.
263. AA.EE.SS., Germania, Pos. 511 P.O. fasc. 24 fo. 11r–v.
264. AA.EE.SS., Germania, Pos. 511 P.O. fasc. 24 fo. 13v.
265. On this see K. Vocelka, *Geschichte Österreichs*, 281; cf. also above, Chapter 2.5.
266. Pacelli to Perosi (18 November 1929), AA.EE.SS., Germania, Pos. 511 P.O. fasc. 24 fo. 15v.
267. AA.EE.SS., Germania, Pos. 511 P.O. fasc. 24 fo. 16r.
268. Jena, 1926.
269. Cf. E. Michel, *Politik*, 46ff. (reference from E. Pacelli).
270. Pacelli to Parosi (18 November 1929), AA.EE.SS., Germania, Pos. 511 P.O. fasc. 24 fo. 16v.
271. AA.EE.SS., Germania, Pos. 511 P.O. fasc. 24 fo. 18r.
272. AA.EE.SS., Germania, Pos. 511 P.O. fasc. 24 fo. 19v.
273. AA.EE.SS., Germania, Pos. 511 P.O. fasc. 24 fo. 20v.
274. AA.EE.SS., Germania, Pos. 511 P.O. fasc. 24 fo. 23r.
275. AA.EE.SS., Germania, Pos. 511 P.O. fasc. 24 fo. 23v.
276. AA.EE.SS., Germania, Pos. 511 P.O. fasc. 24 fo. 26r.
277. AA.EE.SS., Germania, Pos. 511 P.O. fasc. 24 fos 34v, 35v.
278. AA.EE.SS., Germania, Pos. 511 P.O. fasc. 24 fo. 35v.
279. AA.EE.SS., Germania, Pos. 511 P.O. fasc. 24 fos 38v, 39r.
280. AA.EE.SS., Germania, Pos. 511 P.O. fasc. 24 fo. 40r.
281. AA.EE.SS., Germania, Pos. 511 P.O. fasc. 24 fo. 41r.
282. AA.EE.SS., Germania, Pos. 511 P.O. fasc. 24 fo. 41v.
283. AA.EE.SS., Germania, Pos. 511 P.O. fasc. 24 fo. 42r.
284. AA.EE.SS., Germania, Pos. 511 P.O. fasc. 24 fo. 42v.
285. AA.EE.SS., Germania, Pos. 511 P.O. fasc. 24 fo. 43r.
286. AA.EE.SS., Germania, Pos. 511 P.O. fasc. 24 fo. 44r.
287. AA.EE.SS., Germania, Pos. 511 P.O. fasc. 24 fo. 44v.
288. Cf. M. Biffi, *Orsenigo*; Biffi, *Cavalletto*.
289. Cf. on this and the following, *loc. cit.* 16ff.
290. Cf. P. Godman, *Hitler and the Vatican*, 30–1.
291. Cf. S. Adam, *Preysing*; W. Knauft, *Preysing*.
292. O. Chadwick, *Pius XII*.
293. Cf. L. Volk, *Reichskonkordat*, 212ff.
294. H. Winkler, *Weimar*, 477.
295. Orsenigo to Pacelli (9 May 1930), AA.EE.SS., Germania, Pos. 604 P.O. fasc. 112 fo. 3v. Printed in Italian in G. Sale, *Hitler*, 275–6.
296. Ibid.
297. AA.EE.SS., Germania, Pos. 604 P.O. fasc. 112 fos 3v–4r.
298. Cf. Pacelli to Orsenigo (7 June 1930), AA.EE.SS., Germania, Pos. 604 P.O. fasc. 112 fo. 5r.
299. Cf. Orsenigo to Pacelli (4 August 1930), AA.EE.SS., Germania, Pos. 604 P.O. fasc. 112 fo. 20r–v.
300. Ibid.

301. Cf. G. Besier, *Neuansätze*, 194ff.
302. Orsenigo to Pacelli (4 August 1930), AA.EE.SS., Germania, Pos. 604 P.O. fasc. 117 fos 21r–23r; here 23r. Printed in G. Sale, *Hitler*, 279–80 (rendered correctly down to small typing errors).
303. Pacelli to Orsenigo, AA.EE.SS., Germania, Pos. 604 P.O. fasc. 117 fo. 25r–v.
304. Cf. below, Chapter 3.6.
305. Cf. K. Scholder, *Kirchen*, vol. 1, 127ff.; H. Winkler, *Weimar*, 388ff.
306. Cf. to Bruno Doehring, G. Besier, *Dom*, 197ff.
307. Orsenigo to Pacelli (16 September 1930), AA.EE.SS., Germania, Pos. 606 P.O. fasc. 117 fos 18r–19v. Printed by G. Sale, *Hitler*, 282–4 (wrongly ascribed to 18 September 1930 and described with the shelf-mark '605 P.O. fasc. 117').

3. The Foreign Policy of the Vatican under Cardinal Secretary of State Pacelli 1930–39

1. D. Tardini, *Pius XII*, 92.
2. Thus E. von Weizsäcker, *Erinnerungen*, 357.
3. Cf. F. Rossi, *Vatican*, 85–6.
4. Thus Nosengo, cited from F. de Giorgi, *Linguaggi militari*, 265–6.
5. Cf. M. Agostino, *Pie XI*, 443ff.
6. Cited from Fr. Engel-Janosi, *Chaos*, 111.
7. AAS 23 (1931), 285–312; Fitzek (ed.), *Pius XII*, 27ff.; cf. also C. Confalonieri, *Pius XI*, 204ff.; Fr. Engel-Janosi, *Chaos*, 229–55.
8. AAS 23 (1931), 294.
9. Cf. J. Charnitzky, *Schulpolitik*, 3.
10. Cited from G. Gentile, *Grundlagen*, 8.
11. Gentile, *Grundlagen*, 89.
12. Ibid., 90.
13. Ibid., 90.
14. Ibid., 92.
15. Ibid., 96.
16. Ibid., 94.
17. Ibid.
18. Tacchi Venturi was frequently drafted in as mediator in cases of disagreement between Mussolini and Pius XI. When, for example, the fascist press dealt critically with the Pope's Christmas address in 1937, Tacchi Venturi received a letter from Pacelli on 8 January 1938, requesting him to point out to Mussolini 'the regret of the Holy Father at such an attitude in the press, especially after what he had to say in his Christmas address about the persecution suffered by the Church in Germany'. AA.EE.SS., Germania, Pos. 724 P.O. fasc. 339 fo. 58r–v.
19. Text: R. de Felice, *Mussolini*, vol. 1, 269.
20. Cf. J. Charnitzky, *Schulpolitik*, 292–7.
21. Cf. F. de Giorgi, *Linguaggi militari*, 277–8.
22. Cf. below, Chapter 3.2.
23. Cf. on this H. Hürten, *Deutsche Katholiken*, 119–43.
24. Cf. L. Esch, *Neudeutschland*; R. Guardini, *Stationen und Rückblicke*, 14–15; F. Henrich, *Bünde*; F. Raabe, *Bündische Jugend*.

25. Cf. Pacelli to Carlo Perosi (18 November 1929), AA.EE.SS., Germania, Pos. 511 P.O. fasc. 24 fos 4r–49v; here: 7r–8v.
26. Cf. E. Iserloh, *Bewegungen*.
27. Cf. e.g. R. Guardini, *Sinn*, 13.
28. Cf. G. May, *Ludwig Kaas*.
29. Cf. L. Volk, *Kirche*, 543–5.
30. Cf. K. Klemperer, *Ignaz Seipel*; Fr. Rennhofer, *Ignaz Seipel*.
31. Cf. on this and what follows: S. Amann, *Austrofaschismus*; I. Bärnthaler, *Vaterländische Front*; F. Carsten, *Republik*; H. Drimmel, *Kanzlermord*; A. Hopfgartner, *Kurt Schuschnigg*; U. Kluge, *Ständestaat*; L. Meysels, *Austrofaschismus*; A. Suppan (ed.), *Dokumente*; G. Volsansky, *Pakt*; E. Weinzierl, *Prüfstand*; Weinzierl/K. Skalnik (eds), *Österreich*; R. Steininger/M. Gehler (eds), *Österreich*, vol. 1, esp. 153ff.
32. Fr. Engel-Janosi. *Chaos*, 56–7.
33. Cf. E. Hanisch, *Katholizismus*.
34. Cf. W. Wiltschegg, *Heimwehr*.
35. On the support of Italian-Hungarian relations by the Vatican cf. P. Kent, *Pope*, 26ff.
36. Cf. W. Maderthaner, *12. Februar 1934*, esp. 158ff. On the concept of the 'new order' as represented by the home-defence units at their leadership conference on 18 May 1930 in Korneuburg, cf. the book of the Vienna sociologist and national-economist Othmar Spann (O. Spann, *Staat*, esp. 62, 175ff., 237ff.)
37. Thus K. Vocelka, *Geschichte Österreichs*, 276.
38. Cf. by contrast G. Kindermann, *Österreich*.
39. Cf. E. Tálos, *Herrschaftssystem*, 104.
40. Cf. E. Weinzierl, *Prüfstand*, 33–4.
41. Cf. B. Galletto, *Dollfuss*.
42. Cf. K. Schuschnigg, *Kampf*.
43. Cf. in detail W. Maderthaner, *12. Februar 1934*. Mussolini advised him expressly to this step. Cf. Mussolini to Dollfuss (1 July 1933), in W. Maderthaler/M. Maier (eds), *Führer*, 23–7; here: 25.
44. Cited after W. Maderthaner, *12. Februar 1934*, 163.
45. Cited after H. Wohnout, *Regierungsdiktatur*, 430.
46. Cf. above, Chapter 2.5.
47. Cf. Bertram's warning on the forthcoming Reichstag election on 1 September 1930 in W. Marschall (ed.), *Hirtenbriefe*, 428–9.
48. See also Bertram's 'Open Word in a serious moment at the end of the Year 1930', W. Marschall (ed.), *Hirtenbriefe*, 429–34. Here the Breslau Cardinal takes up the Christmas address of Pius XI (AAS 22 [1930], 529–39) and like him warns against 'exaggerated nationalism' and 'glorification of race'. On Pacelli's request, Orsenigo reported on 31 December 1930 on the response to Pius XI's Christmas address in the German press (AA.EE.SS., Germania, Pos. 604 P.O. fasc. 112 fos 52r–53v. Printed in G. Sale, *Hitler*, 286–7, correctly rendered in Sale down to a small typing error and the concluding formula – in Sale identical with the introductory words of the document). After this many papers identified Italian fascism and German National Socialism as the addressees.
49. Report of the German Embassy to the Holy See (30 September 1930) (No. 229; A633), PA/AA, Botschaft beim Heiligen Stuhl, Best. 29, vol. 1/Lfd. Nr. 441 (unfoliated).

50. Cf. K. Scholder, *Kirchen*, vol. 1, 132ff.
51. Orsenigo to Pacelli (8 October 1930), AA.EE.SS., Germania, Pos. 621 P.O. fasc. 138 fos 3r–4r.
52. Ibid.
53. AA.EE.SS., Germania, Pos. 621 P.O. fasc. 138 fo. 10.
54. Cf. AA.EE.SS., Germania, Pos. 606 P.O. fasc. 117 fos 34–77; AA.EE.SS., Germania, Pos. 606 P.O. fasc. 117 fos 22r–33r.
55. AA.EE.SS., Germania, Pos. 606 P.O. fasc. 117 fo. 77r.
56. Matthias Ehrenfried, Bishop of Würzburg, communicated this impression to Pacelli on 2 February 1932 (AA.EE.SS., Germania, Pos. 621 P.O. fasc. 139 fos 22r–v). Cf. Franz Josef Fürst von Isenburg to Pacelli (12 November 1931), AA.EE.SS., Germania, Pos. 621 P.O. fasc. 139 fo. 10r–v; cf. Pacelli to Isenburg (21 November 1931), AA.EE.SS., Germania, Pos. 621 P.O. fasc. 139 fo. 11r; Klara-Marie Prinzessin Georg von Sachsen-Meiningen to Pius XI (12 November 1931), AA.EE.SS., Germania, Pos. 621 P.O. fasc. 139 fos 12r–13r; Pacelli to the Prinzessin von Sachsen-Meiningen (21 November 1931), AA.EE.SS., Germania, Pos. 621 P.O. fasc. 139 fos 16r–v, 17r.
57. Cf. Draft answer of Pacelli to Orsenigo (13 October 1930), AA.EE.SS., Germania, Pos. 621 P.O. fasc. 138 fo. 11r.
58. Orsenigo to Pacelli (29 December 1930), AA.EE.SS., Germania, Pos. 604 P.O. fasc. 112 fo. 49r. Printed in G. Sale, *Hitler*, 285.
59. H. Hömig, *Brüning*, 204ff.
60. Orsenigo to Pacelli (27 January 1931), AA.EE.SS., Germania, Pos. 621 P.O. fasc. 138 fos 25r–26r.
61. AA.EE.SS., Germania, Pos. 621 P.O. fasc. 138 fo. 25r.
62. Ibid.
63. Ibid.
64. Text: W. Marschall (ed.), *Hirtenbriefe*, 429–34.
65. Text: B. Stasiewski (ed.), *Akten deutscher Bischöfe*, vol. 1, 806–9.
66. K. Scholder, *Kirchen*, vol. 1, 133.
67. Vassallo to Pacelli (17 February 1931), AA.EE.SS., Germania, Pos. 621 P.O. fasc. 138 fo. 25r–v.
68. Report of Groenesteyn (16 March 1931), BayHStA, Bayerische Gesandtschaft, Päpstlicher Stuhl, 1030, fo. 99.
69. Thus, for example, the Pastoral Instruction of the Bavarian Episcopate of 10 February 1931, in B. Stasiewski (ed.), *Akten deutscher Bischöfe*, vol. 1, 806–9.
70. B. Stasiewski (ed.), *Akten deutscher Bischöfe*, vol. 1, 832–43.
71. Orsenigo to Pacelli (8 March 1931), AA.EE.SS., Germania, Pos. 621 P.O. fasc. 138 fo. 33r–v.
72. B. Stasiewski (ed.), *Akten deutscher Bischöfe*, vol. 1, 806–9.
73. Ibid.
74. Ibid.
75. Text: W. Corsten (ed.), *Sammlung*, 619ff.
76. B. Stasiewski (ed.), *Akten deutscher Bischöfe*, 806–9.
77. Dollfuss, at the end of his speech in the Trabrennplatz on 11 September 1933, cited from W. Maderthaner, *Legitimationsmuster*, 134.
78. Cf. Hausleithner, *Geist*, esp. 92ff.
79. Cited from E. Huber/W. Huber (eds), *Staat und Kirche*, vol. 3, 304.
80. Ibid.

81. Cited from E. Huber/W. Huber (eds), *Staat und Kirche*, vol. 4, 426.
82. Thus A. Hudal, *Vatikan*, 12.
83. On 23 April 1932 Cardinal Hlond issued a pastoral letter, *Um die Christlichen Grundsätze des Staatslebens* [*On the Christian Foundations of Political Life*] (Poznań, 1932). The principles for which he argued were: the State must acknowledge God and owe him worship; the duties of the State towards God; in public life the divine law is binding (refers to Leo XIII, *Immortale Dei*); relation of the State to the family; the right of parents over their children and their education; State and Church; independence of the Church from the State; the Church a guardian of the morality of public life.
84. Emmerich Tálos holds that in the case of Austria the reference of the encyclical *Quadragesimo Anno* was a farce, "'professional corporative order" signified in reality too authoritarian determination between state and social interests', E. Tálos, *Herrschaftssystem*, 116.
85. See Tom Gallagher, 'Portugal', in Buchanan/Conway, *Political Catholicism*, 128–55.
86. Höcht, *Fatima und Pius XII*, 42ff.
87. Cf. for the following Bernecker/Pietschmann, *Geschichte Portugals*; Birmingham, *History*; Braga da Cruz, *Estado Novo*, 49–63; Golder/Rahden, *Studien*; Linz/Stepan (eds), *Breakdown*; Opello, *Development*; Pinto, *Salazar's Dictatorship*.
88. There were of course also opposite trends. Cf. on this E. Hanisch, *Ideologie*, 26ff.
89. H. Wohnout, *Regierungsdiktatur*, 428.
90. *Wiener Diözesanblatt*, no. 12, 21 December 1933, 104.
91. Cf. J. Kremsmair, *Konkordat*, 291ff. On the relations between Mussolini and Dollfuss, see W. Maderthaner/M. Maier (eds), *Führer*.
92. J. Kremsmair, *Konkordat*, 293.
93. Cf. on Hudal's role below, Chapter 3.10. As a recognition of his pains in bringing the concordat about, Hudal was created bishop in 1933 (J. Kremsmair, *Konkordat*, 304). On the relations between Pacelli and Hudal, cf. Chenaux, 'Pacelli, Hudal', 135ff.
94. Text: AAS 26 (1934), 249ff. Cf. K. Scholder, *Konkordat*. See also the critical SD report 'Kirchen-Staat Österreich' ['The Church-State of Austria'], BA ZB I 1653, fos 387–91. In it is talk of a 'clericalisation of the entire life of the state' (BA ZB I 1653, fo. 391).
95. Cf. Fr. Engel-Janosi, *Chaos*, 133.
96. Cf. E. Tálos, *Herrschaftsytem*, 121. On 30 November 1933 the Austrian bishops' conference passed a resolution on the political activity of the clergy. It was thereafter forbidden to clergy of every level to accept political mandates and take part in politics. *Wiener Diözesanblatt*, no.12 (21 December 1933) 99.
97. Thus K. Vocelka, *Geschichte Österreichs*, 293. On the amendments, corrections and excitements between the signing and the ratification of the concordat, cf. J. Kremsmair, *Konkordat*, 299ff.
98. 'The Concordat', in *Wiener Diözesanblatt*, no. 4 (7 May 1934), 27.
99. Ibid., 28.
100. Cf. E. Hanisch, *Schatten*, 314–15.

101. W. Maderthaner, *Legitimationsmuster*, 142.
102. D. A. Binder, *Ständesstaat*, 211.
103. A. Hudal, *Vatikan*, 12.
104. Cf. E. Hanisch, *Katholizismus*, esp. 53ff.
105. On his Rome visit Göring also succeeded in being received by Mussolini for the first time. Cf. E. Butler/G. Young, *Hermann Göring*, 92–3; R. De Felice (ed.), *Mussolini e Hitler*, 227; A. Kube, *Pour le mérite und Hakenkreuz*, 17–18; W. Maser, *Hermann Göring*, 131.
106. Cf. on this and the following E. Deuerlein, *Katholizismus* 53ff.; Deuerlein (ed.), *Aufstieg*, 351ff.
107. On this and the following, see A. Kube, *Pour le mérite und Hakenkreuz*, 17f.; St. Martens, *Hermann Göring*, 35ff.; J. Petersen, *Hitler-Mussolini*, 44–5, 104.
108. Göring to Pacelli, Rome (30 April 1931), AA.EE.SS., Germania, Pos. 621 P.O. fasc. 138 fo. 38r.
109. 'Under the given conditions [rejection of National Socialism by the German bishops] it was conceivably very painful to Cardinal Pacelli to be requested for an audience by a representative of the National Socialist party'. Report of Groenesteyn (11 May 1931), BayHstA, Bayerische Gesandtschaft, Päpstlicher Stuhl, 1030, fo. 88.
110. AA.EE.SS., Germania, Pos. 621 P.O. fasc. 138 fo. 40r–v.
111. Ibid.
112. M. Feldkamp, *Pius XII*, 73.
113. See, in contrast, E. Deuerlein, *Katholizismus*, 53, 56; L. Volk, *Reichskonkordat*, 65.
114. Cf. K. Scholder, *Kirchen*, vol. 1, 150–1.
115. Cf. H. Fraenkel/R. Manvell, *Göring*, Hannover 1964, 64 (Göring's interview with the *Nationalzeitung*).
116. Göring to Pizzardo (26 May 1931), AA.EE.SS., Pos. 606 P.O fasc. 118 fo. 3r–v.
117. Report of Groenesteyn of 11 May 1931, BayHStA, Bayerische Gesandtschaft, Päpstlicher Stuhl, 1030, fo. 91–2. Cf. BayHStA, Bayerische Gesandtschaft, Päpstlicher Stuhl, 1030, fos 236–7, 238.
118. Cf. on the following M. Feldkamp, *Pius XII*, 73ff.; H. Hömig, *Brüning*, 359–61.
119. Cf. R. Morsey, *Entstehung*; Fr. Müller, *Brüning-Papers*; A. Rödder, *Dichtung und Wahrheit*.
120. A. Rödder, *Dichtung und Wahrheit*, 116.
121. H. Brüning, *Memoiren*, 365.
122. Ibid., 357.
123. Ibid., 357.
124. Ibid., 358.
125. Cf. on army chaplaincy EAM NL Faulhaber, no. 6790.
126. Cf. above, Chapter 2.3.
127. H. Brüning, *Memoiren*, 358.
128. Ibid.
129. Ibid. In fact Pacelli had written to Centoz on the 29 February 1930: 'Whoever is familiar with the attitude of the Protestants towards the concordat concluded between the Holy See and Prussia cannot fail to find it very odd that it should be the Catholics of all people [i.e. the Centre

Party] who seek to further the above-mentioned agreement [i.e. the State–Church treaty], which in view of the special circumstances of this country can be tolerated but not supported' (AA.EE.SS., Germania, Pos. 511 P.O. fasc. 24 fo. 58).

130. H. Brüning, *Memoiren*, 359.
131. Ibid., 359f.
132. Cf. A. Rödder, *Dichtung und Wahrheit*, 82.
133. Cf. R. Morsey, *Brünings politische Weltanschauung*, 333–4; Müller, '*Brüning-Papers*', 142–3.
134. Cited from Fr. Müller, *Brüning-Papers*, 143; cf. H. Brüning, *Memoiren*, 135–6.
135. Cf. J. Stephan, *Begleiterin*. Claire Nix: Heinrich Brünings Eckermann in Neuengland, in *FAZ* no. 54 (4 March 2000), 3, and the readers' letters on it in *FAZ* no. 58 (9 March 2000), 17 (William L. Patch), and *FAZ* no. 66 (18 March 2000), 11 (Claire Nix).
136. Cf. Fr. Müller, *Brüning-Papers*, 143, n. 633.
137. Akten der Reichskanzlei, Kabinett Brüning I und II, vol. 2, 1551; record of Foreign Minister Curtius (9 August 1931), ADAP, B, vol. 18, 248.
138. Cf. R. Morsey (ed.), *Protokolle*, 479–80, 500, 542.
139. Cf. H. Winkler, *Weimar*, 431.
140. Orsenigo to Pacelli (11 October 1931), AA.EE.SS., Pos. 604 P.O. fasc. 112 fos 84r–85v. Printed by G. Sale, *Hitler*, 290–2.
141. AA.EE.SS., Pos. 604 P.O. fasc. 112 fos 92r–94r.
142. P. Godman, *Hitler and the Vatican*, 14.
143. Cf. P. Kent, *Pope*, 193. Cf. also J. Gaillard, *Attractions*, 208, who with Ernesto Rossi (*Manganello*, 210) quotes Pius XI: 'if there is a totalitarian form of government – totalitarian both in fact and in law – it is the form of government of the Church'.
144. Cf. P. Foresta, *Totalitarismus*.
145. See also M. Agostino, *Pie XI*, 76ff.
146. AAS 14 (1922), 673–700.
147. AAS 17 (1925), 593–610.
148. Cf. G. Besier, *Kirche im 20. Jahrhundert*, 14ff.
149. Cf. Ch. Walther, *Königsherrschaft Christi*.
150. Thus P. Foresta, *Totalitarismus*.
151. Cf. Encyclical *Quas primas* (11 December 1925), AAS 17 (1925), 593–610.
152. Cf. K. Frank, *Christkönig*, 1140.
153. F. Malgieri/E. Collotti, *Chiesa*, 174.
154. Cf. R. De Felice, *Mussolini e Hitler*, 272–3.
155. Cf. Bohn, *Verhältnis*, esp. 152ff.
156. Thus F. de Giorgi, *Linguaggi militari*, 266.
157. Cf. above, Chapter 3.3.
158. G. Batelli, *Chiesa*; G. Miccoli, *Chiesa e società*, 1521–2.
159. Thus for Italy, P. Scoppola (ed.), *Chiesa e stato*, 685.
160. AAS 14 (1922), 673–80; cf. A. Rohrbasser (ed.), *Heilslehre*, 1000f.
161. Quoted from *Ecclesiastica: Dokumente und Nachrichten zur zeitgenössischen Kirchengeschichte* no. 2, VI of 9 January 1926.
162. Cf. L. Mangoni, *Patti*, 159.
163. Cf. G. Miccoli, *Italien*, 544. See also the pastoral letter of the Bishop of Linz, Johannes Maria Gföller (27 February 1928). This, in conjunction with

the encyclical of Pius XI of 11 December 1925, was to strengthen the idea of authority – of parental, political and ecclesiastical authority. *Linzer Diözesanblatt* no. 2 (1927), 25–34. Since the bishops throughout the world accepted the Pope's declarations into their own pastoral letters, their effect was greatly increased.

164. Cf. AAS 16 (1924), 133–48.
165. Cf. F. de Giorgi, *Linguaggi militari*, 274.
166. *Rundschreiben unseres Heiligsten Vaters Pius XI zur sechsten Jahrhundertfeier der Heiligsprechung des Thomas von Aquin* (29 June 1923: *Studiorum ducem*), Freiburg/Breisgau 1923, 31. Cf. also *Rundschreiben unseres Heiligen Vaters Pius XI zum 300: Todestag des heiligen Märtyrers Josaphat des Erzbischofs von Polozk ritus orientalis* (12 November 1923: *Ecclesiam Dei*), Freiburg/Breisgau 1923; *Rundschreiben Pius XI über den hl. Franziskus von Assisi zu seinem 700: Todestage* (30 April 1926: *Rite expiates*), Freiburg/Breisgau 1926; *Rundschreiben Pius XI über die Förderung der Missionen* (28 February 1926: *Rerum ecclesiae*), Freiburg/Breisgau 1926; *Apostolischer Brief Pius XI zum 200 jährigen Jubiläum der Heiligsprechung des heiligen Aloisius von Gonzaga* (*Singulare illud*, 13 June 1926), Trier 1926; *Rundschreiben Pius XI über die Förderung der wahren Einheit der Religion* (6 January, on the Feast of the Epiphany, 1928: *Mortalium animos*), Freiburg/Breisgau 1928; *Rundschreiben Pius XI zum glücklichen Abschluss seines fünfzigsten Priesterjahres* (23 December 1929: *Quinquagesimo ante anno*), Freiburg/Breisgau 1930; *Rundschreiben Pius XI über die christliche Erziehung der Jugend* (31 December 1929: *Rappresentanti*), Freiburg/Breisgau 130; *Rundschreiben Pius XI zum 1500: Todesjahres des Heiligen Augustinus Bischofs von Hippo und Kirchenlehrers* (2O April 1930: *Ad salutem humani generis*), Freiburg/Breisgau 1930; *Rundschreiben Pius XI über die christliche Ehe in Hinsicht auf die gegenwärtigen Verhältnisse, Bedrängnisse, Irrtümer und Verfehlungen in Familie und Gesellschaft* (*Casti connubii*, 31 December 1930), Munich 1931.
167. Cf. encyclical *Quas primas* of 11 December 1925, AAS 17 (1925), 593–610; here: 602ff.; cf. A. Rohrbasser (ed.), *Heilslehre*, 67ff.
168. Cf. A. Rohrbasser (ed.), *Heilslehre*, 65.
169. Thus F. de Giorgi, *Linguaggi militari*, 271.
170. A. Rohrbasser, *Heilslehre*, 70.
171. Cf. Ch. Joosten, *Christkönigsfest*, 115–16.
172. Cf. Fr. Engel-Janosi, *Chaos*, 165; A. Mattioli, *Hölle*; see also Mattioli, *Kriegsgewalt*; G. Schneider, *Mussolini*.
173. A. Mattioli, *Hölle*. Further examples and indications of the literature in L. Klinkhammer, *Mussolini's Italien*; here: 88.
174. Cf. Besier, *Kirchen*, 757. In this view of the matter he was supported among others by the right wing of British Catholicism led by Hilaire Belloc. On this see Corrin, *Catholic Intellectuals*, 305ff.
175. It was manifest that after 1929 the Vatican gold coins to the value of 100 lire bore on the one side the image of Christ the King and on the other that of Pius XI.
176. Cf. D. Menozzi, *Regalità*; P. Scoppola, *Storiografia*, 192.
177. Cf. E. Gentile, *Sacralization*.
178. Cf. F. de Giorni, *Linguaggi militari*.
179. Cf. M. Zöller, *Washington und Rom*, esp. 152ff.; Ph. Chen, *Religious Liberty*; Ch. Gallagher, *Patriotism*.

180. Quoted from D. Albrecht, *Notenwechsel*, 69. On 16 November 1918 a letter from the Pope to the Cardinal Secretary of State was published in the *Osservatore Romano* declaring that: 'The Church [is] a perfect society which has as its sole object the salvation of men of all ages and lands; it adapts itself to various forms of government, and it accepts without difficulty the legitimate territorial and political variations of the natons.'
181. Conversation of Bishop Robert Picard de le Vacquerie with embassy councillor Joseph Höfer. Embassy councillor Jaenicke to the [German] Foreign Office (20 November 1954), quoted from M. Feldkamp, *Beziehungen*, 124.
182. Text: E. Huber/W. Huber (eds), *Staat und Kirche*, vol. 1, 246–57.
183. Cf. the correspondence in E. Huber/W. Huber (eds), *Staat und Kirche*, vol. 4, 350–3.
184. Cf. E. Föhr, *Geschichte*, 14–15.
185. Text: E. Huber/W. Huber (eds), *Staat und Kirche*, vol. 4, 354–8.
186. Cf. L. Volk, *Reichskonkordat*, 50ff.
187. Cf. above, Chapter 2.4 and Chapter 3.4.
188. Cf. above, Chapter 2.5.
189. Cf. G. May, *Ludwig Kaas*, vol. 1, 377; vol. 2, 664–86.
190. Cf. above, Chapter 3.2.
191. Cf. on this and the following, W. Becker, *Zentrumspartei*.
192. H. Hömig, *Zentrum*, 269.
193. R. Morsey (ed.), *Protokolle*, 599 (29 November 1932); cf. W. Patch, *Brüning*, 294.
194. Thus G. Treviranus, *Ende*, 374.
195. Cf. H. Winkler, *Weimar*, 536.
196. Orsenigo to Pacelli (11 October 1932), AA.EE.SS., Germania, Pos. 604 P.O. fasc. 113 fos 29r–31r. Printed in G. Sale, *Hitler*, 309–11.
197. Already in 1932 the election of Papen as successor to Brüning had produced a 'shock' at home and abroad. Cf. H. Graml, *Stresemann und Hitler*, 206.
198. Cf. H. Winkler, *Weimar*, 580f.
199. AA.EE.SS., Germania, Pos. 604 P.O. fasc. 113 fos 41r–42v; here: 41v. Reprint of the document in G. Sale, *Hitler*, 314–15.
200. Ibid.
201. AA.EE.SS., Germania, Pos. 604 P.O. fasc. 113 fo. 42r.
202. Ibid.
203. Cited from L. Volk, *Reichskonkordat*, 64, n. 24; cf. ibid., 65.
204. Fr. von Papen, *Wahrheit*, 314.
205. L. Volk, *Reichskonkordat*, 65, n. 26.
206. In the Reichstag elections of 6 November 1932 the SPD had still been able to attract 20.4 per cent of the votes, the KPD 16.9 per cent.
207. Cf. A. Mannes, *Brüning*, 183.
208. Thus G. Schwaiger, *Papsttum und Päpste*, 237.
209. On the afternoon of 23 March 1933 Georg Schreiber communicated the agreement of the Centre to the 'Enabling Act' in a small room in the Krolloper Frick. In this conversation there was no mention of the question of the concordat. Cf. finally on this R. Morsey, *Ende*.
210. A. François-Poncet, *Botschafter*, 125.
211. Thus H. Winkler, *Weg*, vol. 2, 13.
212. R. Morsey, *Ermächtigungsgesetz*, 46–7; the same (ed.), *Protokolle*, 630ff.

213. Cf. R. Morsey (ed.), *Protokolle*, 596 (19 November 1932).
214. Cf. D. Junker, *Deutsche Zentrumspartei*, 197.
215. Cf. L. Kaas, *Konkordatstyp*, 491.
216. Cf. in detail R. Morsey (ed.), *Ermächtigungsgesetz*, 49ff.
217. Cf. R. Morsey, *Ende*.
218. Cited from Morsey, *Ende*, who refers to Karsten Ruppert.
219. H. Brüning, *Memoiren*, 656; cf. J. Becker, *Zentrumspartei*, 359–61.
220. Cf. K. Bracher, *Machtergreifung*; L. Siegele-Wenschkewitz, *Nationalsozialismus und Kirchen*, 90–123; K. Scholder, *Kirchen*, vol. 1, 237–53; Scholder, *Altes und Neues*.
221. Cf. H. Hürten, *Deutsche Katholiken*, 233–4; St. Stehlin, *Weimar*, 451.
222. Cf. K. Repgen, *Entstehung*; Repgen, *Nachwort*; Repgen, *Strategie*; Repgen, *Reichskonkordat-Kontroversen*; Repgen, *Machtergreifung*; L. Volk, *Ökumene*.
223. See, by contrast G. May, *Ludwig Kaas*, vol. 3, 351, 367, who certifies that Kaas acted in good faith, to be very badly deceived.
224. Cf. L. Kaas, *Konkordatstyp*.
225. Cf. K. von Aretin, *Vorbemerkungen*. See also now C. Kretschmann, *Scholder-Repgen-Debatte*.
226. Cf. H. Hürten, *Deutsche Katholiken*, 86ff., 231ff.
227. On 10 April 1933 Vice Chancellor von Papen handed over the Reich government's concordat offer to Rome.
228. Letter of Kaas to von Bergen (19 November 1935), in A. Kupper (ed.), *Staatliche Akten*, 496.
229. Cf. K. Scholder, *Kirchen*, vol. 1, 382ff. Contrast K. Repgen, *Entstehung*.
230. Cf. H. Brüning, *Memoiren*, 655ff. Thus also Brüning in a letter to Franz Dessauer (8 May 1959), in K. Repgen, *Ungedruckte Nachkriegsquellen*, 404–7.
231. Cf. H. Brüning, *Memoiren*, 358ff.
232. R. Morsey (ed.), *Ermächtigungsgesetz*, 60.
233. Cited after E. Huber/W. Huber (eds), *Staat und Kirche*, vol. 4, 467.
234. Thus the embassy councillor at the German embassy to the Holy See, Eugen Klee, cf. R. Morsey, *Zentrumspartei*, 363–4, n. 59.
235. W. Becker, *Zentrumspartei*, 22.
236. Cited from R. Morsey (ed.), *Ermächtigungsgesetz*, 136.
237. R. Morsey (ed.), *Kaas*, 427; cf. ibid., 424.
238. Thus already K. Scholder, *Altes und Neues*, 533.
239. Cf. above, Chapter 3.2.
240. Orsenigo to Pacelli (7 February 1933), AA.EE.SS., Germania, Pos. 641–643 P.O. fasc. 157 fos 13r–14r. Printed in G. Sale, *Hitler*, 316–17. (The date is there given as 4 February 1933, otherwise the text, including the printed enclosures [p. 318–19], is correct.)
241. Cf. F. von Papen, *Wahrheit*, 189ff.
242. Cf. R. Baumgärtner, *Weltanschauungskampf*, 146–7; G. Besier, *Kirchen*, 696; K. Breuning, *Vision*.
243. Cf. K. Breuning, *Vision*, 225ff.
244. Cf. J. Petzold, *Papen*, 193. See now also G. Denzler, *Papen*.
245. Cf. M. Albert, *Benediktinerabtei Maria Laach*, 105–6.
246. Orsenigo to Pacelli (7 February 1933), AA.EE.SS., Germania, Pos. 641–643 P.O. fasc. 157 fos 13r–14v.

247. Report of Orsenigo to Pacelli (16 February 1933), AA.EE.SS., Germania, Pos. 641–643 P.O. fasc. 157 fos 18r–19v.
248. W. Adolph, *Klausener*.
249. Orsenigo to Pacelli (16 February 1933), AA.EE.SS., Germania, Pos. 641–643 P.O. fasc. 157 fos 18r–19v. Printed in G. Sale, *Hitler*, 322–4.
250. Orsenigo to Pacelli (22 February 1933), AA.EE.SS., Gemania, Pos. 621–623 P.O. fasc. 140 fos 62r–63v.
251. Orsenigo to Pacelli (7 March 1933), AA.EE.SS., Germania, Pos. 641–643 P.O. fasc. 157 fos 21r–22r; here: 21r. Printed in G. Sale, *Hitler*, 328–9.
252. Ibid.
253. Ibid.
254. Cf. e.g. B. J. Falter, *Hitlers Wähler*, 177ff., 186ff. Orsenigo's impression was right that, at the March elections 1933, the NSDAP made an unprecedented incursion into the Catholic milieus (Falter, *Hitlers Wähler*, 188).
255. Orsenigo to Pacelli (9 March 1933), AA.EE.SS., Germania, Pos. 641–643 P.O. fasc. 157 fos 26r–27r. Printed in G. Sale, *Hitler*, 330–1.
256. Orsenigo to Pacelli (22 March 1933), AA.EE.SS., Germania, Pos. 621 P.O. fasc. 139 fo. 71r.
257. Orsenigo to Pacelli (22 March 1933), AA.EE.SS., Germania, Pos. 641–643 P.O. fasc. 157 fos 31r–32v. Printed in Sale, *Hitler*, 341–3.
258. Orsenigo to Pacelli (24 March 1933), AA.EE.SS., Germania, Pos. 641–643 P.O. fasc. 157 fo. 29r. Printed in L. Volk (ed.), *Kirchliche Akten*, 4–5. Text of Hitler's Reichstag speech (23 March 1933): P. Meier-Benneckenstein, *Dokumente*, 39–40.
259. Orsenigo to Pacelli (26 March 1933), AA.EE.SS., Germania Pos. 621 P.O. fasc. 139 fos 77r–78r.
260. Cited from Th. Brechenmacher, *Held* (AA.EE.SS., Baviera, ANM Pos. 418 fasc. 4 fo. 39). On 31 March 1931 Vassallo replied to Pacelli's telegram: '[...] spoken to the Archbishop in the sense of the coded message. Push on with the Declarations of the Conference of German Bishops. Half the bishops of Bavaria are now preparing individual further declarations to clergy and faithful'. (AA.EE.SS., Germania Pos. 621 P.O. fasc. 139 fo. 73.)
261. Pacelli to Orsenigo (29 March 1933), AA.EE.SS., Germania, Pos. 621 P.O. fasc. 139 fo. 72r.
262. Orsenigo to Pacelli (29 March 1933), AA.EE.SS., Germania, Pos. 621–623 P.O. fasc. 140 fos 2r–3v; here: 2v. Printed in G. Sale, *Hitler*, 347–8. (Sale's transcription includes various copying errors, one affecting the sense: Orsenigo wished after Hitler's declaration to ascertain not only Bertram's own attitude ['l'atteggiamento dell' Eminentissimo'; cf. Sale, *Hitler*, 347] but also the attitude of the episcopate in general ['l'atteggiamento dell'Episcopato'; cf. AA.EE.SS., Germania, Pos. 621–623 P.O. fasc. 140 fo. 2r] to National Socialism.)
263. Orsenigo to Pacelli (30 March 1933), AA.EE.SS., Germania, Pos. 621 P.O. fasc. 139 fo. 74r.
264. Text: E. Huber/W. Huber (eds), *Staat und Kirche*, vol. 4, 467–8.
265. Text of the instruction of 29 March 1933: B. Stasiewski (ed.), *Akten deutscher Bischöfe*, vol. 1, 33–8.
266. Pacelli to Orsenigo (3 April 1933), AA.EE.SS., Germania, Pos. 621–623 P.O. fasc. 140 fos 13r–14r.

267. Ibid.
268. Faulhaber to Pacelli (10 April 1933), in L. Volk (ed.), *Kirchliche Akten*, 10–11.
269. Cited from B. Stasiewski (ed.), *Akten der deutschen Bischöfe*, vol. 1, 7–8.
270. Cf. above, Chapter 3.6.
271. Cited from B. Stasiewski (ed.), *Akten deutscher Bischöfe*, vol. 1, 9–10.
272. Ibid.
273. Ibid.
274. Ibid.
275. Cf. above, Chapter 3.4.
276. E. Deuerlein, *Reichskonkordat*, 89–90.
277. Thus W. Becker, *Zentrumspartei*, 29.
278. Cf. K. Repgen, *Strategie*, 530ff.
279. Cf. W. Patch, *Brüning*, 295ff.
280. Cf. Hitler's statements on the Lateran treaties in the *Völkische Beobachter* no. 45 of 22 February 1929, cited by K. Scholder, *Kirchen*, vol. 1, 164–5.
281. Cf. J. Molony, *Emergence*; K. Repgen, *Pius XI*, 12; see also above, Chapter 2.2.
282. Cf. R. Schumann, *Geschichte Italiens*, 224.
283. Cf. L. Volk (ed.), *Kirchliche Akten*, 20ff.
284. Cf. H. Hürten, *Deutsche Katholiken*, 235–6.
285. Cf. L. Volk, *Ökumene*, 357.
286. Cf. Bertram to Hindenburg (6 April 1933), in B. Stasiewski (ed.), *Akten deutscher Bischöfe*, vol. 1, 49–50; Bertram to Hitler (16 April 1933), in Stasiewski (ed.), *Akten deutscher Bischöfe*, vol. 1, 60–2.
287. Hitler to Bertram (28 April 1933), in B. Stasiewski (ed.), *Akten deutscher Bischöfe*, vol. 1, 62–4.
288. Cf. Report of Orsenigo to Pacelli (8 May 1933), AA.EE.SS., Germania, Pos. 621–3 P.O. fasc. 140 fo. 107–8.
289. Cf. B. Stasiewski (ed.), *Akten deutscher Bischöfe*, vol. 1, 133–6, 255–6; L. Volk (ed.), *Kirchliche Akten*, 115.
290. Cf. B. Stasiewski (ed.), *Akten deutscher Bischöfe*, vol. 1, 239–48.
291. L. Volk (ed.), *Kirchliche Akten*, 58.
292. Orsenigo to Pacelli (8 April 1933), AA.EE.SS., Germania, Pos. 621–623 P.O. fasc. 140 fos 70–1.
293. Orsenigo to Pacelli (26 June 1933), Orsenigo to Pacelli (20 April 1933), AA.EE.SS., Germania, Pos. 621–623 P.O. fasc. 140 fo. 112.
294. Vice Chancellor von Papen also did this, speaking to Faulhaber 'very optimistically', and thinking that 'the present good will should be exploited for a hasty conclusion'. Faulhaber to Preysing (12 June 1933), EAM NL Faulhaber, no. 7302.
295. L. Volk (ed.), *Kirchliche Akten*, 89.
296. Cf. H. Hürten, *Deutsche Katholiken*, 240.
297. Cf. Scharnagel to Pacelli (10 April 1933), in L. Volk, *Kirchliche Akten*, 12–13.
298. Cf. A. Rhodes, *Papst*, 151–2.
299. Cf. V. Berning/H. Maier, *Dempf*, 12, 116, cf. 82–3, 23–4. There was also a warning from the former Reich Chancellor Josef Wirth, who was in Rome at Easter 1933, and was able to see the first drafts. F. R. Morsey, *Ende*.

300. Cf. K. Repgen, *Strategie*, 530ff.
301. Orsenigo to Pacelli (20 April 1933), AA.EE.SS., Germania, Pos. 621–623 P.O. fasc. 140 fo. 105.
302. Orsenigo to Pacelli (5 May 1933), AA.EE.SS., Germania, Pos. 621–623 P.O. fasc. 140 fos 109–10.
303. AA.EE.SS., Germania, Pos. 621–623 P.O. fasc. 140 fos 109–10.
304. Note of Gasparri, AA.EE.SS., Germania, Pos. 645 P.O. fasc. 163 fo. 20r. Printed in G. Sale, *Hitler*, 20 (there, wrongly attributed to fo. 10). P. Godman, *Hitler and the Vatican*, 6–7, wrongly dates the note to 20 June 1933, and makes a 'Memorandum' out of it.
305. Note of Gasparri, AA.EE.SS., Germania, Pos. 645 P.O. fasc. 163 fo. 20r.
306. Cf. A. Kupper (ed.), *Staatliche Akten*, 199ff.
307. Cf. L. Volk (ed.), *Kirchliche Akten*, 131.
308. Cf. A. Kupper (ed.), *Staatliche Akten*, 215.
309. Cf. ibid., 219–20.
310. Cf. L. Volk, *Reichskonkordat*, 197ff.
311. Cf. M. Feldkamp, *Pius XII*, 95. For the otherwise unresisting attitude of the Vatican, cf. Fr. Sandmann, *Haltung*, 48ff.
312. Pacelli to Schioppa (15 July 1933), AA.EE.SS., Germania, Pos. 645 fasc. 166 fos 71r–73r.
313. Cf. L. Volk, *Faulhaber*, 201ff. On the 26 July 1933 von Papen had written to Faulhaber dedicating himself to the hope 'that this treaty may introduce a new era of flourishing activity of our Holy Church and also of the welfare of the German Reich', EAM NL Faulhaber, no. 7304/1.
314. Cf. Bertram to Pacelli (2 September 1933), AA.EE.SS., Germania, Pos. 645 fasc. 171 fo. 15, cited from P. Godman, *Hitler and the Vatican*, 9.
315. Text from W. Jussen (ed.), *Gerechtigkeit*, 201–16; here: 205.
316. Orsenigo to Pacelli (8 April 1933), AA.EE.SS., Germania, Pos. 621–623 P.O. fasc. 140 fos 70–1.
317. Orsenigo to Pacelli (30 August 1933), AA.EE.SS., Germania, Pos. 643 P.O. fasc. 160 fos 50–1.
318. Cf. on this S. Friedländer, *Jews*, 41–9.
319. Cf. G. Besier, *Kirchen*, 807ff.
320. Cf. S. Friedländer, *Jews*, 42.
321. B. Stasiewski (ed.), *Akten deutschen Bischöfe*, vol. 1, 42, n. 3.
322. L. Volk, *Episkopat*, 77.
323. Cf. B. Stasiewski (ed.), *Akten deutschen Bischöfe*, vol. 1, 43, n. 3.
324. Faulhaber to Pacelli (10 April 1933), cited from L. Volk (ed.), *Kirchliche Akten*, 11.
325. Draft of Pacelli to Orsenigo (4 April 1933), AA.EE.SS., Germania, Pos. 643 P.O. fasc. 158 fo. 4r. On this and the following, see also P. Badde, *Ausschreitungen*; Th. Brechenmacher, *Held*.
326. RGBl. 1933 I, 175.
327. Orsenigo to Pacelli (9 April 1933), AA.EE.SS. Germania, Pos. 643 P.O. fasc. 158 fo. 5r.
328. Cf. W. Stüken, *Hirten*.
329. Orsenigo to Pacelli (9 April 1933), AA.EE.SS. Germania, Pos. 643 P.O. fasc. 158 fo. 5r.
330. B. Stasiewski (ed.), *Akten deutscher Bischöfe*, vol. 1, 51.

242 Notes, pp. 124–30

331. Orsenigo to Pacelli (11 April 1933), AA.EE.SS., Germania, Pos. 643 P.O. fasc. 158 fo. 6r–v.
332. Ibid.
333. AA.EE.SS., Germania, Pos. 643 P.O. fasc. 158 fo. 8.
334. Cited from W. Rauscher, *Hitler und Mussolini*, 197.
335. Cited from J. Petersen, *Hitler-Mussolini*, 157ff.
336. Faulhaber to Pacelli (10 April 1933), L. Volk (ed.), *Kirchliche Akten*, 11.
337. Pacelli's undated note on the document, AA.EE.SS., Germania, Pos. 643 P.O. fasc. 158 fo. 12r.
338. Pacelli to Faulhaber (20 April 1933), in L. Volk (ed.), *Kirchliche Akten*, 23.
339. S. Friedländer, *Jews*, 43.
340. Cf. B. Beckmann/H.-B. Gerl-Falcowitz (eds), *Edith Stein*; G. Wills, *Papal Sin*, 47ff.; cf. also Neyer, *Brief.*
341. On this and what follows, see K. Repgen, *Machtergreifung*, 48, 53, 58ff.
342. Stein to Pius XI (12 April 1933), AA.EE.SS., Pos. 643 P.O. fasc. 158 fos 16r–17r.
343. Cf. B. Stasiewski (ed.), *Akten deutscher Bischöfe*, vol. 1, 100–3.
344. Cf. K. Repgen, *Machtergreifung*, 67–8. On the measures of the Holy Office, cf. below, Chapter 3.11.
345. Schwarz to Pius XI (9 April 1933), AA.EE.SS., Pos. 643 P.O. fasc. 158 fos 29r–30r. Cf. H. Wolf, *Molto delicato.*
346. Note of 26 April 1933, AA.EE.SS., Germania, Pos. 643 P.O. fasc. 158 fo. 32r.
347. Telegram of Margolis to the Vatican (22 April 1933), AA.EE.SS., Germania, Pos. 643 P.O. fasc. 158 fo. 27r.
348. On this and what follows, see B. Stasiewski (ed.), *Akten deutscher Bischöfe*, vol. 1, 87–103 (minutes of representatives of the church provinces in Berlin on the 25/26 April 1933).
349. Cf. documentary note on the visit of Berning to Hitler on 26 April 1933, A. Kupper (ed.), *Staatliche Akten*, 28ff.
350. Orsenigo to Pacelli (8 May 1933), AA.EE.SS., Germania, Pos. 641–643 P.O., fasc. 157, fos 107r–8v. Printed in G. Sale, *Hitler*, 362–4.
351. Ibid.
352. Ibid.
353. Cf. B. Stasiewski (ed.), *Akten deutscher Bischöfe*, vol. 1, 100–3.
354. Contrary to P. Godman, *Hitler and the Vatican*, 32.
355. Orsenigo to Pacelli (28 April 1933), AA.EE.SS., Germania, Pos. 643 P.O. fasc. 158 fos 33r–34r.
356. Ibid.
357. Ibid.
358. Cf. St. Martens, *Hermann Göring*, 35–6.
359. Cf. J. Petzold, *Papen*, 193.
360. Cf. A. Kube, *Pour le mérite und Hakenkreuz*, 35.
361. Cf. A. Kube, *Pour le mérite und Hakenkreuz*, 38.
362. Quoted from W. Rauscher, *Hitler und Mussolini*, 200; cf. B. Stasiewski (ed.), *Akten deutscher Bischöfe*, vol. 1, 107–8.
363. Cf. W. Rauscher, *Hitler und Mussolini*, 199; G. Otruba, *Auswahldokumente.*
364. Orsenigo to Pacelli (25 April 1933), AA.EE.SS., Germania, Pos. 641–643 P.O. fasc. 157 fo. 39r–v. Printed in G. Sale, *Hitler*, 355–6.
365. On 11 April 1933 Goebbels's visit to Rome was announced in the *Völkischer Beobachter.*

366. Interview with the *Nationalsocialistischer Presse-Korrespondenz*, quoted from H. Michels, *Ideologie*, 146.
367. On this cf. Michels, *Ideologie*, 145.
368. Cited from E. Fröhlich (ed.), *Tagebücher*, Part 1, vol. 2, 426.
369. E. Fröhlich (ed.), *Tagebücher*, Part 1, vol. 2, 427–8.
370. Ibid.
371. Cf. letter of Bertram (23 July 133). Cf. B. Stasiewski (ed.), *Akten deutscher Bischöfe*, vol. 1, 270.
372. Pacelli to Orsenigo (3 August 1933), AA.EE.SS., Germania, Pos. 641–643 P.O., fasc. 157, fo. 41r.
373. Orsenigo to Pacelli (23 August 1933), AA.EE.SS., Germania, Pos. 643 fasc. 158 fo. 45r–v.
374. Pacelli to Orsenigo (26 August 1933), AA.EE.SS., Germania, Pos. 643 fasc. 158 fo. 46r.
375. Cf. *The Jewish Chronicle* to the secretariat of the Cardinal Secretary of State of 8 September 1933, AA.EE.SS., Germania, Pos. 643 fasc. 158 fo. 47r.
376. Pfannenstiel to the Munich nunciature (20 November 1933), AA.EE.SS., Germania, Pos. 643 fasc. 158 fo. 47r.
377. Ibid.
378. Pizzardo to Vassallo (16 December 1933), AA.EE.SS., Germania, Pos. 643 fasc. 158 fo. 75r.
379. Vassallo to Pizzardo (7 February 1934), AA.EE.SS., Germania, Pos. 643 fasc. 158 fo. 76r–v.
380. Ibid.
381. Pizzardo to Vassallo (18 February 1934), AA.EE.SS., Germania, Pos. 643 fasc. 158 fo. 77r.
382. Ibid.
383. Cf. G. Besier, *Kirchen*, 881.
384. On this and the following, cf. H. Wolf, *Gottesmord*. The documents used by Wolf are to be found in the Acts of the Holy Office for the pontificate of Pius XI in the archive of the Roman Congregation of the Faith (ACDF, S.O.R.V. 1928 [2]); cf. Wolf, *Pro perfidis Judaeis*; U. Altermatt, *Katholizismus*, 63ff.; see also P. Godman, *Hitler and the Vatican*, 24ff.; Brechenmacher, *Vatikan*, 154ff.
385. Cited from the Missal by Anselm Schott in the edition of 1913 (A. Schott [ed.], *Messbuch*, 281–2).
386. AAS 20 (1928), 103. On the proceedings see also G. Wills, *Papal Sin*, 32–3.
387. Cf. S. Friedländer, *Jews*, 211–40. See also N. Aleksiun, *Polish Historiography*.
388. In Hungary, Rumania, Spain and other European lands an anti-Semitism, partly fanatical, predominated. On this cf. e.g. B. P. Bettelheim, *Antisemitismus*; J. Hoensch, *Judenemanzipation*; M. Kappeler, *Rassismus*; L. Mosse, *Geschichte*.
389. On the situation in the USA, cf. G. Besier, *Contradiction*.
390. Lenten Pastoral Letter (1936), cited from V. Pollmann, *Untermieter*, 174; cf. S. Friedländer, *Jews*, 215–19.
391. S. Friedländer, *Jews*, 216.
392. Ibid., 237.
393. On this cf. J. Sánchez, *Pius XII*.
394. Cf. on this O. Blaschke, *Katholizismus und Antisemitismus*, 78–83; V. Pollmann, *Untermieter*, 212–22.

395. Cf. H. Hürten, *Deutsche Katholiken*, 356ff.; H. Gruber, *Muckermann*, esp. 262ff.
396. Cf. AA.EE.SS., Germania, Pos. 666 P.O. fasc. 221 fos 3ff. Printed in Sale, *Hitler*, 433. See P. Godman, *Hitler and the Vatican*, 35ff.
397. Cf. P. Godman, *Hitler and the Vatican*, 58–9.
398. German embassy to the Holy See to AA (19 June 1937) (no. 131; A187), PA/AA, Embassy to the Holy See, Best. 29, vol. 1/Lfd. No. 441 (unfoliated).
399. Cf. G. Besier, *Kirchen*, 880ff.
400. AA.EE.SS., Germania, Pos. 706 P.O. fasc. 272.
401. Cf. Corrin, *Catholic Intellectuals*, 236ff.; Reinhold, *Autobiography*.
402. AA.EE.SS., Germania, Pos. 706 P.O. fasc. 272 fos 13r–18r. Reinhold of course did not enjoy the support of his Church because he was regarded as a sympathizer with Communism. In New York he was prohibited from preaching, became isolated and was excluded from the refugee work. Cf. Corrin, *Catholic Intellectuals*, 243ff.
403. Cf. letter of the Katholiek Comité voor Vluchtelingen (Utrecht) to Hudal (28 May 1935), AA.EE.SS., Germania, Pos. 722 P.O. fasc. 339 fos 17r–18r, and the memorandum from National Catholic Committees for the Assistance of Refugees from Germany and Austria, AA.EE.SS., Germania, Pos. 722 P.O. fasc. 339 fos 33r–35r.
404. Froelicher to Reinhold (28 May 1936), EAM NL Faulhaber no. 8427 fos 10r–11r.
405. Cf. EAM NL Faulhaber nos 8423, 8425, 8427.
406. Cf. Laghi to Pacelli (27 July 1938), AA.EE.SS., Germania, Pos. 722 P.O. fasc. 339 fos 30r–31v. On the conference at Evian, cf. H. Kohler, *Konferenz von Evian*; J. Mendelsohn, *Holocaust*; J. Stein, *Evian Conference*.
407. Laghi to Pacelli (27 July 1938), AA.EE.SS., Germania, Pos. 706 P.O. fasc. 272 fo. 31r. Cf. *Correspondence Juive* (22 July 1938), Les résolutions et les rapports adoptés à Evian.
408. The official nomination followed in December 1939. Cf. H. Tittmann, *Inside*, 6–7; G. Besier, *Friends*, 54, 6. For the motives of the establishment of an American special ambassador to the Vatican, cf. D. Alvarez, *Spies*, 269ff.; Alvarez, *Information*. See also J. S. Conway, *Pope*.
409. Politis to Pacelli (9 August 1938), AA.EE.SS., Germania, Pos. 706 P.O. fasc. 272 fo. 36r.
410. Cf. G. Besier, *Kirchen*, 884ff. On Grösser's activities, see also EAM Faulhaber NL no. 3692.
411. Grösser to Faulhaber (10 June 1939), L. Volk (ed.), *Akten Kardinal Michael von Faulhabers*, vol. 2, 642–3. Cf. EAM NL Faulhaber, no. 8427. See also no. 8423.
412. Cf. Faulhaber to Bertram (24 March 1939), L. Volk (ed.), *Akten Kardinal Michael von Faulhabers*, vol. 2, 613–14.
413. On this and the following, cf. M. Feldkamp, *Aufhebung*; EAM NL Faulhaber, no. 1320/2.
414. Cf. M. Feldkamp, *Aufhebung*, 192.
415. Cited from M. Feldkamp, *Aufhebung*, 195.
416. Ritter zu Groenesteyn to the Bavarian state chancellery (6 January 1934), in AA Rom-Vatikan, 19, Aufhebung, Vol. 1/Lfd. Nr. 286, cited from M. Feldkamp, *Aufhebung*, 196.

417. Cited from M. Feldkamp, *Aufhebung*, 199.
418. Cf. Besier, *Kirchen*, 159–62.
419. Cf. M. Keipert/P. Grupp (eds), *Biographisches Handbuch*, 471–2.
420. Quoted from M. Feldkamp, *Aufhebung*, 204.
421. Ibid.
422. Cf. E. von Weizsäcker, *Weizsäcker-Papiere*.
423. Text: M. Feldkamp, *Aufhebung*, 208ff.
424. K.-A. Recker, *Berning*, 56ff.; cf. B. Stasiewski (ed.), *Akten deutscher Bischöfe*, vol. 1, 100–2.
425. Cf. also with the meeting of the bishops with Hitler, above, Chapter 3.7.
426. Cf. K.-A. Recker, *Berning*, 68.
427. Ibid.
428. Cited from ibid., 68.
429. Ibid.
430. Ibid., 69.
431. Ibid., 71.
432. Ibid., 74.
433. Ibid.
434. Cf. Besier, *Kirchen*, 115–19. See also the report in the *NZZ* of 21 June 1934 about the 'crisis of mood' in Germany immediately before the 'Röhm-Putsch'.
435. Cf. G. Besier, *Kirchen*, 121–2, 130, 147–8.
436. Cf. report of Orsenigo to Pacelli (24 August 1934), AA.EE.SS., Germania, Pos. 666 P.O. fasc. 220 fo. 12r–v.
437. Cf. H. Winkler, *Weg*, 39–40.
438. Cf. Orsenigo to Pacelli (21 August 1934), AA.EE.SS., Germania, Pos. 666 P.O. fasc. 220 fos 26r–27r.
439. Pacelli to Orsenigo (4 August 1934), AA.EE.SS., Germania, Pos. 666 P.O. fasc. 220 fos 37r–38r.
440. Orsenigo to Pacelli (13 September 1934), AA.EE.SS., Germania, Pos. 666 P.O. fasc. 220 fo. 48v.
441. Cf. H. Müller (ed.), *Katholische Kirche und Nationalsozialismus*, 309, 344, 360–1.
442. Cf. G. Besier, *Kirchen*, 718–25.
443. Cf. Galen to Orsenigo (28 October 1935), AA.EE.SS., Germania, Pos. 666 P.O. fasc. 224 fo. 12r–v.
444. Cf. D. Albrecht (ed.), *Notenwechsel*. See also EAM NL Faulhaber, no. 7307; 7304/2.
445. Cf. U. von Hehl/Ch. Klosters, *Priester*.
446. Orsenigo to Pacelli (24 April 1936), AA.EE.SS., Germania, Pos. 666 P.O. fasc. 224 fo. 30v.
447. Cf. G. Besier, *Kirchen*, 714–18.
448. This conversation was able to take place through the mediation of the Reichsstatthalter in Bavaria, General Ritter von Epp, and Orsenigo. Cf. H.-J. Hecker, *Kardinal Faulhaber*, 28.
449. Cf. G. Besier, *Kirchen*, 762–77.
450. Cf. Fr. Engel-Janosi, *Chaos*, 74ff., 141ff., 185ff.; E. Weinzierl, *Prüfstand*, 57ff.
451. L. Volk (ed.), *Akten Kardinal Michael von Faulhabers*, vol. 2, 196, n. 1. See now in detail Burkard, *Häresie*, 209–22.

452. Cf. Fr. Müller, *Rechtskatholik*, 255.
453. A. Hudal, *Rassenpoblem*.
454. Cf. A. Hudal, *Römische Tagebücher*, 129.
455. Cf. Fr. Engel-Janosi, *Chaos*, 188–9; Chenaux, 'Pacelli, Hudal', 144ff.
456. Pacelli to Faulhaber (16 November 1936), cited from L. Volk (ed.), *Akten Kardinal Michael von Faulhabers*, vol. 2, 198.
457. On this and the following, see K. Scholder, *Kirchen*, vol. 2, 152ff.; R. Baumgärtner, *Weltanschauungskampf*, 42–81; C.-E. Bärsch, *Religion*, 197ff.; G. Besier, *Nationalsozialismus*, 460ff.
458. Cf. Wolf, *Pius XI und die 'Zeitirrtümer'*, 5–6. On the question of who pressed the indexation in Rome, cf. Burkard, *Häresie*, esp. 48–50. On the proceedings see ibid., 63–72.
459. Cf. on this and the following, D. Burkard, *Bergpredigt*.
460. Cf. A. Hudal, *Römische Tagebücher*, 119.
461. Cf. ACDF, S.O. 4304, 1933 i (1). Printed with the drafts: Burkard, *Häresie*, 337–50.
462. Cf. Burkard, *Häresie*, 86–93,110–19, 173–80, 365.
463. *Osservatore Romano* (7 February 1934), 3.
464. Ibid.
465. In the course of the prohibition of the NSDAP in Austria on 19 June 1933, all the propaganda for this party was proscribed. Thus Hitler's *Mein Kampf* was also affected. The book was formally forbidden on 11 December 1933. Plöckinger, *Geschichte*, 297ff.
466. Erzbischöfliches Generalvikariat (ed.), *Studien*.
467. A. Hudal, *Römische Tagebücher*, 120.
468. Thus Hubert Wolf, 'Vertagt auf unbestimmte Zeit', *FAZ* no. 87 (12 April 2003), 8. See also the reader reply by Heinz Hürten, '*Leserbrief*' (*FAZ* no. 93 [22 April 2003], 11), which draws attention to the fact that the draft Syllabus of the Holy Office of Spring 1937 was published, in its essential features, as a rescript of the Papal Congregation of Studies on 1 May 1938 in *La Croix*. Cf. also P. Godman, *Hitler and the Vatican*, 222ff., also below, Chapter 3.10.
469. A. Hudal, *Römische Tagebücher*, 120.
470. Ibid., 120–1.
471. ACDF, S.O. R.V. 1934, 29. Prot. 3373/34, vol. 1, 1, 2–4; 3–4.
472. Cf. P. Godman, *Hitler and the Vatican*, 58ff.
473. Ibid., 43ff., citation, 43. Here he follows Fr. Engel-Janosi, *Chaos*, 187.
474. Godman, *Hitler and the Vatican*, 84.
475. Ibid., 46.
476. Burkard, *Häresie*, 231.
477. Cf. Brechenmacher, *Vatikan*, 222–3.
478. Cf. Ibid., 246–7. Godman indeed mentions this fact but ascribes it only to Hudal's 'ambition', his desire to play an important role, a desire in which he 'briefly' succeeded.
479. Cf. Chenaux, *Pacelli, Hudal*, 153–4.
480. Cf. Ibid., 74–5.
481. Innsbruck, 1935.
482. Innsbruck-Munich-Vienna, 1935.
483. A. Hudal, *Vatikan*, 82

484. Cf. Chenaux, *Pacelli, Hudal*, 137.
485. On the excellent relationship between Papen and Hudal, see Chenaux, *Pacelli, Hudal*, 145ff.
486. Cf. J. Petzold, *Papen*, 250.
487. The completion of this treaty was one of Papen's political objects. On this cf. G. Volsansky, *Pakt*, esp. 22ff., 35–6.
488. Papen to Hitler (28 July 1936), BA ZB I 1653, fos 97–100; citation: 99.
489. Von Bergen to Dieckhoff (16 January 1936), PA/AA, R 103249.
490. Cf. A. Hudal, *Römische Tagebücher*, 129.
491. Cf. J. Charnitzky, *Schulpolitik*, 155–69.
492. E. Weinzierl-Fischer, *Katholiken*, Part II, 497–9.
493. Cited from A. Hudal, *Rassenproblem*, 22–3.
494. Reichsleitung NSDAP, Abt. III (Rosenberg) to SS-Brigadeführer Schaub, Büro der Reichskanzlei (Obersalzburg), of 26 October 1936, BA NS 10/109. Cf. NS-Presseanweisung of 31 October 1936, according to which the book must be announced but not 'further commented upon'. G. Toepser-Ziegert (ed.), *NS-Presseanweisungen*, 1299.
495. Cf. Letter of Hauptstellenleiter Matthes Ziegler to RPM (22 October 1936), BA, NS 10/62, fo. 23.
496. Letter of Reichsgeschäftsstelle of Rosenberg's office to Wiedemann of 13 November 1936, along with Rosenberg's opinion: Bishop Dr Alois Hudal, Die 'Grundlagen des Nationalsozialismus', BA, NS 10/62, fos 15–21. Also Joseph Roth gave warning in his notes for Kerrl's conversation with Hitler of 11 November 1936 of the 'peril of Bishop Hudal and those who were behind him'. Text: L. Brandl, *Neue Quellen*, 442–3. See also M. Huttner, *Britische Presse*, 574; H. Kreutzer, *Reichskirchenministerium*, 220–1.
497. Cf. Hudal, *Schaffen*, 82, 255ff.; cf. P. Godman, *Hitler and the Vatican*, 45.
498. Cf. A. Hudal, *Ecclesiae*, 45.
499. Cf. K. Breuning, *Vision*, 190ff., and above, Chapter 3.6.
500. Cf. Luigi Centoz to Pacelli (4 September 1931), AA.EE.SS., Germania, Pos. 621 P.O. fasc. 138 fo. 43r–v; Fritz to Pacelli (1 September 1931), AA.EE.SS., Germania, Pos. 621 P.O. fasc. 138 44r–46v; Pacelli to Centoz (10 September 1931), AA.EE.SS., Germania, Pos. 621 P.O. fasc. 138 fo. 49r.
501. Cf. on this and the following P. Godman, *Hitler and the Vatican*, 617ff.; Wolf, *Pius XI und die 'Zeitirrtümer'*, 12–13 (ACDF, S.O. R.V. 1934, 29; Prot. 3373/34, vol. 1, 1–3).
502. Cf. Wolf, *Pius XI und die 'Zeitirrtümer'*, 17ff.
503. Cited from P. Godman, *Hitler and the Vatican*, 189–90.
504. Cited from D. Albrecht (ed.), *Notenwechsel*, 146.
505. AA.EE.SS., Germania, Pos. 661–663 P.O. fasc. 210 fos 23ff.; Germania, Pos. 692 P.O. fasc. 260 fos 4–8, 22ff.; Germania, Pos. 692 P.O. fasc. 264 fos 5ff.; Germania, Pos. 666 P.O. fasc. 221 fos 27–8 (printed in G. Sale, *Hitler*, 441); Germania, Pos. 666 P.O. fasc. 223 fos 3ff. (printed in G. Sale, *Hitler*, 447–8).
506. Cf. G. Besier, *Kirchen*, 657.
507. Cf. ibid., 849–56.
508. Orsenigo to Pacelli (14 September 1935). AA.EE.SS., Germania 'scatole' fasc. 9, fos 32–3.
509. Cf. e.g. D. Albrecht (ed.), *Notenwechsel*, 309.

510. E. Pacelli, *Discorsi*, 430ff., cited from P. Godman, *Hitler and the Vatican*, 80. The German embassy to the Holy See sent excellent reports on Pacelli's public statements. Cf. Reports of 29 April 1935 (Budde K 24.IV) and 4 May 1935 (A263), PA/AA, Botschaft beim Heiligen Stuhl, Best. 29, Vol. 1/Lfd. No. 41 (unfoliated).

511. Cf. in general H. Maier, *Totalitarianismus*.

512. List of theses on nationalism, racialism and totalitarianism (May 1935), cited from P. Godman, *Hitler and the Vatican*, 172ff.

513. Cf. H. Hürten, *Deutsche Katholiken*, 370; P. Godman, *Hitler and the Vatican*, 92.

514. Cf. C. Casula, *Tardini*.

515. ACDF, S.O. R.V. 1934, 29, Prot. 3373/34, vol. 2, 4, 9.

516. Cf. G. Ledit, *Paradossi*; Ledit, *Religione*.

517. P. Godman, *Hitler and the Vatican*, 99.

518. Cf. ACDF, S.O. R.V. 1934, 29, Prot. 3373/34, vol. 2, 7ff.

519. Cf. R. De Felice, *Mussolini*, vol. 2.

520. B. Mussolini, *Scritti e discorsi*.

521. M. Missiroli, *Date*.

522. ACDF, S.O. 2935/291.

523. Cf. G. Schneider, *Mussolini*.

524. Cf. above, Chapter 3.5.

525. Cf. ACDF, S.O. R.V. 1934, 29, Prot. 3373/34, vol. 4, 12.

526. Cf. ACDF, S.O. R.V. 1934, 29, Prot. 3373/34, vol. 4, 12, 5–6.

527. ACDF, S.O. R.V. 1934, 29, Prot. 3373/34, vol. 4, 12–13.

528. ACDF, S.O. R.V. 1934, 29, Prot. 3373/34, vol. 4, 12, 16.

529. Text: P. Godman, *Hitler and the Vatican*, 194–9.

530. Ibid., 199.

531. Cf. e.g. G. Besier, *Convictions*, 509–18; E. Rosa, *Internazionale*.

532. Cited from P. Godman, *Hitler and the Vatican*, 128.

533. Cf. Wolf, *Pius XI und die 'Zeitirrtümer'*, 25–6.

534. Cited from L. Volk (ed.), *Akten Cardinal Michael von Faulhabers*, vol. 2, 199; cf. ibid., 228–33.

535. Cf. G. Besier, *Kirchen*, 768.

536. Cf. on this and the following: J. Anderson, *Spanish Civil War*; S. Balfour/P. Preston (eds), *Spain*; S. Ben-Ami, *Dictatorship*; W. Bernecker, *Krieg*; Bernecker, *Religion*; Bernecker /H. Pietschmann, *Geschichte Spaniens*; M. Blinkhorn, *Spain*; Blinkhorn, *Democracy and Civil War*; W. Bowen, *Spaniards*; C. Boyd, *Historia Patria*; R. Carr (ed.), *Spain*; J. Casanova, *Iglesia*; J. Coverdale, *Italian Intervention*; P. Davidson (ed.), *Orwell*; J. Goytisolo, *Spanien*; C. Humleboek, *Zeitgeschichteforschung*; J. Linz, *Regime*; Linz, *Great Hopes*; S. G. Payne, *Falange*; P. Preston, *Franco*; J. Rial, *Revolution*; K.-J. Ruhl, *Spanien*; W. Schieder/Ch. Dipper (eds), *Bürgerkrieg*; E. Straub, *Jahrhundert*; R. Traina, *American Diplomacy*; A. Vinas, *Franco*.

537. Gasparri to Dormer, British embassy (21 September 1923), cited from A. Rhodes, *Papst*, 96 n. 1.

538. Cf. critically M. del Carmen Tapia, *Schwelle*, 417–23.

539. AAS 25 (1933), 261–74; J. Schmidlin, *Papstgeschichte*, vol. 3/IV, 140–1.

540. Cf. Ch. Ealham/M. Richards (eds), *Splintering*.

541. Cf. D. Tierney, *Roosevelt*; R. Traina, *American Diplomacy*, 158–69.
542. Cf. P. Moa, *Guerra civil*.
543. Cf. G. Besier *Kirchen*, 757–61.
544. On the comparison between Poland and Spain, see K. Ruchniewicz/ St. Troebst, *Diktaturbewältigung*.
545. W. Bernecker, *Spanische Geschichte*, 180.
546. Cf. J. Rodrigo, *Campos*, 218–21.
547. Cf. on this and the following, G. Besier, *Kirchen*, 757–61.
548. Quoted from W. Bernecker, *Religion*, 95.
549. Cf. G. Besier, *Kirchen*, 759.
550. Cf. ibid., 765. In this case Pacelli turned against the propagandists of the authoritarian corporative model of the state on the Italian pattern, who had gathered round the Catholic priest Charles Coughlin, and rallied massively against Roosevelt. Cf. Angermann, *Amerika*, 167–8.
551. Cf. G. Fogarty, *Roosevelt*, 15ff.
552. Thus the report of von Bergen to AA (8 October 1936) (no. 266; A 309), PA/AA Embassy to the Holy See, Best. 29, vol. 1/Lfd. no. 441 (unfoliated).
553. Cf. G. Besier, *Kirchen*, 766–7.
554. Text: L. Volk (ed.), *Akten Kardinal Michael von Faulhabers*, vol. 2, 244–52.
555. Faulhaber to Hitler (30 December 1936), in L. Volk (ed.), *Akten Kardinal Michael von Faulhabers*, vol. 2, 261–2.
556. Ibid.
557. Cf. Besier, *Kirchen*, 774.
558. Cf. Bertram to Faulhaber (30 December 1936), in L. Volk (ed.), *Akten Kardinal Michael von Faulhabers*, vol. 2, 263.
559. Cf. Bertram to Pacelli (28 December 1936), in L. Volk (ed.), *Akten deutscher Bischöfe*, 65–6.
560. Cf. Notes of Faulhaber on the audience, in L. Volk (ed.), *Akten Kardinal Michael von Faulhabers*, vol. 2, 275–7. See also Wolf, *Pius XI und die 'Zeitirrtümer'*, 30ff.
561. Cf. on this and the following G. Besier, *Kirchen*, 777–80.
562. Text: L. Volk (ed.), *Akten Kardinal Michael von Faulhabers*, vol. 2, 277–9.
563. AA.EE.SS., Germania, Pos. 719 P.O. fasc. 314 fos 5r–6r.
564. Ibid.
565. 'A letter from the Holy Father to the Reich Chancellor appears inopportune. There was the possibility of a disrespectful reply. Success out of the question. Hitler tolerates only total acknowledgment, no criticism. In any case there is the danger of garbled publication and hence the possible misleading of Catholics'. Ibid.
566. Cf. G. Besier, *Kirchen*, 778.
567. Ibid., 779.
568. Pacelli noted: 'The present moment seems now to be favourable: the conviction of the government's hostility to the Church is very widespread; even Protestant circles will receive the word of the Holy Father sympathetically; world opinion is ripe for such a statement' (AA.EE.SS., Germania, Pos. 719 P.O. fasc. 314 fo. 6r).
569. Cf. M. Agostino, *Pie XI*, 639ff. See on the conditions in Mexico, K.-J. Ruhl/L. Ibarra Garcia, *Kleine Geschichte Mexikos*, 182ff.; G. Schwaiger, *Papsttum und Päpste*, 257–8.

570. Cf. AA.EE.SS., Germania, Pos. 719 P.O. fasc. 314 fos 22r.–27r; see also the report of Faulhaber (L. Volk [ed.], *Akten Kardinal Michael von Faulhabers*, vol. 2, 279ff.) and of Preysing (W. Adolph, *Preysing*, 73).

571. AA.EE.SS., Germania, Pos. 719 P.O. fasc. 314 fo. 23r.

572. P. Godman, *Hitler and the Vatican*, 146.

573. Cf. G. Besier, *Kirchen*, 778.

574. Cf. Faulhaber to Pacelli (21 January 1937), in L. Volk (ed.), *Akten Kardinal Michael von Faulhabers*, vol. 2, 281–2.

575. A synopsis of the draft and the final encyclical is given in D. Albrecht (ed.), *Notenwechsel*, 404–43.

576. Pignatti to Ciano of 8 March 1937, in DDI, 8/VI, 313.

577. Cf. AA.EE.SS., Germania, Pos. 719 P.O. fasc. 313 fo. 43.

578. AA.EE.SS., Germania, Pos. 719 P.O. fasc. 316 fos 4ff.

579. Cf. P. Godman, *Hitler and the Vatican*, 150.

580. Text and commentary: A. Fitzek (ed.), *Pius XI*, 153–209. See also EAM NL Faulhaber, no. 3055.

581. ACDF, S.O. R.V. 1934, 29, Prot. 3373/74, vol. 4, 16.

582. Cf. e.g. the view in the USA: G. Besier, *Friends*, 66ff.

583. Cf. G. Besier, *Kirchen*, 784–5.

584. Cited from A. Fitzek (ed.), *Pius XI*, 169.

585. Ibid., 113.

586. *The Catholic Times*, 27 March 1937.

587. Cf. J. Echeverria, *Kampf*; J. Meyer, *Christiade*; K.-J. Ruhl/L. Ibarra Garcia, *Kleine Geschichte Mexicos*, 182ff.; G. Schwaiger, *Papsttum und Päpste*, 257–8.

588. Cf. G. Besier, *Kirchen*, 785.

589. Cf. ibid., 786ff. On this and the following, see also H.-A. Raem, *Pius XI*.

590. Cf. Orsenigo to Pacelli (1 April 1937), AA.EE.SS., Germania, Pos. 719 P.O. fasc. 316 fos 28r–30r.

591. Cf. Pignatti di Custoza to Pacelli (24 April 1937), AA.EE.SS., Germania, Pos. 720 P.O. fasc. 329 fos 11r–13r.

592. Cicognani to Pacelli (24 April 1937), AA.EE.SS., Germania, Pos. 720 P.O. fasc. 329 fos 40r–42r.

593. Pacelli to Cicognani (28 April 1937), AA.EE.SS., Germania, Pos. 720 P.O. fasc. 329 fo. 43r.

594. Cicognani to Pacelli (4 May 1937), AA.EE.SS., Germania, Pos. 720 P.O. fasc. 329 fos 45r–46r (Citation in the original: '[…] quem Deus vult perdere prius dementat').

595. Cf. G. Besier, *Kirchen*, 799ff.

596. Summary of Attolico's report (21 June 1937), AA.EE.SS., Germania, Pos. 720 fasc. 329 fos 15r–16r.

597. EAM NL Faulhaber, nos 1201/2 and 1201/3.

598. Cf. E. Göring, *Seite*, 121–4; A. Kube, *Pour le mérite und Hakenkeuz*, 224ff.; St. Martens, *Hermann Göring*, 94ff.

599. Cf. A. Kube, *Pour le mérite und Hakenkeuz*, 215ff.

600. Cf. M. Muggeridge (ed.), *Ciano's Diplomatic Papers*, 80–91, esp. 88–9.

601. Cf. W. Maderthaner, *12. Februar 1934*. On the *Anhaltelager* (literally 'halting camp', a term for an internment camp) in Wöllersdorf, cf. D. Binder, *Ständestaat*, 213.

602. Cf. on this and the following R. Steininger, *12. November 1918*.

603. Cf. in detail H. Rein, *Papen*, 61ff.
604. Cf. Fr. Müller, *Rechtskatholik*; Ch. Mentschl, *Tätigkeit*; H. Graf von Kageneck, *Hindenburgs Testament*.
605. Cf. *Neue Freie Presse* (Vienna), 26 July 1934.
606. E. Weinzierl, *Prüfstand*, 56.
607. Cf. Fr. Müller, *Rechtskatholik*, 252.
608. Cf. ibid., 254.
609. Cf. R. Ebneth, *Wochenschrift*, esp. 102ff.
610. P. Enderle, *Grundlagen*. Cf. also W. Rauscher, *Hitler und Mussolini*, 210.
611. L. Noël, *Stresa*.
612. Cf. J. Dülffer, *Weimar*, 325–54.
613. C. R. De Felice, *Mussolini*, 597ff. See also V. Reinhardt, *Geschichte*, 281–2.
614. Cf. W. Rauscher, *Hitler und Mussolini*, 225ff.
615. Cf. R. Moseley, *Mussolini's Shadow*, 28ff.
616. Cf. Ch. Burdett, *Journeys*.
617. W. Rauscher, *Hitler und Mussolini*, 237ff.
618. Cf. Fr. Müller, *Rechtskatholik*, 271ff.; G. Volsansky, *Pakt*.
619. See above, Chapter 3.13.
620. Cf. Petersen, *Vorspiel*, 245.
621. Cf. R. Lill, *Südtirol*, 152.
622. Cf. P. Eppel, *Kreuz und Hakenkreuz*. Even Faulhaber published in *Schönere Zukunft*. Cf. EAM NL Faulhaber, no. 6887.
623. Cf. W. Rauscher, *Hitler und Mussolini*, 245.
624. Cf. G. Ciano, *Diario* (5 December 1937), 65–6.
625. Cf. H. Neuman, *Seyss-Inquart*; W. Rosar, *Deutsche Gemeinschaft*.
626. Cf. W. Rauscher, *Hitler und Mussolini*, 225ff.; cf. also D. Binder, *Ständestaat*, 230ff.; W. Kleindel, *Anschluss*, 20–9; G. Tomkowitz/D. Wagner, *Anschluss*, 8–9; R. Steininger, *12. November 1918*, 125ff.
627. Shorthand Minutes, 733–45.
628. Cf. W. Goldinger/D. Binder, *Geschichte*, 282.
629. Cf. E. Schmiedl, *März 1938*.
630. Cf. on this Chenaux, *Pacelli, Hudal*, 150.
631. Cf. H. Arnberger/W. Garscha/Ch. Mitterrutzner, *Anschluss*, 393ff.; W. Rauscher, *Hitler und Mussolini*, 260.
632. Cf. H. Arnberger/W. Garscha/Ch. Mitterrutzner, *Anschluss*, 379–81, 392–3.
633. Report of Magistrati (summary) transmitted to Pacelli on 19 March 1938. AA.EE.SS., Germania, Pos. 720 P.O. fasc. 329 fos 21r–22r. The following citation, ibid.
634. This general judgement requires, of course, a regional differentiation: cf. J. Thierfelder, *Wahlverweigerer*.
635. Cf. M. Liebmann, *Innitzer*; Liebmann, *Theodor Innitzer*.
636. Cf. M. Michaelis, *Mussolini's Unofficial Mouthpiece*. See below, Chapter 3.15.
637. Quoted from E. Weinzierl, *Prüfstand*, 61.
638. Ibid.
639. Cf. E. Bukey, *Hitler's Austria*, 93ff.
640. Cf. on this and the following: M. Liebmann, *Innitzer*; Liebmann, *Theodor Innitzer*.
641. Quoted from E. Weinzierl, *Prüfstand*, 82.
642. Cf. H. Jablonka, *Waitz*.

643. Quoted from E. Weinzierl, *Prüfstand*, 3035; cf. A. Reichhold, *Kirche*, 136–7.
644. Quoted from E. Weinzierl, *Prüfstand*, 107.
645. Wilson to Secretary of State (7 April 1938), NA LM 197, Reel #2.
646. Quoted from E. Weinzierl, *Prüfstand*, 108.
647. See also A. Hudal, *Katholizismus*.
648. Cf. Hudal's memorandum to Pius XI of 2 November 1938 on the situation of the Church in Austria after 1938, AA.EE.SS., Germania, Pos. 720 P.O. fasc. 336 fos 39ff.; citation, AA.EE.SS., Germania, Pos. 720 P.O. fasc. 336 fo. 60.
649. Cf. AA.EE.SS., Germania, Pos. 720 P.O. fasc. 336 fos 70ff. See also Chenaux, *Pacelli, Hudal*, 152–3.
650. SD-Jahreslagebericht, BA ZB I 1237, 358–74; here 358. In a report on the 'political Church' it says: 'The reincorporation of Austria into the Reich implied a severe blow to Church circles. This collapse of Church authority in the Ostmark occasioned insecurity and powerful confusion in Church circles. On the Catholic side a cleft opened between people and episcopate, between the episcopate and Rome, between the German and the Austrian episcopate, as well as within the German episcopate. The political fighting-power of the Church was thus substantially weakened' (SD-Jahreslagebericht, BA ZB I 1237, 358 fo. 2).
651. Report of Wilson to the Secretary of State (5 March 1938), NA, LM 197, Reel #2 (unfoliated).
652. Ibid.
653. Ibid.
654. A. J. Drexel Biddle, US Embassy Warsaw, to the Secretary of State (14 April 1938), NA, LM 197, Reel #2 (unfoliated).
655. On the relation between Pacelli and Kennedy cf. R. F. de Bedts, *Joseph Kennedy*, 126ff.; T. Schwarz, *Joseph P. Kennedy*, 281ff. The Church archive materials on the Pacelli visit of 1936 deposited in the USA have disappeared since 2002. On the 18 September 2003, Sister Marguerita Smith, Archivist of the Archive of the New York Archdiocese, wrote to the author that this material together with the other contents of Box X–21 and also the microfilm disappeared.
656. On this and the following cf. Th. Brechenmacher, *Widerspruch*; Ch. Gallagher, *Views*.
657. Cf. G. Besier, *Kirchen*, 765.
658. Text: http://www.americamagazine.org/articles/pacelli.cfm (accessed 2 January 2007).
659. Ibid.
660. Ibid.
661. Ibid.
662. Cf. above, Chapter 1.3.
663. Text: http://www.americamagazine.org/articles/pacelli.cfm (accessed 2 January 2007).
664. Ch. Gallagher, *Views*, 9.
665. Central Zionist Archives, Jerusalem, S 25 3759 (26 May 1938), cited from Th. Brechenmacher, *Widerspruch*.
666. Th. Brechenmacher, *Widerspruch*.
667. Quoted from Ch. Gallagher, *Views*, 9.

668. Cf. on this and the following also J. Schwarte, *Katholische Kirche*.
669. Cf. A. Rauscher (ed.), *Rassismus*, 23; G. Passelecq/B. Suchecky, *Enzyklika*, 70–1; Wolf, *Pius XI und die 'Zeitirrtümer'*, 27–8; Burkhard, *Häresie*, 232ff.
670. Thus Grundlach himself, cited from A. Rauscher (ed.), *Rassismus*, 29.
671. Cited from Rauscher (ed.), *Rassismus*, 161, 166.
672. Ibid., 167. Cf. also EAM NL Faulhaber, no. 7091. Like Pius XI, Faulhaber turned against every kind of anti-Semitic actions by the clergy. Cf. his Advent sermon (1933) and his New Year's Eve sermon summarized in his book *Judentum, Christentum, Germanentum* (Munich, 1934). Here he emphasizes among other things the religious values of the Old Testament. Pressure from the Nazis ensured that the book was not sold in many German bookshops. Many of the booksellers undertook in writing not to bring the book into circulation again. Cf. EAM NL Faulhaber nos 7103/1 and 7103/2.
673. Cf. R. Lill, *Katholische Kirche*, 214; see also R. De Felice, *Mussolini*, vol. 2, 489; A. Hoffend, *Kultur-Achse*, 357ff.; Schlemmer/Woller, *Faschismus*, esp. 174ff.
674. See in general V. De Grazia, *Radikalisierung*.
675. Cf. W. Rauscher, *Hitler und Mussolini*, 209.
676. *Il Popolo d'Italia* (26 May 1934) (*Opera Omnia*, vol. 6, 232f.). Quoted from J. Petersen, *Hitler – Mussolini*, 341–2.
677. Cf. M. Agostino, *Pie XI*, 719ff.
678. Roberto Farinacci, *Das Judenproblem in der Geschichte der Kirche* (7 November 1938), BA ZB I 1146 fos 986–1003; here: 989, 96.
679. BA ZB I 1146 fo. 998.
680. BA ZB I 1146 fo. 1003.
681. Preface of 6 January 1939, BA ZB I 1146 fo. 983.
682. On this and the following cf. M. Michaelis, *Mussolini's Unofficial Mouthpiece*; EAM NL Faulhaber, no. 1254.
683. Cf. G. Ciano, *Diario*, 346.
684. Esmonde Robertson (E. Robertson, *Race*, 44) recalls that Mussolini already forced Dollfuss into doing something against the Jews in Austria – of course on political grounds – because they were Left inclined. See also G. Schneider, *Mussolini*.
685. Hudal's denunciation of Cogni's *Il Razzismo* is printed in Burkard, *Häresie*, 371–2. Cf. ibid., 217–18.
686. Cf. *Opera Omnia*, vol. 2, 202–3.
687. Cf. W. Rauscher, *Hitler und Mussolini*, 265ff.; Sturzo, *Fascisme*.
685. Cf. J. Petersen, *Hitler-Mussolini*, 344ff.; W. Rauscher, *Hitler und Mussolini*, 245ff. On the significance of this visit for foreign policy cf. Fr. Müller, *Rechtskatholik*, 37ff. In a Vatican note to a document in an unknown hand it is affirmed that Pius XI had an influence upon Mussolini's journey to Germany. Documentary observation (14 September 1937), AA.EE.SS., Germania, Pos. 724 P.O. fasc. 339 fo. 52r.: see also Documentary note 3 September 1937, ibid., fo. 53r. After this the Holy Father was 'beside himself [...] when he speaks of Germany, and now also of Italy which stands at Germany's side, and of Mussolini on account of his journey to Germany'. According to the Belgian ambassador the relations between the Reich and the Holy See were among the discussion points which Mussolini arranged with Hitler. Documentary note (17 September 1937), ibid., fo. 54r.

689. Cf. above, Chapter 3.4.
690. Cf. von Bergen to Weizsäcker (3 March 1938), ADAP, D vol. 1, 829–30.
691. Cf. A. Giovannetti, *Vatikan*, 176.
692. Cf. Note of Mackensen on conversation with Ribbentrop on 14 February 1938, ADAP, D, vol. 1, 828; Preliminary note of Weizsäcker (9 March 1938), ibid., 830–1; von Bergen to Weizsäcker (23 May 1938), ibid., 841.
693. Weizsäcker to von Bergen (26 February 1938), ibid., 828.
694. Von Bergen to Weizsäcker (3 May 1938), ibid., 829.
695. Preliminary note of Weizsäcker (9 March 1938), ibid., 831. See also Borgongini Duca to Pacelli (27 April 1938), in G. Sale, *Hitler*, 522–3. Shortly before Hitler's visit to Rome Mussolini had once again intervened on account of the persecution of German Catholics in Berlin, as transpires from a letter of thanks from the Vatican to the Duce. Cf. ibid., 525.
696. Cf. Sale, *Hitler*, 524.
697. Cf. ibid., 517.
698. Cf. ibid., 520.
699. Thus Chenaux, *Pacelli, Hudal*, 151.
700. American embassy in Warsaw to the Secretary of State (14 April 1938), NA, LM 197, Reel #2. On 18 May 1938, the Amercan embassy in Rome reported that the Vatican had denied 'that any rapprochement to the Holy See on the side of representatives of the German government to the Holy See before or during Herr Hitler's visit has taken place with a view to having the latter received by the Pope to an audience' (NA, LM 197, Reel #2).
701. M. Feldkamp, *Pius XII*, 121, draws attention to this.
702. Cf. von Bergen to Weizsäcker (18 May 1938), ADAP, D, vol. 1, 839.
703. Cf. Edward L. Reed, Rome, to the Secretary of State (18 May 1938) NA LM 197, Reel #2.
704. Report of Tacchi Venturi to Ratti (10 April 1938), AA.EE.SS., Germania Pos. 720 P.O. fasc. 329 fo. 31r. Cf. Wolf, *Pius XI und die 'Zeitirrtümer'*, 28–9.
705. Cf. J. Pollard, *Vatican*, 190.
706. G. Bottai, *Diario* (6 October 1938).
707. Bottai, *Diario*, 137.
708. G. Ciano, *Tagebücher*, 295.
709. Cf. Pacelli to Mussolini (16 March 1938), AA.EE.SS., Germania, Pos. 735 P.O. fasc. 353 fo. 4. In this letter Pacelli gives thanks for an intervention with Hitler in favour of oppressed German Catholics. Printed in G. Sale, *Hitler*, 525.
710. Contrary to P. Godman, *Hitler and the Vatican*, 156.
711. Cf. the note of Pacelli on an audience with Pius XI on the 24 March 1938. AA.EE.SS., Germania, Pos. 735 P.O. fasc. 252 fo. 7r. Cf. the print in G. Sale, *Hitler*, 517 (with variations from the original).
712. Thus Ciano to Francesco Borgongini (nuncio in Italy) (2 May 1938), AA.EE.SS., Germania, Pos. 720 P.O. fasc. 329 fo. 25v.
713. Cf. report of Borgongini to Pacelli (15 June 1938), on a conversation with Ciano, AA.EE.SS., Germania, Pos. 720 P.O. fasc. 329 fos 27r–28r.
714. Text: P. Godman, *Hitler and the Vatican*, 222ff.; Wolf, *Pius XI. und die 'Zeitirrtümer'*, 2ff. Cf. also Burkard, *Häresie*, 224–7. He describes the putting of Bergmann's book on *Die natürliche Geistlehre* [*The Natural Doctrine of Spirit*] as the hyphen between the adjourned syllabus draft and the Instruction.

715. After the Fulda bishops' conference of August 1938 the theses with comments by the bishops were forwarded to the Catholic clergy. Cf. H. Hürten, *Deutsche Katholiken*, 424ff.
716. Wolf (*Pius XI. und die 'Zeitirrtümer'*, 23) speaks of a 'far-reaching identity'.
717. G. Miccoli, *Dilemmi*, 308ff.; S. Zucotti, *Vaticano*, 11ff. See also above, Chapter 3.15.
718. Cf. P. Gallo, *Love and Country*, 22; G. Miccoli, *Dilemmi*, 309.
719. Cf. P. Godman, *Hitler and the Vatican*, 21ff.; cf. also F. Rossi, *Vatikan*, 44ff.
720. AA.EE.SS., Germania, Pos. 738 P.O. fasc. 354 fos 51r–52r.
721. Orsenigo to Pacelli (15 November 1918), AA.EE.SS., Germania, Pos. 742 P.O. fasc. 354 fos 40r–41v. The following quotation, ibid.
722. Orsenigo to Pacelli (19 January 1938), AA.EE.SS., Germania, Pos. 742 P.O. fasc. 354 fos 42r–43r. On 13 September 1941 Orsenigo reported to Luigi Maglione that Jews in the protectorate of Bohemia and Moravia, in consequence of a decree from the Ministry of the Interior, as well as Jews throughout the Reich, must wear the Jewish star in public places and must not leave their place of residence. 'The baptized non-Aryans feel especially confused and have their worst anxieties realized. These are not ended when they [...] go to Church especially on festival days. The echo of these anxieties reached both [...] Cardinal Innitzer and [...] Cardinal Bertram; they thought of the possibility of reserving the Jews a place of their own in the Church, or even, if they were numerous, of offering them a service of their own'. AA.EE.SS., Germania, Pos. 742 P.O. fasc. 354 fo. 50r–v.
723. Cf. AA.EE.SS., Germania, 1934–44, 'scatole' ['boxes'] 50, fos 59r–71r; here, 65r.
724. Cf. G. Besier, *Friends*, 54–6; M. Carter, *Diplomacy's Detractors*.
725. Drexel Biddle, Warsaw US embassy, to the Secretary of State, Washington DC (8 December 1938), NA, LM 197, Reel #2.
726. Ciano wrote in his diary on 12 February 1939: 'The Duce agreed to take part in the Pope's funeral, which has been fixed by the Nunciature for the seventeenth. That decision pleases me, because it will create a good impression upon the Conclave. In some American circles it is rumoured that Pacelli has a document written by the Pope. The Duce desires Pignatti to find out, and, if it is true, to try to get a copy of the document [Commentary: just before his death the Pope was writing a speech, to be delivered to the bishops of Italy, on the relations between Italy and the Vatican. It was rumoured in Rome that this speech was a strong denunciation of the Fascist violations of the Lateran treaties. Copies of it were destroyed by Vatican officials.] "... in order to avoid a repetition of the Filipelli incident". It may be of some significance in this connection that yesterday Rosenberg in a long speech refrained from his usual, embittered attack upon the Catholic Church' (M. Muggeridge [ed.], *Ciano's Diary*, 28).
727. Gilbert to the Secretary of State (18 February 1939), Na, LM 197, Reel #2.
728. Ibid.
729. Von Bergen to AA (18 February 1939), ADAP, D, vol. 4, 251.
730. After the death of Gasparri, Pacelli became Camerlengo [Chamberlain]; in this office he was at the head of the papal financial administration, and during the vacancy in the See had to care for its temporal rights.

731. Cf. O. Chadwick, *Britain*, 30ff.; M. Feldkamp, *Pius XI*, 121ff. Cf. also the express-telegram no. 592/200 from G. Mameli of 23 February 1939 from Lisbon to the Italian Foreign Ministry about a conversation which took place with the nuncio in Portugal, Pietro Ciriaci: 'The nuncio had no doubt at all that this time the Pope would be an Italian again. According to Monsignor Ciriaci only one single candidature stood out, that indeed of Cardinal Pacelli, be it on account of his past record or on account of his influence, and because, finally, he is supported by a group of cardinals, the so-called "democratic group" headed by Cardinal [Jean] Verdier. According to the nuncio this candidature can only succeed through a very rapid action. Only while the first votes are "blocked" can it hope for success. [...] When he speaks of Cardinal Pacelli, the nuncio brushes aside almost impatiently the widespread objection that tradition forbids the election of the Cardinal Secretary of State. Since this time he had to name a name, Monsignor Ciriaci was especially cautious when he spoke of Cardinal Pacelli. It was a question of a purely formal caution, for the tone in which he described him as "a certainly outstanding man" was sufficient. He then added that, when he [Pacelli] was elected, he "could probably not, or at least not altogether, follow the political line, which many foresee"' (ASMAE, Serie Affari Politici 1931–45, Santa Sede, Busta 43 [1939], fasc. 'Conclave' [unfoliated]).
732. Cf. P. Blet, *Pie XII*, 19.
733. Cf. Report of von Bergen (8 October 1936) (no. 266; a 309), PA/AA, Embassy to the Holy See, Best. 29. vol. 1/Lfd. no. 441 (unfoliated).
734. Cf. H. Hoberg, *Papst Pius XII*, 30; 58; W. Sandfuchs, *Aussenminister*, 124ff.
735. G. Schwaiger, *Papsttum und Päpste*, 272.
736. Von Bergen to AA (13 March 1939), ADAP, D, vol. 4, 525.
737. Warsaw, April 1939.
738. Jena, April 1939.
739. Cf. BA ZB I 1237, fos 83ff.
740. *Giornale d'Italia* (11 February 1939).
741. Cf. O. Chadwick, *Britain*, 27.
742. But cf. the report of Osborne who, after a last visit to Pius XI on 29 January 1939, received the impression that the Pope had developed sympathies for democratic Great Britain and viewed Nazi Germany as on the same level as communism (O. Chadwick, *Britain*, 25–6).
743. Cf. the Gestapo report, Munich (14 March 1939), on 'Judaism and the Death of Pope Pius XI' (BA ZB I 1146, fo. 1060).
744. C. Thoma, *Botschaft*, 241. Another time it says: 'Consider that Abraham, our Patriarch, is called our forbear. Anti-Semitism does not go with the spirit and exalted reality which come to expression in these words. Anti-Semitism is an offensive movement, in which we Christians can have no share. It is not possible for the Christian to take part in anti-Semitism. [...] Anti-Semitism is not to be justified' (Ibid.). On 23 October 1938, Tardini telegraphed the Apostolic Delegation in Washington DC that the Chief Rabbi of Cairo had sent the Pope 'a respectful message of admiration and thanks in the name of Egyptian Judaism for the attitude of His Holiness concerning oppressive measures, which have been put in force by the enemies of justice in opposition to the divine law of love, and love of

neighbour when they deny indefeasible rights. Explains, His Holiness stood for the honour of all mankind – not only because he acts as the supreme head of the Church but before the eyes of the whole world as the highest authority of eternal morality and the human conscience, which cannot be swayed by the worst of blasphemies' (AA.EE.SS., Germania, Pos. 742 P.O. fasc. 356 fo. 38r).

745. 'Pius XII', *The New York Times* (3 March 1939), 20; cf. SD-Lagebericht for the period from 1 January to 31 March 1939 (BA ZB I 1237, fos 83–93; here 86).
746. *L'Humanité* (4 March 1939), title page; Cf. SD-Lagebericht for the period 1 January–31 March 1939 (ibid.).
747. SD-report (17 March 1939), BA ZB I 186, 58–63; here, fos 62–3.
748. Cf. R. Eatwell, *Reflections*, 150.
749. Cf. G. Besier, *Friends*, 63–4.
750. Geist to Secretary of State (9 May 1939), NA, LM 197, Reel #2 (own re-translation).
751. Kirk to Secretary of State (24 May 1939), NA, LM 197, Reel #2 (own re-translation).
752. Von Bergen to AA (5 March 1939), ADAP. D, vol. 4, 522–3.
753. Ibid. See the correspondence between Pacelli and Hitler on the occasion of the election report of Pius XII (EAM NL Faulhaber, no. 1170).
754. Von Bergen to AA (5 March 1939), ADAP, D, vol. 4, 522–3.
755. Cf. D. Zlepko, *Friedensbemühungen*, 13ff.
756. Statement in: EAM NL Faulhaber, no. 1152/1.
757. At the same time the German episcopate prepared a greetings telegram to Hitler. Cf. Volk (ed.), *Akten Kardinal Michael von Faulhabers*, vol. 2, 614.
758. Letter in: EAM NL Faulhaber, no. 1152/1.
759. On the one-sided cancellation of the German-Polish non-aggression pact by Germany on 28 April 1939, cf. A. Kotowski, *Hitlers Bewegung*, 178ff.
760. Cf. on this and the following P. Blet, *Papst Pius XII*, 4ff.; O. Chadwick, *Britain*, 57ff.
761. Cf. e.g. *Catholic Times* (12 May 1939).
762. Radio message of Pope Pius XII, in ADSS, vol. 1, 232.
763. ADSS, vol. 1, no. 160, and AAS 31 (1939), 335–6.
764. Cf. *The New York Times* (21 March 1939). On the connections between the British and American churches, cf. Besier, *Friends*, 63–4. On Protestant criticism of Lang's proposal to act jointly with the Pope, cf. Besier, *Pacelli*, 207.
765. Cf. the Paris nuncio Valeri to Cardinal Maglione, Paris (20 June 1939), in ADSS, vol. 1, 179–80.
766. Cf. the Paris nuncio Valeri to Cardinal Maglione, Paris (4 July 1939), in ADSS, vol. 1, 198.
767. Cf. notes of Msgr Maglione, Vatican (24 August 1939), in ADSS, vol. 1, 239–40.
768. Cf. notes of Msgr Tardini, Vatican (26 August 1939), in ADSS, vol. 1, 249.
769. Cf. Notes of Msgr Montini and of Msgr Tardini, Vatican (28 August 1939), in ADSS, vol. 1, 256–7.
770. Quoted from S. Friedländer, *Pius XII*, 49–50.

771. P. Godman, *Hitler and the Vatican*, 15.
772. Ibid., 18.
773. Cf. G. Miccoli, *Italien*, 549.
774. *Osservatore Romano*, no. 164 (17 July 1937).
775. This was valid for the ruler also. At the papal celebration in Rosenheim, Faulhaber thought that, in relation to Pius XI, 'if the details of the papal election were known, there would be known with the clarity of the sun, how the finger of God clearly, and more clearly and absolutely clearly pointed to the Archbishop of Milan. The finger of God was clearly visible in the Papal election, if I may put it thus' (*Bayerischer Kurier* no. 157 [1922]).
776. Cf. with the problem of knowledge in the exclusive possession of truth. J. Assmann, *Herrschaft und Heil*. See also R. Stark, *One True God*.
777. Declaration of the Belgian episcopate (2 February 1930), EAM NL Faulhaber, no. 2051.
778. P. Godman, *Hitler and the Vatican*, 94.
779. See above, Chapter 3.3.
780. R. Eatwell, *Reflections*, 148.
781. Cf. Gaillard, *Attractions*, 209–10.
782. Cf. for Germany R. Uertz, *Gottesrecht*.
783. Cf. G. Miccoli, *Italien*, 550.
784. By contrast, Mussolini persevered with the political character of the celebrations. Cf. on this A. Nützenadel, *Faschismus*, esp. 29–32; see also M. Berezin, *Fascist Self*, esp. 70ff.
785. Text: E. Huber/W. Huber (eds), *Staat und Kirche*, vol. 3, 336–43.
786. L. Sturzo, *Kirche und Staat*, 17 (own translation).
787. Ibid., 28 (own translation).
788. R. Eatwell, *Reflections*, 148.
789. Thus J. Molony, *Emergence*, 12.
790. See above, Chapter 2.5.
791. Cf. R. Eatwell, *Reflections*, 148.
792. Cf. G. Miccoli, *Italien*, 551.
793. The early Fascists formed teams (*squadre*) to go out and beat up opponents; when applied to Fascism the word *squadrista* was used of persons who took part in these violent activities. Mussolini later tried to tame them (translator's note).
794. R. Eatwell, *Reflections*, 149.
795. Cf. ibid.
796. Cf. on this P. Kent, *Tale*, 593.
797. R. Eatwell, *Reflections*, 151.
798. Cf. H. Maier, *Doppelgesicht*, 46ff.
799. Canepa enrolled in the Fascist Party in 1932 and received, after the publication of his *Sistema*, a chair for the history and doctrine of Fascism and also the (general) history of political theory at the University of Catania in Sicily. He took part under the pseudonym of Mario Turri in the resistance to Fascism, supporting the independence of Sicily from Italy. He and two other fighters fell on 17 June 1945 in an exchange of shots with a unit of the Carabinieri. Sicilian separatism had already at that date passed its zenith, and declined rapidly in significance. Cf. S. Barbagallo, *Rivoluzione*; A. Caruso, *Arrivano*.

800. Already in 1925 the French sociologist Georges Valois emphasized that Fascism was a 'universal phenomenon' and would become 'a synthesis of the positive anti-democratic movements' in Europe. Cf. G. Valois, *Essenza*.
801. A. Canepa, *Sistema*, 96.
802. Ibid., 100.
803. G. Bruni, *Stato totalitario*, 261–2.
804. L. Klinkhammer, *Mussolinis Italien*, 89. Similarly already, J. Gaillard, *Attractions*, 213.
805. Cf. on this E. Gentile, *Sacralization*; Gentile, *Liktorenkult*.
806. Cf. G. Besier, *Kirchen*, 241ff.; E. Gajek, *Feiergestaltung*.
807. L. Klinkhammer, *Mussolinis Italien*, 87.
808. Ibid., 90. Cf. also on the post-war politics of the Vatican, P. Kent, *Cold War*, esp. 87ff., 237ff.
809. Cf. G. Denzler, *Widerstand oder Anpassung*; Denzler, *Widerstand*.
810. K. Breuning, *Vision*, 321.
811. Cf. J. Brokoff/J. Fohrmann (eds), *Politische Theologie*. When it was a question of 'Italian affairs' – for example, the Abyssinian War – national attitudes occasionally show through.
812. On the relation of Protestantism and nationalism as 'political religion', see Th. Kuhn, *Christentum*. See on the relations of political and traditional religion, E. Gentile, *Religioni*, 210.
813. Cf. P. Godman, *Hitler and the Vatican*, 191.
814. R. Niebuhr, *Catholic Heresy*.
815. Cf. Corrin, *Catholic Intellectuals*, 272ff. The spearhead of conservative, militant anti-communist Catholicism was formed by the journal *America* under the editorship of Francis Talbot after 1936.
816. Report of 7 January 1927 on conversation of Groenesteyn with Gasparri. BayHStA, Bayerische Gesandtschaft, Päpstlicher Stuhl, 1005 (unfoliated).
817. Cf. reports of Groenesteyn (15 January 1927) and (24 January 1927), BayHStA, Bayerische Gesandtschaft, Päpstlicher Stuhl, 1005 (unfoliated).
818. Cf. EAM NL Faulhaber, no. 2008.
819. Cf. Will to AA (19 August 1926), PA/AA, R 79640 (unfoliated).
820. Cf. EAM NL Faulhaber, no. 2054.
821. Cf. G. Besier, *Contradictions*; R. Slayton, *Al and Frank*.
822. J. McGreevy, *Catholicism*, 171.
823. Cf. Corrin, *Catholic Intellectuals*, 292.
824. North American Committee to Aid Spanish Democracy, *American Democracy vs. the Spanish Hierarchy*, New York 1937.
825. McGreevy, *Catholicism*, 173.
826. L. Mumford, *Call*, 41.
827. J. Mecklin, *Freedom of Speech*, 170–1.
828. T. Parsons, '*Academic Freedom*'.
829. Cf. U. Lübken, *Bedrohliche Nähe*, esp. 130ff.: Gaudig/Veit, *Hakenkreuz*; Friedman, *Nazis and Good Neighbors*.
830. Cf. AA to von Bergen (9 August 1939 and 19 August 1939), ADAP, D, vol. 7, 114–15.
831. Cf. Stohrer (German ambassador in San Sebastian) to the AA (16 July 1939), ADAP, D vol. 6, 780.
832. AA to von Bergen (19 August 1939), ADAP, D, vol. 7, 114.

260 Notes, pp. 203–4

833. The right wing of English Catholicism could find Fascism very attractive as Corrin, *Catholic Intellectuals*, 188ff., shows. Here, for instance, the Anglo-American criticism of Mussolini's Abyssinian War was seen as part of the strategy of the political Left, who wished to bring Europe under their own rule (ibid., 218).

834. Robertson to Bell (23 September 1937), LPL London, Bell Papers, German Church 9, fo. 3 (own re-translation).

835. Thus Robertson to Bell (25 October 1937), LPL London, Bell Papers, German Church 9, fo. 26. (own re-translation).

836. Nathaniel Micklem to Headlam (7 August 1938), Headlam Papers MS 2643, fo. 272. Cf. N. Micklem, *National Socialism*.

837. Cf. H. Maier, *Revolution und Kirche*; Maier, *Kirche und Demokratie*.

838. Cf. H. Lutz, *Katholizismus und Faschismus*; H. Lutz/C. Amery, *Katholizismus und Faschismus*, 49.

839. Thus K.-E. Lönne, *Historiographischer Rückblick*, 144–5.

840. Böckenförde, *Katholizismus im Jahre 1933*, 215–39, here 237; cf. Böckenförde, *Stellungnahme*, 217–45.

841. Cf. on this P. Kent, *Cold War*, 191ff.

842. Omodeo, *Totalitarismo cattolico*, 332.

Bibliography

Unpublished sources

Archives of the League of Nations, Geneva [LON]
    Bestand R 3906: 41/5154/560; 41/6274/56.
Archivio della Congregazione della Fede Rome [ACDF]
    Bestand S.O.: 535/30; 1413/30 i; 4304, 1933 i (1); R.V 1928 (2); R.V. 1934/12;
    R.V. 1934, 29, Prot. 3373/34, vol. 1, 1, 2–4; 3–4; vol. 1, 1–3; vol. 2, 4, 9; vol. 2,
    7ff.; vol. 4, 12; vol. 4, 16; 2935/291.
Archivio Storico-Diplomatico del Ministero degli Affari Esteri italiano Rome
    [ASMAE]
    Serie Affari Politici 1931–1945: Santa Sede, Busta 43 (1939), fasc. 'Conclave'.
Archiwum Kurii Metropolitalnej w Krakowie [AKMK]
    Bestand AKMK, TS: XI, Akta kard. Sapiehy. Konkordat (1919–1939); XII, 2 List
    R do S wiadomościami o drodze do Warszawy z 3 VI 1918; XII, 3 List r do
    S z wiadomościami p przesyłkach do Wiednia z 14 VI 1918; XII, 4 List R do S o
    konsekracji nowych biskupów z 22 XI 1918; XII, 5 List R do S kondolencyjny
    po śmierci kuzyna z 16 I 1919; XII, 6 List R do S o biskupie polowym z 22 I
    1919; XII, 7 List R do S przyszłej konferencji i o konkordacie z 3 II 1919; XII,
    8 List R do S o sprawie ks. Forysia, Urszulankach i gen. Halera z 28 III 1919;
    XII, 9 List R do S o ambasadorze Kowalskim i liście past. abpa kakowskiego z
    30 V 1919; XII, 11 List R do S o ambasadzie w Rzymie I prasie polskiej z 6 VI
    1919; XII, 12 List r do S o osobie Loreta z 22 VII 1919; XII, 14 List R do S o
    utworzeniu ambasady przy Watykanie II kl. z 19 VIII 1919; XII, 18 List R do S
    o korespondencji z 5 IX 1919; XII, 19 List bpa Sapiehy do nunjusza Rattiego
    o biskupie polowym z 2 XI 1919; XII, 20 List R do S o biskupie Galu z 13 XI
    1919; XII, 21 List R do S o zjednoczeniu paulinów z 24 VI 1919; XII, 22 List R
    do S o przyjeździe abpa Roppa z 24 XI 1919; XII, 25 List R do S w sprawie ks.
    Czyżewskiego z 1 III 1920; XII, 26 List R do S w sprawie nominacji sufragana
    białoruskiego w Wilnie; XII, 27 List R do S o nominacjach z 16 VII 1920; XII,
    28 List R do S w związku z projektem parcelacji ziemi kościelnej z 10 IX 1920;
    XII, 30 List R do S z zaproszeniem na konferencję w sprawie ziemi kośc. z 4 V
    1921; XII, 34 List R do S o opinię o ks. Komarze jako kandydacie na biskupa z 6
    V 1921; XII, 75 List kard. Pacelli do kard. Hlonda z 23 VII 1930 r., list dotyczy
    Kongresu Eucharystycznego.
Bayerisches Hauptstaatsarchiv München [BayHStA]
    Bayerische Gesandtschaft. Päpstlicher Stuhl: 949; 954; 956; 967; 973; 996; 1005;
    1017; 1025; 1030; 1045.
    MA: 99878; 100009.
    MInn: 72442.
    MK: 49127.

Bundesarchiv Berlin [BA]
   Bestand NS 10: 62; 109.
   Bestand ZB I: 186; 1146; 1237; 1653.
Erzbischöfliches Archiv München und Freising. Kardinal-Faulhaber-Archiv [EAM
   NL Faulhaber]
   Nr. 1000; 1051; 1053; 1103f.; 1152; 1170; 1200f.; 1250f.; 1254; 1257; 1300;
   1320; 1330; 1350–2; 1370; 1395; 2008; 2013; 2015f.; 2051–4; 2059; 2062–7;
   2073f.; 2076; 2079; 2200; 2205; 3051; 3054f.; 3154; 3156; 3250; 3503; 3624;
   3692; 3703; 3801f.; 4105; 5537; 5916; 5919; 5922; 5929; 6015–17; 6020;
   6281–4; 6303f.; 6580–2; 6585f.; 6760f.; 6790; 6887; 7001; 7006; 7033f.; 7039f.;
   7088–92; 7103–6; 7150–6; 7182; 7206; 7222; 7228f.; 7261; 7264–7; 7277;
   7302–5; 7307f.; 7407; 7480; 7482–4; 7603; 7609; 7686; 8000–4; 8022; 8024;
   8028f.; 8057; 8060–2; 8106; 8203; 8211; 8216f.; 8301; 8319; 8359; 8373;
   8422–7; 9086; 9268–73; 9276–8; 9364; 9375; 9400f.; 9603; 9899.
Hoover Institution Archives Stanford
   Poland. Ambasada (Catholic Church), Records, 1924–1945.
Lambeth Palace Library London [LPL]
   Bell Papers: German Church 9; 20.
   Headlam Papers: MS. 2643.
National Archives at College Park, MD (Archives II), Washington, DC [NA]
   Bestand LM: 193, Reel # 24; 196, Reel # 2; 197, Reel #2.
Politisches Archiv des Auswärtigen Amtes [PA/AA]
   Bestand R: 9349; 9353; 72079; 72088; 72229; 79640; 103249; 130193; 130195.
   Botschaft beim Heiligen Stuhl (Rom, Vatikan): 8 Nuntius, Vol. 1/Lfd. Nr. 284; 9
   Umwandl., Vol. 1/Lfd. Nr. 283; 19, Aufhebung, Vol. 1/Lfd. Nr. 286; 29, Kardinal
   Pacelli, Vol. 1–2/Lfd. Nr. 441f.
Vatican Secret Archives Rome [Archivio Segreto Vaticano]
   Affari Ecclesiastici Straordinari, Baviera [AA.EE.SS., Baviera]
   Pos. 62, fasc. 40.
   Affari Ecclesiastici Straordinari, Germania [AA.EE.SS., Germania]
   Pos. 507 P.O., fasc. 16–17; Pos. 511 P.O., fasc. 21; 23–4; Pos. 515 P.O., fasc.
   25; Pos. 535 P.O., fasc. 64; Pos. 563 P.O., fasc. 79–81, Vol. I–II; Pos. 565
   P.O., fasc. 81; Pos. 597 P.O., fasc. 17; Pos. 604 P.O., fasc. 112–13; 115; 138;
   Pos. 606 P.O., fasc. 112–18; Pos. 621 P.O., fasc. 138–9; Pos. 621–623 P.O.,
   fasc. 140; Pos. 632 P.O., fasc. 150; Pos. 641–3 P.O., fasc. 157; Pos. 643 P.O.,
   fasc. 158; 160; Pos. 645 P.O., fasc. 163; 166; 171; Pos. 661–3 P.O., fasc. 210;
   Pos. 666 P.O., fasc. 220–1; 223–4; Pos. 692 P.O., fasc. 260; 264; Pos. 706
   P.O., fasc. 272; Pos. 719 P.O., fasc. 312–14; 316; Pos. 720 P.O., fasc. 329;
   336; Pos. 722 P.O., fasc. 339; Pos. 724 P.O., fasc. 339; Pos. 735 P.O., fasc.
   353; Pos. 736–8 P.O., fasc. 354; Pos. 742 P.O., fasc. 354; 356; Pos. 1716 P.O.,
   fasc. 896–7.; Pos. 1718 P.O., fasc. 897; 1935 'scatole', fasc. 9; 50; 1934–1944,
   'scatole' 50.
   Archivio della Nunziatura Apostolica in Monaco (di Baviera) [ANM]
   Pos. 307, fasc. 4; Pos. 328, fasc. 1; Pos. 395, fasc. 1; Pos. 396, fasc. 7; Pos. 397,
   fasc. 1–3;
   Pos. 418, fasc. 4.
   Stati Ecclesiastici
   Pos. 1317, fasc. 470, vol. XII; XVII.

Published sources and references

Acta Apostolicae Sedis (AAS), Roma 6 (1914); 9 (1917); 10 (1918); 12 (1920); 13 (1921); 14 (1922); 16 (1924); 17 1925); 19 (1927); 20 (1928); 21 (1929); 22 (1930); 23 (1931); 25 (1933); 26 (1934); 31 (1939).

Actes et documents du Saint Siège (ADSS), relatifs á la seconde guerre mondiale, Vol. 1: Le Saint Siegé et la guerre en Europe. Mars 1939–août 1940, ed. Pierre Blet, Angelo Martini and Burkhart Schneider, Vatican City 1965.

Adam, Stephan, Die Auseinandersetzung des Bischofs Konrad von *Preysing* mit dem Nationalsozialismus in den Jahren 1933–1945, St Ottilien 1996.

Adolph, Walter, Erich *Klausener*, West Berlin 1955.

—Kardinal *Preysing* und zwei Diktaturen. Sein Widerstand gegen die totalitäre Macht, West Berlin 1971.

Adriányi, Gabriel, Die *Geschichte* der katholischen Kirche in Ungarn, Cologne-Vienna 2004.

Agostino, Marc, Le Pape *Pie XI* et l'opinion 1922–1939 (Collection de l'École française de Rome, 150), Rome 1991.

Akten der Reichskanzlei (Weimarer Republik), ed. Karl Dietrich Erdmann, Das *Kabinett Bauer*. 21. Juni 1919 bis 27. März 1920, ed. Anton Golecki, Boppard 1980.

Akten der Reichskanzlei (Weimarer Republik), ed. Karl Dietrich Erdmann, Die *Kabinette Brüning I und II*, vol. 2:1. März 1931 bis Oktober 1931, Dokumente Nr 253 bis 514, ed. Tilmann Koops, Boppard 1982.

Akten zur deutschen Auswärtigen Politik 1918 bis 1945 (ADAP). Aus dem Archiv des Auswärtigen Amtes, Serie A: 1918–1925, Vol. 14: 14. August–30. November 1925, Göttingen 1995; Serie B: 1925–1933, Vol. 5: 17. März–30. Juni 1927, Göttingen 1974; Vol. 7: 1. Oktober–31. Dezember 1927, Göttingen 1974; Vol. 18: 1. Juli–15. Oktober 1931, Göttingen 1982; Serie D: 1937–1945, Vol. 1: Von Neurath zu Ribbentrop (September 1937–September 1938), Göttingen 1950; Vol. 4: Die Nachwirkungen von München (Oktober 1938–März 1939), Göttingen 1951; Vol. 6: Die letzten Monate vor Kriegsausbruch (März bis August 1939), Göttingen 1956; Vol. 7: Die letzten Monate vor Kriegsausbruch (August bis September 1939), Göttingen 1956.

Albert, Marcel, Die *Benediktinerabtei Maria Laach* und der Nationalsozialismus (VKZG.F, 59), Paderborn-Munich-Vienna-Zurich 2004.

Albrecht, Dieter (ed.), Der *Notenwechsel* zwischen dem heiligen Stuhl und der deutschen Reichsregierung, Vol. 1: Von der Ratifizierung des Reichskonkordats bis zur Enzyklika 'Mit brennender Sorge' (VKZG.Q, 1), Mainz 1965.

Aleksiun, Natalia, *Polish Historiography* of the Holocaust – between Silence and Public Debate, in German History 22 (2004), 406–32.

Altermatt, Urs, Katholizismus und Antisemitismus. Mentalitäten, Kontinuitäten, Ambivalenzen. Zur Kulturgeschichte der Schweiz 1918–1945, Frauenfeld-Stuttgart-Vienna 1999.

Alvarez, David, A Few Bits of *Information*: American Intelligence and the Vatican, 1939–45, in Woolner and Kurial (eds), *FDR*, 253–67.

—*Spies* in the Vatican: Espionage & Intrigue from Napoleon to the Holocaust, Lawrence 2002.

Alvarez, David, and Robert A. Graham, *Nothing Sacred*: Nazi Espionage against the Vatican 1933–1945 (Cass Series: Studies in Intelligence), London-Portland 1997.

Amann, Sirikit M., Kulturpolitische Aspekte im *Austrofaschismus* (1934–1938) unter besonderer Berücksichtigung des Ministeriums für Unterricht, Diss. phil. Vienna 1987.

Amici Israel (ed.), *Pax super Israel*, no place, 1926.

Anderson, James M., The *Spanish Civil War*: A History and Reference Guide, Westport-London 2003.

Angermann, Erich, Die Vereinigten Staaten von *Amerika* seit 1917, 9th edn, Munich 1995.

Anschütz, Gerhard, Die *Verfassung* des Deutschen Reichs vom 11. August 1919: Ein Kommentar für Wissenschaft und Praxis (Stilkes Rechtsbibliothek, 1), 14th edn, Berlin 1933.

Arendt, Hannah, 'Der *Stellvertreter*' in den USA, *NDH* 101 (September/October 1964), 111–23.

Aretin, Karl Otmar von, Einleitende *Vorbemerkungen* zur Kontroverse Scholder-Repgen, in Klaus Scholder, Die Kirchen zwischen Republik und Gewaltherrschaft: Gesammelte Aufsätzem, ed. Karl Otmar von Aretin and Gerhard Besier, West Berlin 1988, 171–3.

Arnberger, Heinz, Winfried R. Garscha and Christa Mitterrutzner (ed.), '*Anschluss*' 1938: Eine Dokumentation, hg. vom Dokumentationsarchiv des österreichischen Widerstandes, Vienna 1988.

Assmann, Jan, *Herrschaft und Heil*: Politische Theologie in Altägypten, Israel und Europa, Munich-Vienna 2000.

Astorri, Romeo, *Diritto comune* e normativa concordataria: Uno scritto inedito di Mons. Pacelli sulla 'decadenza' degli accordi tra chiesa e Stato, in *SCont* 22 (1991), 685–701.

Badde, Paul, 'Antisemitische *Ausschreitungen*', in *Die Welt* (15 March 2003), 28.

Balfour, Sebastian, and Paul Preston (eds), *Spain* and the Great Powers in the Twentieth Century (Cañada Blanch Studies in Contemporary Spain), London 1999.

Barbagallo, Salvo, Una *rivoluzione* mancata, Catania 1974.

Barkowez, Olga, Fjodor Federow and Alexander Krylow, 'Geliebter Nicky': Der letzte russische *Zar Nikolaus II* und seine Familie. Aus dem Russischen von Bärbel und Lothar Lenhardt. Mit 52 historischen Photographien, Berlin 2002.

Bärnthaler, Irmgard, Die *Vaterländische Front*: Geschichte und Organisation, Vienna-Frankfurt/M.-Zurich 1971.

Bärsch, Claus-Ekkehard, Die politische *Religion* des Nationalsozialismus: Die religiösen Dimensionen der NS-Ideologie in den Schriften von Dietrich Eckart, Joseph Goebbels, Alfred Rosenberg und Adolf Hitler, 2nd edn, Munich 2002.

Batelli, Giuseppe, *Chiesa*, societá e 'devozioni politiche', in *StSt* 43 (2002), 611–26.

Batowski, Henryk, Die territorialen *Bestimmungen* von San Stefano und Berlin, in Ralph Melville and Hans-Jürgen Schröder (eds), Der Berliner Kongress von 1878: Die Politik der Grossmächte und die Probleme der Modernisierung in Südosteuropa in der zweiten Hälfte des 19. Jahrhunderts (Veröffentlichungen des Instituts für Europäische Geschichte Mainz. Abteilung Universalgeschichte. Beiheft 7), Wiesbaden 1982, 51–62.

Bauer, Richard (ed.), Kardinal Michael von *Faulhaber*, 1869–1952: Eine Ausstellung des Archivs des Erzbistums München und Freising, des Bayerischen

Hauptstaatsarchivs und des Stadtarchivs München zum 50. Todestag. München 6. Juni bis 28. Juli 2002 (Ausstellungskataloge der Staatlichen Archive Bayerns, 44), Munich-Neuburg 2002.

Baumgärtner, Raimund, *Weltanschauungskampf* im Dritten Reich: Die Auseinandersetzung der Kirchen mit Alfred Rosenberg (VKZG.F, 22), Mainz 1977.

Becker, Josef, Das Ende der *Zentrumspartei* und die Problematik des politischen Katholizismus in Deutschland, in Gotthard Jasper (ed.), Von Weimar zu Hitler 1930–1933 (Neue wissenschaftliche Bibliothek, 25: Geschichte), Cologne-Berlin 1968, 344–76.

Becker, Winfried, Die Deutsche *Zentrumspartei* gegenüber dem Nationalsozialismus und dem Reichskonkordat 1930–1933: Motivationsstrukturen und Situationszwänge, *HPM* 7 (2000), 1–37.

Beckmann, Beate, and Hanna-Barbara Gerl-Falkowitz (eds), *Edith Stein*. Themen-Bezüge-Dokumente (Orbis phaenomenologicus: Perspektiven, 1), Würzburg 2003.

Ben-Ami, Shlomo, The *Dictatorship* of Primo de Rivera: A Political Reassessment, in *JCH* 12 (1977), 65–84.

Berezin, Mabel, Making the *Fascist Self*: The Political Culture of Interwar Italy (The Wilder House Series in Politics, History, and Culture), Ithaka 1997.

Berger Waldenegg, Georg Christoph, Hitler, Göring, Mussolini und der 'Anschluss' Österreichs an das Deutsche Reich, in *VfZ* 51 (2003), 147–182.

Bergmann, Ernst, Die *Deutsche Nationalkirche*, Breslau 1933.

Bernecker, Walther L., *Krieg* in Spanien 1936–1939, Darmstadt 1991.

—*Religion* in Spanien. Darstellung und Daten zur Geschichte und Gegenwart (Gütersloher Taschenbücher 636: Religion in Europa), Gütersloh 1995.

—*Spanische Geschichte* von der Reconquista bis heute, Darmstadt 2002.

Bernecker, Walther L., and Horst Pietschmann, *Geschichte Portugals*. Vom Spätmittelalter bis zur Gegenwart (Beck'sche Reihe, 2156: C. H. Beck Wissen), Munich 2001.

—*Geschichte Spaniens*. Von der frühen Neuzeit bis zur Gegenwart, 3rd edn, Stuttgart-Berlin-Cologne 2000.

Berning, Vincent, and Hans Maier, Alois *Dempf* 1891–1982. Philosoph, Kulturtheoretiker, Prophet gegen den Nationalsozialismus, Weissenhorn 1992.

Besier, Gerhard, 'Berufsständische Ordnung' und autoritäre Diktaturen: Zur politischen Umsetzung einer 'klassenfreien' katholischen Gesellschaftsordnung in den 20er und 30er Jahren des 20. Jahrhunderts, in Gerhard Besier and Hermann Lübbe, Politische Religion und Religionspolitik: Zwischen Totalitarismus und Bürgerfreiheit, Göttingen 2005, 79–110.

—Confessional versus Ideological *Convictions*: The *Fliednersches Evangelisationswerk* and the Ecclesiastical Foreign Office of the German Protestant Church during the Spanish Civil War, *KZG* 15 (2002), 509–18.

—Dogmatische *Neuansätze*, politisch ethische Kontroversen und praktisch-theologisches Handeln in der Kirche und Universitätstheologie, in Gerhard Besier and Eckhard Lessing (eds), Die Geschichte der Evangelischen Kirche der Union: Ein Handbuch, Vol. 3, 142–210.

—Der *Dom* in der Weimarer Republik und im Dritten Reich, in Detlef Plöse (ed.), Der Berliner Dom: Geschichte und Gegenwart der Oberpfarr- und Domkirche zu Berlin (Dokumentation des 'Symposiums zur Geschichte und Gegenwart der Oberpfarr- und Domkirche (Berliner Dom)' vom 19. November 1999 bis 3. März 2000 in Berlin), Berlin 2001, 197–209.

—Eugenio *Pacelli*, die Römisch-katholische Kirche und das Christentum (1933–1945) in historisch-religiöser Kritik, in Rainer Bendel (ed.), Die katholische Schuld? Katholizismus im Dritten Reich zwischen Arrangement und Widerstand, Münster-Hamburg-London 2002, 200–20.

—'The *friends*…in America need to know the truth…': Die deutschen Kirchen im Urteil der Vereinigten Staaten (1933–1941), in *JHK* 1998, Munich 1999, 23–76.

—In *Contradiction* to the Grassroots? The Stance of the Federal Council of the Churches of Christ (FCC) towards the 'Third Reich', in Kyrkohistorisk Årsskrift 1 (2003), 139–156.

—*Kirche*, Politik und Gesellschaft *im 19. Jahrhundert* (EDG, 48), Munich 1998.

—*Kirche*, Politik und Gesellschaft *im 20. Jahrhundert* (EDG, 50), Munich 2000.

—Die *Kirchen* und das Dritte Reich: Spaltungen und Abwehrkämpfe 1934–1937, Berlin-Munich 2001.

—Der *Nationalsozialismus* als Säkularreligion, in Gerhard Besier and Eckhard Lessing (eds), Die Geschichte der Evangelischen Kirche der Union: Ein Handbuch, Vol. 3: Trennung von Staat und Kirche – Kirchlich-politische Krisen – Erneuerung kirchlicher Gemeinschaft (1918–1992), Leipzig 1999, 445–78.

Bettelheim, Peter (ed.), *Antisemitismus* in Osteuropa. Aspekte einer historischen Kontinuität, Vienna 1992.

Biffi, Monica M., Il *cavalletto* per la tortura. Cesare Orsenigo, ambasciatore del papa nella Germania di Hitler, Rome 2006.

—Mons. Cesare *Orsenigo*: nunzio apostolico in Germania (1930–1946) (Archivo ambrosiano, 75), Milan 1997.

Binder, Dieter A., Der 'Christliche *Ständestaat*': Österreich 1934–1938, in Rolf Steininger and Michael Gehler (eds), Österreich im 20. Jahrhundert, Vol. 1, 203–43.

Birmingham, David, A Concise *History* of Portugal (Cambridge Concise Histories), Cambridge 1993.

Blaschke, Olaf, *Katholizismus und Antisemitismus* im Deutschen Kaiserreich (Kritische Studien zur Geschichtswissenschaft, 122), Göttingen 1997.

Blet, Pierre SJ, *Papst Pius XII* und der Zweite Weltkrieg: Aus den Akten des Vatikans, 2nd edn, Paderborn-Munich-Vienna-Zurich 2001.

—*Pie XII* et la Seconde Guerre mondiale d'après les archives du Vatican, Paris 2000.

Blinkhorn, Martin, *Democracy and Civil War* in Spain, 1931–1939 (Lancaster Pamphlets), London 1996.

Blinkhorn, Martin (ed.), *Spain* in Conflict, 1931–1939: Democracy and Its Enemies, London 1986.

Böckenförde, Ernst-Wolfgang, Der deutsche *Katholizismus im Jahre 1933*: Eine kritische Betrachtung, *Hochland* 53 (1960–61), 215–39.

—Der deutsche Katholizismus im Jahre 1933: *Stellungnahme* zu einer Diskussion, *Hochland* 54 (1961–62), 217–45.

Bohn, Jutta, Das *Verhältnis* zwischen katholischer Kirche und faschistischem Staat in Italien und die Rezeption in deutschen Zentrumskreisen (1922–1933), Frankfurt am Main 1992.

Bokenkotter, Thomas, *Church and Revolution*: Catholics in the Struggle for Democracy and Social Justice, New York 1998.

Bottai, Giuseppe, *Diario* 1935–1944, ed. Giordano Bruno Guerri, Milan 1982.

Böttcher, Hans Viktor, Die *Freie Stadt Danzig*: Wege und Umwege in die europäische Zukunft. Historischer Rückblick und völkerrechtliche Fragen (Forschungsergebnisse der Studiengruppe für Politik und Völkerrecht, 23), 3rd edn, Bonn 1999.

Bottum, Joseph, The *End* of the Pius Wars, *First Things* 142 (April 2004), 18–25.

Bottum, Joseph, and David G. Dalin, The *Pius War*: Responses to the Critics of Pius XII, Lanham 2004.

Bowen, Wayne H., *Spaniards* and Nazi Germany: Collaboration in the New Order, Columbia-London 2000.

Boyd, Carolyn B., *Historia Patria*: Politics, History, and National Identity in Spain 1875–1975, Princeton 1997.

Bracher, Karl Dietrich, Nationalsozialistische *Machtergreifung* und Reichskonkordat: Ein Gutachten, in Friedrich Giese, Friedrich August von der Heydte and Hans Müller (eds), Der Konkordatsprozess (Veröffentlichungen des Instituts für Staatslehre und Politik, 7), Vol. 3, 2nd edn, Munich 1995, 947–1021.

Braga da Cruz, Manuel, Der *Estado Novo* und die katholische Kirche, in Fernando Rosas (ed.), Vom Ständestaat zur Demokratie: Portugal im zwanzigsten Jahrhundert (Schriftenreihe der Vierteljahrshefte für Zeitgeschichte, 75), Munich 1997, 49–63.

Brandl, Ludwig, *Neue Quellen* zum Reichskonkordat vom 20. Juli 1933, *ZfP* 38 (1991), 428–49.

Brandmüller, Walter, Ein neuer *Streit* um Pius XII: Zum Desaster der katholisch-jüdischen Historikerkommission, *Die Neue Ordnung* 55 (2001), 371–81.

Braun, Otto, Von *Weimar* zu Hitler, New York 1940.

Brechenmacher, Thomas, Das *Ende* der doppelten Schutzherrschaft: Der Heilige Stuhl und die Juden am Übergang zur Moderne 1775–1870 (Päpste und Papsttum, 32), Stuttgart 2004.

—Er war nicht stark, und er war kein *Held*, *FAZ* 95 (24 April 2003), 42.

—Im *Widerspruch* zum göttlichen Recht. Neue Quellen zeigen: Kardinal Pacelli lehnte 1938 jeden Kompromiss mit dem Nationalsozialismus ab, *FAZ* 238 vom 14 October 2003), 48.

—Pope Pius XI, Eugenio Pacelli, and the Persecution of the Jews in Nazi Germany, 1933–1939: New Sources from the Vatican Archives, German Historical Institute London, Bulletin, Vol. XXVII, no. 2 (November 2005), 17–44.

—*Teufelspakt*, Selbsterhaltung, universale Mission? Leitlinien und Spielräume der Diplomatie des Heiligen Stuhls gegenüber dem nationalsozialistischen Deutschland (1933–1939) im Lichte neu zugänglicher vatikanischer Akten, *HZ* 280 (2005), 591–645.

—Der *Vatikan* und die Juden: Geschichte einer unheiligen Beziehung, Munich 2005.

Breuning, Klaus, Die *Vision* des Reiches: Deutscher Katholizismus zwischen Demokratie und Diktatur (1929–1934), Munich 1969.

Brokoff, Jürgen, and Jürgen Fohrmann (eds), *Politische Theologie*: Formen und Funktionen im 20. Jahrhundert (Studien zu Judentum und Christentum), Paderborn-Munich-Vienna-Zürich 2003.

Bruneteau, Bernard, *Antiliberalismus* und totalitäre Versuchung – Am Beispiel von fünf Intellektuellen des 'Parti populaire français' in den 30er Jahren, in Uwe Backes (ed.), Rechtsextreme Ideologien in Geschichte und Gegenwart (Schriften des Hannah-Arendt-Instituts für Totalitarismusforschung, 23), Cologne-Weimar-Vienna 2003, 123–37.

Bruni, Giulio Ulderigo, Sul concetto di *Stato totalitario*, Lo Stato 10 (1939), 257–89.

Brüning, Heinrich, *Memoiren* 1918–1934, Stuttgart 1970.

Bruti Liberati, Luigi, *Santa Sede* e Stati Uniti negli anni della grande guerra, in Giorgio Rumi (ed.), Benedetto XV e la pace 1918 (Biblioteca di storia temporanea), Brescia 1990, 129–50.

Buchanan, Tom, and Martin Conway (eds), *Political Catholicism* in Europe, 1918–1965, Oxford 1996.

Bukey, Evan Burr, *Hitler's Austria*: Popular Sentiment in the Nazi Era 1938–1945, Chapel Hill-London 2000.

Burdett, Charles, *Journeys* to Italian East Africa 1936–1941: Narratives of Settlement, in *JMIS* 5 (2000), 207–26.

Burkard, Dominik, Die *Bergpredigt* des Teufels. Keine Gnade vor den Augen des Vatikans: Zur Indizierung von Rosenbergs Mythus des 20. Jahrhunderts, *FAZ* 73 (27 March 2003), 48.

—*Häresie* und Mythus des 20. Jahrhunderts: Rosenbergs nationalsozialistische Weltanschauung vor dem Tribunal der Römischen Inquisition, Paderborn 2005.

Butler, Ewan, and Gordon Young, The Life and Death of *Hermann Goering*, Newton Abbot 1989.

Canepa, Antonio, *Sistema* di dottrina del fascismo. Libro terzo: Le basi del sistema, Rome 1937.

Carr, Raymund (ed.), *Spain* A History, Oxford 2000.

Carroll, James, *Constantine's Sword*: The Church and the Jews, Boston 2001.

Carsten, Francis L., Die erste österreichische *Republik* im Spiegel zeitgenössischer Quellen (Böhlaus zeitgeschichtliche Bibliothek, 8), Vienna-Cologne-Graz 1988.

Carter, Michael H., *Diplomacy's Detractors*: American Protestant Reaction to FDR's 'Personal Representative' at the Vatican, in Woolner and Kurial (eds), *FDR*, 179–208.

Caruso, Alfio, *Arrivano* i nostri, Milan 2004.

Casanova, Julián, La *Iglesia* de Franco (Colección historia), Madrid 2001.

Casula, Carlo Felice, Domenico *Tardini* (1888–1961): L'azione della Santa Sede nella crisi fra le due guerre, Rome 1988.

—Le *segreterie di stato* tra le due guerre, in Gabriele De Rosa and Giorgio Gracco (eds), Il Papato e l'Europa, Soveria Mannelli (Catanzaro) 2001, 417–28.

Chadwick, Owen, *Britain* and the Vatican during the Second World War (Ford Lectures, 1981), Cambridge 1986.

—*Pius XII*: The Legends and the Truth, *International Catholic Newspaper* (28 March 1998).

Charnitzky, Jürgen, Die *Schulpolitik* des faschistischen Regimes in Italien (1922–1943) (Bibliothek des Deutschen Historischen Instituts in Rom, 79), Tübingen 1994.

Chen, Philip, *Religious Liberty* in American Foreign Policy, 1933–41: Aspects of Public Argument beween FDR and American Roman Catholics, in Woolner and Kurial (eds), *FDR*, 121–39.

Chenaux, Philippe, *Pacelli, Hudal* et la question du nazisme (1933–1938), *Rivista di storia della Chiesa in Italia* 57 (2003), 133–54.

——*Pie XII*: Diplomate et pasteur, Paris 2003.

Chiron, Yves, *La Vie de Maurras*, Paris 1991.

Cianfarra, Camille M., *The War and the Vatican*, London 1945.

Ciano, Galeazzo, *Diario* 1937–1943, ed. Renzo de Felice, Milano 1980.

——*Tagebücher* 1937/38, Hamburg 1949.

Cimbaev, Nikolay, Die *Russische Kirche* in den Jahren schwerer Prüfungen, in Leonid Luks (ed.), Das Christentum und die totalitären Herausforderungen des 20. Jahrhunderts (Schriften des Zentralinstituts für Mittel- und Osteuropastudien, 5), Cologne-Weimar-Vienna 2002, 175–89.

Codex juris canonici (*CIC*) Pii X pontificis maximi jussi digestus, Benedicti Papae XV auctoritate promulgatus, praefatione, fontium annotatione et indice analytico-alphabetico ab Petri Card. Gasparri auctus, Rome 1918.

Cogni, Giulio, *Il Razzismo* (Piccola Biblioteca di scienze moderne, 415), Milano 1936.

Colas, Dominique, Le *léninisme*: Philosophie et sociologie politiques du léninisme, 2nd edn, Paris 1998.

——Säubernde und gesäuberte *Einheitspartei*: Lenin und der Leninismus, in; Uwe Backes and Stéphane Courtois (eds), 'Ein Gespenst geht um in Europa.' Das Erbe kommunistischer Ideologien, Cologne-Weimar-Vienna 2002, 147–86.

Collectanea S. Congregationis de Propaganda Fide seu decreta, instructiones, rescripta pro apostolicis missionibus. Vol. 2: [Years] 1867–1906, No. 1300–2317, Rome 1907.

Confalonieri, Carlo, *Pius XI* aus der Nähe gesehen, Aschaffenburg 1958.

Conway, John S., *Pope* Pius XII and the Myron Taylor Mission: The Vatican and American Wartime Diplomacy, in Woolner and Kurial (eds), *FDR*, 143–51.

Conway, Martin, Catholic Politics in Europe 1918–1945, London-New York 1997.

Cornwell, John, *Hitler's Pope*: The Secret History of Pius XII, London-New York 1999.

Corrin, Jay P., *Catholic Intellectuals* and the Challenge of Democracy, Notre Dame 2002.

Corsten, Wilhelm (ed.), *Sammlung* kirchlicher Erlasse, Verordnungen und Bekanntmachungen für die Erzdiözese Köln, Vol. 1, Cologne 1929.

Coverdale, John F., *Italian Intervention* in the Spanish Civil War, Princeton 1975.

Dalin, David G., The *Myth* of Hitler's Pope: How Pius XII Rescued Jews from the Nazis, Washington, DC 2005.

Davidson, Peter (ed.), *Orwell in Spain* The Full Text of *Homage to Catalonia*, with Associated Articles, Reviews and Letters from the Complete Works of George Orwell, London 2001.

Davies, Norman, Im *Herzen Europas*: Geschichte Polens, 2nd edn, Munich 2001.

De Bedts, Ralf F., Ambassador *Joseph Kennedy* 1938–1940: An Anatomy of Appeasement (American University Studies Series 9, 12), New York-Bern-Frankfurt am Main 1985.

De Felice, Renzo (ed.), *Mussolini e Hitler*: I rapporti segreti (1922–1933) (Quaderni di storia, 33), 2nd edn, Florence 1983.

——*Mussolini* il Duce, Vol. 1: Gli anni del consenso 1929–1936, Torino 1974; Vol. 2: Lo Stato totalitario 1936–1940, Torino 1981.

De Giorgi, Fulvio, *Linguaggi militari* e mobilitazione cattolica nell'Italia fascista, *Contemporanea* 5 (2002), 253–86.

De Grazia, Victoria, Die *Radikalisierung* der Bevölkerungspolitik im faschistischen Italien: Mussolinis 'Rassenstaat', *GuG* 26 (2000), 219–54.

Del Carmen Tapia, Maria, Hinter der *Schwelle*: Ein Leben im Opus Dei. Der schockierende Bericht einer Frau, 2nd edn, Zürich 1994.

Denzler, Georg, Franz von *Papen* als abtrünniger Zentrumspolitiker und Initiator des Reichskonkordats. Vortrag am 17. 6. 2004 im DHI Rom (Ms.).

—*Widerstand* ist nicht das richtige Wort: Katholische Priester, Bischöfe und Theologen im Dritten Reich, Zürich 2003.

—*Widerstand oder Anpassung?* Katholische Kirche und Drittes Reich, Munich-Zürich 1984.

Deuerlein, Ernst (ed.), Der *Aufstieg* der NSDAP in Augenzeugenberichten, 3rd edn, Munich 1974.

—Der deutsche *Katholizismus* 1933 (Fromms Taschenbücher zeitnahes Christentum, 10), Osnabrück 1963.

—*Reichskonkordat*: Beiträge zu Vorgeschichte, Abschluss und Vollzug des Konkordates zwischen dem Heiligen Stuhl und dem Deutschen Reich vom 20. Juli 1933, Düsseldorf 1956.

Dietrich, Donald J., *Joseph Mayer* and the Missing Memo: A Catholic Justification for Euthanasia, in Remembering for the Future: Papers Presented at an International Scholars' Conference, Vol. 1, Oxford 1988, 38–49.

[I] Documenti diplomatici italiani (DDI). Ministero degli Affari Esteri, Commissione per la Pubblicazione dei Documenti Diplomatici, Serie 4: 1908–1914. Vol. 5–6 (11 dicembre 1909–29 marzo 1911), Rome 2001; Serie 8: 1935–1939. Vol. 6 (1 gennaio–30 giugno 1937), Rome 1997.

Drimmel, Heinrich, Vom *Kanzlermord* zum Anschluss: Österreich 1934–1938, 2nd edn, Vienna 1988.

Dülffer, Jost (ed.), Theobald von *Bethmann Hollweg*, Betrachtungen zum Weltkrieg, Essen 1989.

—*Weimar*, Hitler und die Marine: Reichspolitik und Flottenbau 1920–1939, Düsseldorf 1973.

Ealham, Chris, and Michael Richards (eds), The *Splintering* of Spain Cultural History and the Spanish Civil War, 1936–1939, Cambridge 2005.

Eatwell, Roger, *Reflections* on Fascism and Religion, *TMPR* 4 (2003), 145–66.

Ebneth, Rudolf, Die österreichische *Wochenschrift* 'Der Christliche Ständestaat': Deutsche Emigration in Österreich 1933–1938 (VKZG.F, 19), Mainz 1976.

Echeverria, José, Der *Kampf* gegen die katholische Kirche in Mexiko in den letzten 13 Jahren (Apologetische Tagesfragen, 21), Mönchen Gladbach 1926.

Enderle, Peter, Die ökonomischen und politischen *Grundlagen* der Römischen Protokolle aus dem Jahre 1934, Diss. phil., Vienna 1980.

Engel-Janosi, Friedrich, *Österreich* und der Vatikan 1846–1918, Vol. 2: Die Pontifikate Pius' X und Benedikts XV. 1903–1918, Graz-Vienna-Cologne 1960.

—Vom *Chaos* zur Katastrophe: Vatikanische Gespräche 1918–1938. Vornehmlich auf Grund der Berichte der österreichischen Gesandten beim Heiligen Stuhl, Vienna-Munich 1971.

—Zwischen *Kreuz und Hakenkreuz*. Die Haltung der Zeitschrift 'Schönere Zukunft' zum Nationalsozialismus in Deutschland 1934–1938 (Veröffentlichungen der Kommission für Neuere Geschichte Österreichs, 69), Vienna-Cologne-Weimar 1980.

Epstein, Klaus, Matthias *Erzberger* und das Dilemma der deutschen Demokratie (Ullstein-Buch, 3227), Frankfurt am Main-Berlin-Vienna 1976.

Erzberger, Matthias, *Erlebnisse* im Weltkrieg, Stuttgart 1920.

Erzbischöfliches Generalvikariat (ed.), *Studien* zum Mythus des XX. Jahrhunderts (Amtsblatt des Bischöflichen Ordinariats, Berlin Amtliche Beilage 1934), Cologne 1934.

Esch, Ludwig SJ, *Neudeutschland*: Sein Werden und Wachsen, Saarbrücken 1927.

Falecki, Tomasz, *Stolica Apostolska* a problem ewentualnego zbliżenia polsko-niemieckiego w 1920 r, in Zbigniew Kapaly and Wiesław Lesiuk (eds), Pamięć o Powstaniach Śląskich czy i Komu Potrzebna?, Bytom 2001, 136–54.

Falter, Jürgen W., *Hitlers Wähler*, Munich 1991.

Fattorini, Emma, *Germania* e Santa Sede: Le nunziatura di Pacelli fra la Grande guerra e la Repubblica di Weimar (Annali dell'Istituto Storico Italo-Germanico: Monografia, 18), Bologna 1992.

Feldkamp, Michael F., Die *Aufhebung* der Apostolischen Nuntiatur in München 1934. Mit einem Anhang der Amtsdaten der Nuntien, Internuntien und Geschäftsführer 1786–1934, in Reimund Haas (ed.), Im Gedächtnis der Kirche neu erwachen: Studien zur Geschichte des Christentums in Ost- und Mitteleuropa. Festgabe für Gabriel Adriányi zum 65. Geburtstag (Bonner Beiträge zur Kirchengeschichte, 22), Cologne-Weimar-Vienna 2000, 185–234.

—Die *Beziehungen* der Bundesrepublik Deutschland zum Heiligen Stuhl 1949–1966: Aus den Vatikanakten des Auswärtigen Amtes. Eine Dokumentation (Bonner Beiträge zur Kirchengeschichte, 21), Cologne-Weimar-Vienna 2000.

—*Pius XII* und Deutschland (Kleine Reihe V & R, 4026), Göttingen 2000.

Fink, Carole, The *Genoa Conference*: European Diplomacy 1921–22, Chapel Hill-London 1994.

Fischer, Hans Friedrich, Die *Wiedererrichtung* des Bistums Meissen 1921 und ihre Vorgeschichte (Studien zur katholischen Bistums- und Klostergeschichte, 34), Leipzig 1992.

Fischer, Holger, Eine kleine *Geschichte* Ungarns (Edition Suhrkamp, 2114), Frankfurt am Main 1999.

Fitzek, Alfons (ed.), *Pius XII* und Mussolini, Hitler und Stalin Seine Weltrundschreiben gegen Faschismus, Nationalsozialismus, Kommunismus, Eichstätt 1987.

Fogarty, Gerald T., *Roosevelt* and the American Catholic Hierarchy, in Woolner and Kurial (eds), *FDR*, 11–43.

Föhr, Ernst, *Geschichte* des badischen Konkordats, Freiburg/Breisgau 1958.

Foresta, Patrizio, Der 'katholische *Totalitarismus*': Katholizismus und Moderne im Pontifikat Pius' XI, in Manuel Franzmann, Christel Gärtner and Nicole Köck (eds), Religiosität in der säkularisierten Welt: Theoretische und empirische Beiträge zur Säkularisierungsdebatte in der Religionssoziologie (Veröffentlichungen der Sektion Religionssoziologie der Deutschen Gesellschaft für Soziologie, 11), Wiesbaden 2006, 177–95.

Fraenkel, Heinrich, and Roger Manvell, Hermann *Göring*, Hannover 1964.

François-Poncet, André, *Botschafter* in Berlin 1931–1938, 3rd edn, Mainz 1962.

Frank, Karl Suso, *Christkönig*, LThK 3 (1994), 1140–1.

Franz-Willing, Georg, Die *bayerische Vatikangesandtschaft* 1803–1934, Munich 1965.

Franzke, Hans-Georg, Die *Laizität* als staatskirchenrechtliches Leitprinzip Frankreichs, DÖV (2004), 383–7.

Friedländer, Saul, Nazi Germany and the *Jews*. Vol. 1: The Years of Persecution, 1933–1939, London 1997.

—*Pius XII* und das Dritte Reich: Eine Dokumentation, Reinbek b. Hamburg 1965.

Friedman, Paul Max, *Nazis and Good Neighbors*: The United States Campaign against the Germans of Latin America in World War II, Cambridge 2003.

Fröhlich, Elke (ed.), Die *Tagebücher* von Joseph Goebbels: Sämtliche Fragmente. Hg. im Auftrag des Instituts für Zeitgeschichte und in Verbindung mit dem Bundesarchiv, Teil 1: Aufzeichnungen 1924–1941, Vol. 2: 1. 1. 1931–31. 12. 1936, Munich-New York-London-Paris 1987.

Gaillard, Jone, The *Attractions* of Fascism for the Church of Rome, in John Milfull (ed.), The Attractions of Fascism: Social Psychology and Aesthetics of the 'Triumph of the Right', New York-Oxford-Munich 1990.

Gajek, Esther, *'Feiergestaltung'* – Zur planmässigen Entwicklung eines 'aus nationalsozialistischer Weltanschauung geborenen, neuen arteigenen Brauchtums' am Amt Rosenberg, in Stefanie von Schnurbein and Justus H. Ulbricht (eds), Völkische Religion und Krisen der Moderne: Entwürfe 'arteigener' Glaubenssysteme seit der Jahrhundertwende, Würzburg 2001, 386–408.

Gallagher, Charles R. SJ, A Peculiar Brand of *Patriotism*: The Holy See, FDR, and the Case of Reverend Charles E. Coughlin, in Woolner and Kurial (eds), *FDR*, 269–77.

—'Personal, Private *Views*', *America* (September 2003), 8–10.

Galletto, Bortolo, Vita di *Dollfuss*: Prefazione di S. E. Mons. Luigi Hudal, Rome 1935.

Gallo, Patrick J., For *Love and Country*: The Italian Resistance, Lanham 2003.

—*Pius XII*, the Holocaust and the Revisionists, Jefferson (NC) 2006.

Gaudig, Olaf, and Peter Veit, *Hakenkreuz* über Südamerika: Ideologie, Politik, Militär, Berlin 2004.

Gentile, Emilio, Der *Liktorenkult*, in Christof Dipper, Rainer Hudemann and Jens Petersen (eds), Faschismus und Faschismen im Vergleich: Wolfgang Schieder zum 60. Geburtstag (Italien in der Moderne, 3), Vierow bei Greifswald 1998, 247–61.

—Le *religioni* della politica: Fra democrazie e totalitarismi, Rome-Bari 2001.

—The *Sacralisation* of Politics in Fascist Italy, Cambridge 1996.

—La *via italiana* al totalitarismo: Il partito e lo Stato nel regime fascista, Rome 1995.

Gentile, Giovanni, *Grundlagen* des Faschismus (Veröffentlichungen des Petrarca-Hauses 3, 2), Stuttgart 1936.

Giacometti, Zaccaria, *Quellen* zur Geschichte der Trennung von Staat und Kirche, Tübingen 1926.

Giovannetti, Alberto, Der *Vatikan* und der Krieg, Cologne 1961.

Godman, Peter, *Hitler and the Vatican*: Inside the Secret Archives That Reveal the New Story of the Nazis and the Church, New York 2004.

Golder, Marko, and Manuel von Rahden, *Studien* zur Zeitgeschichte Portugals: Sport- und Jugendpolitik im Estado Novo (1933–1974). Militär und Parteien während der Nelkenrevolution (1974–75) (Hamburger Ibero-Amerika-Studien, 10), Hamburg 1998.

Goldhagen, Daniel Jonah, A *Moral Reckoning*: The Role of the Catholic Church in the Holocaust and Its Unfulfilled Duty of Repair, London 2002.

Goldinger, Walther/Binder, Dieter A. (Bearb.), *Geschichte* der Republik Österreich 1918–1938, Vienna 1992.

Golombek, Dieter, Die politische *Vorgeschichte* des Preußenkonkordats (1929) (VKZG.F, 4), Mainz 1970.

Göring, Emmy, An der *Seite* meines Mannes: Begebenheiten und Bekenntnisse, 4th edn, Coburg 1996.

Goyet, Bruno, Charles *Maurras* (Références/Facettes), Paris 2000.

Goytisolo, Juan, *Spanien* und die Spanier (Suhrkamp-Taschenbuch, 861), Frankfurt am Main 1992.

Graml, Hermann, Zwischen *Stresemann und Hitler*: Die Außenpolitik der Präsidialkabinette Brüning, Papen und Schleicher (Schriftenreihe der *VfZ*, 83), Munich 2001.

Grau, Bernhard, Kurt *Eisner* 1867–1919: Eine Biographie, Munich 2001.

Grau, Bernhard, and Guido Treffler, *Unter Republikanern* und Republikfreunden, in Bauer (ed.), Kardinal Michael von Faulhaber, 176–99

Grentrup, Theodor, Die kirchliche *Rechtslage* der deutschen Minderheiten katholischer Konfession in Europa: Eine Materialsammlung, Berlin 1928.

Gribble, Richard, CSC, *Guardian* of America: The Life of James Martin Gillis, New York 1998.

Gritschneder, Otto, *Bewährungsfrist* für den Terroristen Adolf H: Der Hitler-Putsch und die bayerische Justiz, Munich 1990.

Grössl, Gerhard, *Papst Pius XII* (1939–1958): 'Pastor angelicus' oder 'Hitlers Papst'? Dokumentation eines Widerstreits. Mit einer Bibliographie und einem Autorenverzeichnis, Dipl. phil. thesis, Eichstätt 2000.

Grott, Bogumił, *Polnische Parteien* und nationalistische Gruppen in ihrem Verhältnis zur katholischen Kirche und zu deren Lehre vor dem Zweiten Weltkrieg, *ZfO* 45 (1996), 72–88.

Gruber, Hubert, Friedrich *Muckermann*, S.J. 1883–1946: Ein katholischer Publizist in der Auseinandersetzung mit dem Zeitgeist (VKZG.F, 61), Mainz 1993.

Guardini, Romano, *Stationen und Rückblicke*: Berichte über mein Leben, 2nd edn, Mainz 1995.

—Vom *Sinn* der Kirche: Fünf Vorträge, Mainz 1922.

Hamers, Antonius, Zur *Konkordatspolitik* Eugenio Pacellis: Die nicht vollendeten Konkordate mit Württemberg und Hessen. Vortrag am 17. 6. 2004 im DHI Rom (Ms.).

Hanisch, Ernst, Die *Ideologie* des politischen Katholizismus in Österreich 1918–1938 (Veröffentlichungen des Instituts für Kirchliche Zeitgeschichte am Internationalen Forschungszentrum für Grundfragen der Wissenschaften Salzburg: 2. Serie, Studien, 5), Vienna-Salzburg 1977.

—Der lange *Schatten* des Staates: Österreichische Gesellschaftsgeschichte im 20. Jahrhundert, Vienna 1994.

—Der politische *Katholizismus* als ideologischer Träger des 'Austrofaschismus', in Emmerich Tálos and Wolfgang Neugebauer (eds), 'Austrofaschismus': Beiträge über Politik, Ökonomie und Kultur 1934–1938, 4th edn, Vienna 1988, 53–73.

Hankel, Gerd, Die *Leipziger Prozesse*: Deutsche Kriegsverbrechen und ihre strafrechtliche Verfolgung nach dem ersten Weltkrieg, Hamburg 2003.

Hanus, Franciscus, Die *preussische Vatikangesandtschaft* 1747–1920, Munich 1954.

Härtel, Hans-Joachim, and Roland Schönfeld, *Bulgarien*: Vom Mittelalter bis zur Gegenwart, Regensburg 1998.

Hausleithner, Rudolf, Der *Geist* der neuen Ordnung: Einblicke in das päpstliche Gesellschaftsrundschreiben 'Quadragesimo Anno', Vienna 1937.

Hecker, Hans-Joachim, *Kardinal Faulhaber* und seine Stellung im Wandel der politischen Verhältnisse, in Bauer (ed.), Kardinal Michael von Faulhaber, 19–36.

Hehl, Ulrich von, *Wilhelm Marx* 1863–1946: Eine politische Biographie (VKZG.F, 47), Mainz 1987.

Hehl, Ulrich von, and Christoph Kösters, *Priester* unter Hitlers Terror: Eine biographische und statistische Erhebung, 2 vols (VKZG.Q, 37), 3rd edn, Paderborn-Munich-Vienna-Zurich 1996.

Hein, Heidi, Der *Pitsudski-Kult* und seine Bedeutung für den polnischen Staat 1926–1939 (Materialien und Studien zur Ostmitteleuropa-Forschung 9), Marburg 2002.

Heinemann, Rebecca, *Familie* zwischen Tradition und Emanzipation: Katholische und sozialdemokratische Familienkonzeptionen in der Weimarer Republik (Schriftenreihe der Stiftung Reichspräsident-Friedrich-Ebert-Gedenkstätte, 11), Munich 2004.

Henrich, Franz, Die *Bünde* katholischer Jugendbewegung: Ihre Bedeutung für die liturgische und eucharistische Erneuerung, Munich 1968.

Hildermeier, Manfred, *Geschichte* der Sowjetunion: Entstehung und Niedergang des ersten Sozialistischen Staates, Munich 1998.

Hillmayr, Heinrich, Roter und Weißer *Terror* in Bayern nach 1918: Ursachen, Erscheinungsformen und Folgen der Gewalttätigkeiten im Verlauf der revolutionären Ereignisse nach dem Ende des Ersten Weltkrieges (Moderne Geschichte, 2), Munich 1974.

Hitler, Adolf, Mein *Kampf*, 276th edn, Munich 1937.

Hoberg, Hermann, *Papst Pius XII*: Die wesentlichen Tatsachen seines Lebens und Wirkens, Munich 1949.

Hochhuth, Rolf, Der *Stellvertreter*: Schauspiel mit einem Vorwort von Erwin Piscator (Rowohlt-Paperback, 20), Hamburg-Reinbek 1963.

Höcht, Johannes Maria, *Fatima und Pius XII*: Maria Schützerin des Abendlandes. Der Kampf um Russland und die Abwendung des dritten Weltkrieges, Wiesbaden 1959.

Hoensch, Jörg K. (ed.), *Judenemanzipation* – Antisemitismus – Verfolgung in Deutschland, Österreich-Ungarn, den böhmischen Ländern und in der Slowakei (Veröffentlichungen der Deutsch-Tschechischen und Deutsch-Slowakischen Historikerkommission, 6; Veröffentlichungen des Instituts für Kultur und Geschichte der Deutschen im östlichen Europa, 13), Essen 1999.

Hoffend, Andrea, Zwischen *Kultur-Achse* und Kulturkampf: Die Beziehungen zwischen 'Drittem Reich' und faschistischem Italien in den Bereichen Medien, Kunst, Wissenschaft und Rassenfragen (Italien in Geschichte und Gegenwart, 10), Frankfurt am Main-Berlin-Bern-Vienna 1998.

Höhle, Michael, Die *Gründung* des Bistums Berlin 1930 (VKZG.F, 73), Paderborn-Munich-Vienna-Zurich 1996.

Hömig, Herbert, *Brüning*: Kanzler in der Krise der Republik: Eine Weimarer Biographie, Paderborn-Munich-Vienna-Zurich 2000.

—Das preussische *Zentrum* in der Weimarer Republik (VKZG.F, 28), Mainz 1979.

Hopfgartner, Anton, *Kurt Schuschnigg*: Ein Mann gegen Hitler, Graz-Vienna-Cologne 1989.

Hrabovec, Emilia, Der Heilige Stuhl und die *Slowakei* 1918–1922 im Kontext internationaler Beziehungen (Wiener Osteuropa Studien 15), Frankfurt am Main 2002.

Huber, Ernst Rudolf, and Wolfgang Huber (eds), *Staat und Kirche* im 19. und 20. Jahrhundert: Dokumente des deutschen Staatskirchenrechts, Vol. 1: Staat und Kirche vom Ausgang des alten Reichs bis zum Vorabend der bürgerlichen Revolution, 2nd edn, Berlin 1990; Vol. 3: Staat und Kirche von der Beilegung des Kulturkampfes bis zum Ende des Ersten Weltkriegs, 2nd edn, 1990; Vol. 4: Staat und Kirche in der Zeit der Weimarer Republik, West Berlin 1988.

Hudal, Alois, *Deutsches Volk* und christliches Abendland, Innsbruck 1935.

— *Ecclesiae* et nationi: Katholische Gedanken in einer Zeitenwende, Rome 1934.

—Die *Grundlagen* des Nationalsozialismus: Eine ideengeschichtliche Untersuchung von katholischer Warte, Leipzig-Vienna 1937.

—Der *Katholizismus* in Österreich: Sein Wirken, Kämpfen und Hoffen, Innsbruck 1931.

—Das *Rassenproblem* (Schriftenreihe im Dienste der Katholischen Aktion, 10/11), Lobnig (CŠR) 1936.

—*Römische Tagebücher*: Lebensbeichte eines alten Bischofs, Graz 1976.

—Der *Vatikan* und die modernen Staaten, Innsbruck 1935.

—Vom deutschen *Schaffen* in Rom: Predigten, Ansprachen und Vorträge, Innsbruck-Vienna-Munich 1933.

Hürten, Heinz, *Deutsche Katholiken* 1918–1945, Paderborn-Munich-Vienna-Zurich 1992.

—Kardinal *Faulhaber* – ein Kirchenmann im Meinungsstreit, in *Beiträge zur altbayerischen Kirchengeschichte* 47 (2003), 253–67.

—Keineswegs vertagt, *Leserbrief*, in *FAZ* 93 (22 April 2003), 11.

—*Legenden* um Pacelli: Die Münchener Vatikansgesandtschaft 1918/19, in Konrad Ackermann (ed.), Bayern vom Stamm zum Staat: Festschrift für Andreas Kraus zum 80. Geburtstag (Schriftenreihe zur bayerischen Landesgeschichte, 140), Vol. 2, Munich 2002, 503–11.

Humleboek, Carsten, Die spanische *Zeitgeschichtsforschung* zur Franco-Ära seit 1975, in *Jahrbuch für Europäische Geschichte* 4 (2003), 161–88.

Huttner, Markus, *Britische Presse* und nationalsozialistischer Kirchenkampf: Eine Untersuchung der 'Times' und des 'Manchester Guardian' von 1930 bis 1939, Paderborn-Munich-Vienna-Zurich 1995.

Iserloh, Erwin, Innerkirchliche *Bewegungen* und ihre Spiritualität, in *HKG* VII, 301–37.

Jablonka, Hans, *Waitz* – Bischof unter Kaiser und Hitler, Vienna 1971.

Jaspers, Karl, Nicht schweigen! Zu Hochhuths '*Stellvertreter*', in Mitverantwortlich, Gütersloh, no date, 472.

Jeřábek, Martin, Konec Demokracie V Rakousku, 1932–1938: Politické, hospodářské a ideologické příčiny pádu demokracie, Prague 2004.

Joosten, Christoph, Das *Christkönigsfest*: Liturgie im Spannungsfeld zwischen Frömmigkeit und Politik (Pietas Liturgica, 12), Tübingen-Basel 2002.

Junker, Detlef, Die *Deutsche Zentrumspartei* und Hitler 1932/33: Ein Beitrag zur Problematik des politischen Katholizismus in Deutschland (Stuttgarter Beiträge zur Geschichte und Politik, 4), Stuttgart 1969.

Jürgs, Michael, Der kleine *Frieden* im Großen Krieg: Westfront 1914: Als Deutsche, Franzosen und Briten gemeinsam Weihnachten feierten, Munich 2003.

Jurkiewicz, Jarosław, *Nuncjatura* Achillesa Ratti w Polsce, Warsaw 1955.

Jussen, Wilhelm (ed.), *Gerechtigkeit* schafft Frieden: Reden und Enzykliken des Heiligen Vaters Papst Pius XII., Hamburg 1946.

Kaas, Ludwig, Der *Konkordatstyp* des faschistischen Italien, in Zeitschrift für ausländisches öffentliches Recht und Völkerrecht 3 (1933), Teil 1, 488–522.

Kageneck, Hans Graf von, Wo blieb *Hindenburgs Testament?*, *FAZ* 146 (26 June 2004), 39.

Kappeler, Manfred, *Rassismus*: Über die Genese einer europäischen Bewusstseinsform, Frankfurt am Main 1994.

Karlov, Ju. E., Sovetskaja vlast' i *Vatikan* v 1917–1922 gg., in E. S. Tokareva and A. V. Judina (eds), Rossija i Vatikan v konce XIX–pervoj treti XX veka, Moskva 2002, 158–84.

Keipert, Maria, and Peter Grupp (eds), *Biographisches Handbuch* des deutschen Auswärtigen Dienstes 1871–1945, Vol. 1, Paderborn-Munich-Vienna-Zurich 2000.

Keller, Katrin, *Landesgeschichte* Sachsen (UTB, 2291), Stuttgart 2002.

Kent, Peter C., The Lonely *Cold War* of Pius XII: The Roman Catholic Church and the Division of Europe 1943–1950, Montreal-London-Ithaka 2002.

—The *Pope* and the Duce: The International Impact of the Lateran Agreements, New York 1981.

—A *Tale* of Two Popes: Pius XI, Pius XII and the Rome–Berlin Axis, *JCH* 23 (1988), 589–608.

Kertzer, David I., The *Popes* against the Jews: The Vatican's Role in the Rise of Modern Anti-semitism, New York 2001.

Kindermann, Gottfried-Karl, *Österreich* gegen Hitler. Europas erste Abwehrfront 1933–1938, Munich 2003.

Kleindel, Walter, 'Gott schütze Österreich!' Der *Anschluss* 1938, Vienna 1988.

Klemperer, Klemens, *Ignaz Seipel*: Staatsmann einer Krisenzeit, Graz-Vienna-Cologne 1976.

Klinkhammer, Lutz, *Mussolinis Italien* zwischen Staat, Kirche und Religion, in Klaus Hildebrand (ed.), Zwischen Politik und Religion: Studien zur Entstehung, Existenz und Wirkung des Totalitarismus, Munich 2003, 73–90.

—Pius XII., Rom und der Holocaust, in DHI Rom (ed.), Quellen und Forschungen: Aus Italienischen Archiven und Bibliotheken, Vol. 80, 2000, 668–78.

Kluge, Ulrich, Der Österreichische *Ständestaat* 1934–1938. Entstehung und Scheitern, Munich 1984.

Knauft, Wolfgang, Konrad von *Preysing* – Anwalt des Rechts: Der erste Berliner Kardinal und seine Zeit, Berlin 1998.

Kneifel, Eduard, *Geschichte* der Evangelisch-Augsburgischen Kirche in Polen, Niedermarschacht 1962.

Kochanowski, Jerzy, *Horthy und Piłsudski* – Vergleich der autoritären Regime in Ungarn und Polen, in Erwin Oberländer (ed.), Autoritäre Regime in Ostmittel- und Südosteuropa 1919–1944, Paderborn 2001, 19–94.

Köck, Heribert Franz, *Pius XII* und das Apostolat der Laien, in Schambeck (ed.), Pius XII, 427–33.

Kohler, Helga, Die *Konferenz von Evian* (6.–15. 7. 1938): Erfolgsaussichten und Ergebnisse einer internatonalen Konferenz zur Lösung des jüdischen Flüchtlingsproblems im Deutschen Reich nach dem Anschluss Österreichs im März 1938, Magisterarbeit Stuttgart 1991.

Köhler, Joachim, Adolf Kardinal *Bertram* (1859–1945), in Hans-Jürgen Karp and Joachim Köhler (eds), Katholische Kirche unter nationalsozialistischer und kommunistischer Diktatur: Deutschland und Polen 1939–1989 (Forschungen und Quellen zur Kirchen- und Kulturgeschichte Ostdeutschlands, 32), Cologne-Weimar-Vienna 2001, 175–93.

Kohler, Lotte, and Hans Saner (eds), *Hannah Arendt/Karl Jaspers. Correspondence 1926–1969*, New York-San Diego-London 2006.

Koryna, Andrzej, *Wojna* polsko-sowiecka 1920 roku: Przebieg i tło międzynarodowe, Warsaw 1993.

Kotowski, Albert S., *Hitlers Bewegung* im Urteil der polnischen Nationaldemokratie (Studien der Forschungsstelle Ostmitteleuropa an der Universität Dortmund, 28), Wiesbaden 2000.

—*Polnischer Staat*, katholische Kirche und die deutschen Katholiken 1918–1939, *KZG* 15 (2002), 128–49.

Kovács, Elisabeth, *Österreich-Ungarn* aus der Sicht des Vatikans: Die Instruktion für den Apostolischen Nuntius in Wien, Teodoro Valfré di Bonzo, vom Sommer 1916, *AHP* 33 (1995), 275–98.

—*Papst Benedikt XV* und die Friedensbemühungen des Kaisers und Königs Karl von Österreich, *AHP* 27 (1989), 357–99.

Kowalec, Krzysztof, Roman *Dmowski*, Warsaw 1996.

Kremsmair, Josef, Der Weg zum österreichischen *Konkordat* von 1933/34 (Dissertationen der Universität Salzburg, 12), Vienna 1980.

Kretschmann, Carsten, Die *Scholder-Repgen-Debatte*, Vortrag am 17. 6. 2004 im DHI Rom (MS).

Kreutzer, Heike, Das *Reichskirchenministerium* im Gefüge der nationalsozialistischen Herrschaft (Schriften des Bundesarchivs, 56), Düsseldorf 2000.

Krieg, Robert A., Catholic Theologians in Nazi Germany, New York-London 2004.

Kube, Alfred, *Pour le mérite und Hakenkreuz*: Hermann Göring im Dritten Reich (Quellen und Darstellungen zur Zeitgeschichte, 24), 2nd edn, Munich 1987.

Kuhn, Thomas K., Das neuzeitliche *Christentum* und die Genese des Nationalismus als 'Politischer Religion', in George Pfleiderer and Ekkehard W. Stegemann (eds), Politische Religion: Geschichte und Gegenwart eines Problemfeldes (Christentum und Kultur, 3), Zurich 2004, 131–57.

Kupper, Alfons (ed.), *Staatliche Akten* über die Reichskonkordatsverhandlungen 1933 (VKZG.Q, 2), Mainz 1969.

Lama, Friedrich von, *Papst und Kurie* in ihrer Politik nach dem Weltkrieg dargestellt unter Berücksichtigung der Verhältnisse zwischen dem Vatikan und Deutschland, Illertissen 1925.

Landra, Guido, *Manifesto* della razza, Il Giornale d'Italia (14 July 1938).

[Die] *Lateranverträge* zwischen dem Heiligen Stuhl und Italien vom 11. Februar 1929. Italienischer und deutscher Text. Mit einem Geleitwort von Eugenio Pacelli, Apostolischem Nuntius in Berlin, Freiburg/Breisgau 1929.

Lawler, Justus George, *Popes* and Politics: Reform, Resentment, and the Holocaust, New York-London 2002.

Ledit, Giuseppe [= Joseph] SJ, *Paradossi* del comunismo, Milan 1938.

—La *religione* e il comunismo, Milan 1937.

Lehnert, Pascalina M., Ich durfte ihm dienen: *Erinnerungen* an Papst Pius XII., 10th edn, Würzburg 1996.

Leiber, Robert, *Friedenstätigkeit* Benedikts XV, *SdZ* 100, 4 (1921), 267–80.

Levillain, Philippe (ed.), *Dictionnaire* historique de la Papauté, Paris 1994.

Lewy, Guenter, Die *Katholische Kirche* und das Dritte Reich, Munich 1965.

Liebmann, Maximilian, Theodor *Innitzer* und der Anschluss: Kirche und Nationalsozialismus in Österreich (Grazer Beiträge zur Theologie-Geschichte und kirchlichen Zeitgeschichte, 1), Graz 1982.

—*Theodor Innitzer* und der Anschluss: Österreichs Kirche 1938 (Grazer Beiträge zur Theologie-Geschichte und kirchlichen Zeit-Geschichte, 3), Graz-Vienna-Cologne 1988.

Lill, Rudolf, Die *katholische Kirche* im faschistischen Italien, in Leonid Luks (ed.), Das Christentum und die totalitären Herausforderungen im 20. Jahrhundert. Russland, Deutschland, Italien und Polen im Vergleich (Schriften des Zentralinstituts für Mittel- und Osteuropastudien, 5), Cologne-Weimar-Vienna 2002, 205–16.

—Il *Papato* e la sua recezione nella Germania contemporanea, in Gabriele De Rosa and Giorgio Cracco (eds), Il Papato e l'Europa, Soveria Manelli 2001, 381–91.

—*Südtirol* in der Zeit des Nationalsozialismus, Konstanz 2002.

Linz, Juan José, An Authoritarian *Regime*: Spain, in Erik Allard and Stein Rokkan (eds), Mass Politics. Studies in Political Sociology, New York 1970, 251–83.

—From *Great Hopes* to Civil War: The Breakdown of Democracy in Spain, in Linz and Stepan (eds), The Breakdown of Democratic Regimes, 142–215.

Linz, Juan José, and Alfred Stepan (eds), The *Breakdown* of Democratic Regimes, Baltimore 1978.

Lipiński, Wacław, Josef *Piłsudski*: Erinnerungen und Dokumente. Von Josef Piłsudski, dem Ersten Marschall von Polen persönlich autorisierte deutsche Gesamtausgabe, 2 vols, Essen 1935.

Listl, Joseph, Die *konkordatäre Entwicklung* von 1871 bis 1988, St. Ottilien 1991.

Livre blanc du S. Siège, la séperation de l'Église et de l'État en France, exposé et documents, Paris 1906.

Lönne, Karl-Egon, *Historiographischer Rückblick*, in Ernst-Wolfgang Böckenförde (ed.), Der deutsche Katholizismus im Jahre 1933: Kirche und demokratisches Ethos (Schriften zu Staat, Gesellschaft, Kirche, 1), Freiburg-Basel-Vienna 1988, 121–50.

Lübken, Uwe, *Bedrohliche Nähe*: Die USA und die nationalsozialistische Herausforderung in Lateinamerika 1937–1945 (Transatlantische historische Studien, 8), Stuttgart 2004.

Ludendorff, Mathilde (ed.), *General und Kardinal*: Ludendorff über die Politik des neuen Papstes Pius XII. (Pacelli) 1917–1937, Munich 1939.

Lutz, Heinrich, *Katholizismus und Faschismus*: Beobachtungen und Reflexionen, *Beiträge zur historischen Sozialkunde* 2 (1972), 21–5.

Lutz, Heinrich, and Carl Amery, *Katholizismus und Faschismus*: Analysen einer Nachbarschaft. Heinrich Lutz antwortet Carl Amery (Das Theologische Interview, 16), Düsseldorf 1970.

McGreevy, John T., *Catholicism* and American Freedom: A History, New York 2003.

Maderthaner, Wolfgang, *12. Februar 1934*: Sozialdemokratie und Bürgerkrieg, in Steininger and Gehler (eds), Österreich im 20. Jahrhundert, Vol. 1, 153–202.

—*Legitimationsmuster* des Austrofaschismus, in Maderthaner and Maier (eds), 'Der Führer bin ich selbst', 131–57.

Maderthaner, Wolfgang, and Michaela Maier (eds), 'Der *Führer* bin ich selbst': Engelbert Dollfuss – Benito Mussolini, Briefwechsel, Vienna 2004.

Mai, Gunther, *Europa* 1918–1939: Mentalitäten, Lebensweisen, Politik zwischen den Weltkriegen, Stuttgart-Berlin-Cologne 2001.

Maier, Hans, Das *Doppelgesicht* des Religiösen: Religion – Gewalt – Politik, Freiburg/Breisgau-Basel-Vienna 2004.

—*Kirche und Demokratie*, in Hans Maier, Schriften zur Kirche und Gesellschaft, Vol. 1: Katholizismus und Demokratie, Freiburg/Breisgau-Basel-Vienna 1983, 11–31.

—*Politische Religionen*: Die totalitären Regime und das Christentum, Freiburg/Breisgau-Basel-Vienna 1995.

—*Revolution und Kirche*: Zur Frühgeschichte der christlichen Demokratie (1789–1901), 5th edn, Freiburg/Breisgau-Basel-Vienna 1988.

Maier, Hans (ed.), *Totalitarismus* und 'Politische Religionen': Konzepte des Diktaturvergleichs (Politik- und Kommunikationswissenschaftliche Veröffentlichungen der Görres-Gesellschaft, 16; 17; 21), 3 vols, Paderborn-Munich-Vienna-Zurich 1996–2003.

Malgieri, Francesco, and Enzo Collotti, *Chiesa* cattolica e regime fascista, in Andelo del Boca (ed.), Il regime fascista: Storia e storiografia, Rome-Bari 1995, 166–81.

Mangoni, Luisa, I *Patti* lateranensi e la cultura cattolica, in *StSt* 43 (2002), 153–65.

Mann, Michael, *Fascists*, Cambridge 2004.

Mannes, Astrid Luise, *Brüning*: Leben – Wirken – Schicksal. Mit einem Vorwort von Bundesminister a. D. Dr. Gerhard Stoltenberg, Munich 1999.

Marchione, Margherita, *Consensus and Controversy*: Defending Pope Pius XII, New York 2002.

Marschall, Werner, *Geschichte* des Bistums Breslau, Stuttgart 1980.

Marschall, Werner (ed.), Adolf Kardinal Bertram: *Hirtenbriefe* und Hirtenworte (Forschungen und Quellen zur Kirchen- und Kulturgeschichte Ostdeutschlands, 30), Cologne-Weimar-Vienna 2000.

Martens, Stefan, *Hermann Göring*: 'Erster Paladin des Führers' und 'Zweiter Mann im Reich' (Sammlung Schöningh zur Geschichte und Gegenwart), Paderborn 1985.

Maser, Werner, *Hermann Göring*: Hitlers janusköpfiger Paladin. Die politische Biographie, Berlin 2000.

Mattioli, Aram, Entgrenzte *Kriegsgewalt*: Der italienische Giftgaseinsatz in Abessinien 1935–1936, in *VfZ* 51 (2003), 311–37.

—Eine veritable *Hölle*, in *Die Zeit* 51 (13 December 2001).

May, Georg, Die *Konkordatspolitik* des Heiligen Stuhls von 1918–1974, in *HKG* VII, 179–229.

—*Ludwig Kaas*: Der Priester, der Politiker und der Gelehrte aus der Schule von Ulrich Stutz, 3 vols, Amsterdam 1981–82.

Mayer, Joseph, Gesetzliche *Unfruchtbarmachung* Geisteskranker (Studien zur katholischen Sozial- und Wirtschaftsethik, 3), Freiburg/Breisgau 1927.

Mecklin, John M., *Freedom of Speech* for Clergymen, in *Annals of the American Academy of Political and Social Science* 200 (1938), 165–84.

Meier-Benneckenstein, Paul, *Dokumente* der deutschen Politik, Vol. 1: Die Nationalsozialistische Revolution 1933, 2nd edn, Berlin 1937.

Melloni, Alberto, Das *Konklave*: Die Papstwahl in Geschichte und Gegenwart, Freiburg/Breisgau 2002.

Mendelsohn, John (ed.), The *Holocaust*: Selected Documents in Eighteen Volumes. Vol. V: Jewish Emigration from 1933 to the Evian Conference of 1938 (Garland Series), New York 1982.

Menozzi, Daniele, *Regalità* sociale di Cristo e secolarizzazione: Alle origini della 'Quas Primas', in *CRST* 16 (1995), 79–113.

Mentschl, Christoph, Zur *Tätigkeit* des deutschen Gesandten und späteren Botschafters 'in besonderer Mission' Franz von Papen in Wien, Dipl. phil. thesis, Vienna 1991.

Meyer, Jean M., La *christiade*: L'Église, l'état et le peuple dans la révolution mexicaine 1926–1929, Paris 1975.

Meysels, Lucian O., Der *Austrofaschismus*: Das Ende der Ersten Republik und ihr letzter Kanzler, Vienna 1992.

Meysztowicz, Walerian, La *nunziatura* di Achille Ratti in Polonia, in Ufficio studi arcivescovile di Milano (ed.), Pio XI nel trentesimo della morte (1939–1969): Raccolta di studi e memorie, Milan 1969, 177–201.

Miccoli, Giovanni, *Chiesa e società* in Italia dal Concilio Vaticano I (1870) al pontificio di Giovanni XIII, in Romano Ruggiero and Corrado Vivanti (eds), Storia d'Italia, Vol. 5, 2: I documenti, Torino 1973, 1494–1548.

—I *dilemmi* e i silenzi di Pio XII: Vaticano, Seconda guerra mondiale e Shoah, Milan 2000.

—Das katholische *Italien* und der Faschismus, in Quellen und Forschungen aus italienischen Archiven und Bibliotheken 78 (1998), 539–66.

Micewski, Andrzej, Roman *Dmowski*, Warsaw 1971.

Michaelis, Meir, *Mussolini's Unofficial Mouthpiece*: Telesio Interlandi – Il Tevere and the Evolution of Mussolini's Anti-Semitism, in *JMIS* 3 (1998), 217–40.

Michalka, Wolfgang, Matthias *Erzberger*: 'Reichsminister in Deutschlands schwerster Zeit'. Essays zur Ausstellung, Potsdam 2002.

Michel, Ernst, *Politik* aus dem Glauben, Jena 1926.

Michels, Helmut, *Ideologie* und Propaganda: Die Rolle von Joseph Goebbels in der nationalsozialistischen Aussenpolitik bis 1939 (Europäische Hochschulschriften: Reihe 3, Geschichte und ihre Hilfswissenschaften, 527), Frankfurt am Main-Bern-New York-Paris 1992.

Micklem, Nathaniel, *National Socialism* and the Roman Catholic Church: Being an account of the conflict between the National Socialist Government of Germany and the Roman Catholic Church 1933–1938, London 1939.

Milkowski, Tadeusz Kosciol hiszpanski i Watykan w czasie wojny domowej (Die spanische Kirche und Vatikan während des Bürgerkrieges), in Polski Instytut Spraw Miedzynarodowych (ed.), Polski Przeglad Dyplomatyczny (Polnisches Diplomatisches Review), Vol. 4, 4 (20), July–August 2004, 107–52.

Minnerath, Roland, *L'Église* et les États concordataires (1864–1981): La souveraineté spirituelle, Paris 1983.

Missiroli, Mario, *Date* a Cesare: La politica religiosa di Mussolini con documenti inediti, Rome 1923.

Moa, Pío, Los mitos de la *Guerra Civil* (La esfera: historia), 23rd edn, Madrid 2003.

Möller, Horst, Die *Weimarer Republik*: Eine unvollendete Demokratie, 7th ed, Munich 2004.

Molony, John N., The *Emergence* of Political Catholicism in Italy. Partito Popolare 1919–1926, London/Totowa 1977.

Mommsen, Wolfgang J., *Bürgerstolz* und Weltmachtstreben: Deutschland unter Wilhelm II. 1890–1918, Berlin 1995.

Morsey, Rudolf, *Brünings politische Weltanschauung* vor 1918, in Gerhard A. Ritter (ed.), Gesellschaft, Parlament und Regierung: Zur Geschichte des Parlamentarismus in Deutschland (Veröffentlichung der Kommission für Geschichte des Parlamentarismus und der politischen Parteien), Düsseldorf 1974, 317–35.

—Die *Deutsche Zentrumspartei* 1917–1933 (Beiträge zur Geschichte des Parlamentarismus und der politischen Parteien, 32), Düsseldorf 1966.

—Das *Ende* der Zentrumspartei 1933: Forschungsstand und persönliche Erinnerungen an die Zusammenarbeit mit Zeitzeugen, Vortrag am 17. 6. 2004 im DHI Rom (MS).

—Eugenio *Pacelli* als Nuntius in Deutschland, in Schambeck (ed.), Pius XII., 103–39.

—*Machtkampf* um eine Bibliothek in Münster 1939–1942: Himmlers und Rosenbergs Interesse an den beschlagnahmten Instituten von Georg Schreiber, in *KZG* 18 (2005), 68–120.

—Matthias *Erzberger* (1875–1921), Bonn 1973.

—[Teilnahme an] *Diskussion*, in Ulrich von Hehl (ed.), Adenauer und die Kirchen (Veröffentlichungen der Stiftung Bundeskanzler-Adenauer-Haus; Rhöndorfer Gespräche, 17), Bonn 1999, passim.

—Zur *Entstehung*, Authentizität und Kritik von Brünings 'Memoiren' 1918–1934 (Rheinisch-Westfälische Akademie der Wissenschaften, Geisteswissenschaften, Vorträge, Geisteswissenschaften, 202), Opladen 1975.

—Zur *Vorgeschichte* des Reichskonkordats aus den Jahren 1920 und 1921, *ZRG KA* 44 (1958) 237–67.

Morsey, Rudolf (ed.), Das *'Ermächtigungsgesetz'* vom 24. März 1933: Quellen zur Geschichte und Interpretation des 'Gesetzes zur Behebung der Not von Volk und Reich' (Kommission für Geschichte des Parlamentarismus und der politischen Parteien: Dokumente und Texte, 1), Düsseldorf 1992.

—Ludwig *Kaas* †. Tagebuch 7.–20. April 1933. Aus dem Nachlaß von Prälat Ludwig Kaas, in *SdZ* 166 (1960), 422–30.

—Die *Protokolle* der Reichstagsfraktion 1926–1933 und des Fraktionsvorstandes der Deutschen Zentrumspartei 1926–1933 (VKZG,Q., 9), Mainz 1969.

Moseley, Ray, *Mussolini's Shadow*: The Double Life of Count Galeazzo Ciano, New Haven-London 1999.

Mosse, Georg L., Die *Geschichte* des Rassismus in Europa: Aus dem Amerikanischen von Elfriede Burau und Hans Günter Holl, Frankfurt am Main 1990.

Mróz, Maciej, *Watykan y Ukraina* w okresie kształtowania się systemu wersalskiego w latach 1918–1921, *Dzieje Najnowsze* 36 (2004), Heft 1, 3–19.

Müller, Frank, Die *'Brüning-Papers'*: Der letzte Zentrumskanzler im Spiegel der Selbstzeugnisse (Europäische Hochschulschriften: Reihe 3, Geschichte und ihre Hilfswissenschaften, 557), Frankfurt am Main-Bern-New York-Paris 1993.

—Ein *'Rechtskatholik'* zwischen Kreuz und Hakenkreuz: Franz von Papen als Sonderbevollmächtigter Hitlers in Wien 1934–1938 (Europäische Hochschulschriften: Reihe 3, Geschichte und ihre Hilfswissenschaften, 446), Frankfurt am Main-Bern-New York-Paris 1990.

Müller, Hans (ed.), *Katholische Kirche und Nationalsozialismus*, Munich 1965.

Muggeridge, Malcolm (ed.), *Ciano's Diary* 1939–1943, London 1950.

—*Ciano's Diplomatic Papers*: Being a Record of Nearly 200 Conversations Held during the Years 1936–42 with Hitler, Mussolini, Franco, Goering, Ribbentrop; Chamberlain, Eden, Sumner, Welles, Schuschnigg, Lord Perth, François-Poncet; and Many Other World Diplomatic and Political Figures. Together with Important Memoranda, Letters, Telegrams, etc., London 1948.

Mumford, Lewis, The *Call* to Arms, *New Republic* (8 May 1938), 39–42.

Mussolini, Benito, *Scritti e discorsi*: dal gennaio 1934 al novembre 1935: XII–XIV E.F., Milan 1935.

Myszor, Jerzy, Die polnisch-deutschen *Beziehungen* in Polnisch-Schlesien im Zeitraum 1918–1926 aus der Sicht der Kirche, in *KZG* 18 (2005), 28–39.

Myszor, Jerzy, and Jan Konieczny (eds), *Korespondencja* Augusta Hlonda i Józefa Gawliny w latach 1924–1948 (Studia i Materiały Wydziału Teologicznego Uniwersytetu Śląskiego w Katowicach, 14), Katowice 2003.

Nagy, Zsuzsa L., Über die *Geschichte* der ungarischen Kommune, in József Farkas (ed.), Räterepublik und Kultur: Ungarn 1919, Budapest 1979, 7–17.

Napolitano, Matteo Luigi, *Pio XII* tra guerra e pace: Profezia e diplomazia di un papa (1939–1945) (i volti della storia, 12), Rome 2002.

Napolitano, Matteo Luigi, and Andrea Tornielli, Il *Papa* che salvò gli ebrei: Dagli archivi segreti del Vaticano tutta la verità su Pio XII, Casale Monferrato 2004.

Němeček, Jan (ed.), Mnichovská dohoda: cesta k destrukci demokracie v Evrope (Munich Agreement: The Way to Destruction of Democracy in Europe), Prague 2004.

Neuman, Hendricus Johannes, Arthur *Seyss-Inquart*, Graz-Vienna-Cologne 1974.

Neyer, Maria Amata, Der *Brief* Edith Steins an Pius XI., in *Edith-Stein-Jahrbuch* 10 (2004), 11–29.

Niebuhr, Reinhold, The *Catholic Heresy*, in *ChC* 54 (8 December 1937).

Nix, Claire, *Leserbrief*, *FAZ* 66 (18 March 2000), 11.

Noël, Léon, Les illusions de *Stresa*: L'Italie abandonnée à Hitler, Paris 1975.

Nolte, Ernst, Der *Faschismus* in seiner Epoche: Die Action française. Der italienische Faschismus. Der Nationalsozialismus, 5th edn, Munich-Zurich 1979.

North American Committee to Aid Spanish Democracy, *American Democracy vs. the Spanish Hierarchy*, New York 1937.

Nosov, Sergej N. (ed.), Papstvo i ego bor'ba s Pravoslaviem, Moscow 1993.

Nützenadel, Alexander, *Faschismus* als Revolution? Politische Sprache und revolutionärer Stil im Italien Mussolinis, in Christof Dipper (ed.), Europäische Sozialgeschichte: Festschrift für Wolfgang Schieder (Historische Forschungen, 68), Berlin 2000, 21–40.

Omodeo, Adolfo, *Totalitarismo cattolico* (1945), in Omodeo, Libertà e storia: Scritti e discorsi politici, Turin 1960, 332–8.

Opello, Walter, Portugal's Political *Development*: A Comparative Approach (Westview Special Studies in West European Politics and Society), Boulder 1985.

Opera Omnia di Benito Mussolini, a cura di Edoardo e Duilio Susmel, Vol. 26: Dal Patto a quatro all'inaugurazione della provincia di Littoria: (8 giugno 1933–18 dic. 1934), Florence 1958; Vol. 28: Dalla proclamazione dell'imperio al viaggio in Germania: (10 magg. 1936–30 sett. 1937), Florence 1959.

Otruba, Gustav, *Auswahldokumente* zur Geschichte der 'Tausend-Mark-Sperre' von 1934 bis zum Juliabkommen 1936, in Jahrbuch für Zeitgeschichte 1979, Vienna 1980, 237–57.

Pacelli, Eugenio (Pius XII. Papa), *Discorsi* e panegirici: Con l'aggiunta di nuovi discorsi e panegirici (1931–1938), 2nd edn, Vatican City 1956.

—La *personalità* delle leggi: Specialmente nel Diritto Canonico, Rome 1912.

Pacelli, Francesco, *Diario* della Conciliazione: Con verbali e appendice di documenti, Rome 1959.

Padellaro, Nazareno, *Pius XII*, Bonn 1952.

Papen, Franz von, Der *Wahrheit* eine Gasse, Munich 1952.

Parsons, Talcott, '*Academic Freedom*', in Uta Gerhard (ed.), Talcott Parsons on National Socialism, New York 1993, 98.

Passelecq, Georges, and Bernard Suchecky, Die unterschlagene *Enzyklika*: Der Vatikan und die Judenverfolgung, Berlin 1999.

Passos, Marceliño, Der *Niedergang* des Faschismus in Portugal: Zum Verhältnis von Ökonomie, Gesellschaft und Staat/Politik in einem europäischen Schwellenland (Schriftenreihe der Studiengesellschaft für Sozialgeschichte und Arbeiterbewegung, 65), Marburg 1987.

Pastor, Ludwig von, *Tagebücher* – Briefe – Erinnerungen. Hg. von Wilhelm Wühr, Heidelberg 1950.

Patch, William L., Heinrich *Brüning* and the Dissolution of the Weimar Republic, Cambridge 1998.

—*Leserbrief, FAZ* 58 (9 March 2000), 14.

Payne, Stanley G., *Falange*: A History of Spanish Fascism (Stanford Studies in History, Economics and Political Science, 22), Stanford 1961.

—A *History of Fascism* 1914–1945, London 1997.

Petersen, Jens, *Hitler- Mussolini*: Die Entstehung der Achse Berlin-Rom 1933–1936 (Bibliothek des DHI in Rom, 43), Tübingen 1973.

—*Vorspiel* zu Stahlpakt und Kriegsallianz: Das deutsch-italienische Kulturabkommen vom 23. November 1938, in Karl Dietrich Bracher and Leo Valiani (eds), Faschismus und Nationalsozialismus, Berlin 1991, 243–82.

Petzold, Joachim, Franz von *Papen*: Ein deutsches Verhängnis, Munich-Berlin 1995.

Pfister, Peter, Im *Spannungsfeld* von Orts- und Weltkirche: Freising, Fulda, Rom, in Richard Bauer (ed.), Kardinal Michael von Faulhaber, 200–20.

Pfister, Peter (ed.), Michael Kardinal von *Faulhaber* (1869–1952): Beiträge zum 50. Todestag und zur Öffnung des Kardinal-Faulhaber-Archivs (Schriften des Archivs des Erzbistums München und Freising, 5), Regensburg 2002.

Phayer, Michael, The *Catholic Church* and the Holocaust 1930–1965, Bloomington 2000.

—*Pius XII and the Genocide* of Polish Catholics and Polish Jews during the Second World War, in *KZG* 15 (2002), 238–62.

—*Pope Pius XII*, the Holocaust, and the Cold War, *Holocaust and Genocide Studies* 12 (1998), 233–56.

Pinto, António Costa (ed.), Modern *Portugal*, Palo Alto 1998.

—*Salazar's Dictatorship* and European Fasicm: Problems of Interpretation (Social Science Monographs), New York 1995.

[Pius XII.], Der *Papst* an die Deutschen: Pius XII. als Apostolischer Nuntius und Papst in seinen deutschsprachigen Reden und Sendschreiben von 1917 bis 1956, nach den vatikanischen Archiven hg. von Bruno Wüstenberg, Frankfurt 1956.

Plöckinger, Othmar, *Geschichte* eines Buches: Adolf Hitlers 'Mein Kampf' 1922–1945 (Eine Veröffentlichung des Instituts für Zeitgeschichte), Munich 2006, 297ff.

Pollard, John Francis, The *Vatican* and Italian Fascism 1929–32: A Study in Conflict, Cambridge 1985.

Pollmann, Viktoria, *Untermieter* im christlichen Haus: Die Kirche und die 'jüdische Frage' in Polen anhand der Bistumspresse der Metropole Krakau 1926–1939 (Jüdische Kultur, 9), Wiesbaden 2001.

Pouthier, Jean-Luc, *Émigrés* Catholiques et Antifascisme: Luigi Sturzo et l'internationale blanche, in Perre Milza (ed.), Les Italiens en France de 1914 à 1940, Paris-Rome 1986, 481–97.

Preston, Paul, *Franco*: 'Caudillo de España', 2nd edn, Barcelona 1994.

Prévotat, Jacques, Les *catholiques* et l'Action française: Histoire d'une condamnation 1899–1939, Paris 2001.

Raabe, Felix, Die *Bündische Jugend*: Ein Beitrag zur Geschichte der Weimarer Republik, Stuttgart 1961.

Raem, Heinz-Albert, *Pius XI* und der Nationalsozialismus: Die Enzyklika 'Mit brennender Sorge' vom 14. März 1937 (Beiträge zur Katholizismusforschung: Reihe B, Abhandlungen), Paderborn-Munich-Vienna-Zurich 1979.

Rall, Hans, *Wilhelm II*: Eine Biographie, Graz-Vienna-Cologne 1995.

Rauscher, Anton (ed.), Wider den *Rassismus*: Entwurf einer nicht erschienenen Enzyklika (1938). Texte aus dem Nachlass von Gustav Gundlach SJ, 2nd edn, Paderborn-Munich-Vienna-Zurich 2001.

Rauscher, Walter, *Hitler und Mussolini*: Macht, Krieg und Terror, Graz-Vienna-Cologne 2001.

Recker, Klemens-August, 'Wem wollt ihr glauben?' – Bischof *Berning* im Dritten Reich, 2nd edn, Paderborn-Munich-Vienna-Zurich 1998.

[Die] *Reden* gehalten in den öffentlichen und geschlossenen Versammlungen der 62. Generalversammlung der Katholiken Deutschlands zu München 27. bis 30. August 1922, Würzburg 1923.

Reichhold, Anselm OSB, Die deutsche katholische *Kirche* zur Zeit des Nationalsozialismus (1933–1945) unter besonderer Berücksichtigung der Hirtenbriefe, Denkschriften, Predigten und sonstigen Kundgebungen der deutschen katholischen Bischöfe, St Ottilien 1992.

Reichsgesetzblatt (*RGBl.*). Teil I. Hg. im Reichsministerium des Innern, Berlin 1933.

Rein, Hans, Franz von *Papen* im Zwielicht der Geschichte: Sein letzter Prozess, Baden-Baden 1979.

Reinhardt, Volker, *Geschichte* Italiens: Von der Spätantike bis zur Gegenwart (Beck's historische Bibliothek), Munich 2003.

Reinhold, Hans Ansgar (H. A. R.), The *Autobiography* of Father Reinhold, New York 1968.

Rennhofer, Friedrich, *Ignaz Seipel*, Mensch und Staatsmann: Eine biographische Dokumentation (Böhlaus zeitgeschichtl. Bibliothek, 2), Vienna-Cologne-Graz 1978.

Repgen, Konrad, Hitlers '*Machtergreifung*', die christlichen Kirchen, die Judenfrage und Edith Steins Eingabe an Pius XI. vom [9.] April 1933, in Edith-Stein-Jahrbuch 10 (2004), 31–69.

—*Nachwort* zu einer Kontroverse, VfZ 27 (1979), 159–61.

—*Pius XI und das faschistische Italien*: Die Lateranverträge von 1929 und ihre Folgen, in Werner Pöls (ed.), Staat und Gesellschaft im politischen Wandel: Beiträge zur Geschichte der Moderne, Stuttgart 1979, 331–59.

—*Pius XI* zwischen Stalin, Mussolini und Hitler: Zur Vatikanischen Konkordatspolitik der Zwischenkriegszeit, APuZ 39 (1979), 3–23.

—*Reichskonkordats-Kontroversen* und historische Logik, in Manfred Funke, Hans-Adolf Jacobsen, Hans-Helmuth Knütter and Hans-Peter Schwarz (eds), Demokratie und Diktatur: Geist und Gestalt politischer Herrschaft in Deutschland und Europa. Festschrift für Karl Dietrich Bracher, Düsseldorf 1987, 158–76.

—Über die *Entstehung* der Reichskonkordats-Offerte im Frühjahr 1933 und die Bedeutung des Reichskonkordats, VfZ 26 (1978), 499–543.

—*Ungedruckte Nachkriegsquellen* zum Reichskonkordat: Eine Dokumentation, *HJ* 99 (1979), 375–413.

—Zur vatikanischen *Strategie* beim Reichskonkordat, *VfZ* 31 (1983), 506–35.

Les résolutions et les rapports adoptés à Evian, in: *Correspondence Juive* (22 July 1938), 2.

Rhodes, Anthony, Der *Papst* und die Diktatoren: Der Vatikan zwischen Revolution und Faschismus (Böhlaus zeitgeschichtliche Bibliothek, 3), Vienna 1980.

Rial, James H., *Revolution* from Above: The Primo de Rivera Dictatorship in Spain, 1923–1930, Fairfax 1986.

Richter, Ingrid, *Nationalsozialismus, Kommunismus und die Folgen: Der katholische Moraltheologe, Eugeniker und Caritasfunktionär Joseph Mayer und die rassenhygienische Wende des Jahres 1933*, in Michael Manderscheid and Hans-Josef Wollasch (eds), Die ersten hundert Jahre: Forschungsstand zur Caritas-Geschichte. Dokumentation eines Symposiums der Fortbildungs-Akademie des Deutschen Caritas-Verbandes, Freiburg/Breisgau 1998, 79–86.

Rigoni, Anna, Il *concordato* serbo-vaticano del 1914, in *ASI* 133 (1976), 159–78.

Ring-Eifel, Ludwig, Weltmacht Vatikan: Päpste machen Politik, Munich 2004.

Rittberg, Gräfin Else von, Der preussische *Kirchenvertrag* von 1931: Seine Entstehung und Bedeutung für das Verhältnis von Staat und Kirche in der Weimarer Republik, Diss. phil., Bonn 1959.

Ritter, Gerhard, *Staatskunst und Kriegshandwerk*: Das Problem des 'Militarismus' in Deutschland, Vol. 4: Die Herrschaft des deutschen Militarismus und die Katastrophe von 1918, Munich 1968.

Robertson, Esmonde, *Race* as a Factor in Mussolini's Policy in Africa and Europe, *JCH* 23 (1988), 37–58.

Rodrigo, Javier, Los *campos* de concentración franquistas: Entre la historia y la memoria, Madrid 2003.

Rödder, Andreas, *Dichtung und Wahrheit*: Der Quellenwert von Heinrich Brünings Memoiren und seine Kanzlerschaft, *HZ* 265 (1997), 77–116.

Rogall, Joachim, Die Deutschen im *Posener Land* und in Mittelpolen (Studienbuchreihe der Stiftung Ostdeutscher Kulturrat, 3), Munich 1993.

Rohrbasser, Anton, and Paul Cattin (ed.), *Heilslehre* der Kirche: Dokumente von Pius IX bis Pius XII, Freiburg/Switzerland 1953.

Rood, Wim, *Rom und Moskau*: Der Heilige Stuhl und Russland bzw. die Sowjetunion von der Oktoberrevolution 1917 bis zum 1. Dezember 1989 (Münsteraner theologische Abhandlungen, 23), Altenberge 1993.

Roos, Hans, *Geschichte* der polnischen Nation 1918–1985: Von der Staatsgründung im Ersten Weltkrieg bis zur Gegenwart. Fortgeführt von Manfred Alexander, 4th edn, Stuttgart-Berlin-Cologne 1986.

Rosa, Enrico, L' *internazionale* della barbarie nella sua lotta contro la civiltà, *CC* 87 (19 September 1936), 441–50

Rosar, Wolfgang, *Deutsche Gemeinschaft*: Seyss-Inquart und der Anschluss, Vienna-Frankfurt am Main-Zurich 1971.

Rosenberg, Alfred, Der *Mythus* des 20. Jahrhunderts: Eine Wertung der seelisch-geistigen Gestaltungskämpfe unserer Zeit, Munich 1930.

Rosenfeld, Günter, *Sowjetunion und Deutschland* 1922–1933, East Berlin 1984.

Rossi, Ernesto, Il *manganello* e l'aspersorio, Bari 1968.

Rossi, Fabrizio, Der *Vatikan*: Politik und Organisation (Beck'sche Reihe, 2182; C. H. Beck Wissen), Munich 2004.

Rothenbücher, Karl, Die *Trennung* von Staat und Kirche, Munich 1908.

Ruchniewicz, Krzysztof, and Stefan Troebst (eds), *Diktaturbewältigung* und nationale Selbstvergewisserung – Geschichtskulturen in Polen und Spanien im Vergleich. Materialien eines internationalen Workshops in Wrocław und Krzyzowa, 12.–15. Juni 2003. Wrocław 2004 (= Monografie Centrum Studiów Niemieckich i Europejskich im. Willy Brandta na Uniwersytecie Wrocławskim, t. 5).

Ruhl, Klaus-Jörg, *Spanien* im Zweiten Weltkrieg. Franco, die Falange und das 'Dritte Reich' (Historische Perspektiven, 2), Hamburg 1975.

Ruhl, Klaus-Jörg, and Laura Ibarra García, *Kleine Geschichte Mexikos*: Von der Frühzeit bis zur Gegenwart (Beck'sche Reihe, 1366), Munich 2000.

Rychlak, Ronald J., *Hitler*, the War and the Pope, Huntington (Indiana) 2000.

Sadowski, Konrad, *Catholic Power* and Catholicism as a Component of Modern Polish National Identity 1863–1918 (The Donald W. Treadgold Papers, 29), Seattle 2001.

Sale, Giovanni SJ, Il delitto *Matteotti*, CC 155 (2004), 13–26.

—*Hitler*, la Santa Sede e gli ebrei con documenti dell'archivio segreto vaticano (Di fronte e attraverso, 661), Milan 2004.

Samerski, Stefan, Die *Aufnahme* diplomatischer Beziehungen zwischen dem Hl. Stuhl und dem Deutschen Reich (1920), AHP 34 (1996), 325–68.

—Der geistliche *Konsultor* der deutschen Botschaft beim Heiligen Stuhl während der Weimarer Republik, RQ 86 (1991), 261–78.

—Der *Heilige Stuhl* und der Vertrag von Versailles, ZKG 107 (1996), 355–75.

—Die katholische *Kirche* in der Freien Stadt Danzig 1920-1933: Katholizismus zwischen Libertas und Irredenta (Bonner Beiträge zur Kirchengeschichte, 17), Cologne-Weimar-Vienna 1991.

—Ostdeutscher *Katholizismus* im Brennpunkt: Der deutsche Osten im Spannungsfeld von Kirche und Staat nach dem Ersten Weltkrieg (Historische Forschungen), Bonn 1999.

—*Primat* des Kirchenrechts: Eugenio Pacelli als Nuntius beim Deutschen Reich (1920-1929), Archiv für katholisches Kirchenrecht 170 (2001), 5–21.

—Prof. Richard *Delbrueck* und die Anfänge der Reichskonkordatverhandlungen aus den Jahren 1920 bis 1923, ZKG 104 (1993), 328–57.

Samerski, Stefan (ed.), Das *Bistum Danzig* in Lebensbildern: Ordinarien, Weihbischöfe, Generalvikare, Apostolische Visitatoren 1922/25 bis 2000 (Religions- und Kulturgeschichte in Ostmittel- und Südeuropa, 3), Münster 2003.

—*Wilhelm II* und die Religion. Facetten einer Persönlichkeit und ihres Umfeldes (Forschungen zur brandenburgischen und preussischen Geschichte: Beiheft, N.F., 5), Berlin 2001.

Sánchez, José M., *Pius XII* and the Holocaust: Understanding the Controversy, Washington DC 2002.

Sandfuchs, Wilhelm, Die *Aussenminister* der Päpste, Munich-Vienna 1962.

Sandmann, Fritz, Die *Haltung* des Vatikans zum Nationalsozialismus im Spiegel des 'Osservatore Romano' (von 1929 bis zum Kriegsausbruch), Mainz 1966.

Schäfer, Michael, *Luigi Sturzo* als Totalitarismustheoretiker, in Maier (ed.), 'Totalitarismus', Vol. 1, 37–47.

Schambeck, Herbert (ed.), *Pius XII* zum Gedächtnis, West Berlin1977.

Scheuermann, Audomar, Die *Konkordatspolitik* Pius XII, in Schambeck (ed.), Pius XII, 71–102.

Scheuermann, Martin, *Minderheitenschutz* contra Konfliktverhütung? Die Minderheitenpolitik des Völkerbundes in den zwanziger Jahren (Materialien und Studien zur Ostmitteleuropa-Forschung, 6), Marburg 2000.

Schieder, Wolfgang, *Faschismus*, in Richard van Dülmen (ed.), Fischer Lexikon Geschichte, Frankfurt am Main 2003, 194–221.

Schieder, Wolfgang, and Christof Dipper (eds), Der Spanische *Bürgerkrieg* in der internationalen Politik (1936–1939) (Nymphenburger Texte zur Wissenschaft, 23), Munich 1976.

Schlemmer, Thomas, and Hans Woller, Der italienische *Faschismus* und die Juden 1922 bis 1945, *VfZG* 53 (2005), 165–201.

Schmidlin, Josef, *Papstgeschichte* der neuesten Zeit, Vol. 3, I: Papsttum und Päpste im 20. Jahrhundert: Pius X. und Benedikt XV. (1903–1922), Munich 1936; Vol. 3, II–IV: Papsttum und Päpste im 20. Jahrhundert: Pius XI. (1922–1939), Munich 1939.

Schmiedl, Erwin A., *März 1938*: Der deutsche Einmarsch in Österreich, Vienna 1987.

Schneider, Burkhart, Die *Friedensbemühungen* des Vatikans im Ersten Weltkrieg, *SdZ* 93 (1968), 31–43.

Schneider, Gabriele, *Mussolini* in Afrika: Die faschistische Rassenpolitik in den italienischen Kolonien 1936–1941 (Italien in der Moderne, 8), Cologne 2000.

Scholder, Klaus, *Altes und Neues* zur Vorgeschichte des Reichskonkordats: Erwiderung auf Konrad Repgen, *VfZ* 26 (1978), 535–70.

—Die *Kirchen* und das Dritte Reich, Vol. 1: Vorgeschichte und Zeit der Illusionen 1918–1934, 3rd edn, Frankfurt am Main-Berlin 2000; Vol. 2: Das Jahr der Ernüchterung 1934. Barmen und Rom, 3rd edn, Frankfurt am Main-Berlin 2000.

—Österreichisches *Konkordat* und nationalsozialistische Kirchenpolitik 1938/39, *ZevKR* 20 (1975), 230–43.

Schöppe, Lothar (ed.), *Konkordate* seit 1800: Originaltext und deutsche Übersetzung der geltenden Konkordate (Dokumente, 35), Frankfurt am Main-Berlin 1964.

Schott, Anselm P. (ed.), Das *Messbuch* der hl. Kirche (Missale Romanum) lateinisch und deutsch mit liturgischen Erklärungen, 19th edn, Freiburg/Breisgau 1913.

Schreiber, Georg, Deutsche *Kirchenpolitik* nach dem ersten Weltkrieg: Gestalten und Geschehnisse der Novemberrevolution 1918 und der Weimarer Zeit, *HJ* 70 (1951), 296–333.

Schumann, Reinhold, *Geschichte Italiens*, Stuttgart-Berlin-Cologne 1983.

Schuschnigg, Kurt, Im *Kampf* gegen Hitler: Die Überwindung der Anschlussidee, Vienna-Munich 1988.

Schwaiger, Georg, *Papsttum und Päpste* im 20. Jahrhundert: Von Leo XIII zu Johannes Paul II, Munich 1999.

Schwarte, Johannes, Die *katholische Kirche* und der Rassismus der Nationalsozialisten – konkretisiert am Enzyklika-Projekt Pius' XI gegen den Rassismus, in Edith-Stein-Jahrbuch 10 (2004), 69–98.

Schwarz, Ted, *Joseph P. Kennedy*: The Mogul, the Mob, the Statesman, and the Making of an American Myth, Hoboken 2003.

Schwengler, Walter, *Völkerrecht*, Versailler Vertrag und Auslieferungsfrage: Die Strafverfolgung wegen Kriegsverbrechen als Problem des Friedensschlusses 1919/20 (Beiträge zur Militär- und Kriegsgeschichte, 24), Stuttgart 1982.

Scoppola, Pietro, La *Chiesa e il fascismo*: Documenti e interpretazioni, Rome-Bari 1973.

—La *storiografia* italiana sul pontificio di Pio XI, in École Française (ed.), Achille Ratti, Pape Pie XI: Actes du colloque (Rome 15–18 mars 1989), Rome 1996, 181–93.

Scoppola, Pietro (ed.), *Chiesa e stato* nella storia d'Italia. Storia documentaria dall'unità alla repubblica, Bari 1967.

Senn, Wilhelm Maria, *Katholizismus und Nationalsozialismus*: Eine Rede an den deutschen Katholizismus, Münster 1931.

Severus, Emmanuel von OSB, Abt Ildefons *Herwegen*: Maria Laach gedenkt seines Geburtstags vor hundert Jahren, in Severus (ed.), Was haltet ihr von der Kirche? Die Fragen des Abtes Ildefons Herwegen an seine und unsere Zeit. Beiträge und Würdigungen aus Anlass seines Geburtstages vor hundert Jahren am 27. November 1874 (Beiträge zur Geschichte des alten Mönchtums und des Benediktinerordens. Supplementband, 3), Münster 1976, 10–19.

Siegele-Wenschkewitz, Leonore, *Nationalsozialismus und Kirchen*: Religionspolitik von Partei und Staat bis 1935 (Tübinger Schriften zur Sozial- und Zeitgeschichte, 5), Düsseldorf 1974.

Slayton, Robert A., *Al and Frank*: The Great Smith–Roosevelt Feud, in Woolner and Kurial (eds), *FDR*, 55–66.

Spadolini, Giovanni, Il cardinale *Gasparri* e la questione romana: Con brani delle memorie inedite (Quaderni di storia, 23), Florence 1972.

Spann, Othmar, Der wahre *Staat*: Vorlesungen über Abbruch und Neubau der Gesellschaft, 3rd edn, Leipzig 1931.

Stark, Rodney, *One True God*: Historical Consequences of Monotheism, Princeton 2001.

Stasiewski, Bernhard (ed.), *Akten deutscher Bischöfe* zur Lage der Kirchen 1933–1945, Vol. 1: 1933–1934 (VKZG.Q, 5), Mainz 1968.

Steffen, Franz, Die *Diözese Danzig*, ihr erster Bischof Graf Eduard O'Rouke und ihre Kathedralkirche zu Olivia, Danzig 1926.

Steglich, Wolfgang (ed.), Der *Friedensappell* Papst Benedikts XV. vom 1. August 1917 und die Mittelmächte: Diplomatische Aktenstücke des Deutschen Auswärtigen Amtes, des bayerischen Staatsministeriums des Äußern, des Österreichisch-Ungarischen Ministeriums des Äußern und des Britischen Auswärtigen Amtes aus den Jahren 1915–1922 (Quellen und Studien zu den Friedensversuchen des Ersten Weltkrieges, 2), Wiesbaden 1970.

—Die *Friedenspolitik* der Mittelmächte 1917/18 (Quellen und Studien zu den Friedensversuchen des Ersten Weltkrieges, 1), Wiesbaden 1964.

—Die *Verhandlungen* des 2. Unterausschusses des Parlamentarischen Untersuchungsausschusses über die Päpstliche Friedensaktion von 1917. Aufzeichnungen und Vernehmungsprotokolle (Quellen und Studien zu den Friedensversuchen des Ersten Weltkrieges, 3), Wiesbaden 1974.

Stehle, Hansjakob, *Geheimdiplomatie* im Vatikan: Die Päpste und die Kommunisten, Zurich 1993.

—*Geheimes* aus Bonn für Moskau vom Vatikan: Der vielseitige Agent Monsignore Edoardo Prettner-Cippico und sein Nachlass, *VfZ* 51 (2003), 263–83.

—*Lenins Mann* im heiligen Rom, in Stehle, Graue Eminenzen – dunkle Existenzen: Geheimgeschichten aus vatikanischen und anderen Hinterhöfen, Düsseldorf 1998, 32–9.

Stehlin, Stewart A., *Weimar* and the Vatican 1919–1933: German-Vatican Diplomatic Relations in the Interwar Years, Princeton 1983.

Stein, Joshua B., Great Britain and the *Evian Conference* 1938, *The Wiener Library Bulletin* 37/38 (1976/1977), 40–52.

Steininger, Rolf, *12. November 1918* bis 13. März 1938: Stationen auf dem Weg zum 'Anschluss', in Steininger and Gehler (eds), Österreich im 20. Jahrhundert, Vol. 1, 99–151.

Steininger, Rolf, and Michael Gehler (eds), Österreich im 20. Jahrhundert, Vol. 1: Von der Monarchie bis zum Zweiten Weltkrieg, Vienna 1997.

Steinmaus-Pollak, Angelika, Das als *Katholische Aktion* organisierte Laienapostolat. Geschichte seiner Theorie und seiner kirchenrechtlichen Praxis in Deutschland (Forschungen zur Kirchenrechtswissenschaft, 4), Würzburg 1988.

Stenographische Protokolle über die Sitzungen des Bundestages des Bundesstaates Österreich, Vol. 2, Vienna 1938.

Stephan, Juliane, *Begleiterin* im langen Schatten. Claire Nix: Heinrich Brünings Eckermann in Neuengland, *FAZ* 54 (4 March 2000), 3.

Sternhell, Zeev, Mario Sznaijder and Maia Asheri, Die *Entstehung* der faschistischen Ideologie: Von Sorel zu Mussolini, Hamburg 1999.

Straub, Eberhard, Das Spanische *Jahrhundert*, Berlin 2004.

Stricker, Gerd, *Religion* in Russland: Darstellungen und Daten zu Geschichte und Gegenwart (Gütersloher Taschenbücher, 634: Religion in Europa), Gütersloh 1993.

Stüken, Wolfgang, *Hirten* unter Hitler: Die Rolle der Paderborner Erzbischöfe Caspar Klein und Lorenz Jäger in der NS-Zeit, Essen 1999.

Sturzo, Luigi, Le *Fascisme* et le Vatican en 1938: La visite de Hitler à Rome, *La Vie Intellectuelle* (10 February 1940), 325–50.

—*Kirche und Staat*, Augsburg 1932.

Suppan, Arnold (ed.), Aussenpolitische *Dokumente* der Republik Österreich 1918–1938, Vol. 2: Im Schatten von Saint-Germain 15. März 1919 bis 6. September 1919, Vienna 1994.

Sutton, Michael, Charles *Maurras* et les Catholiques français 1890–1914: Nationalisme et Positivisme (Bibliothèque Beauchesne. Religions – société – politique, 25), Paris 1994.

Tálos, Emmerich, Das austrofaschistische *Herrschaftssystem* 1933–1938, in Wolfgang Maderthaner and Michaela Maier (eds), 'Der Führer bin ich selbst': Engelbert Dollfuss – Benito Mussolini, Briefwechsel, Vienna 2004, 103–27.

Tardini, Domenico, *Pius XII* als Oberhirte, Priester und Mensch, Freiburg/Breisgau 1963.

Thierfelder, Jörg, 'Aber Hände weg von Bibel und Kirche': *Wahlverweigerer* im evangelischen Württemberg bei der Volksabstimmung vom 10. April 1938, in Gerhard Besier and Günther R. Schmidt (eds), Widerstehen und Erziehen im christlichen Glauben: Festgabe für Gerhard Ringshausen zum 60. Geburtstag, Holzgerlingen 1999, 164–81.

Thoma, Clemens, Versteckte und verpasste *Botschaft* für die Juden: Bemerkungen zu einer 1938 vorbereiteten Enzyklika über Rassismus und Antisemitismus, in Freiburger Rundbrief: Zeitschrift für christlich-jüdische Begegnung, *Neue Folge* 4 (1997), 241–9.

Tierney, Dominic, Franklin D. *Roosevelt* and Covert Aid to the Loyalists in the Spanish Civil War, *JCH* 39 (2004), 299–314.

Tittmann, Harold Jr, *Inside* the Vatican of Pius XII: The Memoirs of an American Diplomat during World War II, ed. Harold H. Titmann III, New York 2004.

Toepser-Ziegert, Gabriele (ed.), *NS-Presseanweisungen*: Edition und Dokumentation, hg. von Hans Bohrmann, Vol. 4/III: 1936, Munich-New Providence-London 1993.

Tokareva, Evgenia S., Catholic *Hierarchy* in Russia in the 1920s and the 1930s: New Archival Evidence, *KZG* 14 (2001), 142–7.

Tomkowitz, Gerhard, and Dieter Wagner, 'Ein Volk, ein Reich, ein Führer!': Der *'Anschluss'* Österreichs 1938, 2nd edn, Munich-Zurich 1988.

Topolski, Jerzy, *Polska* dwudziestego wieku 1914–1997, 3rd edn, Poznań 1998.

Tornielli, Andrea, Pio XII: Il papa degli *Ebrei*, Casale Monferrato 2001.

Traina, Richard P., *American Diplomacy* and the Spanish Civil War, Bloomington 1968.

Tretjakewitsch, Léon, *Bishop Michel d'Herbigny* and Russia: A Pre-ecumenical Approach to Christian Unity (Das östliche Christentum, Neue Folge, 39), Würzburg 1990.

Treviranus, Gottfried Reinhold, Das *Ende* der Weimarer Republik: Heinrich Brüning und seine Zeit, Düsseldorf-Vienna 1968.

Tüchle, Hermann, *Pietro Kardinal Gasparri*, in Wilhelm Sandfuchs (ed.), Die Aussenminister der Päpste, Munich-Vienna 1962, 94–108.

Uertz, Rudolf, Vom *Gottesrecht* zum Menschenrecht: Das katholische Staatsdenken in Deutschland von der Französischen Revolution bis zum II. Vatikanischen Konzil (1789–1965) (Politik- und Kommunikationswissenschaftliche Veröffentlichungen der Görres-Gesellschaft, 25), Paderborn-Munich-Vienna-Zurich 2004.

Valois, Georges, L'*essenza* del Fascismo secondo un sociologo francese, *Il popolo d'Italia* (18 October 1925).

Van de Velde, Theodor Hendrik, Ideal Marriage: Its Physiology and Technique. With an Introduction, by J. Johnston Abraham, London 1936.

Verhandlungen des Reichstags. XIII. Legislaturperiode. II. Session. Band 310. Stenographische Berichte. Von der 102. Sitzung am 7. Mai 1917 bis zur 125. Sitzung am 10. Oktober 1917, Berlin 1917.

Verhandlungen des Sächsischen Landtags, 3. *Wahlperiode*, 1928/29; 4. Wahlperiode, 1929/30.

Vinas, Añgel, *Franco*, Hitler y el estallido de la guerra civil: Antecedentes y consecuencias (Alianza ensayo, 171), Madrid 2001.

Vocelka, Karl, *Geschichte Österreichs*: Kultur – Gesellschaft – Politik, Graz-Vienna-Cologne 2000.

Volk, Ludwig, Der bayerische *Episkopat* und der Nationalsozialismus 1930–1934 (VKZG.F, 1), 2nd edn, Mainz 1966.

—Kardinal Michael von *Faulhaber* (1869–1952), in Volk, *Katholische Kirche* und Nationalsozialismus: ausgewählte Aufsätze, hg. von Dieter Albrecht (VKZG.F, 46), Mainz 1987, 201–51.

—Die *Kirche* in den deutschsprachigen Ländern (Deutschland, Österreich, Schweiz), in HKG VII, 537–561.

—*Ökumene* des Versagens?, in Volk, *Katholische Kirche* und Nationalsozialismus: ausgewählte Aufsätze, hg. von Dieter Albrecht (VKZG.F, 46), Mainz 1987, 354–60.

—Das *Reichskonkordat* vom 20. Juli 1933. Von den Ansätzen in der Weimarer Republik bis zur Ratifizierung am 10. 9. 1933 (VKZG.F, 5), Mainz 1972.

Volk, Ludwig (ed.), *Akten deutscher Bischöfe* über die Lage der Kirche 1933–1945, Vol. 4: 1936–1939 (VKZG.Q, 30), Mainz 1981.

—*Akten Kardinal Michael von Faulhabers*, Vol. 1: 1917–1934 (VKZG.Q, 17), Mainz 1975; Vol. 2: 1935–1945 (VKZG.Q, 26), Mainz 1978.

—*Kirchliche Akten* über die Reichskonkordatsverhandlungen 1933 (VKZG.Q, 11), Mainz 1969.

Volsansky, Gabriele, *Pakt* auf Zeit. Das Deutsch-Österreichische Juli-Abkommen 1936 (Böhlaus zeitgeschichtliche Bibliothek, 37), Vienna-Cologne-Weimar 2001.

Wagner, Oskar, Zwischen Völkern, Staaten und Kirchen: Zur *Geschichte* des Protestantismus in Ostmitteleuropa, West Berlin 1986.

Wahrmund, Ludwig, Die kaiserliche *Exklusive* im Konklave Innozenz XIII. mit einem Anhang betreffend die Akten des päpstlichen Konsistorialarchivs über Sedisvakanz und Konklave (Sitzungsberichte der Kais. Akademie der Wissenschaften in Wien, Philosophisch-Historische Klasse, 170, 5), Vienna 1912.

Walther, Christian, *Königsherrschaft Christi*, TRE XIX (1999), 311–23.

Walz, Angelus M., *Andreas Kardinal Frühwirth* (1845–1933): Ein Zeit- und Lebensbild, Vienna 1950.

Warszawski, Józef, *Piłsudski a religia*, 2nd edn, Warsaw 1999.

Wedemeyer-Kolwe, Bernd, 'Der neue Mensch': *Körperkultur* im Kaiserreich und in der Weimarer Republik, Würzburg 2004.

Weinzierl, Erika, *Prüfstand*: Österreichs Katholiken und der Nationalsozialismus, Mödling 1988.

Weinzierl, Erika, and Kurt Skalnik (eds), *Österreich* 1918–1938: Geschichte der Ersten Republik, 2 vols, Graz-Vienna-Cologne 1983.

Weinzierl-Fischer, Erika, Österreichs *Katholiken* und der Nationalsozialismus, Teil I: 1918–1933; Teil II: 1933–1945, *WuW* 18 (1963), 41–439; 493–526.

Weizsäcker, Ernst von, *Erinnerungen*, Munich 1950.

—Die *Weizsäcker-Papiere* 1933–1950, ed. Leonidas E. Hill, Frankfurt am Main 1974.

Wende, Erich, *C. H. Becker*: Mensch und Politiker. Ein biographischer Beitrag zur Geschichte der Weimarer Republik, Stuttgart 1959.

Wenger, Antoine, *Rome et Moscou* 1900–1950, Paris 1987.

Wilhelm II, *Ereignisse und Gestalten* aus den Jahren 1878–1918, Leipzig 1922.

Wilk, Stanislav, Der Heilige Stuhl und die *Staaten* Ostmitteleuropas nach dem 1. Weltkrieg (Abriss der Problematik), in Jerzy Kłoczowski, Wojciech Lenarczyk and Sławomir Łukasiewicz (eds), Churches in the Century of the Totalitarian Systems (Proceedings of the Commission Internationale d'Histoire Ecclésiastique Comparée, 5, 2), Vol. 2, Lublin 2001, 247–59.

Wills, Garry, *Papal Sin*: Structures of Deceit, New York 2000.

Wiltschegg, Walter, Die *Heimwehr*: Eine unwiderstehliche Volksbewegung?, Vienna 1985.

Winkler, Heinrich August, Der lange *Weg* nach Westen: Deutsche Geschichte 1806–1933, Vol. 2: Deutsche Geschichte vom 'Dritten Reich' bis zur Wiedervereinigung, Munich 2000.

—*Weimar* 1918–1933: Die Geschichte der ersten deutschen Demokratie, Munich 1993.

Wohnout, Helmut, *Regierungsdiktatur* oder Ständeparlament? Gesetzgebung im autoritären Österreich (Studien zu Politik und Verwaltung, 43), Vienna-Cologne-Weimar 1993.

Wolf, Hubert, Denn für *Gottesmord* gab's in der Kurie kein Pardon, *FAZ* 91 (17 April 2003), 44.

—*Molto delicato*, *FAZ* 60 (12 March 2003), 40.

—*München* als Reichsnuntiatur? Aus Anlass der vollständigen Öffnung des Archivo della Nunziatura di Monaco, *ZKG* 103 (1992), 231–42.

—*Pius XI und die 'Zeitirrtümer'*: Die Initiativen der römischen Inquisition gegen Rassismus und Nationalismus, *VfZG* 53 (2005), 1–43.

—*'Pro perfidis Judaeis'*: Die 'Amici Israel' und ihr Antrag auf eine Reform der Karfreitagsfürbitte für die Juden (1928). Oder: Bemerkungen zum Thema katholische Kirche und Antisemitismus, *HZ* 279 (2004), 611–57.

—Vertagt auf unbestimmte *Zeit*, *FAZ* 87 (12 April 2003), 8.

Wolf, Hubert, and Klaus Unterburger (eds), *Eugenio Pacelli*: Die Lage der Kirche in Deutschland 1929 (Veröffentlichungen der Kommission für Zeitgeschichte, A, 50), Paderborn 2006.

Wollasch, Hans-Josef, War der katholische *Priester* und Eugeniker Joseph Mayer ein Wegbereiter der NS-Euthanasie?, in caritas 1991. Jahrbuch des Deutschen Caritasverbandes (1991), 411–29.

Woolner, David B./Kurial, Richard G. (eds), *FDR* [= Franklin Delano Roosevelt], the Vatican, and the Roman Catholic Church in America, 1933–1945 (The World of the Roosevelts), New York-Hampshire 2003.

Wucher, Albert, Postwendend eine *Antwort* aus Rom, *FAZ* 86 (11 April 2003), 44.

Zimniak, Stanislaw, Il cardinale *August J. Hlond*, primate di Polonia (1881–1948): note sul suo operato apostolico; atti della serata di studio: Roma 20 maggio 1999 (Piccola bibliotheca dell'Instituto Storico Salesiano, 18), Rome 1999.

Zittel, Bernhard, Die *Vertretung* des Hl. Stuhles in München 1785–1934, in Der Mönch im Wappen – Aus Geschichte und Gegenwart des katholischen München, Munich 1960, 490–3.

Zlepko, Dmytro, Die *Friedensbemühungen* Pius' XII. vom Pontifikatsantritt bis zum Kriegsausbruch (2. März–1. September 1939), Leverkusen-Opladen 1980.

Zöller, Michael, *Washington und Rom*: Der Katholizismus in der Amerikanischen Kultur (Soziale Orientierung, 9), Berlin 1995.

Zuccotti, Susan, Il *Vaticano* e l'Olocausto in Italia, Milan 2001.

Index of Persons

Achille, Ratti *see* Pius XI
Adenauer, Konrad (1876–1967)
  57, 224
Alphonse XIII, King of Spain
  (1885–1931) 155–6
Alvensleben, Werner von (1875–1949)
  75
Andrieu, Paulin (1849–1935) 51
Aquinas, Thomas (1225–74) 100
Arco auf Valley, Anton Count
  (1897–1945) 17–18
Arendt, Hannah (1906–75) vii–viii
Aretin, Karl Otmar von 109
Aron, Raymond Claude Ferdinand
  (1905–83) 152
Asseldonk, Anton van (1892–1983)
  134
Attolico, Bernardo (1880–1942) 168
Auer, Erhard (1874–1945) 17–18, 211
Aversa, Giuseppe (1862–1917)
  9, 26–7

Balbo, Italo (1896–1940) 129
Baumgartner, Eugen (1879–1944)
  103
Beck, Józef (1894–1944) 186
Becker, Carl Heinrich von
  (1876–1933) 36
Becker, Winfried 109
Bell, George (1883–1958) 203
Bellarmine, Robert (1542–1621) 100
Benedict XV (Giacomo della
  Chiesa)(1854–1922) 2, 5, 7–11, 13,
  23–30, 34, 38–9, 41–4, 52–3, 68, 86,
  209, 216, 228
Benigni, Umberto (1862–1934) 5
Berenguer, Dámaso (1873–1953) 156
Bergen, Diego von (1872–1944) 24,
  29–30, 36–7, 58–9, 70, 125, 130,
  139, 148, 187, 190, 202
Bergmann, Ernst (1881–1945) 144–5

Berning, Wilhelm (1877–1955) 74,
  124, 127, 139–43, 149
Bertram, Adolf (1859–1945) 32, 36,
  40–2, 55, 65, 73, 84–5, 114–16, 118,
  122–3, 130–1, 140, 164, 223, 231
Bethmann Hollweg, Theobald von
  (1856–1921) 8, 10–11, 14
Beyerle, Josef (1881–1963) 63
Binder, Dieter A. 90
Blet, Pierre (*1918) ix
Bludau, Augustin (1862–1930) 73
Blum, Léon (1872–1950) ix, 159, 162
Böckenförde, Ernst-Wolfgang (*1918)
  203
Boelitz, Otto (1876–1951) 53–4, 61
Bok, Nikolai (1880–1962) 44
Bolz, Eugen (1881–1945) 63
Bonzano, Giovanni (1867–1927) 214
Bornewasser, Franz Rudoph
  (1866–1951) 176
Bose, Herbert von (1893–1934) 169
Bottum, Joseph x
Brandmüller, Walter (*1929) 208
Bratman-Brodowski, Stefan
  (1880–1937) 48–9
Braun, Otto (1872–1955) 34, 37
Braun, Wilhelm von (1883–1941) 45
Brechenmacher, Thomas (*1964)
  178
Brentano di Tremezzo, Clemens von
  (1886–1965) 28
Breuning, Klaus 200
Brockdorff-Rantzau, Ulrich Count von
  (1869–1928) 45–6, 48, 50
Bruni, Giulio Ulderigo 198
Brüning, Heinrich (1885–1970)
  83–4, 91, 94–6, 105, 108–9, 117,
  119, 182
Buck, Wilhelm (1869–1945) 60
Bünger, Wilhelm (1870–1937) 61
Bürckel, Joseph (1895–1944) 172–5
Burkard, Dominik (*1967) 146

Wiedemann, Fritz (1891–1970)
    174
Wilhelm II, Kaiser (1859–1941)
    10–11, 14, 25–7
Wilson, Hugh R. (1885–1946)
    176
Wilson, Thomas Woodrow
    (1856–1924)   8, 12, 24–5, 175,
    214
Wirth, Josef (1879–1956)   45–6, 54,
    56–9, 92, 95, 224, 240
Wolf, Hubert   133–4

Wolf, Wilhelm (*1897)   175
Worowski, Wacław (1871–1923)
    44–7, 221

Yurenev, Konstantin K. (1888–1938)
    47

Zech-Bukersroda, Julius Count von
    (1885–1946)   19, 29, 58
Zimmermann, Arthur
    (1864–1940)   27
Zimmermann, Kurt Otto von   61